Developmental Dictatorship
and the
Park Chung-hee Era

The Shaping of Modernity
in the Republic of Korea

A Note about Terms and Spelling

The Korean peninsula has been divided into South and North since the end of World War II. The official terms for them are "The Republic of Korea (ROK)" and "The Democratic People's Republic of Korea (DPRK)." In this book, they are stated as South Korea and North Korea to conform to the international convention except in a few cases.

Though the South Korean government officialized the spelling of "Park Cheong-hee" for the president of the third constitutional republic in South Korea, "Park Chung-hee" is used in this book as it has been widely accepted in international communities.

Developmental Dictatorship
and the
Park Chung-hee Era

The Shaping of Modernity
in the Republic of Korea

Edited by
Lee Byeong-cheon

Translated by
Eungsoo Kim and Jaehyun Cho

HOMA & SEKEY BOOKS
Paramus, New Jersey

Library of Congress Cataloging-in-Publication Data

Kaebal tokchae wa Pak Chæong-hæui sidae. English
Developmental dictatorship and the Park Chung-hee era: the shaping of modernity in the Republic of Korea edited by Lee Byeong-cheon ; translated from the Korean by Eungsoo Kim, et al.
    p. cm.
Includes bibliographical references.
ISBN 1-931907-28-5 (hardcover)—ISBN 1-931907-35-8 (pbk.)
1. Korea (South)—Economic policy—1960- 2. Korea (South)—Politics and govern-ment—1960-1988. 3. Park, Chung Hee, 1917-1979. I. Yi, Pyæong-ch'æon, 1952- II. Title.
HC467.95.K3413 2006
338.95195'009'046—dc22
                    2005019693

Homa & Sekey Books
3rd Floor, North Tower
Mack-Cali Center III
140 E. Ridgewood Avenue
Paramus, NJ 07652

Tel: 201-261-8810; 800-870-HOMA
Fax: 201-261-8890; 201-384-6055
Email: info@homabooks.com
Website: www.homabooks.com

Edited by Gail N. Chalew
Printed in U.S.A.
1 3 5 7 9 10 8 6 4 2

CONTENTS

Preface for the English Edition   *vii*
Preface for the Korean Edition   *ix*

PART ONE
Introduction and Overview

1. The Political Economy of Developmental Dictatorship   3
   Lee Byeong-cheon

PART TWO
The Lights and Shadows of Economic Development

2. Industrialization in South Korea   51
   Seo Ick-jin
3. Industrial Policy in the Park Chung-hee Era   80
   Lee Sang-cheol
4. The *Chaebol* Regime and the Developmental
       Coalition of Domination   108
   Cho Young-chol
5. Political and Institutional Conditions of
       Financial Repression   134
   Yoo Chul-gyue
6. Labor Policy and Industrial Relations
       in the Park Chung-hee Era   153
   Kim Sam-soo
7. Developmental Dictatorship   185
   Lee Joung-woo

PART THREE
Political Sociology of
the Developmental Dictatorship Regime

8. The Yushin Regime and the National
       Division Structure   215
   Lee Chong-suk
9. South Korea and the Vietnam War   248
   Han Hong-koo
10. Oppressive Modernization and the Risk Society   271
   Hong Seong-tae
11. The Dead Dictator's Society   294
   Chin Jung-kwon
12. Park Chung-hee in the Age of Democratization   312
   Hong Yun-gi

About the Contributors   339
Bibliography   342
Glossary   365
Chronology   368
Index   378

Preface for the English Edition

Lee Byeong-cheon

The lights and shadows of the Park Chung-hee regime have long been a subject of deep interest and wide debate for the general public, as well as for the academic community both within and without Korea. As a matter of fact, the 18 years of the Park period laid the economic foundation for the accelerated modernization of South Korea. As a result, Korea has been transformed from a weak state in the periphery of East Asia, which had suffered from protracted colonial rule and civil war, into a strong, industrialized one. Yet, the "growth-first" and "speed-first" strategies of modernization involved brutal political oppression, hostile ideological confrontation with the North, the rapid concentration of economic resources, and serious ecological degradation. Thus, the period witnessed the transformation of the Republic of Korea into the so-called Republic of *Chaebol*, Republic of Seoul, or Republic of Construction.

What is the key to the successful economic modernization that occurred during the Park regime? How can the relationships between the "miracle" of industrial and economic breakthrough and the "debacle" of political and social breakdown under the Park regime be understood in a more balanced perspective? How can the political regime of brutal oppression and the economic regime of rapid development be evaluated in a rather holistic perspective? In fact, the Janus-faced nature of the Park regime is reflected in the profound ambivalence of contemporary Koreans: Although supporters praise him as a great leader, antagonists curse him as a brutal dictator. The prolonged controversy in Korea centering on a projected memorial for Park, who is despised enough to deserve "spit on his grave," has revealed the width and depth of the ambivalence prevailing throughout the nation. In this regard, indeed, our central argument is that Park's regime can best be understood and evaluated in terms of *developmental dictatorship*.

This book is the outcome of a joint study on the dynamics of developmental dictatorship during Park's reign from 1961 to 1979, focusing on its contradictory aspects of modernization and anti-modernization. To date, economic success stories predominate in the literature abroad on the modern Republic of Korea. It is our deep belief that a more balanced perspective on the interactions of economic growth and political oppression would help both insiders and outsiders derive more relevant theoretical and practical implications from the Korean experience of developmental dictatorship. It is, thus, our great hope that this book will help both supporters and antagonists understand the lights of breakthrough and the shadows of breakdown under the Park regime from a rather dynamic perspective. The success or failure of our collective intellectual endeavor to integrate the positive and negative aspects of developmental dictatorship in a coherent and organic framework will depend on readers all over the world.

The English edition of this book has been translated by Kim Eungsoo and Cho Jaehyun and completed under the supervision of Park Sa-myoung. It is my great pleasure to acknowledge their invaluable contributions. In particular it is very fortunate that my good friend, Professor Park at Kangwon National University, took charge of the burdensome supervision work and worked very hard during the final stage of translation. The bibliography, chronology, and glossary could not have been prepared without the gracious assistance of Miss Choi Eun-kyoung at the graduate course in Kangwon National University and Doctor Choi Hyun at the Institute for Participatory Society.

Our deep gratitude is expressed to the "100 Books from Korea" Selection Committee and the staff members of the Korea Literature Translation Institute for their support in presenting this book to the Frankfurt Book Fair. Finally, I sincerely thank my wife Lee Kyounghee and daughter Lee Myoung-jee for their deep love and spiritual support, not only for the adventure of this book but for all my life.

May 18, 2005

Preface for the Korean Edition

Lee Byeong-cheon

It has frequently been observed that the Republic of Korea benefited enormously from a "double revolution" for modernity during the last four decades of the 20th century after 8.15 liberation — a dual process encompassing both late industrialization and late democratization. Thus, it could be construed that the nation is now emerging from a dark tunnel and entering a bright phase in its history. Such an extraordinary success, the narrative of which reveals a number of eccentric characteristics, has been both the fruit of great pain and sacrifice on the part of a large segment of the Korean populace and the focus of much international attention. In common with all other histories, the trajectory of this Korean-style "double late revolutions" has both a light and a dark side. The so-called IMF financial crisis, which had an important impact on Korean society during the closing years of the 20th century, forced all Koreans to reflect deeply on the dark side of their nation's history.[1]

When we consider both the phenomenon of South Korean late modernization and the protean relationship between North Korea and South Korea, it is toward the lights and shadows of the late industrialization of South Korea that the focus of our attention must be directed. Undoubtedly, the Park Chung-hee epoch (1961-79) was pivotal in defining the vector and the nature of the Korean modernization process. The central purpose of this book is to critically reexamine the achievements and the disasters of the *developmental dictatorship* regime in the Park Chung-hee era.

There are many reputable studies on the Park era, originating from within Korea and abroad, as well as a large number of research papers published by government-sponsored institutions, including

---

[1] For diverse and complex reasons the South Korean economy virtually collapsed at the end of 1997, necessitating the intervention of the International Monetary Fund.

the Korea Development Institute (KDI). However, there are relatively few comprehensive and accessible works on the subject, either academic or popular. A complementary objective of this book, therefore, is to address that shortcoming and thereby enable as many people as possible to gain a fuller and more balanced understanding of this critical period in the nation's modern history. It is also anticipated that the work will prove useful in both the popular forum in the public space and as an academic textbook on campus. However, it is not written simply for easy understanding; regrettably, circumstances are not yet conducive to the production of a book that would perfectly achieve that goal.

Although much research has already been accomplished, there remain many empirical, theoretical, and ideological issues to resolve. One of the most important factors in this debate is the tension that exists between starkly polarized viewpoints. There are those who see the Park era from the perspective of democratization movements against developmental dictatorship, whereas others regard it from the perspective of the "miracle of East Asia." This unresolved tension plays a significant role in the confusion that exists about the historical period under consideration. Although, in recent years, the "miracle of East Asia" perspective has been somewhat accepted in domestic academic circles, even that ostensible consensus is riddled with dissent. These quite opposite perspectives in academic circles create great confusion about how to understand and evaluate the Park Chung-hee era. Thus, with each side being characterized by passionately held, yet internally discordant, beliefs and opinions, the need for calm and rational dialogue to gain a true understanding of Korean modernity is very clear. However, it would appear that there has been neither a diversity nor an abundance of academic discussions concerning fundamental matters regarding, for example, what linked development and dictatorship or the economic miracle and the political oppression of the period, or where this developmental dictatorship and the movements for democracy ought properly to be located in the history of Korean modernity.

Of particular concern is what may be termed a "fundamentalist ultra-criticism," which unwittingly ignores most of the achievements of the Park Chung-hee era. More than that, however, the great obstacles to a correct understanding of the Park era is the view that might be regarded as "unreflecting triumphalism," which idolizes Park and which discourages fragile Korean democracy and civil society in the current post-Cold War era. Taking into account the historical gravity of the period under review and the bruising political and ideological controversies regarding it, it is clear that there is a distinct shortage of fully coherent academic research; as a consequence, this is not the time to attempt a hasty evaluation. Sadly, up until now the Korean social sciences have not succeeded in taking the lead in this controversy concerning the development of Korean society. However, studies centered on the late president are at last being undertaken.

Another incentive for writing this book is the hope that it will contribute to a rational and comprehensive understanding of the era of Park Chung-hee's national stewardship, helping develop a clearer awareness, beyond both the Cold War rightists and leftists, of the history of this "era of extremes" and ultimately developing a historical conception of the post-Cold War age and post-extremism leading into the 21st century. Readers should notice, however, that the research papers in this book were not written from a single point of view; although they have basic similarities. It is hoped that this feature will be regarded not only as a positive one but also as confirmation of the previous observation that the study of the Park Chung-hee regime is an ongoing process.

This book has three parts. The first part is an introduction and overview of the theoretical and empirical issues of developmental dictatorship in the Park Chung–hee era. The salient features of developmental dictatorship in Korea and the factors involved in its success of economic development are explained from several angles in the second part. The reader may note that these analyses reveal that the success of Korea, which had evident institutional and strategic bases, was not in any sense a mirage but certainly had its imbalances and deviations at the same time. In the third part, what may be regarded as the dark side of developmental dictatorship, in social and political terms, is addressed in concert with a discussion of the Park syndrome in the period of democracy.

In the first part, Lee Byeong-cheon develops a theory of developmental dictatorship and shows that Park's system was an eccentric form of that phenomenon. Lee also provides a comprehensive overview of the benefits and the drawbacks of Park's version of developmental dictatorship. A developmental dictatorship, with its strong dictator-driven character, is defined as one of passive revolution for statist modernization, which allocates the highest national priority to economic growth centered on industrialization while, at the same time, oppressing or controlling the development of civil society and democracy. Although Korea's developmental dictatorship had these dual components, it also had differences in the extent to which Park Chung-hee created a highly centralized and distorted system by using the Cold War and the national division of the Korean peninsula. The writer sees in this phase a Korean edition of the Japanese ultra-nationalism of the pre-World War II era. He argues that the Korean model, however, reflects universal elements contributing to the success of the industrialization process.

In chapter 2 in Part II, Seo Ick-jin discusses the broad outline of the industrialization regime of Korea on the basis of regulation theory. This developmental model combines an accumulation regime on a borrowing-export economy with the state-led regulation mode of a developmental dictatorship. Seo analyzes, through the mutual correlation of various elements, how the Korean economy constructed an autonomous national production system and was able to escape from its original position on the periphery.

In the third chapter, Lee Sang-cheol deals with Park Chung-hee's industrial policy and, in the process, illustrates very clearly the inherent features of Korea's development policy. Analyzing the comprehensive history of Park's industrial policy, Lee shows that Korean industrial policy was consistent and continuous throughout the 1960s and 1970s, contrary to the market-centered view, and that government-controlled import substitution industrialization continued even after the shift to an export-driven policy in the mid-1960s.

The industrialization of Korea was dominated and directed by the dual engine of the government and the *chaebols* (very large vertically and horizontally integrated Korean conglomerates). The extent to which this alliance had almost absolute control over all aspects, both bright and dark, of the "miracle on the Han River" cannot be overstated. So, in the fourth chapter, Cho Young-chol describes how this nexus of government and *chaebols* worked as a growth system. He then offers a critical analysis of its structural limits. Cho also notes that state capital, which to all intents and purposes basically means debt, was poured into the *chaebols* through channels of financial privileges. As a result, the development of "fortress *chaebols*" with extraordinary power was accelerated and culminated in the subservience of the post-developmental dictatorship market economy to overbearing *chaebols*. In addition, Cho lays a foundation for the historical basis of a democratic reform argument against the *chaebols*, in contrast to the limitations of a shareholder value-centered reform approach, necessary since the financial crisis in 1997.

In the fifth chapter, Yoo Chul-gyue deals with finance repression, one of the core elements of the Korean developmental system. Financial repression by the government, as can be seen typically in the heavy chemical industrialization period of the 1970s, secured investment from the private sector for fostering those industries as a strategic priority and became a mechanism for socializing investment risks. This also meant that the policy suppressed the interests of the financial rentier class, when seen merely from the aspect of the financial system itself. However, as is shown in the fourth chapter, under the Korean-style developmental system, financial repression turned into financial benefits for the *chaebols*. As this financial system entailed such dangers that profits went to the *chaebols* and costs went to society as a whole, how then could this be justified? In Yoo's opinion, the national consensus for growth, which was a collective will of the people, may be one explanation.

The darkest side of this high-growth system can be found in the labor sector, and in the sixth chapter Kim Sam-soo analyzes labor policy and the labor system extant under the Yushin dictatorship of the 1970s. What he emphasizes most strongly is the importance of the legal recognition of labor unions and, above all, their right to strike, because this is a major step in the integration of workers into civil society, which is an ineluctable prerequisite for the establishment of a nation-state. With this in mind, Kim asserts that not only were the rights of assembly of workers completely ignored but workers were also excluded from eligibility for those elements necessary to become a nation-state. This situation predated the labor constitution of 1953 and continued throughout the military regime of Chun Doo-hwan,[2] until the law was amended in 1987.

The Korean developmental pattern has been acknowledged internationally as a model for so-called shared growth, and other countries have emulated it effectively. In chapter 7, however, Lee Joung-woo proposes an alternative assessment. Beginning with a discussion concerning the distinction between growth and development, he points out that even if Park Chung-hee's model succeeded in terms of quantitative growth, that success came at the expense of qualitative development. Lee then looks into the distribution of wealth in the three areas of wages, income distribution, and real estate assets. The growth rate in real wages consistently lagged behind that of labor productivity, which, in turn, indicated a low distribution rate. From the point of view of income distribution, there are significant barriers to research because of the poor quantity of data. Thus, Lee argues that it is more effective to gain access to information in terms of a distributional justice theory, rather than depending on tenuous statistics. In particular, he notes that *chaebol* families are omitted in the household income surveys. The most noticeable element, however, which cannot be seen in income statistics, is the distribution of real estate assets. Lee argues that the rise in the price of real estate is the greatest single factor in the inequality of home assets, as well as in the phenomenon of the rich getting richer and the poor getting poorer.

---

[2] Following the assassination of President Park Chung-hee in October 1979, General Chun Doo-hwan assumed power by military coup. He was succeeded by General Roh Tae-woo in 1987.

Although Part II focuses mainly on the bright and dark sides of the economic miracle of the Park Chung-hee era, Part III concentrates on the risks and inhumanity of that period, on which critical reflection, from both political and social aspects, must be focused. Chapters 8-10 review socio-politically the brutal nature of the time, and chapters 11 and 12 critically analyze the "Park syndrome" in the era of democracy.

In chapter 8, Lee Chong-suk reveals how the national division of the Korean peninsula was used in the formation of Park Chung-hee's Yushin (revitalizing) system and how that system served Park's long-term dictatorial power. With the introduction of two core concepts, the hostile interdependence and the mirror image effect, Lee reveals how President Park used dialogue between the two Koreas to set up his rule for life and how the North Korean-style infiltrated the Yushin system. Lee's criticism is directed at Park Chung-hee, as well as at the North Korean leader at the time, Kim Il-sung. According to Lee, the Yushin regime and the *Yuil* (only one person in power) regime (dictatorship) were merely hostile twins with an identical intent; that is, to facilitate the long reign of an authoritarian leader while oppressing as well as mobilizing the population. Each side used the dialogues between North and South, and the North-South division, for ulterior motives.

It is only recently that Park Chung-hee's dispatch of South Korean soldiers to Vietnam has begun to draw attention and be included in the process of evaluating the Park era. For that reason, academic studies concerning the issue are still very preliminary. Han Hong-koo, in the ninth chapter, discusses the historic implications of the Vietnamese involvement on the deployment of developmental dictatorship and the lives of the Korean people. He emphasizes the fact that the decision to send troops to Vietnam was driven primarily by the imperatives of the Park regime, rather than by U.S. pressure. In his analysis of its effects, Han argues that the benefits in terms of the Korean economy were not as great as the sacrifices made. This differs from the conventional view, which places emphasis on the particular benefits of the military dispatch. What interests Han, though, is that the Park regime, underpinned by strong support from the Korean military and the U.S. government, utilized the Vietnam situation to assist in militarizing Korean society, heightening tensions on the Korean peninsula, and therefore paving the way for Park's Yushin regime.

To reduce the development of the Park era to a simplistic dichotomy between poverty and growth would be a naïve and one-dimensional approach. In the tenth chapter, Hong Seong-tae explains the contradictory nature of the Korean modernization process, in which development and destruction, and high growth and high risks have all occurred simultaneously. Hong attaches importance to Korea-specific circumstances while accepting Ulrich Beck's "risk society" (*risikogesellschaft*) theory. According to his perspective, Korea has become a risk society, which is much more complex than Western societies, as a result of oppressive modernization combined with destructive industrial development. His analysis of the influence of destructive development includes the two aspects of society and nature.

In the eleventh chapter, Chin Jung-kwon critically examines the Park Chung–hee syndrome and believes that its ideology has three dimensions: discourse, public opinion, and habitus. Of the three, Jin pays particular attention to habitus. He regards Park's regime as a sort of bio-power like fascism. He believes that President Park's ethos has been deeply ingrained into the collective psyche of the Korean people. Jin goes on to say that even though Park Chung-hee's body has perished, his soul remains deeply embedded in every sector of Korean society and continues to exert significant influence; this continuing influence is the means by which the Park Chung-hee syndrome has developed. Accordingly, Chin insists that it is of immediate importance to go beyond this "micro-fascism" and effect a cure for the Park inheritance.

In the twelfth chapter, by Hong Yun-gi, the discourse of Park Chung-hee is divided into two kinds for the purpose of critical analysis. First, there is the power discourse, idolizing Park Chung-hee, which has led to the Park Chung-hee syndrome in the period of democracy and which is very different from the simple justification discourse of the past. According to Hong, the idolization discourse contains not only ideological features, which manufactured a mythical leader figure far removed from historical reality, but also an offensive against the fragile democracy of Korea. The idolization discourse is, therefore, anti-democratic, anti-civil society, immoral, and inhumane. Hong then raises the question of the so-called fascism within us. He admits that it has the character of a critical discourse on power. The really important consideration, though, is that this discourse has exaggerated public support for the Park's regime and the foundation of national consensus.

It has taken a very long time for this book to come to fruition. The contributors have sacrificed much of their busy and valuable time to prepare their chapters, and I, as editor and organizer of this book, am deeply grateful to them all for the outstanding quality of their completed works. I also would like to express my appreciation to Professor Takizawa Hideki at Shoukyoku University in Japan and Professor Paek Young-seo at Yonsei University in Korea for their invaluable help. Last, but not least, I would like to extend my thanks to the publishing company, Changbi, for waiting patiently for the manuscripts and for agreeing to publish this book.

October 15, 2003

PART ONE

Introduction and Overview

Chapter 1

The Political Economy of Developmental Dictatorship:

A Korean Experience

Lee Byeong-cheon

I. INTRODUCTION

Among a number of remarkable achievements of the Republic of Korea during the second half of the 20th century are its liberation from the bondage of slavery under Japanese colonial rule; the establishment of a nation state, albeit not a unified one; and the successful completion of the dual revolutions of modern times: industrialization and democratization. For Koreans, industrialization means far more than simply being in a position to enjoy the benefits of a modern industrial civilization. It encompasses a much less tangible value, one that extends beyond physical satisfaction. Through the process and experience of industrialization, a physical foundation for the economic and political independence of the Korean people has been laid. Based on this foundation, the nation has proudly taken its place within the international community and made its voice heard. Successful industrialization has led to the formation of a national economy, helping establish its substantial and coherent political framework.

Turning the focus toward the international arena, the failure or stagnation of capitalistic industrialization in other parts of the globe can be seen in contrast to the path of Korean industrialization and the establishment of a national economy. Furthermore, the Korean

3

narrative presents a striking contrast to the failure of experiments with state socialism for more than 70 years in the 20th century and to system transformation from state socialism to capitalism in the East. Most striking of all, the economic success of South Korea compared with the economic failure of North Korea, and the elective democracy of Seoul in contrast with the hereditary dictatorship of Pyongyang, challenges the conventional historical consciousness regarding the legitimacy of the two Koreas by putting an end to ideological competition between the two.

As a matter of fact, the successful industrialization of South Korea and the subsequent growth of the national economy are matters of great significance. The actual mechanisms and processes whereby they took place are equally important. The costs in human terms of industrialization and the suffering endured by the great majority of the Korean people, although relatively small when measured on a global historical scale, should never be discounted or underestimated. Furthermore, attempts should not be made to validate the argument that the long dark shadows cast over the Korean people during the developmental period were an inevitable consequence of leading the country onto the right path. Although industrialization was successful, the dictatorial regime used it as a means of consolidating its Cold War ideology of anti-communism, reinforcing its political power and exacerbating the hostile confrontations between the South and the North of the Korean peninsula. The flower of the so-called miracle on the Han River bloomed amidst the compounded tragedies of national division, political oppression, popular revolt, and the Cold War.

The government's unjustifiable diplomatic normalization with Japan and its participation in the "dirty war" of Vietnam also contributed to the miracle. In addition, economic growth took place in a highly concentrated, unbalanced, distorted, and reckless manner, encouraging conservative collusion between two dominant forces: the dictatorial regime and privileged conglomerates called *chaebols*. The "era of extremes" exerted a negative influence on the generation not only at the time but also continued to do so on the next. It left a deep scar on the historical trajectory of the modern Korean society, which

4

is now manifested by the flawed framework of democracy in contemporary Korea.

In this context it is no exaggeration to say that developmental dictatorship is a core concept integrating the Korean experience of modernization in the era of extremes, as well as a key notion characterizing the Park Chung-hee regime throughout its entire 18 years. Making use of this key concept, this chapter examines the lights and shadows, benefits and penalties, of the Park regime, which created the Janus-faced framework of Korean modernity.

II. THE POLITICAL ECONOMY OF DEVELOPMENTAL DICTATORSHIP

Developmental Dictatorship: The "Passive Revolution" Regime of Statist-Nationalist Modernization

Developmental dictatorship is a key concept in analyzing the transitional period of modernization characterized by industrialization and the establishment of a national economy. However, although the concept is widely used and is gaining public credence in East Asia as well as in Korea, it has yet to be an established term in the academic community. A skeptical attitude toward developmental dictatorship as a scientific concept is widespread in academic circles, where it has yet to be afforded a stamp of approval.

The conventional definition of developmental dictatorship is that it is "a system used to justify a dictatorship that restricts the people's participation in politics based on the reason that political security is a prerequisite to economic growth" (Ko Song-guk 1980). However, this simple definition has been criticized because it only indicates the legitimacy principles of political power, falling short of being a scientifically analyzable conception of the politicoeconomic regime as a whole. First, it does not explain why such a specific dictatorial regime emerges and declines nor does it examine the relationships between the causes and effects of dictatorship. Second, it fails to clarify why the necessary conditions for national development could only be provided by developmental dictatorship, and not by a more democratic system. Furthermore, it does not analyze the socioeconomic structures and their transformations that could serve as the basis of developmental dictatorship.

Nevertheless, the term "developmental dictatorship" should not be ignored, but instead be granted "scientific citizenship" by proactively constructing it as a bona fide academic concept. The concept of developmental dictatorship is particularly useful for a full understanding of the statist-nationalist modernization of East Asian societies. It should be regarded as both coherent and valid for several reasons. First, it can provide a political economy approach by which to comprehend the economic and political aspects of the historical process of modernization in East Asian societies in an organic and holistic manner. In other words, it combines the approaches of state-economy relations and of state-society relations in analyzing the transitional era of modernization. It also helps us understand political and economic dynamics in East Asian societies, because it focuses on the political economy of nation-states with the help of the world system and dependency approaches.

Second, the concept of developmental dictatorship can deal with the triangular relationships among development, democracy, and nationalism, which are long-drawn issues in the studies of economic development and political change (Table 1.1). It brings within its theoretical scope such subjects as the dilemmas between economic and political development, between growth and distribution, and between democracy and nationalism. The transitional period of industrialization tends to demand a centralized government for quick decision making and stable politics, because national harmony, long-term stability, and effective coordination among social groups are, to a certain extent, essential for the development of an integrated national economy. However, decentralized power, procedural legality, and public space are prerequisites for liberal democracy. For that reason, the emergence of conflicts between the demands of democratization and the demands of industrialization in the transitional period seems somewhat inevitable.

Third, the concept of developmental dictatorship critically deals with two major arguments: One insists that oppressive politics is necessary for economic development, and the other expects that political dictatorship will decline as a result of economic development. A political regime of developmental dictatorship might provide the political basis for the "primitive accumulation" of industrial capitalism. At the same time, however, it could deteriorate into a monster-like Leviathan, oppressing and monitoring the growth of civil society from below; it could become an apparatus of domination serving those in state power in the name of national interests and sovereignty. This indeed did occur in the anti-communist developmental dictatorship in the Cold War era of East Asia (Yoo 1987). In this regard a developmental dictatorship might meet the historic needs of the primitive accumulation of industrial capitalism while being characterized by an inherently reactionary oppressiveness. Thus, the concept of developmental dictatorship implies a critique of the double-edged, Janus-faced contradictions of the modernization regime as in East Asia. In short, the concept offers insight into economy and politics as an organic whole in dealing with the tensions between economic development and political democratization while providing a critical perspective on the double-edged nature of primitive accumulation and reactionary oppression, which can be called developmental contradictions or developmental antinomies (Lee Byeong-cheon 2000b).

To set the concept and the formation of theory on a solid ground, it is necessary to clarify the definitions of development and dictatorship and the relationships between the two. Then, what is development in this context? Development here, though including such other connotations as cultural development, human development, and the like, above all means the industrial development that takes place during the transformation of an agrarian society into an industrialized one. One factor that should not be missed, however, is that development in East Asia, by definition, is not only confined to economic industrialization. As development in the region is inseparable from a uniquely East Asian nationalism, the ideology of developmentalism includes strong statist-nationalism to achieve national integration and enhancement through economic development. Therefore, development here means the development of a nation and places national interests above all else, thereby justifying nationwide mobilization and the hierarchical incorporation of the people for national development. During the Cold War, moreover, East Asian developmentalism served as a means of the "politics of survival" against the threats of communism. Thus, it encompassed the characteristics of strong anti-communist developmentalism against external security threats (Castells, 1998:267, 272-76; Johnson 1995:38-50).

Now, let us turn to the term "dictatorship" as used in this chapter. Since Juan Linz (1970) first conceptualized authoritarianism, dictatorship has been divided into two types: authoritarianism and totalitarianism. For greater clarity, Linz assigned authoritarianism to the elusive gray area between democracy and totalitarianism. He compared totalitarianism with authoritarianism in four categories: pluralism, ideology, leadership, and mobilization. In authoritarianism Linz saw a political pluralism with a vague yet limited division of responsibility and a unique mentality without a leading, or focal, ideology. In this system, one person or a small group of people wield vaguely defined power in "predictable" ways without the power of concentrated or wide-ranging mobilization.

Thus, Linz's authoritarianism could provide a theoretically useful element in the concept of developmental dictatorship. His theory makes it possible to distinguish developmental dictatorship based on authoritarianism with political pluralism from one based on monolithic totalitarianism; for example, South Korea represents the former, whereas Taiwan represents the latter (Table 1.2). As can be seen in the case of South Korea, this distinction is very important. A political system with limited pluralism and the consequent contestation for public power carries within itself certain degrees of instability and contradictions and can initiate the political dynamics of transition toward democracy through confrontation between ruling and opposition coalitions. For this reason, an authoritarian developmental dictatorship cannot depend for its political legitimacy solely on its economic performance and its consequential logic that the end justifies the means. In this context, it can be defined as a regime in which its logic of performance legitimacy faces constant challenges by the principle of procedural legitimacy, and as a result, it is subject to inherent tensions and contradictions. In fact, authoritarianism encompasses a wide political spectrum, just as an imperfect free market does in the economic system. Therefore, it is necessary to distinguish a relatively more institutionalized, stable authoritarianism from a less institutionalized, unstable one to which the praetorian regime of ancient Rome belongs (Han Bae-Ho 1993).[1]

Second, as Linz has argued, authoritarianism does not have a leading ideology, but simply musters up a group mentality; hence, it lacks the political capacity to mobilize the masses. It is important at this stage to differentiate positive political mobilization and negative repressive control. According to this categorization, developmental dictatorship is not fascism because it fears, and thus avoids, the political mobilization of people. To the contrary, fascism attempts positive political mobilization. At the same time, developmental dictatorship also differs from Linz's authoritarianism, which is based on group mentality, rather than ideology. Developmental dictatorship in East Asia, however, is founded on the basis of a strong anti-communist statist modernization ideology. This ideology, although not as strong as that of totalitarianism, is able to provide socialization norms for political legitimacy or authority that integrate and mobilize national energy from above, which differs from positive political mobilization in fascism.[2]

In summary, development-centered dictatorship takes root in a nonhegemonic society, with no bourgeois or other social hegemony yet established in a transitional era of modernization. It is a highly discretionary and strategic dictatorship pursuing statist-nationalist modernization while seeking national integration and mobilization through the suppression of political liberty and public participation in the name of national interests and development. In short, it reveals two characteristics: a development-oriented Caesarism (Cox 1987:218, 237-38) and a statist Machiavellism. With regard to Caesarism, developmental dictatorship takes up state-driven political authority

---

[1] For a more refined classification of nondemocratic regimes, see Diamond et al. (1989).

[2] Although Linz also refers to "mobilization authoritarianism," it is insubstantial (Linz 1970:260-1).

and order while unifying and mobilizing national energy to secure the "primitive accumulation" of industrial capitalism. With its Machiavellian strategies and tactics, it incorporates the life of people ceaselessly under the banner of national interests to accumulate dictatorial power for itself. It is a kind of statist dictatorship in the name of the enhancement of the national interests and sovereignty in a transitional era of modernization.

Thus far, we have dealt with political aspects of developmental dictatorship. Let us now consider it in terms of a social development regime as a whole that includes an economic growth regime. To that end, Jessop's contribution (Jessop 1990), which exhibits a more advanced and logical development of Gramsci's theory of hegemony, is useful. He proposes structural determination, strategic orientation, and relations of accumulation as three conditions for a successful hegemonic project in resolving conflicts between particular and general interests for the sake of social development. According to Jessop, the structural determination of hegemony refers to the structural or strategic selectivity of the state, or structural privileges in a given state form for certain forces and their interests at the expense of other forces and interests. The second key element, strategic orientation, infers that the ruling forces should develop certain programs and projects that will not only lead in the long term to the realization of the particular interests of the ruling forces but also will ensure certain benefits for the popular masses. Hegemony here involves political, intellectual, and moral leadership. The third element, relations of accumulation, means that a hegemonic project should be backed by a successful growth regime or an accumulation strategy, and thus, it depends on material concessions for the ruled masses.

Of course, Jessop's theory of hegemonic projects and accumulation strategies does not deal specifically with the transition period of modernization. Therefore, it does not cover the specific hegemonic role, discretionary autonomy, and strategic capacity of the state in late development, particularly in East Asia.[3] However, his conception

---

[3] Jessop's state theory is criticized by state-centered theorists following Weber (Skocpol 1985). Jessop counterattacks (1990: Chapter 10; 1999:

clearly presents three ingredients that enable a developmental dictatorship regime to become a regime of passive revolution oriented toward modernization: (1) a development-oriented ruling bloc of political power elites and dominant socioeconomic forces, oppressing political freedom and public participation; (2) a political authority or societal paradigm of national interests, taking not legal procedures but economic performance as the basis of its legitimacy;[4] and (3) an economic growth regime that makes it possible to build efficient national industries and dynamic competitive advantages. It decidedly depends on state-led institutional forms, which include property rights and accumulation, governing the market and sharing the risks of investments, and regulating the integration of the national economy into the world market.

The above definition of developmental dictatorship implies that it embraces more than the legitimacy based on economic performance and developmental orientation. A political dictatorship, in order to survive, must be combined with a successful economic growth regime for national interests. In addition to factors connected with legitimacy and orientation, therefore, the concept of developmental dictatorship should encompass all aspects of such a highly plausible and actually working regime as shown in the history of late modernization in East Asia. The definition above includes the explanation of the why and the how of development, as well as the presentation of a workable model of development. Moreover, it encompasses the conditions of regime legitimacy, the purposes of ruling forces, and the causes of regime consolidation.

In summary, developmental dictatorship can be defined as a regime of passive revolution for statist or sovereign "reactionary modernization" with its inherent contradictions contained by the

---

2003). Both critiques may be regarded as relevant because they each note the weak points of the other (Lee Byeong-cheon 1997:8-9).

[4] See Castells (1998), who understands a developmental state from the perspective of the legitimacy principle or the historic project. He indicates that the social project of a revolutionary state seeks the fundamental change of the social order, whereas the project of a developmental state is the fundamental change of the economic order.

coercive and mobilization apparatus of the state, wherein successful economic growth and oppressive, sovereign political dictatorship mutually reinforce each other. That is why a study of developmental dictatorship should take into consideration the structural privileges for the discretionary exercise of political power and the strategic coalitions of mutually interdependent political and economic forces, in addition to the political authority and the effective economic performance. Furthermore, the developmental dictatorship regime should be analyzed in a dynamic perspective as a continuously changing one with inherent cleavages, contradictions, and crises. Because it is not a static regime but a changeable one with innate developmental contradictions, the examination of the dynamics of developmental dictatorship should be focused on its dilemmas, risks, crises, and transformations.

Table 1.1 Economic Development and a Political Regime

	Dictatorship	**Democracy**
Growth	Developmental dictatorship	social democratic, welfare capitalism
Stagnancy	Poor, predatory state	Soft market democracy

Table 1.2 Developmental Dictatorship: Comparison between Korea and Taiwan

	Korea	**Taiwan**
Politics	Authoritarian, unstable	Totalitarian, stable
Economics	Large conglomerate-centered	State-run companies in parallel with small/medium-sized enterprises

Beyond the Theory of the Developmental State

Up to now, it seems that the best clue to answering the question how developmental dictatorship can work successfully is located in the developmental state theory. However, the developmental dictatorship theory should encompass the contributions of the developmental state theory and go beyond it. The developmental state theory provides state-centered interpretations of late catch-up industrialization in East Asia, in contrast with the neoclassical market-centered theories, on the one hand, and the world system or dependency theories, on the other. The historical model that supports the theory was derived from the experience of Japan and later applied to the rest of East Asia. So far several prominent researchers have contributed to the elaboration of the developmental state theory, the core elements of which include the high autonomy and capacity of the state, the close cooperation of the government and the market, and the selective integration into the global market (Amsden 1989; Castells 1998; Evans 1995; Johnson 1982, 1995; Lee Byeong-cheon 2003a; Leftwich 1995; Wade 1990; Woo-Cumings 1999). These theoretical elements can be summarized as follows:

- Development-oriented state power: A state holds and exercises power over the public to integrate and mobilize national energy from above in the name of economic modernization. A state is characterized as developmental when it establishes its ability to promote development as the basis of its legitimacy.

- Authoritarian politics in which industrialization outweighs democratization: To maintain political stability and order, the government controls open conflicts of interests in society and suppresses public participation and freedom.

- Institutional coherence in state structures, state autonomy free from the pressure of private interest groups, and bureaucratic autonomy and competency with long-term horizons used in economic policy.

- Public-private cooperation and partnership for development: This is the so-called embedded autonomy of the state with private enterprise.

- Governing the market by the state and bilateral cooperation based on national interests: The government selects and nurtures strategic industries while pursuing dynamic competitive advantages.

- Capital discipline by the government: Government subsidies are, in principle, linked to the performance of beneficiaries.

- Financial restraint, mobilization of financial resources, and support for national strategic industries.

- Selective integration into the global economy beyond the dichotomy of simple protectionism and reckless opening: A developing country can take advantage of the various benefits that accrue from being a latecomer while avoiding and coping with the disadvantages.

The first four elements are mainly concerned with political sociology and last four elements with economics. Taken together, they constitute the developmental state theory, which helps explain the successful development of East Asia. Furthermore, this theory helps us understand the history of European industrialization while providing valuable lessons for other developing countries.

There are, however, many difficulties and problems in applying the theory to our developmental dictatorship conception. First, the theorists of the developmental state consider society as the private sector, which is divided by a multiplicity of individual interests, and so the state sector is the only party that can represent the public good. This is a sort of state and sovereignty fetishism. It also equates economic modernization with a quasi-revolution in which the legitimacy of political procedure can be ignored easily. These two critical fallacies make it possible to inhibit horizontal communication in the civil society and its ratification regarding political authority or the legitimacy of the exercise of state power.[5] The theory thereby

---

[5] See Lee Byeong-cheon (2003:107) for a critique of Johnson on this point. Johnson criticizes market fetishism, but is indifferent to the risks of state fetishism or policy priority for national interests. In terms of the net function of dictatorship, the views of Johnson and Wade do not differ from Huntington (1968). Indeed, Wade (1990:373) accepts Huntington's ideas. Skocpol (1985:31, n. 7) also mentions Huntington favorably. However, Huntington's opinion may be regarded as dangerous, because he places a priority on order over freedom and even insists that a common aspect as an effective political system is more important than a differentiation between

ignores the fact that the state is, by its nature, a discordant and unstable combination of legitimacy and violence. State power can serve both as a means of maintaining political authority and order and as a violent monster for power accumulation and consolidation of the dominant ruling bloc. The theory overlooks the discretion and arbitrariness of a dictatorial power and the resulting reaction. It also neglects the differences between authoritarianism and totalitarianism, and between a highly institutionalized authoritarianism and a less institutionalized one. Therefore, it cannot clarify what significance, if any, political pluralism and public space can hold in such a society. For that reason, it makes it difficult to explain the inner cleavages and contradictions of developmental dictatorship and, moreover, the dynamics of democratic transition that follows (Lee Byeong-cheon 2003a).

Second, without giving proper consideration to the diversity of capitalism, the developmental state theory becomes entangled in the dichotomy of capitalism versus socialism. In reality, however, the institutions of capitalism, which include the regime of private rights, business organization, mode of socialization of risks, the financial system, and public-private relations, varies in different eras. These diversities result in various levels of efficiency, fairness, and perform-ance. Furthermore, it seems that even socialistic developmentalism could be possible, as can be seen in the successful transformation experience of China.[6] Therefore, it is essential to take a comparative perspective on the national diversity of capitalism, even when studying the transition period of late modernization. It is also necessary to look beyond common factors of success stories to the advantages and disadvantages of different institutions and of modes of state intervention. In this regard, it is very important to compare

---

totalitarianism and liberal democracy. He appears to see only the effective power of dictatorship while overlooking its formidable violence. It seems to me that there is no discernible difference between the strong state theory of Johnson and Huntington and the theory of Carl Schmitt about fascism and sovereign dictatorship.

[6] See Castells (1998:287-93).

and evaluate the developmental dictatorship of South Korea and Taiwan in their achievements and failures (Table 1.2).

Third, the developmental state theory highlights the state governance or regulation of the market, as well as the synergy of the state and the market, on the premise of capitalist private ownership as a given. Hence, the theory ignores many complicated problems in the practices of capital regulation by the state and the ensuing friction or coalition between state and capital. It takes out of consideration the fact that the state is faced with capital as a structural power that is resistant to state guidance. In other words, it should be recognized that the state exists in society, and thus, the state is never a monolithic entity of united, homogeneous people, but rather a condensed outcome of certain relations of historical forces emerging from never-ending struggles, where a failure to secure the people's consensus sows the seeds of further conflicts. In a nutshell, the social and economic bases of state power, the various types of ruling blocs, and the specific characteristics of each type should all be taken into account (Jessop 1990, 1999, 2003; Jo 1998; Koo 1993; Lee Byeong-cheon 2003a; Migdal 1994; Park 1999; Pempel 1999; Poulantzas 1978).

In contrast to the developmental state theory, public and private cooperation or the embedded autonomy of the state with society has to be accompanied by the disciplining of capital by the state, which in turn entails the resistance of capital and, as a result, the conflict, competition, negotiation, and compromise of the two partners. In this situation, we can ask, Who can monitor their partnership? If society is not sufficiently empowered and enabled to monitor the state-capital partnership, weak discipline certainly will prevail and thus will predatory ties based on privileged subsidies, corruption, and rent-seeking (Lee Byeong-cheon 2003a).

Fourth, the developmental state theory correctly points out the importance of the strategic management of integration into the global market by going beyond the simple dichotomy of protectionism and openness. However, it still falls well short of defining international conditions for successful growth and neglects to consider the following points: In addition to the abstract logic of capital and market in the global economy, the post-war situation gave late industrializers unique opportunities for successful industrialization. The hegemonic structure of the Cold War led by the United States offered them opportunities as well as pressures. Therefore, the theory should have dealt with the effect of the organic interdependence of political, military, and economic factors on the Cold War structure.

More often than not, nonetheless, the theory encompasses not only latecomers' catch-up industrialization but also firstcomers' industrialization and economic development (Murakami 1996; Weiss and Hobson 1995). For example, the Japanese scholar Murakami defines developmentalism as "a policy or theory for industrialization from the viewpoint of nationalist development." He also calls it "an economic system wherein capitalism is regarded as the basic economic framework, but government's market interference is acknowledged for the long-term growth horizon." According to Murakami, industrialization in the East and the West alike has shown universal characteristics of developmentalism, but not those of classical liberalism. The advancement of capitalism provides industrialization with a hospitable environment, but industrialization is not a necessary product of capitalism. He believes that the capitalist ethos that allows liberty in private accumulation activities could undermine social and national integration; hence the necessity for a strong political and economic unity: developmentalism.

The developmental dictatorship as seen by Murakami traces its origins to absolutism. In his viewpoint, from the 16th to the 18th century European empires experienced a phenomenon called pre-industrialization or proto-industrialization based on mercantilism under absolutism. Absolutism here means "the first developmental dictatorship attempting to connect, combine, and promote a nation state and an industrial capitalism." The first success of developmentalism was achieved in England under the absolute monarchy. Regarding such developmentalism as a universal road in the political economy of nationalist industrialization for advancing into the modern era, Murakami disapproves of a widely recognized classification of modernization: the firstcomer model of democratization before industrialization and the latecomer model of democratization after industrialization. He believes that the former is difficult to identify even in Europe, including England.

In a similar vein, Weiss and Hobson also criticize the arguments of the well-known development economist Gerschenkron (1962) for late industrialization. They extend the developmental state theory to cover the experiences of firstcomers' industrialization (Weiss and Hobson 1995:127). They admit that governmental roles are more critical in developing countries that are following in the path of their advanced peers. However, unlike Gerschenkron, they do not dismiss the importance of the strong state in early industrialization. Therefore, they consider the strong developmental capacity of the state in the mercantilist era to be the main factor in England's lead in industrialization. However, there exists a significant gap between their view and Murakami's. First, Weiss and Hobson pay attention to late or parliamentary mercantilism after civil revolution, rather than absolutism. Second, they believe that the key to the state coordination capacity is not a one-way process, but one based on its competitive cooperation with the capitalist class. Third, they emphasize the importance of the government protection of private ownership (Weiss and Hobson 1995:72-3). Fourth, although they distinguish between the firstcomers' developmentalism and the latecomers' developmentalism, they contrast the decline of the Anglo-Saxon type of capitalism with the rise of East Asian capitalism.

Nevertheless, all three scholars above subscribe to the view that the developmental state and developmentalism have been universal phenomena in the processes of industrialization and national wealth building throughout the modern world: a view that is considered sustainable. It is true that nationalism and the nation-state tended to be marginalized by both the right and the left in their discourse on modernity. The same is true of the combination of nationalism and industrialization. In the viewpoints of Murakami, Weiss, and Hobson, developmentalism may be seen as a rite of passage for a nation as it establishes a basis for a modern industrial society and a national economy. Nonetheless, the diverse and unique characteristics of developmentalism deserve attention as much as do its universal traits.

18

Although concentrating more on the universal history of the capitalist mode of production in general than on the national histories of
capitalism, Karl Marx even argued that the primitive accumulation of
capital takes different routes depending on the era and the country
concerned. The three scholars' studies undoubtedly contribute to a
better understanding of developmentalism and help us place the East
Asian type of developmentalism in the comparative historical
perspective. However, they do not acknowledge sufficiently the dual
character of developmentalism, fail to make a distinction among the
various types of historical developmentalism, and above all show a
lack of awareness of the contradictions and risks in the statist-
nationalist type of developmentalism in particular.

III. DEVELOPMENTAL DICTATORSHIP IN SOUTH
   KOREA

Historical Origins and Conditions

The ways in which social systems originate, evolve, and sometimes
decline are matters of profound interest to many observers, and
South Korea's development-oriented dictatorship is no exception.
Such is the extent of the attention paid to the Korean case that some
scholars have developed an argument called the "colonial origin of
the developmental state" to explain its history and particular features
(Cumings 1984a, b; Eckert et al. 1990:403-4, 1991:255-9; Kohli 1999;
Woo-Cumings 1991). The argument is based on the pattern of
Korea's economic growth under Japanese colonialism, especially on
the wartime industrialization process that took place during the 1930s
and the first half of the 1940s.[7] Supporters of this argument view the

---

[7] Furthermore, Cumings traces the origin of the North East Asian political
economy after the Second World War to the colonial period, suggesting that
the regional structure of "center" (Japan), "semi-periphery" (Korea and
Taiwan), and "periphery" (Manchuria) was revived along with the product
cycle after World War II. It is safe to say that his view is highly contentious
in regard to the influence he assigns to external factors, such as Japan.

developmental state model of South Korea under President Park as a type of revival of the development that took place during the colonial period, particularly the war eras. However, such a focus on colonial origins is problematic and falls victim to the fallacy of retroactively projecting such origins onto the subjective and objective elements of the period in question. It fails to take into account the fact that there were other alternatives for development after Korea's liberation from Japan. It almost excludes the viewpoints of actors in the historical process as well.

Let us examine the "colonial origin of the developmental state" argument in more detail, beginning with the remnants of ideology and policy paradigms that Park learned and inherited from his experience during Japanese colonial rule. These are not mere industrial relics from the colonial period, because what is essential to discover is what ideological and experiential lessons Park himself learned from the Japanese and what roles those lessons played in Park's own national stewardship after the military coup of May 16, 1961. According to the studies of primary sources, his ideology of developmental dictatorship was based on what he absorbed from the courses he took in the military schools of Manchuria and Japan. He also learned much from the fascist coup carried out by young Japanese ultra-rightist military officers and the subsequent establishment of the Manchurian state by the Japanese military. Park revered Japanese-style imperialism and fascism and saw the Japanese Meiji restoration and the establishment of the Manchurian state as ideal models for South Korea. He also believed that Adolf Hitler was a man who had worked for the true national interests of Germany. In short, Park's colonial experiences and lessons are crucial factors in understanding his political and socioeconomic outlook and development paradigm (Jin Chung-gwon 1998; Jo 1998:103-35; Lee Chun-sik 2002).

Second, though similar in appearance, Park's developmental dictatorship differed in essence from the wartime industrialization model during Japanese colonial rule. Indeed, it is very hard to understand why those colonial relics would even be considered for revival in the 1960s, so long after Korea's liberation from Japan. Instead, the origin of the Park model should be located in the Korean War (1950-53), which brought about major societal and economic shifts. To illustrate, before the war the constitution of the Republic of Korea included a provision that the government should run major industries, but after the war they were sold and handed over to several favored groups, resulting in the rise of the large Korean conglomerates called *chaebols*. Moreover, the colonial origin argument can explain neither the marked differences in the post-war development of South and North Korea nor the significant differences between South Korea and Taiwan. During the colonial period industrial development occurred mainly in the North, whereas the South remained stagnant as a predominantly agricultural economy. This pattern of industrial development is opposite to what emerged since the 1960s. In the meantime, after the liberation from Japanese rule and a civil war, Taiwan moved toward an ownership system divided into large state-run corporations and small and medium-sized private enterprises, unlike South Korea where the ownership of large corporations was almost monopolized by *chaebols*.

Third, Park Chung-hee's developmental dictatorship was not influenced solely by Japanese colonialism, regardless of the fact that he had been blessed with a Japanese education and related experiences. No less important factors were the complex circumstances of the time: the democratic movements in Korea and the waves of nationalism spreading throughout the nation and East Asia, the influence and interference of the United States, the Cold War structure, the division of the Korean peninsula between South and North, popular resistance and Park's reaction to it, the resulting changes within the Korean state and society, and the exemplary growth of the post-war Japanese economy and its lessons for the economic bureaucrats of the Park Chung-hee era. Most important, Park clearly learned from previous mistakes and, as a consequence, constantly modified his policies. In short, the Park model was as much a creature of its day as it was a legacy of history.

There are two important sociopolitical questions that should be addressed. The first is how Park's governmental power became so strong in the national power structure. He was able to gain enormous power because, after the Korean War and throughout the Cold War period, the Army of the Republic of Korea (ROKA), which was Park's primary support base, became the largest and best-organized element in the national power structure (Choi Jang-jip 1996:81-2). Second, as land reform had weakened the traditional propertied classes, no resistance came from those established forces. Moreover, the land reform measures turned farmers into rightist supporters. Third, although the *chaebols* emerged as significant players during the "U.S. aid economy" of the 1950s, their burgeoning power supported the government because they were considered by the public to have accumulated assets illicitly. In addition, the government controlled the flow of domestic credit as well as foreign exchange. Fourth, South Korea became an extreme rightist, anti-communist nation after the triple upheaval of liberation from Japan, the division of the peninsula, and the Korean War. Leftist forces and movements still existed in the country, but they were sparse and were almost rooted out.

The second question to answer is what conditions were needed for the junta to earn legitimacy for its developmental dictatorship. It seems that the Korean people had suffered too much from the many decades of colonialism and Korean civil war. In other words, for the great mass of the population, the matters of pressing concern were liberation from poverty and nationalist imperatives, for which Park's "national modernization" slogan struck a chord. In contrast, the government of Chang Myon, which was installed after the April 19th student uprising in 1960, did not show either the capacity or the autonomy to deal with many post-revolution tasks, including economic development, social stability, the restoration of the Korea-U.S. relationship, and the establishment of an inter-Korean peace structure. Such incompetence and incapability paved the way for Park's military coup (Chong Yun-jae 2001; Seo 1994).

There is no denying that Cold War anti-communism after the Korean War provided an ideal seedbed for Park's developmental dictatorship. However, we should be aware that there was also a leftist Progressive Party with Jo Bong-am as its leader, which gained significant support just 3 years after the civil war. In other words, Cold War anti-communism was not the only pillar of post-war Korea.

Therefore, Park's battle cry against communism cannot be thought to have had absolute strength and unanimous support from the people. To be sure, that rallying cry had echoes of the 1950s and the Korean War, but it was not a direct descendant. Rather, its origin can be found in the post-May 16, 1961 process. For example, Park restored diplomatic ties with Japan and sent troops to the Vietnam War. Against that backdrop he could invoke the past specter of war and horror to generate what is now called the "red complex." That made possible his power strategy of developmental dictatorship. Such a strategy, however, carried within it such consequences as crises of legitimacy, resistance, and control. The crucial issue of legitimacy recurred throughout Park's presidency, and not only in its initial phases. His legitimacy was never established unequivocally, but remained contestable and had to be reasserted over and over again. Therefore, it is necessary to look beyond the triumphalism of developmental dictatorship and pay proper attention to the historical context, structural contradictions and legitimacy crises of the system, and conflicts that took place between major players (Lee Byeong-cheon 2003a:120-1).

Two Types of Developmental Dictatorship: Continuities and Discontinuities

Some commentators claim that the Chang Myon administration, which lasted for about 18 months from 1960-61, would have been able to achieve both democracy and economic development, if only it had not been interrupted by the May 16th coup of 1961. Unfortunately, historical reality does not allow us to test such speculations. What can clearly be seen, however, is that Park's military junta entered on the scene as a conservative alternative, with the power to overcome Chang Myon's weak and internally divided liberalism. The arrival of Park Chung-hee heralded major and dramatic changes, ranging from state governance ideology to the relationships among the state, society, and the market and between South Korea and other countries, including North Korea.

Although all such changes may be collectively categorized as Park's developmental dictatorship, his 18-year rule went through numerous metamorphoses. For clarity, his leadership can be divided into three phases: (1) the era of national reconstruction (1961-63), (2) the era of "modernizing the fatherland" (1964-71), and (3) the era of "all-out national security" (1972-79). During the first phase, in which there was a transitional junta, Park failed to establish a hegemonic structure. After re-establishing an elected government, Park moved on to the next two phases, which demonstrated continuities as well as discontinuities.

The important element here is our historical viewpoint regarding Park's regime. Earlier in this chapter Park's claimed legitimacy was labeled a "contestable" legitimacy. This term implies that there were ideological collisions between the goals of the May 16th (*Oh-il-yuk*) military coup of 1961 and the April 19th (*Sa-il-gu*) democratic revolution of 1960; that is, between Cold War anti-communism, inter-Korean confrontation, and the statist-nationalist developmental dictatorship, on the one hand, and post-Cold War civil democracy, inter-Korean reconciliation, and people's nationalism, on the other. Park's regime can be distinguished even from those of other East Asian nations on several counts. His power structure was built on a fragile basis and a weak legitimacy (Han Bae-ho 1993). Hence, it had to face democratic resistance and the opposition of broad coalitions, including students, workers, farmers, and civic and church leaders, originating from the tradition of what is called a "contentious society" (Koo 1993). To overcome such challenges, Park's regime had to focus on growth while taking advantage of the ideology and strategy of anti-communism that was, in turn, ardently protested against by democratic alliances. From such dynamism resulted unprecedented economic growth, dubbed the "miracle on the Han River," which later became the frontier of the wider East Asian economic expansion.

At the same time, this process was also regressive in its conservatism against the progressive orientation of the April 19th movements (Lee Gwang-il 2001a, b; Lim and Song 1994). During the first phase, Park softened his advocacy of Cold War anti-communism and statism rooted in Japanese military fascism to a certain extent because of the influence and legacy of the April 19th movements. In contrast, in the second phase of his leadership, he promoted anti-communist statism vigorously so as to strain further the already tense inter-Korean confrontations after crushing the June 3rd (*Yuk-sam*) student uprising of 1964 that was staged to protest the humiliating normalization talks with Japan. He thus removed obstacles in the path to diplomatic relations with Japan and participation in the Vietnam War as a faithful ally of the United States.

Developmental Dictatorship Model A: The Era of "Modernizing the Fatherland" (1964-71)

It has been shown that Park's ideology had its roots in Japanese imperial fascism. However, democratic desires triggered by the April 19th student uprising forced him to concentrate on creating legitimacy for his regime at the expense of his own ideology (Lee Byeong-cheon 2001b; Park Hyon-chae 1987). Moreover, his career as a leftist magnified doubts about his ideological orientation in the presidential campaign against Yun Po-sun, as well as in the diplomatic relations with the United States (Jo 1999:316-23; Lee 1993:120-53). In fact, having praised Japanese imperial statist-nationalism and Hitler's fascism, those problems of Park were not unanticipated. The May 16th coup placed Park's regime on an ideological collision course with the April 19th movements, in that its so-called national democracy was willing to take advantage of the Cold War ideology, whereas the April 19th movements tried to overcome it. Nevertheless, Park managed to secure considerable support for his early orientation of nationalism and populism (Lee 1998:49-51). At the beginning of his regime, indeed, nationalism and populism were represented by his economic policy of state-governed capitalism and his diplomatic policy of distancing Korea from the United States.

On June 3, 1964, the Korean students rose up against his subservient diplomacy with Japan. In response, Park, with the support of the United States, declared a state of emergency, crushing the student uprising and facilitating his developmental dictatorship. This laid the ground for the liberation from poverty and even the miracle on the Han River, and the nationalist and populist elements in the ideological orientation of the military elite at the beginning of the coup lost ground (Kim 1986; Lee Gwang-il 2001b). The initial success and take-off in economic growth brought Park a landslide victory in the May 1967 presidential election.

How, then, did developmental dictatorship model A emerge in the mid-1960s, and what were its main characteristics? First, after the election, Park shifted his top priority to that of *Joguk-geundaehwa* ("Modernizing the fatherland") under the catch phrase *Jal-sara-boshe* ("Let's live a rich life") to compensate for the lack of legitimacy or authority of his regime. Abandoning his earlier distancing diplomacy with the United States, Park became a subordinate partner like a vassal; he cooperated with his new "senior partner" in the U.S.-led anti-communist alliances in Northeast Asia against the USSR-led communist alliances. In step with these strategic shifts, he restored diplomatic ties with Japan and dispatched troops to the Vietnam War. As a result, Park completed two diplomatic circles of critical importance for economic take-off: one involving the United States, Japan, and Korea and the other involving the United States, Vietnam, and Korea. Against this backdrop, Park's Cold War anti-communism was reorganized and transformed into a rather offensive state ideology (Han Bae-ho 2003). Only after this time was the relationship of state and society realigned to become, in name and in reality, one of a strong state and a weak society.

It is important that a uniquely Korean, dual-track growth policy was born out of the trial-and-error of Park's initial state-governed capitalism, selectively accepting the advice and responding to the pressure of the United States and learning from the post-war experiences of Japan in the neighborhood. The two-track industrial and trade policy was designed to combine export promotion with import substitution and improve the quality of the combination through export substitution (Lee 1999). For that purpose, Park forged a new alliance of the state, *chaebols*, and banks while oppressing and mobilizing labor: The new alliance and labor constituted the two pillars of authoritarian developmentalism adapted to suit the South Korean context. However, model A of the 1960s differed greatly from model B of the 1970s. The former was relatively flexible and was less rigid in its industrial policy, the state guidance of the banking and financial sector, and its labor policy on strike and assembly. In addition, the proportion of public ownership in the economy was much larger in the 1960s than in the 1970s.

Developmental Dictatorship Model B: The Yushin Regime of "All-Out National Security" (1972-79)

Phase Two of the developmental dictatorship arose from the contradictions of model A and later emerged as Park's reactionary response to the legitimization crisis of Phase One caused by the new domestic and international circumstances. Park Chung-hee was bewitched by an all-too-familiar obsession of dictators: the belief, "I am the nation," as well as the desire for perpetual reign and dictatorial power accumulation. To realize his ambition, Park attempted a series of emergency measures: In October 1969, the Constitution was amended to allow a third presidential term; on December 6, 1971, a national emergency was declared; on December 27, 1971, a law on special measures for national security was passed; on July 4, 1972, a joint declaration of the North and the South on peaceful reunification was issued; and in October 1972, a martial law for the Yushin Constitution was declared. Therefore, Phase Two can be called the era of *Chongryeok-anbo* ("all-out national security"). The word *Yushin* was borrowed from Japanese history, suggesting a deep influence of Japanese statist-nationalism and imperialism. It referred to the Meiji Restoration, which gave the Emperor full authority over the government and the nation. Although Park interpreted Yushin as a revitalizing reform, it was indeed a Korean version of perpetual dictatorship. The process of the primitive accumulation of sovereign and dictatorial power culminated in an emergency decree on May 13, 1975, which prohibited any attempt to protest or criticize the Constitution.

As the June 3rd incident in 1964 had done for model A, so the Constitutional amendment for a third presidential term in 1969 caused a significant shift in Park's developmental dictatorship model.

As various contradictions were unveiled from model A, there arose a series of conflicts between the oppressive regime and social resistance movements protesting against the amendment, repressions, and class and sectoral cleavages. Park's attempt to secure legitimacy for his dictatorship through economic performance faced fundamental obstacles, and the regime was in danger of losing its legitimacy when popular discontent became politicized. Indeed, students, intellectuals, workers, and religious activists openly resisted the dictatorial power of the regime and the privileged interests of the *chaebols*. With the self-immolation of Chun Tae-il, who was a leading worker in a Peace Market sweatshop, as a dramatic turning point, the various protest movements against political oppression and economic exploitation converged. The spread of a new anti-hegemonic discourse of *Minjung* (people) provided a broad though class-based ideological foundation for the solidarity and cementing of diverse social sectors. The ideology of modernizing the fatherland could no longer serve national integration from above (Han Bae-ho 1993:242-3; Jo 2003; 63-5; Lee Byeong-cheon 2000c). In this situation, the then-opposition politician Kim Dae-jung emerged as a threatening, progressive competitor with a rallying cry for inter-Korean reconciliation and the "mass economy" (*Daejung-kyeongje*) for the greater benefit of the people (Kim 1986; Kim 1999).[8] In the 1971 presidential election, Kim Dae-jung nearly defeated Park Chung-hee, an outcome completely disappointing in comparison with the 1967 election (Choi Jang-jip 2002:86).

On the other hand, Park was faced with external challenges, and the utility of security threats as a justification of his dictatorial power became remarkably weak. Then U.S. President Richard Nixon announced a major reformulation of U.S. foreign policy regarding East Asia; that is, the "Guam Doctrine." According to the doctrine, the United States would no longer take primary military responsibility for defending East Asian nations against communist aggression.

---

[8] Park Hyun-chae's economics of *Minjung* (people) and nationalism based on it, which represented Korean progressive economic thoughts against the developmental dictatorship and its ideology, was first introduced at this time (see Lee 2000:100-1).

Actually, it was an attempt to isolate communist Vietnam from communist China, and there followed the establishment of Sino-U.S. diplomatic ties. The combination of these external factors dealt a severe blow to anti-communism, one of the two pillars of Park's dictatorial regime, resulting in a profound legitimization crisis. In this situation, Park ignored an opportune moment for greatly improving inter-Korean relations and chose instead to proceed more stubbornly with his Cold War anti-communism. This synchronized national security with economic growth under the martial law rule.[9]

Model B was built on the structural conditions of the Cold War and the national division needed to harness those conditions effectively for developmental dictatorship. As the United States declared a new Asian policy to break away from its earlier Cold War hegemony, the Cold War structure gripping East Asia, including Korea, started to crumble, creating a rare opportunity for the countries in the region to find peace and reconciliation. However, Park Chung-hee elected to look the other way and stick to martial rule based on Cold War ideology under the banners of national unity and all-out national security. The Yushin era was marked by a tremendous realignment of state-society relations, which deteriorated into an oppressive dictatorship with almost no room for political freedom or human rights. The Korean Central Intelligence Agency (KCIA) penetrated almost every arena of Korean society. Thus, Park completed an inter-Korean structure of confrontations, which was combined with his ideological orientations of militarism and statist-nationalism. In this period a real political problem for Park was not bondage under the U.S. hegemonic sphere, but self-containment in a fascist-like anti-communist nationalism against North Korea. In addition, the United States helped give rise to model B by giving tacit acknowledgement to Park's power

---

[9] It is true that the Park regime gained a majority of votes when the Yushin Constitution was put to a national referendum on November 21, 1972. However, political activities and freedom to oppose the government were prohibited under the state of emergency, and the regime used somewhat sinister means to lead the population to believe that opposing the Yushin Constitution meant rejecting peaceful coexistence between the North and the South and eventual re-unification.

strategy and its focus on heavy and chemical industrialization. This change in direction, in fact, was made primarily to buttress anti-communist national security and military self-reliance against North Korea; thus, it exacerbated Park's developmental dictatorship as justified by the Cold War and the national division. Model B was to produce an extremely unbalanced and distorted pattern of growth, varying by classes, businesses, regions, and industries.

IV. OUT OF THE PERIPHERY

Domestic Industrialization Regime

Park Chung-hee's developmental dictatorship was conflict-ridden and laden with innate contradictions and unstable factors, which led to frequent crises. His regime was not just a passive revolution. It had to rely on emergency decrees to deal with popular resistance and calls for democracy. Nevertheless, there is no denying the fact that Park's developmental dictatorship regime fulfilled the goals of industrialization and building up the national economy. On the domestic side, the catch phrases of "modernizing the fatherland" and "Let's live a rich life" found timely resonance with the people's desires and also had relevance as a historical project at the time. Unlike the program of his predecessor, Chang Myon, Park's all-out economic drive was based on strong nationalism from above. This ideological rallying cry made it possible to mobilize the entire nation's energy and to forge a collective will for development. However, the people united not just because they were motivated from the top. It should be recognized that a strong passion and collective will for national achievement became an intrinsic part of the modern Korean people constituted against Japanese colonial experience.[10]

---

[10] Choi Jang-jip (1996:26-27, 2002:81) emphasizes that the ideological mobilization using the confrontation between the two Koreas attained public support and contributed to economic development. However, the dangerous confrontation and fierce competition between the two Koreas were in full swing in the 1970s, so it is open to question whether he is

In addition to collective will, there needed to exist a dominant power bloc and institutional forms to make a passive revolution for modernization possible and to create a sustainable growth regime for industrialization. Park reconstructed the bureaucracy, and the political regime was equipped with competent bureaucrats. To his relief, the developmental bloc was not like a rent-seeking or predatory coalition that could have rendered detrimental outcomes for the general population. Instead, it formed an industrialist and productionist partnership that, in the fullness of the time, ushered the nation out of the backwoods into the global arena. Two key policies and their institutional pillars underpinned this success. One is the so-called two-pronged industrial policy combining export promotion and import substitution. Second, there was a capital accumulation regime and corresponding class relations and institutional forms whereby the state formed a cooperative nexus with *chaebols* and banks, all at the expense of the oppressed and exploited labor force.

Contrary to the allegations of the IMF and the Washington consensus, the Korean development model was not a market-conforming one; that is, a "getting the prices right" model that conformed unconditionally to the logic of the global market. Neither did, however, South Korea rely one-sidedly on the import substitution policy nor on a self-reliance strategy. Rather, it developed its own policy paradigm by combining import substitution with export promotion.[11] Such a two-pronged industrial policy was not confined

---

describing the economic functioning of the competition during the Yushin dictatorship. Further, Choi observes the discontinuity between the 1960s and the 1970s, but not the continuity, thereby neglecting the possibility that the orientation and contradiction of the developmental dictatorship regime during 1960s led to the Yushin regime both ideologically and politically.

[11] According to Imaoka Hideki (1985), Taiwan and Japan also implemented the two-pronged development policy, whereas Thailand and the Philippines did not. Kawakami Tadado (1991) puts more emphasis on the establishment of the cotton industry than on the two-pronged industrialization. He shows, however, that from a comparative perspective the industrial types of Korea and Japan are very different from other types. He notes that Japan exported raw silk to earn foreign currency, then succeeded in the import substitution of cotton industry, and moved up to the export promotion of

to the 1960s, but extended to the heavy and chemical industrialization of the 1970s. By the way, some argue that Park's developmental dictatorship was founded on his colonial experience in Manchuria, the Asian equivalent of the North American "Wild West" (Han Hongu 2003:89; Jo 1998:122-3). This argument is not totally groundless in that Park did graduate from a Japanese-run Manchurian military academy during the colonial period, subsequently appointed a number of his ex-schoolmates from the academy to key military positions, and also maintained the Manchurian connection both in Korea and Japan. Therefore, it was inevitable that the Park model would be greatly influenced by his Manchurian experience. However, it is necessary to look more closely into the aforementioned two-pronged industrial policy in the era of heavy and chemical industrialization. As already noted, this industrialization line was chosen partly for South Korea's military needs against North Korea. More interestingly, however, it was an evolved and expanded version of the industrial policy of the 1960s, not one from the colonial period.[12]

Thanks to the two-pronged growth policy of the Park administration, South Korea did not suffer from the troubles that haunted the hasty import substitution drives of such Third World areas as India and Latin America (Lanzarotti 1992a, b). The nation also circumvented the huge problems caused by the socialist self-reliance and heavy industry-first strategy of Mao's China and Kim Il-sung's North Korea. South Korea managed to secure a dynamic competitive advantage in the international scene and succeeded in establishing a national manufacturing regime consisting of two sectors that in-

manufactured goods. Conversely, those late industrializing countries in the West and the United States developed their cotton industry just for the domestic market while exporting only agricultural products.
[12] See Kim (1995:322-2, 368); O Won Chol (1999:457-93, 507-80); and Lee Byeong-cheon (2000c:121). The heavy and chemical industrialization was conducted mainly for military self-reliance, but a military arsenal was not actually produced. In addition, it was based not only on net security motives but also on economic considerations. Seven industry-nurturing laws dating from the late 1960s and early 1970s had particular relevance for the heavy and chemical industrialization (Lee et al. 1989: 16-8; Korea Institute for Industry, Economics and Trade 1997:168-70).

cluded light industries and heavy industries. Additionally, Korea made successful use of the strategic harmony between protection and opening toward the global market, which allowed the nation to escape from a self-inflicted delinking strategy and achieve a rare historic success in utilizing expertly the so-called advantages of lateness and a silk road of the seal, thereby effectively controlling the disadvantages of lateness.

Park's model was, in brief, a market-governing one whereby the government selectively fostered strategic industries with a dynamic competitive advantage while avoiding excessively steep growth that was beyond the conditions and capacities of the country at the time, as in the failed examples above. However, the model was not confined to industrial policy, but went beyond it. The Korean industrialization regime included state intervention in property and class relationships, the mobilization and management of national saving resources toward industrial sectors, and the incentive system linking state subsidies to business performance. In the process, *chaebols* became major investors, and thus, the government provided privileged subsidies to *chaebols* out of socially mobilized capital.

For the accumulation regime for industrialization to emerge and work successfully, the government needed to eliminate traditional obstacles and to establish an incentive as well as disciplining mechanism for industrial production activities.[13] As a result of the land reform of all tenanted properties in South Korea, Park did not need to deal with the resistance problems of the traditional landlord class toward industrialization. However, he had to prepare a positive governance and disciplinary mechanism for industrial capital accumulation. To that end, Park conducted industrial policy and nurtured

---

[13] Brenner (1997) and Amsden (1989) are well-known for their views on the incentive or discipline mechanisms required for successful industrialization. The former emphasizes that the profit opportunity for industrial capital accumulation should be created on the ground that social production relations need to be transformed in the context of the transition from feudalism to capitalism in the West, The latter observes that performance discipline should be linked to the protection and subsidy of the state as a successful condition of late industrialization after 1945.

chaebols as developmental partners. The *chaebols* received government subsidies mainly through bank credits and were encouraged through financial and fiscal means to support the two-pronged industry policy. This industrial policy was combined with financial repression. The state's financial control became an effective means to "guide" *chaebols* toward productive investments in areas of national priority. Protected by the state's firm guarantee, moreover, the property rights and governance structure of *chaebols* were virtually untouchable for outsiders as well as workers.

One of the significant characteristics of Korea's development drive was its performance-based subsidies. We know very well that there have been numerous attempts, in the economic history of the modern world, of government intervention to overcome market failures and to substitute for a capitalist structural power. However, in many cases, such attempts have been to no avail. Fundamentally, one of the reasons for their failure is because government intervention was not harnessed correctly to the disciplinary mechanisms to create new industrial wealth and encourage innovation. Therefore, it is safe to say that tying subsidies to performance was one of the keys to Korea's economic success.

So far, four key policy and institutional mechanisms behind Korea's successful industrialization have been presented: (1) the developmental partnership between the state and *chaebols*, (2) the two-pronged growth policy, (3) the state's support for *chaebols'* property rights and governance structure of accumulation, and (4) the disciplinary mechanism. In addition, the *chaebols* were family-owned businesses with intra-group cross-shareholding and transactions and octopus-like diversification. In an incomplete, less-developed market, they could utilize the intra-group transfer of money and personnel. With state subsidies, a diversification structure, and intra-group transfer, they were willing and able to undertake investment risks. As a result, the big businesses of scale and scope, which had a specific investment and growth orientation, arose. In line with the government policy, they pursued mass productive investments and market shares.

On the other hand, Korean growth successes were, in fact, the product of the huge sacrifice and dedication of laborers. In particular, the labor-intensive export industries, most notably the garment industry, treated poorly educated young female workers merely as parts of a machine, an employment philosophy that led directly to the death of many workers. The self-immolation of Chun Tae-il in a Peace Market sweatshop of Seoul in 1970 — who shouted, "Human beings are not machines!" and "Observe the Labor Standard Law!" — highlighted the plight of workers in Korean modernization. In short, *chaebols* were the main engines of Korea's development drive, and the workforce depended on them under the military-like state control of labor. Their high productivity with low wages called for labor sacrifices under the slogan of "growth first, distribution later." However, it is also true that such rapid growth created employment opportunities and a relatively rapid rise in wages, which in turn stimulated the voluntary participation of workers.

It is now time to attempt to explain the relation between development and dictatorship or, more accurately, how much Korea's economic success depended on its political dictatorship. Answers to such difficult questions can be found, to some extent at least, in the material presented so far. In particular the two-pillar growth policy was not closely related to political dictatorship. The success of that policy, however, depended on the way the government mobilized the social potential of the country in the name of development and then concentrated that potential on industrialization as a national top priority. Considering the Korean historical conditions of 1960s, some sort of authoritarianism might be a necessary part of Korean capitalist industrialization (Choi Jang-jip 2002:86-8; Kim 1999:193-4). In this regard, Park's regime yielded comparatively good results for 5 years from 1964, when the June 3rd martial law was terminated, to 1969, when the Constitution was amended for the third time under his rule. Despite the success of the period, however, there were many more democratic options for Park.[14] In this regard the Yushin dictatorship of Phase Two, quite unlike that of Phase One, had no

---

[14] See Lee Gwang-il (2001b:176) for a study of the political oppression in that period.

historic legitimacy. There were other possibilities and alternatives to move toward more open and democratic development path, a matter addressed in Section V.

External Environments: Two Triangular Opportunities for Development

External environments alone, no matter how favorable they are, cannot bring about national development; an appropriate domestic regime for development is also required. Similarly, without favorable environmental circumstances, the domestic regime alone cannot produce as good a result as it otherwise might. For Korea, the external environments can be divided into that of the East Asia region and that of the world as a whole. As for the former, Korea greatly depended on and made the best possible use of the Northeast Asia policy of the United States. Korea's success would have been quite unattainable had it not been for the help given by the United States, as it was too great a task for South Korea to juggle inter-Korean confrontations and participate to advantage in the world capitalist arena. It is important to recall that the international community continued to focus on the unstable situation of the Korean peninsula at the time.[15] The United States provided money and market to Korea. Under the overwhelming influence of the United States, Japan provided money, technology, equipment, and markets. Korea processed goods and exported mainly to the United States; this was the main external growth triangle for South Korea.[16] Backed by the United States, in particular, the normalization of Korea-Japan diplomatic relations provided South Korea extra money and goods for development and access to Japanese technology and markets, thus, demonstrating the "neighbor effects."

The Korea-U.S.-Japan triangle became possible because of Korea's geopolitical location during the Cold War. It occupied the front-

---

[15] See Oh Won-chol (1995a, b).
[16] See Kawakami (1991:19-31) for his comments on the importance of foreign capital to the Korean economy from a comparative perspective.

line of ideological confrontation, whereas Japan was shielded well away from it. The Cold War standoff between the two Koreas resulted in risks as well as opportunities for South Korean development. On the one hand, South Korea was not able to fully enjoy peace, democracy, or independent diplomacy. Moreover, its military and security situation reduced its room to maneuver even further. On the other hand, however, the situation made the United States realize that South Korea's economic success might also be beneficial to it; hence, its aid to South Korea as a development and security partner against the communist bloc of the North.

Although it is an issue that has often been ignored, there existed a strong, though concealed, motivation for the United States to give aid to South Korea and to pressure Japan to normalize diplomacy with and support the economic reconstruction and development of South Korea. That is, the United States forced Japan to support South Korea in order to secure the military help from the latter for the Vietnam War. That was what lay behind the "Rostow doctrine" (Kim 1986:64-9; Lee Byeong-cheon 2000b:180; Lee Sang-woo 1987:134-43; Lee 1993:131-7; Lee 1995:52-4; Lee 1995:120-1). In Park's perspective, the war in Vietnam provided a timely opportunity for securing a better footing for his U.S. diplomacy and added leverage to raise and compensate Korea's status as a weak state in relation to the United States. As a result, there emerged the Korea-U.S.-Vietnam growth triangle in addition to the Korea-U.S.-Japan triangle (Chong song-jin 2000; Han Hon-gu 2003; Park 1993; Shin Gwang-young 1999).[17]

---

[17] Experts differ on the development effect of South Korea's joining the Vietnam War. Park Keun-ho (1993) points out that Korea had major benefits in the fields of export promotion, financing, governmental role, and the rise of new chaebols. He also indicates that by participating in the war, Korea not only promoted exports to Vietnam but also greatly increased the amount of exports to the United States. On the contrary, Han Hong-gu insists that Korea's gain did not much exceed its loss and also that America was parsimonious with its rewards. On the other hand, Kimiya (1991) notes the gap between Korea's expectation and the actual result. Korea did not achieve its original goal to make inroads into Southeast Asian

As for the global economy, South Korea could secure autonomy for its economic policy for industrialization under the Bretton Woods system, with "embedded liberalism" based on fixed exchange rates and capital controls across the border. The General Agreement on Tariffs and Trades (GATT) also allowed dumping and export subsidies for developing countries. Furthermore, the advanced countries in the West changed into welfare states and enjoyed the so-called golden age of growth and distribution, which entailed the expansion of global trade. All these factors provided South Korea with the best possible foreign market conditions. In addition, there was another favorable factor. The modernization and protectionism of the agricultural sector in advanced countries made it extremely difficult for import substitution through agricultural exports to succeed, leaving labor-intensive manufacturing for export as the only viable alternative. South Korea and other leading latecomers in East Asia effectively utilized this opportunity, whereas their counterparts in Latin America, relying on agricultural export, could not. That was, indeed, a major difference between them.[18] If other competitors had jumped on the bandwagon, South Korea would have had to survive much more cutthroat competition. In this regard, timing was crucial, and Park took advantage of the opportunity as a springboard to move up the growth ladder of the global economy.

However, the external environment of South Korea in the 1970s was substantially different from that of the 1960s. Its relations with the United States worsened, the golden era of the welfare capitalism of Europe and the expansion of the international trade ended, and the global depression began. Despite the harsh circumstances, Park opted for foreign exchange-consuming heavy and chemical industrialization, mainly for security reasons. Fortunately, although the protection and support under the Bretton Woods system and the Cold War were removed, some favorable conditions were created. Oil dollars in the European money market placed Korea and other NICs in an exceptionally advantageous position. Moreover, when advanced countries accepted demands of the Third

---

markets, and the United States did not relax its "buy-American" policy.
[18] See Hwang Byong-dok (1990:115-6); and Lee (1996: 98-99).

World to accord duty-free status to their exports under the General System of Preferences (GSP), Korea unwittingly became a free rider as one of the most favored nations. In addition, thanks to the fierce competition among advanced countries, Korea could import plants for equipment investment on cheap credit. Lastly, the construction boom in the Middle East offered another impetus for the rapid growth of exports in the 1970s.

In short, Park's gamble to shift the focus to heavy and chemical industries was successful thanks, in large part, to a sequence of fortuitous circumstances. Numerous potential difficulties and pains along the road were avoided by dint of major favorable conditions. For example, the significantly undervalued currency under the Plaza Accord of September 1985 contributed to the export boom in the troubled heavy and chemical industries, and the political economic supports granted by the United States and Japan to General Chun Doo-hwan after the assassination of Park Chung-hee ensured a certain degree of political stability. Had it not been for this combination of factors, South Korea's economy might have become enmeshed in a trap of debt similar to the one that Brazil's indebted industrialization experienced in 1981.[19]

V. THE DARK SIDE OF DEVELOPMENTAL DICTATOR-SHIP

Yushin Dictatorship and the Crippled Big Push

Park's imposition of martial law was a manifestation of an all-out anti-communist statist or sovereign dictatorship under which the Korean people were simply commanded to be subservient to the state power and to do as they were told. Meanwhile, Park was dreaming of perpetual rule. This suffocated Korean democracy and stifled any realistic possibility of a peaceful reconciliation with the North. The heavy and chemical industrialization undertaken to achieve

---

[19] See Hart-Landsberg (1993:222-4).

military self-reliance created a close and illicit alliance between the dictatorial power and large conglomerates that functioned for their mutual benefit and reinforcement. The national economy was transformed into a *chaebol* republic. Huge gaps opened up between *chaebols* and small and medium-sized enterprises (SMEs) and also between the eastern and western provinces of South Korea. The economy became more unstable and more dependent on overseas markets; it was increasingly tainted by environmental pollution, high-risk business practices, and many other detrimental side effects of the martial law regime.

At the same time, the Cold War was drawing toward its end, evidenced by the development of diplomatic ties between the United States and China and the commencement of the U.S. withdrawal from Vietnam. It was clear, therefore, that the U.S.-led Cold War anti-communist policy in East Asia was about to undergo a radical transformation. There can be little doubt that, in the circumstances, Park Chung-hee could have abandoned the Cold War-based confrontation with the North and taken the initiative in fostering a balanced development path with growth, stability, and equitable distribution. Instead, he not only ignored the opportunity, but actually went to extremes.[20]

There is another reason why the Yushin dictatorship regime cannot be excused by economic or political necessity. Unlike in the 1960s, Park Chung-hee in the 1970s had other rational alternatives to the dictatorship model. During the presidential election in April 1971, the opposition candidate Kim Dae-jung made many proposals for the achievement of peace on the peninsula and for a more equitable economy called "mass economy" in line with global trends at the time of the termination of the Cold War. Kim's suggestions put pressure on Park to try other alternatives at his disposal, but Park was determined to continue with his saber-rattling posture and the

---

[20] Both Park Chung-hee in the South and Kim Il-sung in the North utilized the division of the Korean peninsula and the intricacies of the North-South dialogue to consolidate their dictatorship and to forcibly mobilize their people. The Yushin dictatorship and *Yuil* (sole) dictatorship may be regarded as "hostile twins" (Lee Chong-sok 2003).

suppression of the Korean people's desire for democracy and peace. Such was the extreme nature of this dictatorship that it brought suffering not only to the mass of the general population but to members of the ruling circle as well. After its failed attempt to establish a hegemonic party system to maintain political power, the ruling circle had to rely solely on Park Chung-hee, the dictator as an individual; hence, the emergence of the rule of martial law and emergency decrees (Han Bae-ho 1993; Kim 1999). In the final act, however, it would engulf Park himself.

At this point, it is important to consider whether the move to heavy and chemical industrialization necessarily had to entail martial rule. Can we assess the heavy and chemical industries separately from the issue of political dictatorship? The view could be supported to a certain extent. It seems to be somewhat unreasonable that the political Yushin dictatorship and economic heavy chemical industrialization are included in the same category and put on the same scales. There, however, existed other alternatives, and more flexible and balanced routes for development that could, at the same time, have guaranteed growth, stability, and more equitable distribution. Kim Dae-jung's ideas of development were representative of that alternative path.

When compared with the Taiwanese pattern, that of Park's Korea was markedly trouble-ridden (Table 1.3). There is further confirmation that developmental dictatorship in Korea and Taiwan exhibited as many differences as they shared common factors. Unlike Korea, Taiwan pursued a development pattern balancing growth, stability, and welfare with state regulation of private capital while, at the same time, harmonizing state-run companies and SMEs. Its economic policy line led to a gradual, flexible industrial policy; a sound monetary policy; low debt-to-equity ratios for companies; and an accumulation of foreign exchange reserves. In contrast, Korea's growth-first and high-speed developmentalism ignored stability and welfare and generated risky development, created colossal *chaebols*, a rigid and reckless industrial policy, high inflation, and abnormal government banking with negative interest rates. Most of these problems originated from the economic policies focused on the heavy and chemical industrialization of the 1970s. Therefore, had it not been for exceptionally favorable external circumstances, South Korea's economy might have sunk into disaster.[21]

Table 1.3 Comparison between Taiwan and South Korea

South Korea	Taiwan
Statism, growth-only, high-speed strategy	Statism based on "Three Principles of the People," balance of growth, stability, and welfare
State-*chaebol* domination alliance strong ties, weak network and on components multi-unbalanced developments	State-run big companies and private SMEs, guanxi capitalism, emphasis on rural industry
Reckless, rigid industrial policy, top-down policy, overstretched and abnormal window dressing, financial repression	Gradual, flexible industrial policy, autonomy of the private sector (SMEs), sound monetary policy, state-run banking and unofficial financial sector
High inflation	Price stability
Debt-ridden expansion of *chaebols*	Soundness of corporate financial structure
Accumulation of trade deficits and foreign debts	Accumulation of trade surpluses and financial reserves

One factor that is highly noteworthy in the Taiwanese model is the ideology behind its developmental dictatorship, the "Three Principles of the People." The then-president of Taiwan, Chiang Kai-shek, raised his nation from the ashes of civil war on clearly defined social principles. It was this socially based recovery and development that differentiates Taiwan so distinctly from Japan, and

---

[21] Considering the sequential process from the implementation of the heavy and chemical industrialization through the structural adjustment of overinvestments in the industry after Park's death to the economic crisis of 1997, it is difficult to concur with Amsden's one-sided, overly optimistic view regarding heavy and chemical industrialization.

from Korea under Park Chung-hee. It is a distinction that adds further credence to the view that Park's ideology and desire for permanent rule had its roots in Japanese military fascism, which was combined with aggressive anti-communism against North Korea.

Regression and Barbarism in the Relationships with Japan and Vietnam

In fact, most of the problems of Park's developmental dictatorship occurred during Phase Two of the 1970s. Had he not gone down the path of the rule of martial law and emergency decrees, he might well have been accorded a different place in history. Nevertheless, Park's problem was not confined to the consequences of martial rule. Indeed, his trouble began to appear even during the heyday of developmental dictatorship, from 1964 to 1969. For example, there occurred a series of "red complex" incidents initiated by the government against supposedly pro-communist activities, such as those involving the so-called People's Revolution Party, the East Berlin Association, and the Unification Revolution Party. Park also created what were known as the "local reserve military forces," initiated military drills for university students, declared a charter of national education, and established other laws aimed at transforming schools and civil society into anti-communist semi-military organizations (Lee 2001:176). Park's economic growth in Phase One was not without problems either. Under his stewardship, numerous politicians formed corrupt alliances with business, allowing the insiders special privileges. Because of such covert arrangements, privileged companies, with financial problems that were concealed by dint of their political protection, became insolvent and bankrupt, eventually forcing the government to issue the "Emergency Decree for Economic Stability and Growth" (August 3, 1972). This August 3rd Order did all that the business circle asked and wanted at the time.

The economic benefits of the normalization of diplomatic relations with Japan and the involvement in the Vietnam War need to be seen in a critical perspective. Those were, in fact, crucial external factors that made developmental dictatorship model A work, providing a springboard for the take-off of the South Korean economy in the 1960s. These factors, however, produced regressive elements in a historically reflexive perspective. The distorted normalization treaty effectively banished a precious chance for resolving legacies of the colonial past, both for Korea and for Japan. Whereas they should, of course, live as friendly neighbors, it was necessary, first, for them to come to terms with their dark and tragic past. However, the ruling blocs of the two countries made an agreement behind closed doors to avoid, rather than resolve, the issues of the colonial past. Because of this, Korea, as the victim, could not point an accusatory finger at the factors and personalities responsible for its colonial subjugation, and Japan lost a golden opportunity to apologize (Institute for Research in Collaborationist Activities 1995; Lee Won-dok 1996a, b).

As for the Vietnam War, Korea joined the U.S.-led domination strategy over Asia against the communist bloc and, arguably, over the world, not merely because it was forced to in any way. Virtually from the outset, the Park Chung-hee regime was willing to offer the participation of Korean troops in one of the bloodiest wars in modern history, in which most of the rest of the world, including European countries, did not wish to participate. Only Australia, New Zealand, the Philippines, Thailand, and South Korea responded positively to the U.S. request, and South Korea emerged as the most important contributor, dispatching a total of 300,000 troops, called "mercenaries" by critics, to Vietnam. Such a warfare developmental dictatorship had much to do with Park's Japanese fascism-grounded statist-nationalism, which was much different from Chiang Kai-shek in Taiwan. In return for his military commitment, the United States formally acknowledged Park and helped him lay the groundwork for the amendment of the Constitution and then the highly oppressive Yushin dictatorship. Consequently, Park's developmental dictatorship, helped greatly by participation in the Vietnam War in Phase One of the mid-1960s, showed innate symptoms of degeneration in Phase Two of the 1970s (Han Bae-ho 2003; Lee 1996:92; Lee 1998:226).

VI. CONCLUSION

This introduction and overview presents a theory, as well as a concept, of developmental dictatorship as a model of the nationalist modernization regime by presenting and analyzing the lights and shadows of the Korean experience. Developmental dictatorship can be understood as a statist-nationalist, passive revolution regime oriented toward modernization. Under the regime, the ruling forces give national priority to economic modernization or industrialization over everything else, oppressing the development of democracy and civil society. In modern history, a typical model of developmental dictatorship appeared in the late industrialization and late democratization of Germany and Japan in the 19th century. Park's approach was essentially a derivative of its historical precedents.

Nevertheless, Park's version was not simply a copy of the Japanese or German model of late industrialization and late democratization, but a new version of post-colonial East Asian countries. Depending on and actively taking advantage of the Cold War and national division, Park combined statist-nationalism with anti-communism. Although Japan and Germany formulated a way of catching up with advanced countries and pursued an imperialist road, the developmental dictatorship of Korea was one on the semi-periphery, protected and controlled by the U.S. hegemony. Another characteristic of Park's model of catch-up industrialization with its magnified advantages and disadvantages as a latecomer, which is distinct from the Japanese or German model, lies in the active entrepreneurial role of the state and its close alliance with big businesses.

In Korea, moreover, industrialization was followed by rapid social changes. The so-called miracle on the Han River enabled the Korean society to break out of the vicious circle of poverty and deprivation and enjoy the many boons of industrialization. Moreover, the establishment of a strong national economy saved Korea from having to beg in international society and allowed it to have a real voice as a sovereign nation in the global society. Although there still remains controversy over whether, overall, the transformation was

45

beneficial or harmful, industrialization was what Korea had been aspiring for since it first opened up to the West in the second half of the 19th century, and it was a hard-earned achievement. Furthermore, the modern history of the Korean peninsula as a whole since the August 15th liberation of 1945 has changed direction sharply, with the rise of the South and the decline of the North. Changes are still under way on the peninsula, and there is a clear imperative for further study of the implications.

The success of Korean economic modernization depended on a combination of various factors, and there were similarities as well as differences in the industrialization regime even within the 18 years of the Park regime. The Korean case reveals certain general lessons of successful catch-up industrialization for latecomers. The dual track or two-pronged growth policy combining export promotion and import substitution; the cooperative nexus between the government, the market and institutions; and the selective or strategic opening up to the global market were of sufficient significance to require a new paradigm of industrialization that would go beyond the dichotomy of state and market. For successful industrialization, however, substantial capital needed to be mobilized, advanced technologies introduced, and foreign markets opened to latecomers. It should be emphasized that Korea enjoyed to the full extent external opportunities at the time, which was highly exceptional.

Despite rapid industrialization, Park's model was no more than a combination of contradictions between high growth and high risk, between modernization and anti-modernization, and even between modernization and retro-modernization. There are many reasons for this. First, Park's model, based on the specters of ultra-nationalism, militarism, and warfare, tried to imitate the imperial fascism of pre-1945 Japan. Model B in the Phase Two of developmental dictatorship went to further extremes when Park ignored an opportunity to choose a direction of democratic transition and peaceful reconciliation with North Korea. Instead, he used scaremongering tactics about external threats, particularly those from the North, to legitimate his regime and consolidate his power. Second, the subservient resumption of diplomatic relations with Japan and the unjustified involvement in the Vietnam War dealt severe blows to the nation's collective colonial memory and historic conscience as an oppressed nation, leaving indelible scars on the modern history of Korea.

Third, Park's development model had an extremely concentrated, unbalanced structure. In addition to its economic efficiency, the triangular nexus among the state, *chaebols*, and banks under the banner of "growth first, distribution later" divided the members of the nation into insiders and outsiders. It resulted in a *chaebol* republic, causing severe socioeconomic imbalances and institutional failures throughout Korean society. Fourth, Park's regime aggravated social and environmental risks through the "growth first, high-speed" strategy, resulting in the superficial expansion of the economy in the shortest time period possible. On the other side of the growth-first policy, frequent "whitewash" practices barely managed to conceal the rising risks passed on to the lives of the people and the natural environment, which would be inherited by generations to come.

In the meantime, history was repeated when the assassination of Park Chung-hee on October 26, 1979 was followed by the new military dictatorship of Chun Doo-hwan, who crushed the Kwangju civil uprising of May 18, 1980 in collaboration with the United States. In response, the incessant struggle, sacrifice, and dedication of democratic and nationalist movements against the anti-communist statist dictatorship since the Park regime played a critical enlightening and civilizing role in the shaping of modernity in the Republic of Korea. This struggle is reflected in the particular dynamic features and significance of the Korean model of modernization or the model of dual revolutions of industrialization and democratization, which is in contrast to the Japanese or other East Asian models of modernization.

Now at the beginning of the 21st century, South Korea is facing the task of moving from the stage of statist mobilization from above into a new stage of civil or societal initiatives from below. That means the nation must overcome the dichotomous dilemma of the statist developmental dictatorship and the neo-liberal free-market despotism. Korea should pursue a democratic republic of horizontal relationships and communication among citizens based on such norms as justice, solidarity, peace, and ecology. In that way the state should undergo a radical shift from the dictatorial mobilizational state from above to a participatory civic state from below. Nevertheless, the nation-state can serve as both a liberating public space and a suffocating prison camp for our lives at the same time. Thus, our efforts to go beyond the dichotomy of developmental dictatorship and neo-liberalism should not be confined to recreating a nation state, but should be extended to rearranging relationships with other nations on the basis of civic cosmopolitanism. Now is the time for the Korean people to reflect on the accustomed national spirit of catching up with developed countries in the era of national competition for short-sighted national interests, which was dominated by the law of the jungle.

Ulrich Beck (1992), a well-known German sociologist, differentiates reflexive modernization from simple modernization propelled by industrialization. In the former, as a society becomes more modernized, members of the society tend to reflect on the condition of modernity and gain the capacity to transform it by themselves as reflexive civic subjects. The Republic of Korea needs to build a democratic nation for civic participation and empowerment, on the one hand, and a post-Cold War peace hub for the Korean peninsula as well as East Asia, on the other, so as to overcome its past extremes. Then, what kinds of self-reflection and self-enlightenment are needed for us Koreans to achieve those goals? One sure starting point is to undertake a critical reflection on our past experiences of developmental dictatorship.

PART TWO

The Lights and Shadows of Economic Development

Chapter 2

Industrialization in South Korea: Accumulation and Regulation

Seo Ick-jin

I. INTRODUCTION

A heightened awareness of the relationship between developmental dictatorship and economic development is nothing new. That relationship was the crux of a long-lasting controversy concerning the "miracle on the Han River" that took place during the 1960s and 1970s. The question was again placed in the spotlight by the unprecedented economic crisis that Korea faced a generation or so later. There has been an assertion that the remarkable economic achievements of Korea would not have been possible without the authoritarian government led by Park Chung-hee. In fact, this argument is well founded. At the same time, some people insist that the 1997-8 IMF economic crisis actually originated from the legacy of that authoritarian administration. Their argument seems to carry weight as well. In still another viewpoint, Professor Amartya Sen (2000), economist and Nobel laureate, has insisted that it was democracy that served as the basis for economic development. It is true that the financial turmoil of the late 1990s occurred at a time when Korea was seeking openness and liberalization and was following the trend of so-called neo-liberal globalization. Despite these various interpretations, few efforts to clarify systematically the relationship between developmental dictatorship and economic development have been made. To correct that omission, this chapter considers the development process during the period of develop-mental dictatorship as a development model and attempts to clarify its logic of functioning. Here no value judgments are made, and a positive attitude is taken throughout.

On the basis of a theory of developmental state, I apply basic concepts of regulation theory (here, regulation considered in French terms) in this chapter. If the theory of developmental state empha-sizes an active role of the state in the process of development, clarifying various intervention mechanisms (Amsden 1989; Wade et al. 1999), the regulation approach offers conceptual tools that can be used in the acceptance of developmental dictatorship as a develop-ment model.[1] A development model is the combination of both an accumulation regime and a mode of regulation. An accumulation regime indicates the macroeconomic mechanisms required to attain stable growth, whereas the mode of regulation is a series of norms to control the activities of microeconomic actors for the purpose of ensuring the smooth operation of the accumulation regime, with these norms being concretized as various institutions.

According to this analysis, the development model of develop-mental dictatorship that is perceived as having worked in Korea from the early 1960s to the mid-1980s can be defined as a combination of the accumulation regime based on a borrowing and export-oriented economy, on the one hand, and the government-led mode of regula-tion having the characteristics of developmental dictatorship, on the other. This chapter shows how the elements necessary for the operation of this development model interact with each other to establish coherence in the model on the whole. The macroeconomic growth mechanisms consisting of this accumulation regime are dealt with first. The chapter then shows, through the perspective of different institutions, how the mode of regulation characterized by developmental dictatorship corresponded to this accumulation regime.

---

[1] Attempts to apply the regulation approach to the domain of economic development have been made by Ominami (1986), Lanzarotti (1992a), Cordova (1994), Boureile (1994), Seo Ick-jin (2000), and Thala (2002).

II. THE ORIGINAL ACCUMULATION REGIME

The macroeconomic growth mechanisms of a borrowing and export-oriented economy are shown in Figure 2.1. It should be noted that the internal and external fronts are closely interconnected to make an ensemble.

Figure 2.1 Mcroeconomic growth mechanisms of a borrowing and export-oriented economy

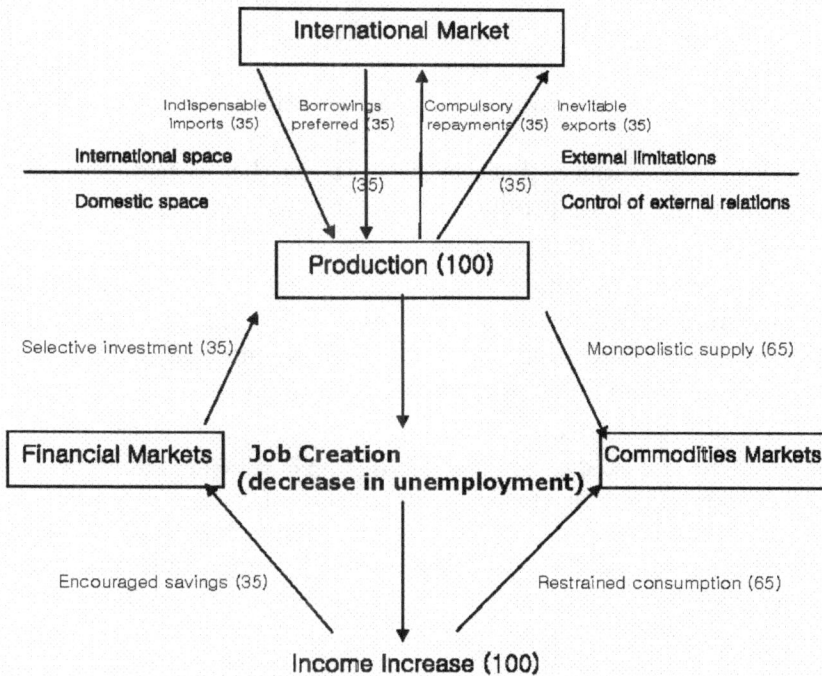

Note: The numbers inside the parentheses are selected to show the quantitative relationship among macroeconomic variables more clearly.

Our argument starts from one of the critical characteristics of underdeveloped economies; that is, the nonexistence or insufficiency of the means of production (producers' goods). Therefore, producers' goods (machines, equipments, intermediate goods, technology, raw materials, and petroleum) must be imported. Such indispensable imports are made possible by attracting foreign capital (overseas savings). However, when foreign capital flows into a country mainly through borrowing from abroad, a borrowing economy develops. The accelerated industrialization rapidly triggers imports, leading to an increase in commercial deficits and overseas debt. Under these circumstances, exports are vital because they are the only normal means to obtain the foreign capital necessary for financing the deficit and paying off the debt.[2] This means that exports are inevitable. In this way, an export-oriented economy and a borrowing economy are inseparable. If the borrowing and export-oriented economy proves effective as a way of overcoming debt crises that tend to occur periodically, the industrialization process can be sustained until an autonomous national production system, as a final goal of the development course, is established.

This external mechanism is accompanied by a specific internal mechanism. The greater the magnitude of exports, the lower will be the part of domestic production absorbed by internal consumption. Therefore, to maintain an appropriate level of inflation and a balance

---

[2] There are two external constraints imposed on developing economies. The one is economic: the maintenance of the balance of international payments. Imports should be matched by exports, or a commercial deficit should be offset by a capital surplus. The other constraint is monetary: The equilibrium of external balances should be realized in terms of international currency. The latter constraint is applied only to the countries with currencies that do not function as international ones (unlike the United States.). Such external constraints become greater when the liberal conversion of a national currency into another international currency is not guaranteed. However, even if this conversion is permitted, for it to be actually realized, the domestic foreign currency market must be stable or foreign exchange reserves so sufficient as to ensure the stability of the foreign exchange market. There is no doubt that the most sound and certain method of increasing reserves is to expand the trade surplus.

in the domestic commodities market, the rate of domestic consumption to national income should decrease, whereas that of savings should increase. A high savings rate is a precondition for increased investment, which leads to a reduced dependence on overseas savings. Investment not only contributes directly to boosting international exports but also indirectly to the development of the export sector by strengthening the national production structure. In addition, an investment in imports substitution can reduce the pressure resulting from external constraints. When an expanded production capacity accompanies job creation (or a decrease in unemployment), socio-political stability, a condition especially important for the development model of developmental dictatorship, is attainable.

The complete mechanism resides in the connection of external and internal components. For a quantitative expansion process to contribute to the establishment of a national production system, the final goal of the development process, the substitution process of imports for national products should be continued until structural deficits in the commercial balance disappear and, at the same time, an autonomous sector of means of production should be constructed.

External Aspects of Accumulation

The establishment and operation of a borrowing and export-oriented economy can be divided into two elements: a borrowing economy and an export-oriented economy.

First, an examination of such factors as the role of imports, import financing methods, and overseas borrowing is necessary to define the borrowing economy. In a borrowing economy, imports act as a kind of production sector of producers' goods; their primary function is to supply from the outside those producer's goods that are indispensable for industrialization, but the production of which is not possible within the country. When the imported producers' goods are used in the construction of domestic production facilities for producers' goods, they can make a contribution to the building of an autonomous national production system. Furthermore, imported goods frequently come with associated technologies and thus constitute one method of technology transfer. Imports are not suppressed, but rather controlled to make them serve such functions. This is a crucial point for the smooth operation of a borrowing and export-led economy.

During the 1960s and 1970s, producers' goods accounted for two-thirds of annual imports (machinery 24-36%, intermediate goods 38-43%), whereas consumers' goods accounted for a meagre 8-10% (Economic Planning Board, *Major Economic Indicators*). During the same period, imports of light industrial goods fell sharply (from 30% in the 1960s to 10% in the 1970s), but imports of heavy industrial goods remained in excess of 50% from the mid-1960s (Bank of Korea, *Input-Output Table Analysis*). In his research on productive imports, Professor Chong Song-jin (1990) noted that imports in the production sector of means of production reached an annual 86-92% of total imports. His research makes sense on two counts in the context of this chapter. First, the indices related to import dependence on producers' goods in all sectors were very high. In particular, those of the heavy and chemical industries were far higher than those of light industries. Second, the indices of imports rose rapidly from 1963. They began to fall steadily after recording an all-time high around 1973. This shows that the progress of industrialization caused a sharp increase in imports. In addition, after industrialization of the heavy and chemical industries, signifying a development of the production sector of producers' goods, went into full swing, the ratio of imports decreased. However, even in the early 1980s producers' goods continued to constitute the largest share of total imports.

This significant role of imports raises questions about the method of import finance. For example, high economic growth and ongoing industrialization increase imports more rapidly than exports, resulting in an accumulation of commercial deficits, which need to be dealt with appropriately. The ideal way of paying imports is through exports. In step with the development of an export-oriented economy, the proportion of exports rose dramatically (14.5% in 1962, 96.4% in 1977, and 85.4% in 1981), but no year saw a commercial surplus. The current account deficit also accumulated because the commercial deficit was offset decreasingly by the surplus in the invisible trade balance and the balance of transfer transactions. With regard to this deficit, two points need to be emphasized. During that period, the balance of transfer transactions remained in the black thanks to a combination of various elements: U.S. economic aid, U.S. payments for the intervention of Korean troops in the Vietnam War, the influx of money resulting from Korean property claims against Japan's colonial occupation, and remittances from Koreans working in the Middle East and Germany. In the meantime, invisible trade balances that had been in the black in the 1960s went into the red in the 1970s. This shift was caused by a rapid increase in insurance and shipping costs paid to foreign companies, profit remittances by foreign companies operating in Korea, and increased repayments of short- and long-term principal and interest (Bank of Korea, *Economic Statistics Yearbook*, 1987). In these circumstances, the basic balance was maintained by a long-term capital balance surplus; that is, a net influx of long-term capital. Foreign investment was very meager, and overseas borrowing took the lion's share. The ratio of overseas loans had increased rapidly in the 1960s, but began to decrease in the early 1970s and fell below international credits in the mid-1970s (Korea National Statistical Office 1991). It is clear that during the developmental dictatorship era imports for industrialization expanded, and the ensuing deficit was supplemented mainly by overseas borrowing.

One other factor in defining the borrowing economy is the ratio of overseas borrowing to the overall economy. In Korea, the ratio of total investment to GNP increased by an annual 15.1% during the period 1962 to 1966 and by 35.5% from 1976 to 1981, whereas the ratio of overseas savings as a financial source for investment rose to approximately one-half of total investment in the 1960s, and to one-third of the 1976 to 1981 figure. The ratio of overseas borrowing to total imports reached an all-time high of 24%, but its ratio to the commercial deficit soared from 15.5% in the early 1960s to 74.5% in the late 1970s. Additionally, the ratio of overseas borrowing to total fixed capital went up by more than double, from 10.6% in the early 1960s to 23.5% in the early 1970s. After that, it fell to 13.3%. It has been pointed out that the same figures concerning the manufacturing sector were twice as high as these ones (Lee Song-hyong 1985).

The operation of an export-oriented economy now needs to be reviewed. As pointed out earlier, an export-oriented economy is both a logical and a practical outcome of a borrowing economy. At the same time, it is one element that completes the external mechanism of a borrowing and export-oriented economy and serves as a driving factor for growth. There are many indices demonstrating the establishment of the Korean export-oriented economy. The ratio of exports to GNP increased sharply (3.3% in 1963, 11.6% in 1971, 36.8% in 1981), and total output also went up (that of light industries from 2.3 to 19.3% during the period 1960-80, and for the heavy and chemical industries from 2.9 to 19% during the same period). The export-oriented economy was not confined to special export areas, especially Free Export Zones for foreign companies, but was connected directly or indirectly to all industrial activities, and international subcontracts, such as original equipment manufacturing (OEM), were prevalent.

There are two statistical categories testifying to the existence of an export sector: bonded processing exports in export data and intermediary goods for exports in import data. The ratio of each category showed a certain stability at a high level after earlier increases (the former stood at 1.8% in 1962, 21.7% in 1975, and 12% in 1981, whereas the latter was recorded as 2.2% in 1965, 27.3% in 1972, and 17-20% until 1983). These figures show that the contribution of the export sector to economic growth reached 27.8% during 1961-70, in stark contrast to 4.1%, the contribution of the sector for imports substitution (Lanzarotti 1992a). According to statistics from the Korea Trade-Investment Promotion Agency (KOTRA), the contribution of exports sector rose to 48.4% in 1981 (Kim Il-gon 1986). There was also a change in the products that were exported. The main products shifted markedly from light industrial ones to heavy-chemical ones during the 1960s and 1970s. The proportion of light and heavy categories of products in total export stood at 18.3% and 9.2%, respectively, in the 1960s, and increased to 33.3% and 40.2%, respectively, in the 1980s. This change is also confirmed in the change in the annual list of the nation's ten major exported products.

In an export-oriented economy, exports play an important role. They are necessary not only for the existence of production units but also for acquiring foreign exchange to pay for imports indispensable to industrialization. Setting aside the criticism that an export-oriented doctrine leads to "exports for export," the situation can be translated more realistically into "exports for import of producers' goods" and "exports contributing to industrialization." Exports exclusively directed at foreign markets can even bring about an increase in domestic production, which results in job and income creation. For exports through OEM, necessary equipment is provided by foreign firms giving orders or can be purchased on long-term credits, so that foreign currencies are rarely needed; furthermore, technological learning occurring during the production process can make a contribution to the production of other products. Therefore, unlike an export-oriented economy that specializes in primary products, an export-oriented economy specializing in manufactured products is not susceptible to the criticism that it is an "enclave economy."[3]

Meanwhile, despite the necessity to export, there is no guarantee that exports can be shipped to foreign countries. Because Korean exports did not have an international competitive advantage at the time, they should have been supported by the government. There is sufficient evidence supporting the assertion that so-called hunger exports and below-cost exports took place. Kuznets (1977) estimated that, in 1977, exporters spent, on average, $1.50 on every $1 worth of exports in the late 1960s. Amsden (1989) emphasized several times in his famous book, *Asia's Next Giant: South Korea and Late Industrialization,* that major export products, such as textiles, were subsidized to complement their weak competitiveness. Leading exporters of heavy-chemical products in the 1970s confessed that it would not have been possible to ship products overseas without governmental subsidies because of their low productivity. They also added that among 246 products dispersed in 28 industries only 14% were competitive and

---

[3] The term "enclave economy" indicates a country's industries or areas that are related more to the global economy than to the domestic production system both in the procurement of producers' goods and in the sale of products.

about 70% had zero, or only slight, competitiveness (Federation of Korean Industries 1978). All this empirical evidence highlights the fact that the competitiveness of exports should be supported, revealing clearly the limits of the static comparative advantage theory and supporting the dynamic comparative advantage theory. Finally, considering high unemployment rates in developing countries, the export-oriented economy laid the foundation for social and political stability through job creation. This applies both to the industrialization centered on labor-intensive light industries in the 1960s and that centered on capital-intensive heavy and chemical industries in the 1970s.

Internal Aspects of Accumulation

The external mechanisms of a borrowing and export-oriented economy should be accompanied by corresponding internal mechanisms.

The first mechanism concerns consumption, savings, and investment that are related to the disposal of income. The more dynamic the export-oriented economy is, the more production and income the economy generates. However, if the ratio of exports to GNP increases, the portion captured by consumption declines and so the savings rate increases. As shown in Figure 2.1, the degree of dependence on exports and on the saving rate is the same, 35%, which is not a coincidence. The high savings rate translates into high investment under the centralized banking system. However, during the period of high economic growth, the investment rate always exceeds the savings rate, so that the gap between them is filled with foreign savings. In Korea, therefore, the gap between domestic savings and investment is the same as the amount of the trade deficit. However, this is only the case when the trade deficit is caused by the import of producers' goods and not by the import of consumers' goods. This is because expenditures for consumption reduce savings.

Second, the borrowing and export-oriented economy can also cause a horizontal expansion and vertical deepening of the production structure. This is most important in that this expansion is the raison d'être of this accumulation regime in a national economy. The ultimate goal of the development process is to establish an autonomous production system, the crucial part of which sets up the production sector of producers' goods, with the focus on machinery. This fact needs again to be borne in mind.

The following are critical points with regard to change in the production structure. It is natural to see the role of agriculture decrease in an economy that is industrializing rapidly; so it is too great a simplification to say that agriculture was sacrificed for industrialization. Nevertheless, the excessive import of cheap American agricultural products in the 1960s broke down the base of Korea's production, and the resultant deficits in the balance of agricultural products accumulated to such an extent as to impede industrialization. This was one of the reasons why the government re-launched agriculture-promotion policies in the 1970s. As a result, the country became self-sufficient in its staple food, rice, whereas the increase in agriculture productivity was attributed to intermediate goods for agriculture (fertilizer, farming chemicals, vinyl, etc.) and agricultural equipment (machines for agriculture, etc.) supplied from industry. In the meantime, there was a marked demographic shift away from the rural areas into the cities, where new arrivals provided a cheap labor force for industries, creating a pressure for industrial wages to diminish or to stagnate. At the same time, the average income of farming households increased gradually, contributing to an expansion of the domestic market for manufactured goods. It was from the early 1980s on that the government began to cease to give any priority to the agricultural sector and agriculture's role in relationship to manufacturing was ignored. From that time on, the government adopted an open-door attitude in respect to economic policy. It is noteworthy that the turnaround in governmental attitude occurred just as the influx of rural migrants into the cities petered out, and there was an undersupply of cheap labor for industries. Eventually, agriculture lost its beneficial function in the export-based economy.

The generally accepted idea about Korea's industrialization is summarized by the phrase, "the industrialization centered on light industries in the 1960s and on heavy and chemical industries in the

1970s." The statistics about the changes in the industrial structure do not support this conclusion. The rate of contribution of heavy and chemical industries to the economy rose from 8.8% in 1960 to 14.5% in 1970 and to 28.2% in 1980, whereas that of light industries remained almost unchanged (22.3% in 1960, 21.2% in 1970, and 22.8% in 1980). As a result, the ratio of the output of heavy and chemical industries to that of light industries increased from 0.392 to 0.686 and then to 1.238 (Bank of Korea, *I-O analysis*). As shown by the above figures, changes in export and production structures did not occur simultaneously. This occurred because, even during the 1960s, the heavy and chemical industries continued to develop in order to supply producers' goods necessary for the exports of light manufactured products. In the 1970s, the development of heavy and chemical industries reached full swing. At the same time, heavy and chemical products started taking the lion's share of Korea's exports. During this period, when industrialization centered on heavy and chemical industries continued to expand, the industrial linkage between the production sector of consumers' goods and that of producers' goods grew first. After that, such a linkage grew even within the producers' goods industry. A continuous industrialization centered on heavy and chemical industries is related to the lasting import structure focused on producers' goods.

The industrialization of Korea can be described as a parallel process of development of export substitution and of import substitution. This so-called double track industrialization theory has been raised as a critique of the export-oriented industrialization theory supported by the main stream of economics. A *dual double-track theory* is proposed in this chapter by addressing a parallel en-forcement of the ascent in industrial affiliations and a descent in industrial affiliations, another aspect of double-track industrialization.

Two aspects need to be focused on in particular. First, export and import substitutions had been implemented together. It was felt that Korean export-oriented industrialization was successful mainly because of the dynamism of exports; namely, the continuous changes in products to export. However, this success would not have been possible without an import substitution process, including the domestic production of imported producers' goods. That is because the absence of domestic producers' goods industries would lead to successive imports of the corresponding goods. If Korea had depended on imports of producer's goods, especially equipment, the autonomous dynamism of domestic production would not have appeared. When export industries resort to imported equipment and intermediary goods for further development, unfavorable fluctuations in the price of imported goods, which are beyond the country's control, may threaten the price competitiveness of exports. Furthermore, trade deficits increase when industrialization does not progress in concert with import substitution. In this case, a slowdown of exports or a sluggish influx of foreign capital can trigger a crisis of foreign debt. (Some Latin American countries are cases in point. However, it should be emphasized that Korea too faced such a crisis twice, in the end of the 1960s and again in the end of the 1970s).

Under a borrowing and export-oriented economy the dynamism of exports is only a requirement for the continuous function of the accumulation regime. The condition sufficient for the system to achieve the aims of the development process is effective imports substitution. In this context, the most meaningful development was made in the machine industry. This industry reached a balance in international payments in the late 1970s. In the early 1980s, when the industry's self-supply rate [production/domestic consumption (production + import − export)] exceeded 100%, imports of equipments were balanced by exporting domestic machinery. For example, high-tech equipment, including machine tools and general machinery, were imported with foreign currency earned by selling electronic appliances and transportation machinery. Nevertheless, during this period the industry's dependence on imports (imports/domestic consumption) stood at 47%, which was high compared with other countries (Kim Il-gon 1986). However, this remarkable development in the machinery must bear a close relationship with the dynamism of technological learning, to be reviewed later.

Second, the simultaneous ascent and descent in industrial affiliations needs to be examined. Here, industrial affiliation means a group of industries related in terms of technology. Ascent is described as a way of industrialization that moves from the production of final products to that of intermediate goods and then to that of raw materials and equipment, using the backward linkage effect of related industries. In descent, on the other hand, industrialization moves from raw materials to final goods, using forward linkage effects. In the consumer goods-centered export industries, the industrial affiliation is generally established on downstream industries first and then on upstream industries. At the same time, this establishment strengthens the competitiveness of consumer goods. In the garment industry, the process of affiliation ascent progressed from spinning and weaving to chemical fibers to chemical raw materials, and in the automobile industry from assembling auto parts to producing them. Such an industrialization strategy was reasonable in the early stage of industrialization when the relationships between domestic industries were very loose and domestic markets did not exist.

However, when domestic markets for imports substitution did exist or when most products could be exported, then the process of affiliation descent could have occurred. In this regard, it must be emphasized that the industries with only forward effects, such as chemicals, petroleum, steel, cement, and chemical fertilizers, are primary industries important enough to determine the success of industrialization. One of the characteristics of Korea's industrialization is considered to be its way of establishing industries. Namely, the construction of industrial affiliations was pursued intentionally from upward to downward and synchronously vice versa. For instance, to maximize both forward and backward linkage effects, both the steel industry as an upstream industry and the automobile and ship industries as downstream industries were developed at the same time. This was true also in the textile and clothing industry and in various affiliations existing between agriculture and manufacture. Here, it needs to be emphasized that the forward and backward linkage effects increase as the elements of each industrial affiliation make up.

Evidence suggests that the role of technological catch-up and learning dynamics in the Korean industrialization process has not received sufficient attention. Developing countries that find it necessary to initiate industrialization require a tremendous effort and

CHAPTER TWO

much time to develop the necessary technology independently. Therefore, it is advantageous for them to import the necessary technology from other countries, because standardized technology can be imported at a relatively low cost, and imported equipment usually comes with technology embedded in it. What is of greater significance, however, is that learning dynamics should follow to make the technical advance pay off. Learning dynamics depend more on the ability to internalize, imitate, and adapt than on the capacity to develop basic technology and creativity for innovation. Learning dynamics are also closely related to the country's specific educational system. For example, a "cramming-style" education in schools and learning about technology in the workplace are closely interconnected. Government-run institutes conduct research and development activities principally to internalize or adapt imported technology, rather than to develop new technology. It is also worthy of note that the technological catch-up in Korea showed its limitations when the industrialization process came to an end.

The accumulation system based on a borrowing and export-oriented economy was established on extensive accumulation first and then on intensive accumulation. The former was implemented by augmenting the quantity of input of production factors, whereas the latter was based on technological changes and productivity increases. In extensive accumulation, increased production does not accompany the difficulties of extending markets even without wage increases, because it can be absorbed by income obtained by additionally injected capital and labor. With extensive accumulation, a borrowing and export-oriented economy can expand quantitatively without weakening export competitiveness. However, in the case of intensive accumulation, an expansion of production occurs through techno-logical innovation and productivity increase with a given quantity of input of production factors. Therefore, the problem of shortage of demand will appear if wages increase as productivity grows. In this case too, if wage increases can be controlled by any means, price cuts can be possible as productivity increases improve international competitiveness. Therefore, the two accumulation regimes can be in accordance with the growth mechanisms of a low-wage-based borrowing and export-oriented economy. As long as a large enough workforce exists, extensive accumulation can be an admirable method for dealing with unemployment as well as seeking quantitatively high growth. In this context, it is understandable that developing countries focus on extensive accumulation.

In Korea, too, extensive accumulation prevailed during the period of the developmental dictatorship. As Paul Krugman (1994) has pointed out, this way of augmenting the quantity of input of production factors cannot last forever, and its efficiency faces limitations without technological development. With a completion of industrialization and, in particular, with the disappearance of a labor oversupply, this creation of absolute *surplus value* becomes more. This eventually leads to the conversion from extensive accumulation to intensive accumulation. In the Korean case, this conversion seems to have begun in the mid-1980s. An increase in domestic consumption through wage increases is necessary for accumulation to continue when exports lose their momentum. As a result, the conditions for Fordist accumulation based on the productivity-wage system are placed. However, the execution is not a natural process, but a social process and even a technical process accompanied by violent sociopolitical struggles. As advanced countries begin to avoid technology transfers, a new external setback is added to the process of technological catch-up, and so the learning dynamics founded on imitation should be replaced by innovation dynamics, based on research and development, and the cramming style of education should be replaced by education for creativity. However, these changes are far from easy.

III. DEVELOPMENTAL DICTATORSHIP AS AN EXTREME FORM OF STATE-LED REGULATION

An accumulation regime can function only if it is guaranteed that economic agents act in accord with macroeconomic growth mechanisms. Here, the mode of regulation corresponding to the accumulation regime based on a borrowing and export-oriented economy is defined as developmental dictatorship, an extreme form of state-led regulation. How the state-led regulation guaranteed a stable operation of the accumulation regime is explained by reviewing a variety of regulation mechanisms. As in the case of the accumulation regime discussed previously, both external and internal aspects are considered in order.

External Aspects of State-Led Regulation

As long as the accumulation regime is defined as a borrowing and export-oriented economy, regulation mechanisms corresponding to this accumulation regime are primarily characterized by state control of all external activities. At the heart of this external control is the imperative to control imports and foreign currency for the borrowing economy and to support exports for the export economy. To that end, various mechanisms exist to decouple the domestic relative price system (a productivity system corresponding to the domestic level of technology) from the international relative price system (international norm of productivity) for the establishment of the autonomous national production system (De Bernis 1984).

Systems for the control of imports and foreign currency work according to the following logic: The producers' goods necessary for industrialization take up the majority of imports, and as much foreign currency as possible is used for imports and repayment of foreign debt. With regard to imports, advocates of market opening have insisted that Korea's market opening and import liberalization policies adopted in the mid-1960s made its export-led industrialization successful. Surely, for Korea seeking outward and export-led economic growth under the GATT system, trade liberalization was a external compulsion that was difficult to disobey. However, this evaluation arose out of ignorance of historical facts or was based on insufficient grounds. When he examined the relationship between import controls and export-oriented growth in Korea during the period 1968-82, Luedde-Neurath (1986) found that, although the number of products that could be liberally imported increased, the overall amount that was actually imported decreased. He came to the conclusion that the Korean government had exercised a selective control of imports widely and systematically and that it was a necessary and effective measure for dealing with a lack of foreign currency and promoting.

All imports were processed through a strict and complex sequence involving the issuance of import licenses, quantity controls, allocation of foreign currency, settlement methods, deposits in advance, and customs clearance (Yoo Hak-sang 1985). Such protective measures paid off well in the Korean case. According to the Korea Development Institute (1982), the average effective rate of protection [(value added in domestic price — value added in international price)/value added in international price] reached 31.7%, and the resultant burden on consumers was estimated to be 13% of GNP. The fact that the essential characteristics of the systematic control of imports were the extensive use of indirect control measures and the selection of control tools did not receive much attention. According to contemporary government policymakers, the reason why indirect control measures were mainly used was that direct controls could have had severe negative effects on domestic prices and could also have generated frictions with international organizations (Economic Planning Board 1982). The selectivity of protectionist practice can be divided into two types: selectivity by industries or products and selectivity by periods. The study on the average effective rate of protection, cited above, shows that there was a substantial difference between products of heavy and chemical industries (71.2%) and light industries' goods (-2.3%). This testifies to the selectivity by products for import controls and the bringing of heavy and chemical industries under systemic protection and support. The timing of the implementation of protection reveals that the list of import-restricted items changed as the national productive apparatus expanded and deepened and especially as the process of imports substitution advanced. For example, at a given point of time, the import of some products, especially intermediate goods for export that could not be manufactured in Korea, was liberalized and that of products competing with Korean ones was restricted or banned. After that, the products that were able to be produced domestically were put on the list of import restriction, and those that were presumed to be sufficiently competitive were exposed to competition with imports. This is a typical example of the theory of protection of infant industries after F. List.

It is clear that foreign exchange is critical in a borrowing and export-oriented economy. The control of foreign exchange is designed to prevent its flight and to encourage its productive use. At the same time, such control is inevitable as long as a trade deficit and an excess demand on foreign exchange exist. The former dictatorial government in Korea chose direct controls over the supply and demand of foreign exchange. In this regard, two systems are important. One was a centralized management system of foreign exchange, under which the general public was banned from holding or using foreign exchange; the central bank managed all of it, and the authorities allocated it according to their own development. The other was a deliberation and permission system of the introduction of foreign capital, supervised by the Economic Planning Board. Shim (1992) has shown how strictly and systematically this system was enforced. The governmental guarantee system for repayments of private borrowing from overseas had a special meaning. The part guaranteed by government or banks — in the place of the government — reached 88% of all overseas borrowings in the 1950s and 1960s (Economic Planning Board 1982). Even though this public guarantee had been requested by foreign lenders, the system was an effective tool for government to control not only foreign capital but also domestic private capital. The government's management of the supply of, and demand for, foreign capital meant an absence of a foreign exchange market. Considering the excess demand for foreign capital, a development of black markets of foreign exchange and high informal exchange rates were inevitable corollaries.

It is now time to examine the export support systems employed during the period under consideration. The purpose of export support is to enhance the competitiveness of exports. Below-cost exports can become an option only when there are other measures designed to offset the loss or to ensure more profits. What is crucial here is that most of the measures adopted were devised and managed by the government. The most widely used were foreign exchange rates and subsidies. From the time of Korea's liberation from Japanese occupation up to the mid-1980s, the South Korean *won*-to-dollar exchange rate rose continually. The general notion was that a low valuation of the *won* was needed to facilitate export-led growth strategies because of the difference between price increase rates at home and abroad. The high inflation in Korea can be explained in terms of growth (or development) inflation mechanisms.

However, the fact that foreign exchange rates actually increased occasionally requires further comment. Under the fixed exchange rate system, a stair-form rise in exchange rates occurred because the government applied the difference in prices at home and abroad to the rates in the middle and long term. (The *won*-to-dollar exchange rate during 1975-79 was fixed at 484 *won*). This shows that the *won* was always highly overvalued. As a result, the gap between nominal and real exchange rates widened until the government judged it excessive. At this point, the government reduced the gap through a "maxi-devaluation" (Lanzarotti 1992b). This highly valued *won* must have triggered imports and hindered exports. However, at the same time, it weakened import inflation pressures, reduced the cost burden of both imported raw materials and intermediate goods for exports, and worked favorably in paying for imports and repaying foreign debt. Therefore, a high valuation of the *won* was in accordance with the borrowing economy, but did not fit into the export-oriented economy. To offset the side effects on exports of the high valuation, subsidies were provided. Export subsidies took various forms, including direct subsidies, preferential financing, and tax exemptions on export income, to consume a huge amount of capital. For example, the real subsidy rate of exports per dollar stood at 58.7% in 1963, 23.4% in 1965, 37.9% in 1970, and 31.4% in 1975 (Lanzarotti 1992b). The rate of tax exemptions to the total amount of exports can be described in *won*-to-dollar terms: 41.1 in 1966, 62.5 in 1968, and 69.7 in 1970 (Lee Jae-hui 1984). The combined operation of the maxi-devaluation and these massive subsidies had the following characteristics: First, the subsidies were designed to resolve the conflict between the effects on the borrowing economy and on the export-oriented economy brought about by the manipulation of foreign exchange rates. Second, a graded subsidy system engendered the same effects as the internationally banned "double foreign exchange rate" system would have caused. Third, despite the certain rationality of this policy mix, the maxi-devaluations were launched predominantly during times of economic difficulties, so that the recovery of an economic equilibrium tended to take violent forms.

Other measures included monopoly benefits that some domestic companies enjoyed in protected markets, as well as special favors for large exporters. The *chaebol* conglomerates charged higher prices for domestic products than exports to reduce their losses or increase profits. The exports-linked import system gave great benefits to large exporters, such as general trading companies of *chaebols*.

Internal Aspects of State-Led Regulation

The internal aspects of the state-led regulation executed by the Korean developmental dictatorship were also diverse. Among them, economic planning, mobilization and allocation of surplus resources, and the government's management of labor forces were crucial. The purpose of all these three elements was to ensure smooth accumulation in a borrowing and export-oriented economy. It was usually achieved through coordinating various government policies and making private actors observe the rules.

First, with regard to the planning of the economy, it is necessary to examine the salient traits of organization of the government and industrial policies. The Economic Planning Board (EPB), nicknamed a "locomotive of the economy," was installed to supervise the entire economic regulation mechanism and to lead economic development on the basis of planning. The minister of the EPB, having the status of a vice premier minister in charge of the economy, had the authority to mediate different views of the ministries concerning the economy to execute coherently a growth-drive economic policy mix. In addition to full autonomy in policy planning, the EPB had full budgeting authority to secure funds necessary for implementing the economic development plans. Its minister, as chairman of the Monetary Board, the highest deliberative organization in the centralized financial system, could control even the monetary and financial policies of the Central Bank.

Second, the basic characteristics of industrial policies lie in the clarity of their objectives and their systematic step-by-step execution. Industrial policies aiming at establishing an autonomous basis of accumulation were implemented clearly and consistently. To that end, the production bases, first of consumer goods and later of producer goods, were established. In the case of consumer goods, production progressed from nondurables to durables and in the case of producer goods from raw materials and intermediate goods to machinery and equipment. According to successive 5-year plans for economic development, Korea pursued the construction of light industries, heavy and chemical industries, and machinery and its parts industries. The main objective of the industrialization centered on heavy and chemical industries was to establish the production sector of producers' goods. However, in Korea, this industrialization was deeply dominated by a politico-military need to construct a defense industry (O Won-chol 1994). In the meantime, the Korean government set up a logistic infrastructure, including highways and ports, essential to export-led industrialization and built industrial complexes that were offered at low cost to the enterprises. It also played a role of producer by founding large government-run companies in areas of heavy and chemical industries where private companies could not enter at that time. These government-run companies were subsequently privatized as they became profitable. The government set up public research institutes by industry, which focused on research and development for enhancing the use and application of imported technology. The government also provided companies with various support measures while enforcing industrial policies. However, to benefit from such measures, favored companies had to comply with strict rules (especially the setting of goals and systems of rewards and penalties according to performance). In this way, governmental measures generated positive outcomes.

Third, the government devised various mechanisms to mobilize and allocate surplus resources. The so-called centralized financial system was a central mechanism of the mode of regulation adopted by developmental dictatorship and illustrates well its characteristics. The government could dominate even the most powerful private actors by taking control of the financial system. The characteristics of that centralized system are now examined, after which attention is turned to the logic dominating the coordination of savings and investments.

Administrated finance was a common characteristic of both developed and developing countries when the wave of financial liberalization gained momentum in the 1980s. There were, however, differences among countries. For example, in the developed countries, administrated finance focused on preventing instability or failure in the financial markets and keeping progress on track. On the other hand, in developing nations the focus was on making the financial system serve the production sector by controlling directly the mobilization and allocation of capital. From this perspective, Korea's centralized administrated finance had the following features:

- Monetary and financial policies of the Central Bank, which was reduced to being a governmental department, were implemented so as to contribute to real growth and industrialization. In this way, the two sorts of policies, monetary and financial policies, on the one hand, and industrial and trade policies on the other hand, could be consistently growth-oriented.

- The government established many specialized banks, such as the Korea Development Bank, Export-Import Bank of Korea, and Korea Exchange Bank, to mobilize and allocate capital, including the foreign currency exchange, necessary for industrialization and export support.

- Commercial banks played a role in allocating policy credits. They were owned by the government, having been seized by the Park Chung-hee military junta in 1960, until the 1980s, when they were privatized. Even in the case of banks' ordinary operations direct intervention prevailed, including the control of interest rates.

- In addition to this seizure of indirect finance (or intermediating finance), the government was able to control the development of direct finance (or market finance), which tended to be more difficult to handle. The development of the securities market (stocks and corporate bonds) was pursued at one time, but its purpose was to give a social appearance to the *chaebols* fostered by the government. The absence or limits of direct finance deterred depositors from turning to means other than bank deposits for their financial portfolios. In this situation the government could mobilize the maximum surplus resources.

- The mobilized deposits and created credits were mostly funneled into financing for development and export, but financing for ordinary consumers barely existed. This was a part of the coordination mechanism of deposits and investment.

- Administrated finance was usually accompanied by financial repression and a development of preferential finance and illegal finance. The repression was natural as long as autonomous functioning of the banks was not allowed. Without crony connections and intentions of securing concessions, credits themselves tended to have the characteristic of special favors because of the excess demand for funds and the preferential character of policy credits. The black financial market became a funding source for companies and consumers who had no access to official finance systems.

Such characteristics illustrate specific methods for coordinating savings and investment in a borrowing and export-oriented economy. As explained earlier, the operation of this economy demanded the encouragement of savings and the restraint of consumption. Therefore, various measures to increase savings were taken, and the mobilized funds were used for productive purposes through the administrated finance. The high savings rate, usually described as one of the crucial factors in Korea's economic growth, was an outcome of both voluntary and compulsory savings. Even without the savings ethic being regarded as a laudable custom or social virtue (national campaign for savings), it was adopted voluntarily because Korean people had to prepare themselves for health care, retirement, and the possibility of unemployment in a society devoid of a social welfare system. It is also of the greatest importance for Korean parents to save money for the education, marriage, and housing of their children. Compulsory saving, able to be explained in terms of growth or development inflation, was a mechanism through which income was transferred from the households as depositors, creditors, and consumers to the enterprises as borrowers, debtors, and producers. That was because households had no means of coping with a decrease in purchasing power caused by inflation, other than through attempts to secure wage increases, whereas companies, especially the monopolistic *chaebols*, could transfer any increase in cost to the selling price of their own products. Compulsory savings reduced the purchasing power of consumers, but improved producers' capacity to invest, so that they contributed to the operation of the export-oriented economy. As a result, growth inflation became a component of the regulation mechanism in the borrowing and export-oriented economy.

Fourth, wage labor norms ensured the export competitiveness of labor-intensive manufactured products and also the entire operation of the borrowing and export-oriented economy. Here, the analysis focuses on low wages in order to propose the thesis of state control of the labor force. It is necessary to compare wage levels among different countries when one discusses wage-based international competitiveness. During the period of the developmental dictatorship, the salary per hour of Korean workers in the manufacturing industry was lower than that of Asian competitors: On the basis of 100 (Korea), in 1965 Taiwan was 160, Singapore 305, India 165, and the Philippines 210; in 1984, the Taiwan figure was 123 and that for Singapore 150 (Ko Chun-sok 1989). Low wages were routinely accompanied by long working hours, which increased from 50.3 per week in 1963 to 53.2 in 1981 (Kim Hyong-gi 1990). At the same time, night and weekend work was commonplace. In some cases, wives and children were forced to work for additional income. This fact provides an answer to the question of how a labor force can be reproduced in a low-wage system (Chong I-hwan 1987). Wages differentials are another representation of low wages; in particular, the gap between wages in the export sector and the nonexport one, between heavy and chemical industries and light ones, between large companies and small-medium ones, and between men and women. There were also wage components connected to length of service and school career (Kim Hyong-gi 1990).

There is, however, a rising doubt about the efficacy of low wages as a method to maintain durable international competitiveness. Coutrot and Husson (1993) pointed out that a low wage system not only prevents technology transfer and ascent in industrial affiliations but also hinders the development of domestic markets, resulting in social division between the sluggish domestic demand sector and the dynamic export sector. The question of how South Korea's export-oriented economy overcame this contradiction inherent in a low-wage system can be answered by reference to the specific relation between real wages and productivity, and the resultant relative poverty. An increase in the rate of nominal wages compared to living expenses (23.2% in 1960, 42.8% in 1980) and a continuous increase in real wages cannot be translated into an improvement in living conditions. However, the rate of increase in real wages always hovered below that of labor productivity (1.7:2.1 during 1965-70, 2.2:2.6 during 1970-80),[4] and the wage distribution rate (wage/national income) continued to fall (26.2% in 1963, 20.8% in 1980). Providing that real wages increase and living conditions improve, regardless of the unfair distribution of productivity gains to workers, the eruption of social conflict can be delayed for a certain period. In the meantime, the income distributed favorably to the enterprise sector can be injected into the investment for productivity's increase.

That low wages exist in an overcrowded labor market may be natural. The relative overpopulation theory and the thesis of the free management of labor forces derive from Lewis's famous hypothesis of the unlimited supply of labor (Lewis 1954). With regard to the

---

[4] According to a report released by the Federation of Korean Trade Unions, this gap is much larger. On the basis of 100, the real wage index stood at 134.7 in 1971, but the labor productivity index was 341 (Kim Tae-il 1985). S. M. Suh estimated that absolute poverty decreased from 40.9% to 9.8% from 1965 to 1980, whereas comparative poverty increased from 12.1% to 13.4% (Kim 1994).

accumulation of capital, Kim Hyong-gi (1990) insisted that a relative overpopulation existed as three different forms during the industrialization of Korea: mobile, potential, and stagnant. He came to the conclusion that, despite a rapid decrease in the potential overpopulation in farming villages, all three forms, especially static, increased in the cities. Salama introduced the thesis of free management of labor forces to clarify a particular way of industrialization of East Asian semi-industrialized economies (Salama 1980; Salama and Tissier 1982). Ominami (1986) even considered overpopulation as a condition of success for export-led industrialization in a Taylor-style economy.

However, these arguments fail to take into account the fact that wage labor norms were managed by the government because they have a point of view of market regulation on labor and wages. The Korean government seemed to have known well both the economic contradictions (restrained increases in domestic consumption) inherent in a low-wage system and the sociopolitical contradictions (workers' resistance and democratization movements). The management by the state of labor forces suggested here neither denies nor replaces the previous propositions. Rather, it complements them to show one aspect of state regulation through developmental dictatorship. The state management in this domain can be divided into two types: direct and indirect. The former consists of direct intervention in the determination of wages and the latter of indirect measures aiming at a decrease in the value of the labor force. A case in point for direct intervention is the policy of wage guidelines. According to this policy, the government first limits or freezes wage increases in the public sector and then requests the private sector to follow suit. To improve the negotiating power of company management, the Korean authorities maintained or strengthened repressive articles of labor-related legislation and sent riot police to the scenes of labor disputes (collapse of labor unions, pro-enterprise corporatism, violent repression of strikes, etc.). The most important indirect method was the control of prices for such basic needs as water, electric power, telephone service, and public transportation, which determine the reproduction cost of the labor force. Considering consumption norms (a high Engel's coefficient) of that period, the importance of a policy of low-price grain, especially rice, is clear. The policy needs to be emphasized in that relative decreases in the value of the labor force could reduce the wage burden on companies, and reproduction of the labor force under the low-wage system became possible. From this perspective it was ineluctable that the low-wage and low-price grain systems had to coexist. In the same vein, price stabilization was always one of the major priorities for the administration (Economic Planning Board 1982). This fact testifies to the existence of continuous inflationist pressures in the export-led high-growth economy.

IV. CONCLUSION

Two such phenomena as development and dictatorship cannot be dealt with through a market-centered approach separating political theory from the economy. As long as all historical experiences show the inseparable combination of politics and economy, the basic conception of the developmental state theory and regulation theory concerning politics and economy do appear to be appropriate. Furthermore, if even the retreat of the state from the economy is one of its policies, one must admit the fact that there may be various combinations of politics (state) and economy (market). Only if this is admitted can all unnecessary controversies about the nation-state and the market be overcome.

This chapter concludes by emphasizing two points. First, because it has focused on clarifying the logic of operation of the development model under developmental dictatorship, it lacks research on possible contradictions of the model. However, this kind of research is needed to understand fully the economic crisis that occurred in 1997. We think the period from the mid-1980s until the onset of the crisis cannot be included in the timeframe of developmental dictatorship. In other words, there were significant changes both in the accumulation regime and in the mode of regulation of the Korean economy (Seo Ick-jin 1999, 2002).

The second point is that the development model characterized by developmental dictatorship discussed here is at the heart of the so-called Korean model. So, can this model be exported or applied to other developing countries? The answer to this question is likely to be in the negative (Seo Ick-jin 2002), because the basic conditions for its application are very difficult to satisfy today. They can be summarized as internal circumstances, such as the existence of a strong government, and external factors, such as the international acceptance of overall protectionist measures (Lee Byeong-cheon 2000). In the meantime, because of the wave of democratization sweeping around the world, an authoritarian government cannot easily appear, and globalization makes the open enforcement of protectionism difficult, if not impossible. Therefore, the issue of development needs to be approached from a different angle in the 21st century. Although the global economy is fettered by the issue of development of the developing countries, now the North-South issue does not receive the attention it merits. It will, however, emerge as a new topic in the global economics or the global political economy beyond the domain of development economics.

Chapter 3

Industrial Policy in the Park Chung-hee Era

Lee Sang-cheol

I. INTRODUCTION

The industrialization of South Korea took place in circumstances characterized predominantly by extreme intervention on the part of the government of President Park Chung-hee. Research to identify and analyze individual strategies and detailed mechanisms that together comprised that intervention is ongoing. However, at this time there remains a difference of opinion among researchers with regard to the precise nature of the content, characteristics, and effects of the governmental industrialization policies adopted in South Korea during the 1960s and the 1970s (Amsden 1989; Kim Nak-nyeon 1999; Lee Byeong-cheon 1999; Lee Sang-cheol 1998; Stern et al. 1995).

Generally speaking, *industrial policy* means the various schemes used by governments to arrange priorities in the allocation of resources among different categories of industry and to direct the economic activities of individual companies. When applied, these strategies tend to accelerate production, investment, research and development, modernization, and industrial reorganization in certain industries. At the same time, however, they can place restraints on the economic activities of other industries. Thus, such policies can achieve the selective fostering of certain industries.

The first question to arise is whether there were any significant differences between the industrial policies of the 1960s and those of the 1970s. Most scholars who belong to the neo-classical school see the 1960s as an era of export-oriented industrialization and the 1970s as the era of heavy industry. They believe that the selective fostering of certain industries was initiated in the 1970s when state attention was turned to the development of heavy industry. The following statement represents this view: "Korea's first 5-year development plan (1962-66) placed great emphasis on export promotion.... In most cases, exports in the 1960s were from light industries, and the government targeted specific industries to foster." In fact, however, the policy of favoring those industries that could substitute for imports was already in place in the initial stages of the economic development plan. Possibly, experience with the export substitution industries in the 1960s was carried over into the policy planning of the heavy chemical industry. The answer to this first question is sought from the conclusions reached in recent studies.

The second question to be addressed in this chapter is whether there is any correlation between the series of policies implemented immediately after the May 1961 military coup and those adopted after 1964. Most studies regard the policies introduced shortly after the coup as being largely tentative and uncertain interventions lacking in positive direction, which occurred in the process of shifting the economy to an export-oriented focus; they see the 3 years between the coup and 1964 as the period when concrete plans for national growth through export-oriented industrialization were established. In other words, they believe that the government turned to an export-oriented economy only after the experimental policies attempted immediately after the coup ran into difficulties. However, subsequent research suggests that the salient characteristics of the measures put in place soon after the coup were not abandoned completely, but were modified and adjusted in the light of experience, and formed the patterns for those policies implemented. In this chapter it is shown that the interventionist character of the series of policies introduced immediately after the military coup was actually rein-forced throughout the 1960s and 1970s.

The third question to be considered is how precisely to under-stand the industrial policies of the 1960s and 1970s. It is pertinent because to discover the true motivations and wider intent of the Park

Chung-hee regime it is essential to take into account the reasons that underpinned the array of state interventions in the industrialization process that took place throughout that regime's incumbency. As yet, however, little work has been accomplished in this area.

In this regard, there have been some attempts to explain Korea's industrialization process by reference to Gerschenkron's (1962) *late industrialization theory*, which suggests that substitution mechanisms could be effective in specific historical situations. Explaining Europe's industrialization in the 19th century, he argued that some countries in Europe that lacked the essential pre-conditions present in Great Britain could nonetheless carry out rapid industrialization successfully by securing "substitutes," such as conglomerates, a universal banking system, and government. Depending on the stage of its development, each nation employed different substitutes, although they all shared the common characteristic of a hierarchy that could replace the mechanisms of the market. As Gerschenkron pointed out, the substitutes fulfilled important roles in the early stages of late industrialization in Europe but had to relinquish their roles to the market as late industrialization proceeded.

If significant costs are involved in market transactions, and uncertainties arise because of the immaturity of the market, something that can allocate resources hierarchically is needed instead of the market. However, because this approach lacks the effectiveness of the market, tools to make up for its shortcomings are necessary. This chapter focuses on how hierarchical structures that replaced the market were developed.

II. EMERGENCE OF INDUSTRIAL POLICY

First 5-Year Development Plan

On July 22, 1961, the Committee for Comprehensive Economic Rehabilitation Planning (CCERP) announced that, by following a 5-year comprehensive economic rehabilitation plan, the nation would achieve 7.2% annual economic growth from 1962 to 1966 and secure the basis of a self-supporting economy by boosting exports, fostering industries that could substitute for imports, and improving the balance of payments by increasing the influx of foreign currency.

The 5-year plan was drawn up by two members of the CCERP, Yu Won-sik and Park Hui-bom; it began by presenting a list of factories to be constructed under the auspices of the Ministry of Commerce and Industry. The plan had three characteristics. First, it highlighted the shortcomings of a free market system and proposed a shift to government-driven capitalism. Second, to build the basis for a self-supporting economy, it placed its main focus on key industries, such as cement, fertilizer, steel, and oil refining. Third, it identified the boosting of exports as the primary means of restructuring the balance of payments. It was a very ambitious plan and there were many difficulties in its execution; one of the most serious of which was the securing of sufficient capital to build the requisite number of factories. The then-finance minister, Chun Byeong-gyu (1988), confirmed the severity of this obstacle in his memoirs: "The success of the economic development plan lies in the mobilization of domestic capital and attracting foreign capital. Of these two, we are likely to have great difficulties in securing foreign capital.... The mobilization of domestic capital and the consequent imperative to nominate appropriate agencies and players to lead the investment effort were extremely sensitive issues."

On July 17, 1961, 9 "speculators," including Kim Ji-tae, who had been released from police custody on June 30, 1961, on the grounds that his continued detainment would be detrimental to the industrial development process, joined with 13 other entrepreneurs who were determined to play leading roles in the implementation of the government's development plan. On August 16, the Federation of Korean Industries (FKI),[1] an organization that had been set up by these 13 individuals, produced a "First Private Development Plan for Key Industries" and proposed its adoption at a meeting of the CCERP. On September 14, FKI General Secretary Kim Ju-in an-

---

[1] Among the founding members of the FKI were: Chairman Lee Byong-chul, Vice Chairmen Cho Song-chol and Nam Gung-ryon, Lee Chong-lim, Sol Gyong-dong, Park Hong-sik, Hong Jae-son, Choi Dae-sob, Lee Han-won, Chong Jae-ho, Kim Ji-tae, Lee Yang-gu, and Ham Chang-hee.

nounced that the FKI was planning six joint second-stage investment projects and suggested that the necessary foreign capital could be raised through foreign loans and investment capital from the redemption of illicitly made wealth. Other previously established conglomerates became actively involved in national economic development activities following the announcement of the 5-year plan.

On September 27, 1961, the government published the criteria to be employed in the selection of development projects eligible for access to foreign capital. In so doing, the Park Chung-hee regime clarified both its intention to have private companies carry out those projects and the principles on which it would select the enterprises. According to the criteria, a pre-condition of acceptance was the proven capability to mobilize domestic capital, and economic and technical inspections would be conducted to verify that ability. The government also established the principle that, except for projects that, because of their unique characteristics, needed to be carried out by government agencies, suitable private companies would receive prior rights.

On October 30, 1961, the Economic Planning Board (EPB) began to assemble the private companies who would qualify to receive foreign capital. Priority was afforded to applicants with the biggest share of equity and those with comprehensive business plans and good conditions for receiving foreign capital. As for those with the same or similar business proposals, those with direct foreign investment would have prior entitlement. In accordance with the first criterion, existing conglomerates, specifically speculators, were destined to be selected. Selection results were announced on January 23, 1962, by the Committee to Introduce Foreign Capital (CIFC).

Meanwhile, in mid-September, the EPB had completed drawing up the first 5-year economic development plan based on the 5-year Comprehensive Economic Rehabilitation Plan announced in the previous July. Following review by the newly established Central Economic Committee and National Rehabilitation Meeting, the plan was announced on January 13, 1962. It focused on exports through the construction of fertilizer plants, steel mills, and oil refineries and concentrated on the use of domestic rather than foreign capital. The plan also emphasized the role of state-owned, rather than private, businesses.

During the period between 1962 and 1966, 72.2% of required capital was drawn from domestic sources and 27.8% from overseas. The government took charge of 55.6% and the private sector took 44.4%. The government also considered ways to make maximum use of domestic capital and to fully utilize domestic labor in carrying out development projects. To be specific, the government intended to secure domestic capital through currency reform and to be involved directly in the economic development process by establishing the Industrial Development Corporation.

Supplementary Plans

On November 26, 1962, the EPB held a joint meeting to supplement the first 5-year economic development plan. Present were officials from the National Rehabilitation Meeting, the cabinet, and related bodies. The supplementary work consisted of two stages: first, to clarify problems arising from the original plan, and second, to set up measures to deal with those problems. As a result of this meeting, primary and secondary industry departments that could handle financial and balance of payment matters were organized; these bodies reported their results in December 1962.

One of the main reasons why the government found it necessary to devise "supplementary" arrangements just one year after the original plan was launched was that it had experienced great difficulty in mobilizing planned domestic capital. The currency reform that had set the exchange rate between the old and new South Korean *won* at 10:1 and had frozen deposits was the prime policy the government had implemented to secure domestic capital. The government applied a 15% interest rate to the frozen deposits and intended to build the Industrial Development Corporation in 6 months by replacing those savings with stock in the corporation.

However, the United States expressed displeasure with the currency reform, which Korea had carried out without consultation, and regarded it as a means to create a government-driven economy and impose restrictions on corporate activity. Furthermore, the United States threatened that it would not sit idly by watching policies put in place that it considered detrimental to the capitalist economy. Against this backdrop and through the establishment of the Korea-U.S. Joint Economic Cooperation Committee (JECC), the United States secured the basis for direct participation in Korea's economic policymaking process, as well as a means of conveying its preferences directly to President Park.

The supplementary plan focused primarily on financial stabilization and the adjustment of average annual economic growth to 5%. Plans to construct steel mills and machine plants were canceled, and the role of the private sector was strengthened. The portion of private sector capitalization was increased to 49.2%, whereas that of the government was decreased to 50.8%. As for the mobilization of domestic and foreign capital, the proportion of foreign capital was increased slightly.

Another reason the government needed a supplementary plan was that the export items and targets in the original plan had to be adjusted. In the original plan, the export target was set at $138 million,[2] an increase of 4.2 times compared with the base year. Agricultural, fishery, and livestock products took an overwhelming 69%, whereas manufacturing and bonded processing exports took 13% and 15%, respectively. The results were better than in the original plan, but there were big variations in the exports of goods. Compared with the original plan, the actual exports of manufactured goods were twice as high, whereas the much-anticipated bonded processing exports made slow progress. In other words, agricultural and mineral products failed to meet expectations, but manufactured goods performed unexpectedly well.

Based on these unanticipated results, export plans were radically altered. As Table 3.1 shows, although export targets for other items were adjusted downward, targets for manufactured products alone

---

[2] First 5-Year Economic Development Plan (Outline). 1962. *Chosa Wolbo* (Monthly Report) 16 (1).

were moved up. This means that, because of the differences between the original plan and actual results, priorities were changed from primary industrial products to manufactured goods. In particular, the supplementary plan indicated that labor-intensive light industry should be fostered for exports and its competitiveness increased by lowering production costs through tax incentives and other financial support. Furthermore, it also indicated that conventional investment policies emphasizing import substitution industries should be changed to support export industries.

Table 3.1 Export Targets in Original and Supplementary Plans (million $US)

	1962		1963		1964		1965		1966	
	O *	S **	O	S	O	S	O	S	O	S
Foods	20.1	21.9	23.2	22.9	27.5	24.7	31.6	27.9	35.8	33.3
Nonfood-related raw materials	25.8	19.4	29.4	22.3	32.3	33.7	46.9	36.8	50.9	45.1
Mineral fuels	1.8	2.8	1.8	1.7	2.7	3.2	3.6	2.6	3.6	3.5
Animal and plant oils and fats	0.9	0.0	1.1	1.0	1.2	1.0	1.3	0.5	1.6	0.6
Chemical goods	1.9	1.0	2.5	2.4	2.9	3.0	3.2	1.0	3.7	1.1
Raw materials	5.8	6.2	6.4	15.7	8.3	19.2	9.2	36.4	10.0	43.0
Miscellaneous	4.6	2.0	70.3	8.7	9.1	9.2	9.9	7.6	12.0	9.0
Bonded processing	5.0	n.a.	8.0	n.a.	12.0	n.a.	16.0	n.a.	20.0	n.a.
Total	65.9	54.8	79.7	81.7	96.0	94.0	121.6	112.8	137.5	135.6

* Original; ** Supplementary

Source: (Kim Dal-hyon 1962; Kimiya 1991)

Note: Foods include beef, pork, fish, cereals, fruit, and vegetables. Nonfood materials include textiles, mineral ore, salt, metals, and animal and plant raw materials. Mineral fuels include anthracite. Animal and plant oils and fats include cod-liver oil. Chemical goods include saccharine, ginseng, and menthol crystals. Raw materials include veneer board, yarn, and nonmetallic materials. Miscellaneous includes straw goods, athletic shoes and rubber shoes, and craftwork.

Export Support Policy

After the 1961 military coup, there were no great shifts in export support policy except for an increased export bounty. As the list of export items receiving export bounties show, the items the government intended to foster were primary industry and bonded processing products.

As mentioned, however, if a dramatic increase in the export of manufactured products was one reason for changing the primary export items, the direct cause of the rapid shift to promote the export of manufactured products was a financial crisis. Since 1956, foreign currency reserves had been steadily increasing, but in late-March 1962 the trend began to reverse. At the end of 1962, reserves had decreased by $39 million from the late 1961 figure to $167 million, and in 1963 this downward movement continued. The decreasing foreign currency reservoir created a mood of crisis, and from 1963 a *trade link* system was introduced.

In the trade link system implemented in January 1963 exporters were given the right to use all the profits generated by exports to import more goods. Because this import right was transferable, a premium market for import rights was created. The rapid increase in exports recorded in 1963 was triggered by this link system, it being used as a compromise for promoting the export of manufactured goods. In a situation in which the domestic currency is overvalued, it is more profitable to import raw materials and sell them on the domestic market after processing, rather than in overseas markets. However, because this direct export support policy violated the General Agreement on Tariffs and Trade (GATT), Section 16, Subsection 4, which does not allow any kind of subsidy, it was difficult to promote exports though this method.

Exchange rate reform was announced in May 1964 against this backdrop, although actual implementation did not take place until March 1965. The reform involved changing the existing fixed exchange rate system to a single floating system and raising the basic rate from 130 *won* to 1 U.S. dollar to 255:1. After introducing the floating system, the rate increased to 280 *won* against the dollar in May but, with the intervention of the Bank of Korea, stabilized at 270:1, where it remained until 1967. With the introduction of the new exchange rate system, the trade link system was ostensibly abolished.[3] After the exchange rate reform, imports were greatly restrained, and exports increased dramatically. It is believed that a series of indirect export promotion policies, such as low interest rates for export financing, payment guarantees offered by financial organizations for import credit memoranda, and customs and commodity tax incentives, also aided this marked increase in exports.

Foreign Capital Regulations

In Subsection 4 of the emergency economic policy announced on July 18, 1961, the following statement regarding the importation of foreign capital was included: "Based on the understanding that importation of foreign capital is necessary for the rapid development of domestic industries, the government has decided to abolish unrealistic restrictions on investment items and investors."

This statement highlighted the fact that existing regulations on the importation of foreign capital were inappropriate for accomplishing the goals of the economic development plan. They were unsuitable, first of all, because the Foreign Capital Management Act of 1958 was placed on the statute book for the purpose of effectively managing aid received from other nations; however, there were no related regulations for controlling foreign loans or factories built with foreign direct investment and technical services. The Act effectively restricted foreign investment, rather than promoting it. According to its provisions, only those foreign citizens from nations with which

---

[3] In fact, the system was not abolished. Even after 1964, whenever the Ministry of Commerce, Employment and Trade announced quarterly import quotas, it noted in its trade guidelines that import application limits could be adjusted according to export results.

Korea had normal diplomatic relations and had made amicable trade relationships, and Korean citizens who had lived for longer than 10 years in nations designated by presidential decree, could conduct investment activities. The result was to eliminate all nations except the United States from investment activities.[4] Moreover, the Act set a lower limit for foreign investment and restricted the withdrawal of profits from investments in Korea.

With the amendment of the two acts these problems were resolved, but the changes were not sufficient to attract foreign capital. Private companies lacking international confidence had particular difficulties attracting sufficient foreign capital to meet all the commitments of the 5-year comprehensive economic rehabilitation plan. At a meeting held between government representatives and entrepreneurs on October 18, 1961 the issue of the importation of foreign capital was discussed. Entrepreneurs from the Federation of Korean Industries and the Korean Chamber of Commerce & Industry (KCCI) demanded that the government provide "certificates of payment guarantee" for all foreign capital and loans for shortfalls in equity capital. They argued that government payment guarantees were essential for attracting foreign capital. The entrepreneurs also demanded greater transparency in the selection by government of "favored" businesses and a more comprehensive sharing of relevant information.

The payment guarantees demanded were made available through the Payment Guarantee Act for Foreign Loans, announced on July 18, 1962. The Act provided payment guarantees for those projects that required foreign capital, after approval from the Committee to Promote Foreign Capital Importation, and enabled companies to borrow needed capital by using planned facilities as collateral.

Shortly after the 1961 coup, the military government nationalized the commercial banks by seizing bank stock held by large speculators and by restricting the voting rights of private stockhold-

---

[4] In the 1960s, when the Foreign Capital Act was put in place, the United States was the only country with which Korea had amicable trade relations.

ers who owned less than 10% of the shares. By mobilizing domestic capital through the nationalized industrial and commercial banks, the regime secured a systematic basis for allocating foreign capital by consolidating the regulations governing it.

Private companies with no international credit unquestionably needed government payment guarantees to raise foreign capital. In the process of providing payment guarantees, the government seized the distribution and deliberation rights over foreign capital and, through the banks, became directly involved in the capital mobilization process of individual companies. The authorities used this financial power to select and foster businesses in the process of developing import substitution industries. For example, Park Hong-sik, who was selected to participate in Viscose Rayon, one of the textile industry's 5-year development projects, was only able to mobilize 43% of needed domestic capital from his own business, Heonghan Chemical Fiber Spinning and Cutting, and the collateral rate needed to attract foreign capital was 76.1%. Heonghan thus had to take out loans from the industrial bank to acquire the capital needed for factory construction and initial operations.

III. EVOLUTION OF INDUSTRIAL POLICY

The government's original plan to use primarily domestic capital and be involved directly in the economic development process as a primary investment body was vastly revised in the supplementary plan. In the process of constructing factories for import substitution, the role of private companies was increased. The principal export items were also changed from the originally planned primary industrial products to manufactured goods, and as a means to acquire foreign capital, exports became even more important.

The idea of *government-directed capitalism* was reflected in the process of domestic capital mobilization, industrialization to substitute for imports, and the distribution of foreign capital. As time went by, government intervention was expanded not only to capital distribution but also to resource allocation, distribution of manufactured goods in the domestic market, and pricing.

Foreign Capital Inducement Act

The Foreign Capital Inducement Act (FCIA) unified the existing Foreign Capital Promotion Act, the Loan Payment Guarantee Act, and the Special Act on Long-term Payments. The FCIA eliminated the inconvenience of dealing with foreign direct investment, credit financing, and payment guarantees for loans under separate acts. However, it went beyond being a simple unification of existing law.

First, the FCIA abolished the lower limit on foreign investment and exempted foreign investors from income, corporate, property, and acquisition taxes for 5 years. Foreign investors could also remit the profits they made to their own nations, and it legalized cash loans that had been prohibited. Of these changes, the most important concerned the payment guarantees. Under the FCIA the government restricted its payment guarantees to the following: businesses that belonged to key industries, agricultural and fishery businesses, businesses producing items and services essential for people's lives, and businesses needed for economic development and the improvement of international payments and that could not attract foreign capital without payment guarantees. With these changes, the government stopped payment guarantees for private commercial loans.

It was impossible for private companies that could not receive government-backed payment guarantees to attract foreign capital with their own credit, and therefore those companies had to look for payment guarantees from commercial banks. Because the approval of the National Assembly was required for government payment guarantees, the reduction in scope of payment guarantees allowed the government to (1) reduce the number of complicated applications for approval to the National Assembly, and (2) strengthen its power regarding the inducement of foreign capital. Because commercial banks were owned by the state, payment guarantees by those banks were actually decided by the government.

The example of a chemical fiber manufacturing company illustrates how individual enterprises introduced foreign capital by means of the FCIA. According to the business plan submitted by Korean Polyester in 1968, 1.523 billion *won* in domestic capital was needed to

92

build a polyester manufacturing company with 20 tons of daily capacity. Korean Polyester planned to obtain 500 million *won* from capital payments, 536 million *won* through cash loans, and 500 million *won* through loans from the Korea Development Bank.[5] An audit conducted by the Hanil Bank, which was in charge of payment guarantees for Korea Polyester Co. Ltd., showed that individual dividends, real estate, textile products, and even subsidiaries' reserves for capital increases and the owner's private note were all included as sources of the 500 million *won* capital payment. Thus, the capital payments of Korea Polyester Co. Ltd. were not current holdings, but entities that could change according to Korean Polyester's future management.[6]

As can be seen from this example, even an existing company that had been the first to build and operate a nylon company in Korea did not hold sufficient capital, and the methods used to mobilize domestic capital in its business plan actually relied on cash loans and loans from development banks. "Given the scale of business in the plan, capital mobilization through cash loans is required, but review by government organizations, including the Economic Planning Board, is needed. The applicant has suggested borrowing 500 million *won* from the Korea Industrial Bank. Considering the scale of its business, it is thought to be appropriate."[7]

The role of the Hanil Bank, which supervised payment guarantees, was limited to summarizing the papers submitted by applicants and evaluating the estates, real and movable, offered as collateral.

As the above summary by the Hanil Bank shows, work on payment guarantees was transferred to commercial banks, but final decisions on foreign capital importation were still made by the government. When construction plans developed by the EPB for four key factories (producing pig iron, specialty steels, ships, and heavy machinery) faced difficulties in attracting foreign capital, the

---

[5] Economic Planning Board, Minutes of the 34th Consultation on Foreign Capital Inducement, November 28, 1968.
[6] Hanil Bank, "Written Opinion on the Financial Strength of Korean Polyester," *Hanilwegwan* 182, August 14, 1967.
[7] Ibid.

Secretary to the President's office at the Blue House stepped in on November 10, 1971, and started to play a leading role in policy establishment and implementation.

Import Substitution Industries and Economies of Scale

Under the first 5-year economic development plan, made on the basis of the 5-year Comprehensive Economic Rehabilitation Plan, facility expansion policies for individual industries focused primarily on estimating domestic demand for each product, calculating supplies needed to meet demand, and approving commercial loans required for expansion and new facilities. Therefore, the first considerations on the part of government in the process of loan approval were the proportion of domestic demand to be met by each product, the quantity of foreign currency that could be saved, and the number of jobs that could be created. However, as an increasing number of businesses applied for commercial loans for expansion and for new entry into the market, policies on import substitution were changed.

Let us return to the chemical fiber manufacturing company, Korea Polyester Co., Ltd. The company submitted a business plan in which it would build polyester types SF and F factories, each with 10 ton/day capacity, using commercial loans and technology from Mitsui and Chemtex. The EPB scrutinized the plan and estimated that the future domestic demand in 1971 for polyester type SF would be 15,906 tons (45.4 tons daily) and 3,243 tons (9.3 tons daily) for polyester type F. Therefore, if the construction received loan approvals as proposed, there would be a shortfall of 140 tons (0.4 ton daily) in the production of polyester SF, whereas 3395 tons (9.7 tons daily) of polyester F would be oversupplied. The additional capacity for making polyester SF and F created by newly established polyester factories would each be 10 tons daily, and thus, if all facilities were built as proposed, polyester SF and F would show daily oversupplies of 9.6 tons and 19.7 tons, respectively (Table 3.2).

Table 3.2 Economic Planning Board Polyester Supply and Demand Estimates (Tons/Day)

		1967		1969		1970		1971	
		SF	F	SF	F	SF	F	SF	F
Demand (calculation)		19.8	4.5	30.3	6.5	37.4	7.8	45.4	9.3
Supply capacity (plan)	Daehan synthetic fiber	6.0		11.0	4.0	11.0	4.0	18.0	12.0
	Samyangsa			12.0	1.0	12.0	1.0	12.0	1.0
	Daehan Sanub					7.0	3.0	7.0	3.0
	Chosun textile manufacturing							8.0	2.0
	Total supply	6.0	0.0	23.0	5.0	30.0	8.0	45.0	18.0
Overs & shorts (demand-supply)		-13.8	-4.5	-6.7	-1.5	-7.4	-0.2	-0.4	9.7

Source: Economic Planning Board, "Minutes of the 34th Foreign Capital Inducement Committee," November 28, 1968; "Review of Economic Feasibility of Applications for the Introduction of Capital Goods and Foreign Investment," December 23, 1968; "Minutes of the 35th Foreign Capital Inducement Committee," December 30, 1968.

The Ministry of Commerce and Industry reviewed Korea Polyester's business plan and suggested approval of the commercial loans on the condition that all production would be exported.[8] In addition, the ministry also suggested expanding the factories to international scale, which was an essential step in acquiring price competitiveness because, with small production facilities, production costs were

---

[8] Ministry of Commerce and Industry, "Employment and Trade, Application to Receive Approval for Cash Loans and for the Introduction of Capital Goods to Build Polyester Factories (Reply)," *Sangilseom*:1334-77, July 31, 1967; "Minutes of the 34th Foreign Capital Inducement Committee," November 28, 1968.

inevitably high. The Foreign Capital Inducement Committee approved commercial loans for Korea Polyester and supported the condition concerning the export of all production. The government policy to foster import substitution industries was thereby transformed to foster export industries.

The policy was changed because the plan to foster import substitution industries did not achieve good results, and there was a possibility that too many small companies that had received approvals for commercial loans would only add to the confusion. The Ministry of Commerce and Industry stressed that the government should allow those companies that could readily attract foreign capital to participate in development projects while preventing a number of small-sized enterprises from randomly applying for foreign capital by imposing strict conditions on such applications.

In particular, the ministry argued that the scale of chemical fiber manufacturing factories should be expanded to meet international competition. Its argument was the result of a Blue House meeting on January 12, 1967, which concluded that construction plans for chemical fiber plants should be reviewed and put into effect on the assumption that the industry would be helped to compete internationally.

With the enactment of temporary legislation concerning textile manufacturing facilities in March 1967, the government took control of investment in chemical fiber manufacturing plans based on its own demand forecasts and maneuvered companies into expanding to international scale. However, securing international competitiveness by realizing economies of scale ran counter to the idea of a market economy, because it blocked entry of newcomers into the market. Even though the scale of companies was expanded, there were problems caused by the difficulty in reducing production costs and meeting international standards in the initial stages, the high interest rates attached to commercial loans, and the low level of technology.

Import Substitution and Export-Oriented Policies

As manufactured products took a bigger proportion of exports, the import of raw materials needed to produce these products was increased, and the foreign exchange earning ratio deteriorated accordingly. The foreign exchange earning rate that had reached 82.2% in 1962 decreased to 65.1% in 1963 and to 64.7% in 1964.[9] To increase the foreign exchange earning rate, raw materials currently imported needed to be obtained domestically. However, domestically supplied goods had to be competitive in terms of price and quality. To make this possible, as it had with Korea Polyester, the government adopted the strategy of controlling the investment plans of chemical fiber manufacturers based on demand forecasts and securing export competitiveness by realizing economies of scale. However, supplying raw materials domestically required additional systematic measures. Because exporters who used imported raw materials enjoyed a comparative advantage in terms of financing and taxation, existing systems of export support had to be revised. Reforms of the export support financing and taxation system in the late 1960s were carried out in this context. However, these systematic supports did not lead directly to supply replacements. Textile exporters distrusted the quality of domestic chemical fiber and doubted whether domestic manufacturers could make deliveries on time. They were also concerned that they might have to face additional price increases because of the high production costs of the domestic material. Therefore, they did not have any overwhelming incentive to switch to domestically produced fiber. Meanwhile, the government felt keenly the necessity for domestic sourcing of raw materials, but it could not risk destabilizing textile exports. Domestic sourcing could be realized gradually as the productivity and quality control of the domestic chemical fiber industry improved, but the government wanted this shift to take effect as soon as possible. Thus, a prior approval system for imported raw materials and a regulation committee were introduced.

The Ministry of Commerce and Industry announced guidelines for the prior approval of imported raw materials in July 1971,

---

[9] Office of the Prime Minister, "Evaluation of the 1st 5-Year Economic Development Plan," 1967, p. 750.

restricting imports of acrylic, nylon, and polyester by demanding prior approval from the ministry when importing raw materials to produce export goods. The Regulation Committee, which consisted of raw material manufacturers, exporters, and officials from related organizations, reviewed and controlled the quality and price of domestic raw materials used to make export goods. With this committee and the prior approval system, the ministry had the right to decide supply prices based on international price changes and import prices, and the import of raw materials was blocked systematically. Only when the price of domestically supplied raw materials rose above international prices or the quality of domestic goods was poorer than that of foreign equivalents were imports allowed after consultation with the Regulation Committee. In other words, the administrative decisions of the committee replaced the role of the market.

However, because this hierarchical structure lacked the effectiveness of the market, it needed some kind of tool to facilitate the allocation of resources. At a time when the government allowed construction of additional facilities that would cause oversupply in the domestic market, it demanded that all products made by the newly built facilities be exported. With the Foreign Capital Inducement Act, the government could demand changes from the companies that had received foreign capital if they did not follow the conditions imposed at the time of investment approval. If companies did not follow the orders to change, the government could collect otherwise exempt corporate income and property taxes. In addition, if companies violated given conditions regarding loans and technology introduction, the government could impose fines. With these measures, the government forced the companies in receipt of foreign capital to meet export quotas and punished those who failed to do so by collecting taxes from which they would otherwise have been exempt. To avoid this penalty, companies strove to meet the given export quotas and, in the process, inevitably faced competition in the international market. This competition acted as a motivation to improve productivity and prevented companies from sitting complacently in the domestic market.

IV. HEAVY AND CHEMICAL INDUSTRIALIZATION POLICY

Implementation

In August 1973 the EPB published the "Long-Term Outlook for the Korean Economy 1972-1981." That outlook differed substantially from the third 5-year economic development plan in the areas of growth, stability, and trade balance and signaled the beginning of a shift toward heavy chemical industrialization. Most significantly, there were major disparities in macroeconomic indices. The 1976 export target in the long-term outlook, at $4.47 billion, was markedly higher than the $3.5 billion of the third 5-year plan, whereas the target for 1981 was set at $10.97 billion. The 1976 GNP per capita figure in the outlook was $488, which was $100 higher than that of the third plan. Accordingly, GNP growth in the outlook was also higher than in the plan. In addition, and as can be seen in Table 3.3 below, heavy chemical products took a higher portion of export manufacturing and added value as compared with the third plan. The long-term outlook for the Korean economy thus focused on the sophistication of industrial structures through the promotion of heavy chemical exports.

Unlike the third economic plan, with its emphasis on stability and balance, the long-term outlook was more akin to a "material mobilization" plan. Whereas the 5-year plan had focused on the import substitution of heavy chemical items based on the progress of industrialization and demand forecasts, the long-term outlook focused primarily on six industries — steel, nonferrous metals, shipbuilding, machinery, electronics, and chemicals — and set production targets for each.

A series of political and military incidents after 1968 led the Park Chung-hee administration to feel keenly the importance of developing the defense industry; thus, an awareness of the political and military situation in South Korea at that time is essential for a full understanding of the Park government's sudden policy changes.[10]

The plan to achieve annual 10% GNP growth by 1981 and drive economic growth through the development of manufacturing industries, which in turn would be driven by industrialization of the heavy chemical industry, was adjusted once and then postponed due to shortages caused by the oil shock in the early 1970s. It was however, implemented aggressively after 1976. To foster the six industries — steel, nonferrous metals, shipbuilding, machinery, electronics, and chemicals — the government planned to invest a total of 2.98 trillion *won*, constituting 22.1% of total investment and 63.9% of investment allocated to the manufacturing sector, from 1973 to 1981. In an attempt to nurture the heavy chemical industry, the government reorganized institutional bodies, improved social overhead capital, and provided tax and financial incentives.

In May 1973 the Heavy Chemical Promotion Committee (HCPC) was set up by presidential decree and mandated to provide comprehensive support and direction for heavy chemical industrial development; a Heavy Chemical Planning Board (HCPB) was formed as a subsidiary of the committee. The HCPB was formally under the authority of the Prime Minister, but in reality, was an influential

---

[10] Various incidents, including the capture of the USS Pueblo, raised concerns over Korea's national defense capability, and a local defense force was established in April 1968. As a result, military procurement for the forces was required. Meanwhile, with the infiltration from North Korea of armed guerrillas into Oljin and Samcheok, tension between the two Koreas increased. In July 1969, U.S. President Richard Nixon announced the Guam Doctrine, which declared that Asian countries should be responsible for their own national security. Soon after the questions on the withdrawal of two army divisions of the U.S. forces stationed in Korea were raised, one division completed its withdrawal in March 1971. On July 4, 1972, the Joint Declaration between the two Koreas was announced, but relations were soon broken off. A South Korean group that visited the North was overwhelmed by the development of the heavy chemical industry there. A reassessment of South Korea's economic development strategies that had focused on light industry since the 1960s was begun (Ishizaki 1996:72-4).

organization under the direct control of the President. It comprised officials from the Blue House, the Ministry of Commerce and Industry, the Ministry of Construction, and the EPB and, until it was disbanded in 1980, was responsible for all heavy chemical-related policies and their implementation.[11]

Table 3.3 Third 5-Year Economic Development Plan and the Long-Term Outlook

	Elements of the Plan	Long-Term Outlook
Characteristics	Focused on stability and balance	Materials mobilization plan
Industrial policies	Presented demand forecasts, production targets and investment plans. Strategic industries were not selected	Six industries (steel, nonferrous metals, shipbuilding, machinery, electronics, and chemical) selected as strategic industries
Annual GNP growth	1972-76 8.6%	1972-76 9.0% 1977-81 11.0%
Exports	1976-$3.5 billion	1976-$4.47 billion 1981-$10.97 billion
GNP per capita	1976-$389	1976-$488 1981-$983
Heavy chemical industry/ value-added manufacturing industry	1970-35.9% 1976-40.5%	1972-35.2% 1976-41.8% 1981-51.0%
Heavy chemical products/ export of manufactured goods	1972-23.3% 1976-33.3%	1972-27.0% 1976-44.0% 1981-65.0%

Source: Ishizaki 1996:69.

---

[11] Ministry of Finance, "White Paper on Financial Investment and Loans," 1982.

In terms of support, more loans were allocated to the heavy chemical industry. In particular, the national investment fund, created by the National Investment Fund Act, was turned over to the heavy chemical industry. From 1974 to 1980, 67.1% of the national investment fund, which represented 80-90% of the financial loan fund, was allocated to the heavy chemical industry.[12]

In terms of taxation, the chemical industry also received special favors. Under the Customs Act and the Tax Exemption Act, 14 key industries, including steel, nonferrous metals, petrochemical, and shipbuilding, could choose from a 100% direct tax exemption for 3 years and a 50% exemption for the following 2 years, an 8-10% deduction on invested funds, or a 100% special depreciation. In addition, a 70-100% customs exemption was available. With the enactment of a series of laws to help the heavy chemical industry, such as the Steel Industry Promotion Act, the Electronics Promotion Act, the Petrochemical Promotion Act, and the Nonferrous Metals Refining Act, further incentives, including customs exemptions and corporate tax exemptions, were also given to the industry. Much of the available finance also went to the chemical industry, and loans from the industrial banks between 1973 and 1980 reached 1.2302 trillion *won* and accounted for 80% of all loans to the manufacturing sector.

Social overhead capital was improved for the heavy chemical industry. Between 1972 and 1976 financial investment given to social overhead capital was 1.6 trillion *won*, which represented 67.4% of total financial investment. Compared with the 54.9% allocated between 1962 and 1966, this was a significant increase. Investment in social overhead capital rose even more between 1977 and 1980, when it reached 5 trillion *won*.

According to the heavy chemical industrialization plan, the government chose industrial sites for each type of industry and provided

---

[12] The Economic Planning Board, "White Paper on the Economy," 1981, p. 107.

the necessary roads, ports, and water facilities. In addition, it provided financial and tax incentives for those who located at these sites.

Market Replacement

As has been shown in the case of Korea's chemical fiber industry, in the process of replacing imports of chemical fiber the government established a plan to achieve international competitiveness by realizing economies of scale and, to that end, intervened in the distribution of foreign and domestic capital and in pricing decisions. In the same vein, the Park government wanted to replace imports of heavy chemical products and realize heavy chemical industrialization as speedily as possible. It is unsurprising, therefore, that the level of government intervention increased. This section examines the import substitution process and price control policies in the petrochemical industry.

On April 11, 1972, the Korea Chemical Fiber Association (KCFA) held its board meeting at the Kookje Hotel. The chair of the KCFA, Park Chong-sik, reported that the Ministry of Commerce and Industry had changed chemical fiber policies and that new policies would be adopted from the second quarter of the year. Heads of corporations requested that officers of the KCFA draft countermeasure proposals to deal with the policy changes, but the association was helpless.[13]

Let us look a little closer at the government's policy changes and their effects on access to raw materials. Up to that time, companies had imported all the raw materials (caprolactam, acrylonitrile monomer, dimethyl terephthalate) needed for manufacturing. Though fiber raw materials for domestic use required import approval, with the recommendation of the KCFA, raw materials to make export goods could be imported without its recommendation. Therefore, even though domestic demand had increased and production rates had gone up as a result, there was no problem obtaining supplies of raw

---

[13] Korea Chemical Fibre Association, "Minutes of the 4th Board Meeting," April 11, 1972.

materials. However, subsequent to Announcement 8311 by the Ministry of Commerce and Industry, made on March 13, 1972, companies needed a recommendation from the KCFA even when importing raw materials to make export goods; furthermore, the Ministry could reject requests for recommendations. As a result, the government assumed absolute power in the allocation of imported raw materials for the chemical fiber industry. With this announcement, the government showed its intention to put in place systematic measures to operate petrochemical factories built in accordance with its second 5-year economic development plan. In March 1972, the Dongseo Petrochemical Company, which produced the raw material for acrylic fiber, acrylonitrile monomer, was putting the final touches on its construction, well ahead of its October goal. Korea Caprolactam, which produced the raw material for nylon fiber, caprolactam, was completed in 1974, and Samsung Petrochemical and Honam Petrochemical, which manufactured the raw materials for polyester terephthalate and EG, were completed in 1979.

The government was now faced with the new task of developing the petrochemical industry as an import substitution industry. On July 25, 1972, the Ministry of Commerce and Industry submitted a report to President Park entitled "Sales Price of Petrochemical Products" (Table 3.4). This report detailed the discussions that it had had with the Finance Ministry and the EPB regarding ways to build up the petrochemical industry. It focused on two issues: protection of immature industries and monopoly restriction. To deal with these two concerns the ministry suggested government regulation of the supply price of petrochemical products. The report noted, "The supply price of petrochemical products is established to protect the six newly built petrochemical factories and to prevent monopolistic price-setting by those companies."[14] The ministry divided domestic production of petrochemical goods into domestic uses and export

---

[14] Ministry of Commerce, Employment, and Trade, "Price Decision on Petrochemical Goods Report," No. 238, July 25, 1972; Presidential Secretary's Office, "Report on Commerce and Trade, Record Keeping Office of the Ministry of Government Administration and Home Affairs," 1972.

uses and adopted a dual-pricing system. The price of exported raw materials was set based on the price of tax-exempt imported goods, and losses were made up by increased local prices. In addition, the ministry set the sales ratio between domestic and exported raw materials.

Table 3.4 Petrochemical Products Supply Prices (July 25, 1972)

Classification item		Sales price (dollars/ton)		Ratio of domestic to exported raw materials
		Domestic	Export	
Polyethylene		363.04	301.35	95:5
VCM		161.77	129.60	95:5
Acrylonitrile monomer		551.24	308.56	50:50
Polypropylene	fiber	379.08	270.11	70:30
	resin	364.35	248.06	70:30
SBR	tire	506.41	362.46	60:40
	shoe	447.78	296.52	60:40
Alkyl benzene		313.10	156.00	70:30

Source: Ministry of Commerce and Industry, "Price Decision on Petrochemical Goods Report," No. 238, July 25, 1972.

Future sales prices were to be adjusted based on previous years' performance, and the prices of exported raw materials were to be changed according to international prices. Whenever the prices of ethylene, propylene, butane, and benzene supplied by naphtha-cracking factories were changed, the prices of petrochemical products were also to be adjusted. To lower the price of petrochemical products, customs duties on imported raw materials and catalysts were waived.

On the strength of Announcement 8311, the government was able to force chemical fiber manufacturers to buy high-priced domestic petrochemical goods, and with the system of recommendations required for importing petrochemical raw materials, the government could control the use of chemical fiber raw materials consumed by chemical fiber manufacturers. The government made the manufacturers buy locally made, high-priced raw materials to manufacture domestic chemical fiber and to use the rest of the raw materials for exports.

V. CONCLUSION

Strategies for import substitution industrialization, carried out in circumstances of strong government intervention after the 1961 military coup, took concrete shape in the first 5-year economic development plan. The original plan was substantially modified in a supplementary plan, which emphasized the role of private companies and shifted major export items from primary industrial products to manufactured goods and exports as a means of acquiring foreign capital, which was assumed to be of even greater importance.

However, the basic idea of capitalism under strong government management was reflected in the process of mobilizing and distributing domestic and foreign capital and in the process of industrialization to substitute for imports. The government restricted the entry of newcomers into the market so that existing companies could grow to the scale necessary for international competition, and it also regulated investment for expansion.

Expansion of some companies built to substitute for imports triggered oversupply in the domestic market. Oversupplies were to be exported, but high interest rates for commercial loans, less sophisticated technology, and poorer quality had unfavorable effects, making it impossible to lower production costs.

As has been shown, import substitution policies for chemical fiber raw materials were carried out to solve the oversupply issue and improve foreign exchange earning rates. However, textile exporters who distrusted the price, quality, and reliability of domestic raw material producers were reluctant to buy domestically, and the government could not force them to do so, and thus hamper the exports of textiles, one of the main export items. The Prior Approval System for Imported Raw Materials and the Regulation Committee were the solutions put forward in the quest for prompt resolutions of these problems. Instead of waiting for the market to solve them naturally, the government exercised its administrative powers. It divided domestic petrochemical goods into domestic uses and export uses and adopted a dual-pricing system for the two categories, systematically blocking imports of raw materials for making export goods.

The heavy chemical industrialization actively carried out from 1973 onward had the goal of achieving import substitution of heavy chemical products and of quickly making heavy chemical goods an export item. Therefore, in the process of resource allocation, government intervention was enhanced even further. The government was involved directly in the mobilization and distribution of the domestic and foreign capital needed to build heavy chemical factories, and it selected and developed industrial sites for each industry. When production began of heavy chemical products, the government restricted import of those goods and established the dual-price system. Sales ratios between domestic and export goods were also set by the government.

Intervention by the Park Chung-hee regime increased exponentially from the time immediately following the military coup of May 1961 and proceeded unabated throughout the 1960s and the 1970s; in so doing, the administration used its various departments most effectively to allocate resources and assume the role of the market.

Chapter 4

The *Chaebol* Regime and the Developmental Coalition of Domination

Cho Young-chol

I. INTRODUCTION

The legacies inherited by the South Korean nation from its experience of developmental dictatorship are many and varied. In terms of finance and business, however, there can be little doubt that the most important creation in that era was that of *chaebols*: the family-owned conglomerates that constitute a core element in defining the modern capitalism of South Korea. One of the main reasons why Korea suffered a severe economic crisis in the final years of the 20th century was that financial liberalization and capital market openness had been pursued by the government without much consideration to how financial liberalization gave rise to severe financial instability. The decisive error lay in seeking financial liberalization without first clearing out the vestiges of the government-led financial system from which the *chaebols* benefited and then establishing an autonomous and transparent bank's governance system in its place. Overinvestment of the *chaebols* was yet another factor contributing to the crisis. The comprehensive and coherent reform of the *chaebol* structure is one of the most crucial tasks facing South Korea today, and a number of proposals aimed at achieving this fundamental objective have been made. However, to engage in a meaningful discussion concerning the reform of the *chaebols* it is necessary first to look at their historic background.

The strategy of state-led development, as conducted in South Korea during the Park Chung-hee era (1961-79), achieved explosive economic growth in spite of a corrupt coalition between the state and the *chaebols*. At that time, the Korean people accepted the government's strategy of "growth first, distribution later" and bore the brunt of extreme economic sacrifice to achieve industrialization; therefore, the *chaebols* bear a clear moral obligation to the population because their accumulation of huge corporate and private fortunes was achieved only by means of patronage by the state and suffering by the people.

There is a danger of minimizing the seriousness of the historical circumstances surrounding the *chaebols* and overlooking the foundation on which they are based, on the grounds that these are merely property issues between *chaebol* owners and minority shareholders. As an extension, if an attempt is made to reform the *chaebols* while assuming the existence of their "vested rights," truly effective measures to deal with their resistance to reform are unlikely to be formulated.

This chapter examines the historical background to the formation of the *chaebols* and suggests a basis for their democratic reform.

II. ECONOMIC DEVELOPMENT PLANS AND THE MAKING OF *CHAEBOLS*

Although the Korean *chaebols* began to emerge as recognizable entities in the 1950s, they grew more because they were the favored recipients of U.S. aid than by their own "producer enterprise." After the military coup in 1961, those *chaebol* families who actively cooperated with the Park Chung-hee regime's industrialization policies were rewarded by a whole raft of highly advantageous and exclusive patronage measures, whereas those who had not followed Park's industrial policies were excluded. Unlike during the 1950s, industrial capital began to accumulate under government leadership in the 1960s. For this reason, inter alia, it can be said that there are both continuities and discontinuities between the *chaebols* of the 1950s and those of the 1960s.

After the April 19th student revolution of 1960, which overthrew the government of Rhee Sung-man, the Korean people recognized that with an economic structure so heavily dependent on foreign aid, they could not realize a self-supporting economy. The military government that seized power a year later shared common views regarding economic development strategy with the administration of Premier Chang Myon, which it had usurped. However, the Park Chung-hee administration believed that to build a self-supporting economy it was necessary to develop key industries — heavy and chemical industries that could be fostered not by the free market, but only by strong government intervention and support. That was the main difference in economic development strategy between the Chang Myon government and its military successor.

The Park administration followed the economic development plan drawn up by the previous government, but differed from it only at the point where it implemented selective industrial policies to regulate and support the *chaebols* by nationalizing the banks owned by *chaebols*. Under the previous arrangements, the government and the *chaebols* had simple collusive ties based on the exchange of economic rents and political funds. After 1961, however, a developmental state that pursued industrialization and the *chaebol* families, who pursued their empire-building, came to a mutual agreement regarding economic growth and together established a vertical coalition in which the government-controlled financial system regulated and supported the *chaebols*.

Because government-directed banking was a key political measure that enabled the government to take the initiative in carrying out its industrial policies, it was the primary means by which the developmental state was able to successfully bring about industrialization. Yet, at the same time, it was the predominant cause of the economic crisis that was to hit South Korea a generation later, demonstrating historically that underdevelopment of the industrial finance system constitutes one of the biggest obstacles facing underdeveloped countries in the process of industrialization.

For example, in Germany, which began capitalist industrialization later, huge amounts of investment funding were raised and immature industries were protected to overcome German inferiority when compared to Great Britain, which had achieved industrialization earlier. In this process and because of the underdevelopment of the German capital market, most of the investment funds were raised through long-term lending by the major commercial banks. These banks had internal departments that examined the loans to be extended to companies. Officially, they provided only short-term loans, but through maturity extensions, long-term loans were, in fact, given to companies. During the late 19th and early 20th centuries, the board of directors of Deutsche Bank were industrial experts in charge of the examination of those major companies that had close relations with banks. Therefore, in the process of German industrialization, German commercial banks served to provide venture capital. That is to say, in nurturing the German heavy chemical industry, for example, trade protectionism based on the protection of immature industries played its part, but the financial commitment of large commercial banks made a substantial contribution.[1]

Thus when developing countries are to carry out industrialization by fostering key industries, they should secure a corporate financing system that can provide dedicated capital in the long-term horizon. In Korea, however, domestic savings rates in the 1950s and the early 1960s were very low, and most commercial banks were owned by the *chaebols* characterized by commercial capital. There were, therefore, few inducements for commercial banks to bear high-risk investments in the long-term horizon.

In 1961, the Park government took statutory measures to restrain the voting rights of private shareholders through the Temporary Act on Financial Organizations, which virtually nationalized the *chaebol*-owned banks, established new development banks, and expanded existing special banks. In a situation in which there were no financial institutions to provide venture capital, the government had to create the requisite industrial finance system and itself become an active investor. Of course, the nationalization of banks left a negative

---

[1] Financial commitment, in contrast to financial liquidity, is neither a short-term nor an arm's length notion that stresses "exit effects," but rather long-term corporate financing.

legacy, most notably the wider implications of government-directed lending, but it was, nevertheless, a key factor in making possible the radical industrialization achievements of Park's developmental dictatorship.

In 1961 the military government did not have any clear strategies for export-oriented industrialization, but it did have a clear understanding that to overcome the external dependency that characterized the Korean economy in the 1950s it needed to develop key industries, such as electricity, coal, oil refining, fertilizers, and steel. Though the investment projects of the First Economic Development Plan could not be carried out because of funding limits, the plan did point the way toward fostering heavy industries through import substitution.[2] Of the loans directed toward the manufacturing sector from commercial and industrial banks, a considerable amount, 52.9%, was allotted to the heavy chemical industry in 1965; this amount increased to 54.5% and 50.4% in 1970 and 1975, respectively. In addition, most of the long-term facilities investment was also given to the heavy chemical industry.

It was the United States that strongly recommended export-oriented industrialization strategies to the Korean administration, but in the early stages at least, the Park government had the relatively passive view that the export of light and primary industrial goods was needed only to solve the shortage of foreign currency.[3] The government did not become actively involved in promoting exports until it

---

[2] The industrialization strategies that the government implemented in the 1960s to substitute for imports focused on capital goods, rather than light industry. This was because import substitution for durable consumer goods had been completed in the early 1960s (Kim Gwang-sok and Cha Dong-se 1995:49).

[3] The main goals of the First 5-year Economic Development Plan were the fostering of energy industries, such as electricity and coal; enhancement of agricultural productivity; expansion of key industries and Social Overhead Capitals (SOCs); utilization of idle resources; job creation; land development and preservation; improvement of the balance of payments through export growth, and technology development (Gang Gwang-ha 2000:28).. Although export growth was included in these goals, it was not regarded as a major target in the pursuit of industrialization.

realized the extent to which they could be a strong driving force for economic growth. One researcher, Chang Ha-won (1999), argues that, though the military government became aware of the export potential after completion of the first 5-year economic development plan, it did not fully appreciate the growth potential of exports and, even in the second 5-year plan, simply regarded them as a means to improve the balance of payments.

In the early 1960s the Park government experienced certain difficulties in its relationship with the United States concerning economic policy. This was mainly because Park set out to build a self-supporting economy by implementing policies to foster key industries under strong government leadership. If he had accepted the light industry-centered export policies recommended by the United States, there would have been no grounds for conflict, at least in the realm of economic matters. However, from the moment it assumed national leadership, the military government was determined to focus on key industries and, to that end, implement industrialization strategies to achieve import substitution. Light industry-centered export strategies were adopted after the government became aware of the growth potential of exports; from that point on, the Park industrialization strategy was transformed into a dual one combining import substitution and export promotion, and the ideas of Friedrich List and Adam Smith.[4]

As exports showed unexpectedly good results, the government gained confidence in the dual strategies and, in carrying out its heavy chemical policies in the 1970s, opted to continue to invest with an export-oriented focus. Rather than targeting the small domestic market, the government elected to aggressively commit large investments to the export sector and, in so doing, enable the *chaebols* to secure a foundation for their future growth.[5]

---

[4] Friedrich List supported an export-oriented industrialization strategy that protects immature key domestic industries, and Adam Smith supported the pursuit of competitiveness in world markets.

[5] When pursuing an industrialization strategy to substitute for imports in the 1960s, foreign experts and foreign loan providers were opposed to building large factories because of the small domestic market (O Won-chol

When the military government first came to power it attempted to penalize the *chaebols* that had accumulated illicit fortunes under the aegis of the Rhee Sung-man government between 1948 and 1960. The endeavor was not continued, however, and the government soon changed its position, having come to the conclusion that the *chaebols* would be essential partners in fostering the heavy chemical industries and in putting into effect its broader industrial strategies. The United States, which communicated with the *chaebol* families, also pressured the Korean government not to penalize illicit speculators insensitively for fear that there would be related socialist developmental strategies.

Within the military government some leaders, such as Park Hee-bom[6] and Yu Won-sik, argued that a self-supporting economy could be built by mobilizing domestic capital and fostering key industries under strong government leadership,[7] but the United States, which supported a free market economy, strongly opposed the idea. In addition, and as Park Chung-hee had severely criticized government-owned companies in the 1950s as being hotbeds of inefficiency and

---

1996). The government built the small-scale factories that would still meet international standards and be internationally competitive in the 1960s and expanded its plan to build the largest scale factories that met international standards and export targets in the 1970s (Lee Byong-cheon 1999: 175).

[6] Criticizing the colony modernization theory, Park Hee-bom argued that industrialization that focused on consumer goods would deepen the monopolization of a few existing large companies. He stressed that the government should focus on establishing key industries utilizing foreign capital and accepting the international division of labor (Hong Sok-ryul 1999: 221).

[7] Core members of the military government, including Park Chung-hee, devised a plan to establish the Industrial Development Corporation to carry out the state's direct investment activities based on domestic capital, acting as a kind of national holding company. The United States strongly opposed the idea, believing it to be a socialist economic development. Though the Chang Myon democratic government had set the goal of fostering key industries through its 5-year development plan, in terms of government-led economic development strategies the military government placed greater emphasis on the role of government than had its democratic predecessor (Park Tae-gyun 2000).

corruption,[8] the government recognized that it was unrealistic for government-owned companies to play a leading role in fostering key industries. After the failure of currency reform, it became even clearer that fostering key industries through the mobilization of domestic capital was an unrealistic proposition. Desperately in need of foreign capital, the government could not resist the U.S. recommendation to establish development strategies based on private companies and the free market. As a result, the construction of such key industries as energy and steel that would be difficult for private companies because of the heavy investments involved was undertaken by government-owned companies,[9] and private companies constructed other heavy industries so that private capital mobilization and management capabilities were utilized.

Far from penalizing all those who had accrued illicit fortunes, 18 speculators received approval from the military authorities to build factories and become involved in the development of key industries. Construction of these facilities did not proceed according to plan, however, because of the limited fund-raising capabilities of *chaebols*. Though the military government could have received considerable popular support by punishing wealthy speculators, it did not do so because it needed the management expertise of these entrepreneurs to achieve its industrialization targets in the heavy chemical sphere. The vertical coalition between the government and the *chaebols* was formed in this context, and government-sponsored speculators went on to build fertilizer plants, power generators, steel mills, chemical

---

[8] "State-owned companies clearly showed the old politicians' corrupt characteristics.... If the state-owned companies had been operated rationally, the economy could have had the strength to carry out industrialization. However, the performance of state-owned companies was disappointing. For example, the financial statements for the second half of 1955 revealed big losses. (Park Chung-hee 1963)

[9] Of the total domestic investment, state-owned enterprises absorbed 27.8% between 1963 and 1966, 19.8% between 1967 and 1971, 24.2% between 1972 and 1976, and 25.2% between 1977 and 1977. Public sector (government and government-owned companies) investment accounted for an average of 35.2% of the total domestic investment between 1963 and 1979 (Sa Gong-il 1993: 48).

fiber plants,[10] and cement factories, clearly illustrating the role of the *chaebols* in the construction of the heavy chemical sector.

Although it was not until the 1970s that heavy chemical industrialization policies were implemented in earnest, given that several acts designed to foster the industry, such as the Engineering Industry Promotion Act, the Shipbuilding Industry Promotion Act, the Electronics Industry Promotion Act, the Steel Industry Promotion Act, and the Petrochemical Industry Promotion Act, were passed between 1967 and 1970, and considering that considerable time was required between policy determination and the enactment of laws, it is reasonable to assume that government policy directions for the heavy chemical industry had already been decided by the mid- to late 1960s. Although in Taiwan small and medium-sized enterprises produced light industry-centered exports and government-owned companies carried out heavy chemical industrialization to substitute for imports, in Korea government-owned companies, together with *chaebols*, implemented the process of heavy chemical industrialization. Thus heavy chemical industrialization was conducted more aggressively in Korea, and as a result, the *chaebols* were formed in Korea, but not in Taiwan.[11]

III. A DEVELOPMENTAL COALITION OF DOMINATION AND ITS LIMITS

State-directed banking and the growth of *chaebols*

The relationship between the government and private companies was a vertical one and exhibited all the characteristics of government-guided capitalism. After dealing with the illicit speculators, the

---

[10] Although Hong Kong focused on a cotton-centered textiles industry, Korea fostered the chemical fiber textile industry, which was decisive in the development of the Korean textile industry as a pre-eminent export contributor.

[11] In the case of the ten largest *chaebols*, the proportion of corporate assets of the heavy chemical industry already reached 70.6% in 1972 and 84.7% in 1979 (Cho Dong-song 1990: 194).

government maintained its dominance over the *chaebols* and, by nationalizing the banks, directly controlled the distribution of capital. Through the sequence of economic development plans, the government also unilaterally selected winner industries and winner companies.

Within this vertical relationship the Korean *chaebol* conglomerates showed both opportunistic and dependent characteristics, and by accepting government guidance, they sought to accumulate capital and economic power. Because the government provided economic incentives to companies that faithfully followed their directives, the relationship between the two was cooperative as well as vertical, and cronyism between politicians and businesses was inevitable. A close relationship with business was also needed by politicians because the Park government, which lacked political legitimacy, needed much political funds. With the introduction of the Political Fund Act in 1965, the government brought political fund raising out into the open, but until 1979 political funds legally raised according to the Act only amounted to 1.8 billion *won*, with most monies being delivered to politicians through individual and informal ties between *chaebols* and government.

By following government directions to the letter, the *chaebols* could enter new business fields, secure growth opportunities and management stability under government protection, and receive financial incentives. In driving economic development, the government provided financial rents based on government-directed lending. Most foreign commercial loans went to big companies and greatly contributed to their accumulation of capital. The growth of the companies in receipt of foreign commercial loans changed the *chaebol* landscape in the 1960s, and Korea's major *chaebols* started to become pre-eminent. Government payment guarantees were specifically targeted at government-owned companies and the favored *chaebols*, and this very special benefit played a decisive role in the growth of the conglomerates.[12]

---

[12] Because Korean companies were not known in the international financial market, it was impossible for them to obtain foreign loans without govern-

In the 1960s and 1970s, initial public offerings were not generally available, and company owners held a large proportion of company equity. Because of the immaturity of the capital market it was difficult to attract investment capital from outside shareholders through capital increase, and corporate bonds were not issued on the capital market until 1971. Therefore, the *chaebols* had to rely on bank loans, and the high debt rate of Korean companies was created during this period. Until 1965, when the savings rate was less than 10%, the debt-to-equity ratio was less than 100%. Later, in 1967, the savings rate was 12.8%, whereas the debt-to-equity ratio was 151.2%. From 1968, the debt-to-equity ratio began to exceed 200%, recording a 15.1% savings rate with a debt-to-equity ratio of 201.3%.

Because banks were nationalized and foreign commercial loans were made with guarantees from the nationalized banks, it is fair to say that investment capital was, to all intents and purposes, supplied by the government, and with the high debt and high investment system, the government had to bear the high risks. In an economic structure that relied on foreign loans, the government — the first and, at the time, the last — lender had to be able to overcome the *information asymmetry* and control the two shortcomings of a loan-based economy: high risk and the *chaebols'* moral hazard. The information asymmetry between government and company should ideally be as narrow as possible, and there should be a network to bridge it. In the mid-1970s, when the heavy chemical industry was being developed, the information gap between the government and heavy chemical companies was not very wide for several reasons. First, because the industries that the government was trying to foster were of a type already established in developed countries, the Korean government could acquire much information by studying the industrializing

---

ment payment guarantees. Therefore, the government created an unprecedented payment guarantee system. When private companies required foreign loans, the Bank of Korea and the Korean Development Bank agreed on payment guarantees, providing that the applicant received approval from the Economic Planning Board (EPB) and the National Assembly. Subsequently, special banks and other commercial banks were given the right to underwrite payment guarantees.

history of those countries. Second, the government received reports on the performance of the companies, and it directed the companies to follow industrial policies through vertical information networks. The Industrial Association and the Export Promotion Association are examples of network structures built between government and companies to facilitate two-way communication and to stimulate competition among the *chaebols*.

In the 1960s and 1970s, when selective industrial policies were most prevalent, the government gave approval to companies after closely examining their business investment program; such approval was sufficient authority for banks to provide loans without further credit assessment. Because the government strictly examined business investment appropriateness, fund-raising capabilities, current market trends, potential future changes, and technology development, the government approval was a kind of credit assessment, and approved companies were given "contingent rents" and were also likely to have fewer risks.[13] Before the 1980s, when the banks were privatized, the government owned all banking institutions, and it was, therefore, realistically impossible for banks to refuse to lend to companies that possessed government investment approval.

By bearing the high investment risks and ensuring that the Korean workforce had no alternative but to accept low wages and excessively long hours, the Park government gave enormous help in maximizing their profits to companies that faithfully followed its directions. In turn, the regime demanded that companies meet given export targets by building large factories and achieving economic efficiency so that they could repay the interest and principal on the loans they had received. *Chaebols* that could not meet government standards were not allowed to enter new business fields and, as a consequence, tended to fall further behind in performance and favor, as shown in Table 4.1.[14] Though there were clear collusive ties

---

[13] Because rents were only given to *chaebols* that met performance standards, such as exports performance and international price competitiveness, they were not monopolistic rents but contingent rents (Aoki et al. 1997).

[14] Among the 50 largest companies in 1965, only 12 remained in that category in 1975; and among the 10 largest companies in 1965, only 1

between government and *chaebols*, the latter companies had to meet certain performance standards set by the government to benefit from government incentives, because the competition for "special favors" was fierce.

Table 4.1 Changes in Ranking of the 10 Major *Chaebols*

	1960	1972	1979	1987
1	Samsung	Samsung	Hyundai	Hyundai
2	Samho	LG	LG	Samsung
3	Gaepung	Hanjin	Samsung	LG
4	Taihan Electronic Wire	Sinjin	Daewoo	Daewoo
5	LG	Ssangyoung	Hyosung	SK
6	Dongyang	Hyundai	Kookje	Ssangyoung
7	Geokdong Shipping	Taihan Electric Wire	Hanjin	Hanhwa
8	Hankook Glass	Hanhwa	Ssangyoung	Hanjin
9	Donglib	Geokdong Shipping	Hanhwa	Hyosung
10	Taechang Spinning	Daenong	SK	Lotte

Source: Fair Trade Commission.

As the government set export results as the screening standard for credit allotment for the general trading companies in the 1970s, the *chaebols* were understandably inclined to boost their export performance by increasing their size and to boost export capability through mergers and acquisitions. As a result, the number of small and medium-sized enterprises (SMEs) that were absorbed or acquired by the *chaebols* increased rapidly from 96 in 1976 to 208 in 1979. Through this largely unregulated process of acquisition based on government incentive and support, the *chaebols* diversified their

reminded in that category in 1975 (Kong Byong-ho 1993).

businesses to an extreme degree. The dangers implicit in such a widespread and competitive corporate practice are not difficult to discern.

Companies highly dependent on loans were susceptible to cash flow problems, and whenever an economic recession or external shock, such as an oil crisis, occurred, a number of companies became insolvent. The Park government dealt with these insolvent companies by having *chaebol* corporations acquire or merge with them. In this process, the *chaebols* were granted various special favors, such as interest or tax exemptions, and they had extremely useful opportunities for expansion.

The *chaebols* were able to achieve rapid growth through a combination of imported foreign technology and a degree of price competitiveness made possible by low-wage labor, rather than by dint of their own technological development. Because their growth was not based on their own special technologies, the industrial life-cycle (growth →maturity→ decline) was comparatively short. Furthermore, they changed the industrial structure from light to heavy industries and from labor-intensive to capital-intensive industries through the process of diversification, rather than specialization. By using cash flow from their core businesses, the *chaebols* expanded their subsidiaries to such an extent that the Korean *chaebol* structures became immensely sophisticated and complex. Large enterprises could achieve even faster growth through *cross-shareholding* among subsidiaries and liability guarantees that other independent companies could not match. For example, when Hyundai Motors faced a liquidity crisis between 1969 and 1972, it was able to avoid bankruptcy thanks to human resource and material support given from another core company of the Hyundai *chaebol*, Hyundai Construction. With that support, it was able to put into production a new model, the Pony, and thereby overcome its difficulties. It went on to become the leader of the Korean automobile industry and one of the leading companies in the Hyundai group. Because the internal capital market of the *chaebols* and their diversified structures provided a certain level of immunity from external shocks, they were able to reduce the financial risks of high debt-to-equity ratios.

The high debt-to-equity ratio companies were able to record high growth in boom times, but in recession, they could easily become insolvent. High debt-to-equity ratios increased the risk of bankruptcy for individual companies and, in turn, posed a similar threat to the banks. The profits remaining after paying back interest and principal belong to debtors who, unlike creditors, prefer risky investments that offer high yields. As the debt-to-equity ratio rises, the conflict of interest between debtors and creditors also increases; therefore, if creditors had been strict about these venture investments there would have been difficulties in achieving high growth in the heavy chemical industry. Given these factors, high growth in the 1960s and 1970s was made possible because the government supervised directed lending to specially selected and regulated enterprises.

Coalition Limits

There were, however, limitations to the government's selection and control capability. Despite the efforts made to bridge the information gap between state institutions and business and the setting up of information networks with the characteristics of corporatism, it was not possible to monitor every facet of corporate moral hazard. Once businesses were selected based on industrial policies, credit assessments were carried out for the sake of form, and after loans were granted the government did not monitor how the businesses used the capital. That is, the government could control credit allocation, but it could not control how the credit was used. Some *chaebols*, through collusive ties, undermined the monitoring system conducted by banks and the government. Excessive credit given to a few selected businesses created a credit imbalance among different businesses and industries, which triggered enlargement of the curb market. Businesses that received policy lending favors tended to invest in the real estate market and, in an attempt to gain favorable interest rates, lent the money in the curb market, whereas businesses excluded from such patronage became increasingly dependent on curb markets. According to the government's 15th Emergency Order on Economic Stability and Growth of August 3, 1972, curb loans accounted for

42% of bank loans. For tax evasion, businesses disguised as if their internal capital was obtained from the curb market, and in extreme cases business owners lent curb loans to their own companies; that is, used internal capital to increase their properties. Given that 30% of curb loans reported after the August 3rd Order were proven to be disguised curb loans supplied by business owners and executives, it could be said that the credit allocation system had suffered a marked deterioration.

An economy heavily dependent on loans should have systematic mechanisms in place for countering financial inflexibility, because companies could suddenly face liquidity problems caused by cash flow inadequacies. Though a liquidity crisis may render a company technically insolvent, some enterprises may have more value by continuing operations than by liquidating. In such cases, creditors could help businesses cope with periodic financial difficulties through flexible management, instead of forcing them to meet their liabilities, regardless of the effect on the business. Therefore, a loan-based economy can operate properly only when banks and businesses have well-established cooperative relations. The primary trading bank system in Japan and the Hausbank system in Germany are prime examples of good cooperative relations between the parties. The Park government did introduce the primary trading bank system in the mid-1970s to strengthen credit assessment.[15] Because big companies borrowed money using different names for their affiliates and subsidiaries, it was clearly inappropriate to set credit limits on individual companies. The primary trading bank system was introduced not to meet the needs of business or the banks, but to meet the government need to delegate management functions for industrial specialization, to prevent excessive loans being made to *chaebols'* affiliates, and to preclude the *chaebols* from investing loans in real

---

[15] The primary trading banks system was carried out under the Agreement on Credit Assessment for Affiliate Companies, enacted in 1974, and the Agreement on Primary Trading Bank System Management, enacted in 1976. In 1982, when the Bank Act was revised, a legal basis for credit management was arranged, and gross credit restraints for the affiliates began to have legally binding status (Cho Young-chol 1998:156).

estate. Therefore, instead of solving agency problems between creditors and debtors, the primary trading bank system carried out supervisory and monitoring functions that belonged to the government. In other words, the banks were not developed to monitor businesses from a long-term cooperative relations perspective, but instead they were simply used as a means of carrying out Park's industrial policies. The "related bank" system should have developed as one that could supplement the fragility of a government-led economy and regulate the *chaebols*, but as time went on the system was reduced to a formality.[16] With the state exercising its enormous power in the screening and monitoring of businesses, the banks lost any motivation to oversee the investment activities of businesses; they also failed to adhere to the strict monitoring that should be the bedrock of all financial institutions.

IV. FINANCIAL FAVORS AND CONSOLIDATION OF THE *CHAEBOL* STRUCTURE

Whether they were special or commercial banks, the nationalized banks supplied investment funds to the *chaebols* by mobilizing private savings and providing payment guarantees for foreign loans. Thus it can be said that the growth of the *chaebols* hinged on indirect and direct financial support from the Korean government.[17] As far as public sector companies were concerned, investment profits were fed

---

[16] In the 1980s, although lending from primary trading banks to related companies decreased, lending from other banks increased. In other words, the relationship between primary trading banks and related companies gradually deteriorated (Cho Young-chol 1998:156).

[17] Kim Song-sok (1986) stresses the importance of the role of national capital, such as provided by the Korea Development Bank, in the growth of the *chaebols*. Actually, between 1962 and 1971, the Korea Development Bank provided 53-75% of the total bank loans extended to facilities investment (Korean Development Bank 1984:99). However, because special banks, such as Korea development banks, and commercial banks were all owned by the state in the 1960s and 1970s, they all had the characteristics of national capital.

back into government coffers, whereas all the profits made by the *chaebols* went to the *chaebol* owners.

The resource mobilization system under the developmental dictatorship was based on government coercion; however, having endured the April student revolution in 1960 and the military coup in May of the following year, a national consensus to build a self-supporting economy and break free from poverty was formed. By presenting detailed economic development plans the military government managed to garner the people's passionate commitment to economic development. The government was also able to create national consensus for its "growth first, distribution later" policy.

In 1960 and 1970s, when there was overpopulation, the developmental state could enforce low wages and long working hours only by repressing the trade union movements. In addition to ensuring the availability of cheap labor, it prohibited capital outflows by capital control and making sure that company profits went to the industrial sectors with high productivity, high job creation potential, and high added value. Because the political leaders of the developmental state can force companies to invest economic surpluses in productive sectors, a positive cycle (wage restraints → profit increases → investment increases → future hiring and wage increases) can be created. With this positive cycle as a background in South Korea, the labor and the wider general public were able to maintain a positive outlook on the future.

Because the blue-collar labor market was a competitive market, the labor turnover rate was high, and wages were determined by supply and demand. In the 1960s and 1970s wage differentials between large and small companies and between industries were not excessive, and except for the wage discrimination between male and female workers, wages in the blue-collar labor market were mainly determined by supply and demand.[18] This balance between supply

---

[18] The blue-collar labor market was a competitive market until the early 1980s. In the mid-1980s, when labor shortages became serious and trade unions began to have actual negotiating power, wage differences between large and small companies became more apparent. Though wage differences between men and women in different occupational categories are

and demand, rather than between sectors with high or low productivity, played a decisive role in determining wages. Thus, conflicts between labor and management concerning the distribution of the company's value-added were suppressed, and in highly productive sectors, capital could be accumulated rapidly. As a result, resources were moved from low-productivity sectors to high-productivity sectors, and the industrial restructuring was accelerated. The cheap labor provided international competitiveness to export industries in the 1960s and 1970s and enlarged the economic power of *chaebols*. The developmental state intentionally distorted the capital and product markets and replaced market discipline. In the labor market, however, the developmental state maintained competitive labor market discipline to use cheap labor by prohibiting the organization of labor unions.

In the process of state-led economic development, employment and real wages increased continuously; it was therefore possible for the state to mobilize labor. However, the "growth first, distribution later" policy came to be seen as an empty slogan. Except for a period of a few years, the growth of real wages was generally lower than that of labor productivity. Workers began to realize that the Korean economic development model increased workers' real wages but could not realize justice in distribution. As economic development got underway, and the *growth* element became apparent, workers started to demand evidence of the *distribution* aspect, with the result that the labor mobilization structure came under threat. The developmental state focused only on fostering businesses by mobilizing resources and was not concerned about reducing economic inequality by creating a system that could fairly distribute investment performance. In Korea, most of the economic performance went to the *chaebols*, adding to their burgeoning economic power.

The government pushed forward an Initial Public Offering (IPO) policy to improve companies' capital structures and separate management from ownership through stock dispersion. In November 1968, the government set basic guidelines for speeding up IPOs

clearly illustrated, wage discrimination between genders occurs even in a competitive labor market (Cho Young-chol 1998: 159).

by enacting laws fostering the capital market. Though various incentives, such as 50% exemptions on corporate taxes, other tax incentives, and the enlargement of authorized capital, were given to corporations, IPOs did not, in fact, assume major significance during this period. However, following the 15th Emergency Order on Economic Stability and Growth of August 3, 1972 (see above), the IPO Promotion Act came into force in December of the same year, and IPO policies were then implemented vigorously.

The government gave tax or financial favors to those companies that followed the August 3rd Order and also pushed them to create IPOs. With the IPO Promotion Act, the government allowed the revaluation of assets to protect founders' interests while, at the same time, corporations that refused to go public suffered from new tax and financial penalties. Over a 6-month period, and primarily as a result of government coercion, 297 corporations went public. However, because 30 of those that had been forced to go public went bankrupt subsequently, the government drafted management regulations for listed corporations in January 1979, strengthening the conditions for IPOs and allowing only sound corporations to go public. Later, the coercive IPO policy was transformed into a "guidance" policy that respected corporate autonomy. As a result of a continuous IPO policy, 309 large companies had gone public by 1979, and the number of listed companies increased to 355. Meanwhile, the government announced the expansion of the Employee Share Ownership Program (ESOP) and provided tax exemption and financial benefits to employee stock ownership associations. Supported by these government efforts, two employee stock ownership associations were established in October 1974, and the number of associations increased to 385 and association membership to 200,000 by 1980.

However, a considerable number of corporations that had been forced to go public maintained their closed ownership structure. Controlling stockholders artificially dispersed their shares or repurchased stocks after the IPO. On the one hand, IPOs speeded up dispersion of ownership, but on the other hand, they reinforced the power of controlling shareholders by providing tools to protect management rights, such as setting upper limits on holdings at the time of stock purchase. In the 1970s, cross-shareholding between affiliate companies was already widespread, and the planning and coordination offices, or the secretary's offices, to assist controlling shareholders began to direct the affairs of affiliates.

In the 30 years since the inception of IPOs, decentralization of ownership has proceeded steadily. As of April 2000, the shareholding percentage held by owners of the *chaebols'* corporations was 1.5%, and shareholding by people in special relations with these corporations was 3%. Because company owners and related people held only a total of 4.5% of shares, it could be said that IPOs had succeeded in their original aim. Nonetheless, although the ownership structure of the *chaebols* is decentralized, they are still not free from an owner's control system because company owners still control 36.6% of equity in their affiliates and 2.3% of treasury stocks. Equity investment in their affiliates enables company owners to control their company group, including affiliates, without bearing any direct risks. That is, though the company owners with mere 1.5% equity are not actual owners in terms of ownership structure, closer examination does reveal an owner-controlling structure in all but name. Therefore, the Park Chung-hee government's IPO strategies, continuously implemented since the 1970s, together with other industrial policies devised by the state, contributed substantially to the establishment of today's Korean *chaebol* structure.

Despite the fact that IPOs helped lower the corporate stake held by founders and their family members, it failed to reform the corporate governance of *chaebols*, which had arisen through oppression and exploitation of the Korean workforce and the patronage of a state-led regime. Whether intentional or not, IPOs forced company owners and external shareholders to share corporations and consolidated the *chaebols'* private property bases. Before IPOs, there were multiple conflicts of interest involving the *chaebols*, the government, and the public, but after their creation, *chaebol* issues were restricted to property right problems between internal controlling shareholders and external minority shareholders. Therefore, the reform of corporate governance to facilitate the democratic control of *chaebols* and foster economic democracy remains an assignment has yet to be completed.

V. RETREAT OF THE STATE AND *CHAEBOL* POWER

In the coalition between government and the *chaebols*, the government both supported and regulated the *chaebols*. However, since the late 1980s and the commencement of the democratization process, successive governments have come to play a smaller role in economic regulations and the role of the free market has grown. At the same time, the private property bases of the *chaebols* have consolidated. Against this backdrop, the following question must be asked: What mechanism can replace the role of the government in regulating the *chaebols*?

Since the 1980s, Korean banks have been privatized, and the *chaebols* have radically improved their fund-raising capabilities by securing the nonbank financial sector.[19] Policy lending was mainly given to agriculture, fisheries, livestock farming, housing, and SMEs, but not a great deal in the way of policy lending was allocated to the *chaebols*. To secure capital, therefore, the *chaebols* found it necessary to activate the stock market and raise funds through direct financing. Because of this shift in fund raising, the influence that government had over the *chaebols* by dint of policy loan allocation started to decrease sharply, and the vertical ties between the two parties loosened accordingly.[20] The *chaebols* became increasingly independent of

---

[19] In late 1987, the 10 largest companies had 21, and the 50 largest companies had 39 affiliates in the nonbank financial sector. However, the numbers increased such that the 10 largest companies had 25 and the 50 largest companies had 43 affiliates in 1995.

[20] At the time when the government provided capital, relations between the state and the *chaebols* assumed more or less the relationship between principal and agent. However, with the change in methods of fund raising, the relationship also changed. That is, financial deregulation strengthened *chaebols'* capabilities to raise funds through normal financing rather than through policy lending. As a result, the agency problems between state and *chaebols* weakened and the ones between private investors and *chaebols* grew.

government direction and, through IPOs, consolidated their property bases.

As the wave of liberalization gathered speed, deregulation weakened the relationships between banks and business. In this situation, the banks should have strengthened their monitoring functions over business investment activities to replace the state discipline, and financial supervisory organizations should have played a more active role. However, the banks could not break free from government direction and were unable to establish an autonomous management system. The primary trading bank system existed for form's sake only, and it was in reality impossible for banks to regulate the big corporations. Interest groups and political groups filled the gaps left by the retreat of government intervention. The Korean economic development model based on the three-party relations — the government, banks, and business — should have rid itself of government-directed lending during the liberalization process in the late 1980s and should have established horizontal cooperative relations between banks and business. The banks' supervisory function should also have been strengthened during this time. However, the model failed to accomplish any of these aims, and the loan-based Korean economy became even more fragile. As a result, the collusion between politicians and *chaebols* increased the social costs of corruption.

Although the developmental dictatorship system in the 1960s did have foreign dependency characteristics, it was comparatively independent of the domestic private sector, including the *chaebols*. However, as industrialization proceeded, the dependency between government and *chaebols* deepened, and collusive ties between the two intensified.

As Korean politics were democratized, economic policies were influenced by parliamentary politics, and interest groups started to exercise their power in policy decision-making processes. Under the developmental dictatorship, labor movements had been strictly proscribed, and the civil society could not be organized into interest groups; meanwhile, the *chaebols* grew virtually unhindered to become social and political power groups. The civil society that could restrain the *chaebols'* economic power was not developed, and neither was corporate governance that could restrain company owners. The media were the public voice of the *chaebols*, especially those with controlling interests in the advertising industry; some *chaebols* themselves actually ran media businesses. Though the gate to democratization was opened in 1987, the process itself started to develop within an unbalanced and turbulent social structure characterized by tensions between strong *chaebols*, on one hand, and weak banks, trade unions, and various organizations of the civil society, on the other. Political democratization proceeded in a less than ideal way, which reflected aspects of money politics and the strong influence of the collusive ties between the government and *chaebols*. Inevitably, problems of corruption became ever more serious. In the past, the government had regulated the *chaebols* by means of state-directed lending, but industrial policy regulations were weakened and, in the mid-1980s, the government came increasingly under the influence of the *chaebols*, rather than the other way around, thereby markedly reducing governmental autonomy.

VI. CONCLUSION

Because many elements of the Park Chung-hee developmental dictatorship were formed extemporaneously, they had diverse characteristics. However, his key, heavy industry-fostering policies cannot be viewed as extemporaneous. As the inflow of public aid from the United States was reduced, the problems of a foreign-dependent economy became clearly apparent, and after the April student revolution, the Korean people began to appreciate the importance of establishing a self-supporting economy. This idea was well reflected in the policies of both the "democratic" government of Chang Myon and the military government of Park Chung-hee. According to the self-supporting economy and intensive industrialization strategy, the military government consistently fostered the heavy chemical industry subsequent to the First 5-Year Economic Development Plan, and this was a focus of disagreement between Korea and the United States in regard to economic policy.

The Park government used the *chaebols* as strategic tools to nurture the key export industries while negotiating with the United States, which had recommended implementing light industry-centered export-oriented industrial policies; it carried out export-oriented heavy chemical industrialization more aggressively in the 1970s. Therefore, unlike Taiwan, in which development was balanced between private and public sectors, Korean development was centered on the heavy and chemical industries, and the *chaebols* played an important role in the industrialization process as the government's partner.

The military government nationalized the banks and provided extensive patronage to selected *chaebols* through payment guarantees for foreign loans and policy loans. The special coalition between the government and the *chaebols* spearheaded economic growth. However, all the investment profits returned to the *chaebols*, and the government's "growth first, distribution later" policy turned out to be illusory. Though the *chaebols* accumulated virtually all of their wealth from government's supporting investment, they claimed all the fruits of investment. To solve this problem, the government implemented the IPO policy, which was a failure, and the *chaebols* were able to build the owner-centered corporate governance that remains extant today. Most equities were held by external stockholders, and the *chaebol* owners, who hold small shares, maintain the controlling status without bearing any commensurate risk.

If only systematic measures to restrain the arbitrariness of the *chaebols* tycoons are discussed — measures such as establishing shareholder capitalism or minority shareholder's rights — the historic background from which the *chaebols* structure was formed will have been overlooked and the danger of settling for purely functional reform of the *chaebols* will remain. *Chaebol* reform should not be discussed from a narrow standpoint, such as the conflict of interest between minority shareholders and the *chaebols'* ownership, or purely from the perspective of economic efficiency. Because the *chaebols* were formed on the dual basis of Park Chung-hee's infamous "growth first, distribution later" mantra and the Korean people's enormous sacrifice in the process of developing a heavy chemical industry, the *chaebols* have moral and unequivocal liabilities to the nation at large. Accordingly, *chaebol* reform must be debated in the context of overcoming the legacy of developmental dictatorship. In other words, whatever shape the reform of the Korean *chaebols* may ultimately take, its outcome must, first and foremost, be to the benefit of the people of South Korea.

Chapter 5

Political and Institutional Conditions
of Financial Repression

Yoo Chul-gyue

I. INTRODUCTION

One of the prime reasons for the continuing interest in the South Korean experience of developmental dictatorship must be the fact that throughout the period, from 1961 to the mid-1980s, Korea achieved a level of industrialization unparalleled in any other developing country. However, a purely historical interest is particularly meaningful when it is related directly to the social development challenges faced in South Korea today. Simply stated, those challenges are the development of substantive democracy and the establishment of a secure foundation for the lives of the entire population. The significance of any discussion of Korean industrialization hinges on the question whether a society can intentionally and determinedly create an effective economic structure that violates global market principles and the economic logic of world capitalism. This is the question faced by most developing nations, the former Soviet nations, and the Eastern European nations, as they move toward a market economy under the direction of the U.S. government, the IMF, and the World Bank, but who are not satisfied with the outcomes. This question is also essential for Korean society as it progresses to a level of social development beyond industrialization.

In the process of addressing this question, fundamental disputes arise over whether the rapid changes in the Korean industrial structure were the result of market principles or social intention. There is even disagreement on the precise definition of the term "market." From one perspective, the market in Western societies, especially Britain and the United States, is a system based on the order of natural law; from a different viewpoint it is regarded as a social system or institution invented to give substance to social values, such as justice, order, and freedom. If the former is the case, it would not be rational to speak of social intentions, but if the latter perspective is used, our task is somewhat clearer and can be encapsulated in this question: What are the social values that should be materialized through social systems and regulations?

This chapter examines South Korea's industrialization experience in terms of the characteristics and apparent contradictions that are suggested by the following supplementary questions. How can the government economic intervention that fostered the Korean *chaebols* and provided social support that enabled them to achieve economic growth be socially and politically justified? How could the government policies of "maximization of investment (minimization of consumption)" and "growth first, distribution later" not evoke opposition from the working population? How could *financial repression*, as represented by the strong government intervention that regulated reserve-require ratio, interest rates, foreign exchange trade, and the composition of bank assets and that imposed heavy taxes on financial revenues, deal with potential inefficiency for such a prolonged period? Did the Korean government suffer fewer policy failures, in comparison with other developing countries, because it was fortunate enough to have been blessed with talented and "clean-handed" dictators?

This chapter argues that the characteristics and conflicts that the South Korean financial system exhibited during the developmental dictatorship era cannot be fully explained by neo-classical market logic alone. In the first section, the formation and organization of the developmental dictatorship and the politicoeconomic meaning of financial repression are examined. In the second section, special aspects of the Korean financial system are analyzed in the context of the formation of the industrial structure. Finally, the mechanisms that justified unbalanced cost sharing among businesses, and between businesses and workers, are considered.

II. DEVELOPMENT DICTATORSHIP AND FINANCIAL REPRESSION

Understanding Developmental Dictatorship

To discuss the process of Korean industrialization, it is necessary to divide it into several discrete phases; of those phases, the rapid industrialization period illustrates most clearly the systems employed by the developmental dictatorship administrations. Korean heavy chemical industrialization began officially in January 1973 with a formal "declaration of heavy chemical industrialization," and, in terms of industrial structure, it reached its peak in the mid- to late 1980s. This period, then, is the first area of investigation.

Economic policy in the dictatorship period consistently emphasized manufacturing and identified growth as the top priority. Western observers frequently point out that the Korean economic system, at least in terms of ideology, seemed naturally to accept political control of business, especially the *chaebols*. As Fukagawa (1997) notes, the consistency of political ideology and policy orientation is what enabled the flexibility of Korean economic policy, and analysis shows that there was an element of social consensus as the basis for the policy consistency.

The colonial experience and the popular resistance to it were believed to have played an important role in creating popular sympathy for the imperative to achieve nation-statehood. The establishment of a modern nation-state meant the dissolution of the feudal social structure through democratization and industrialization. It should also be mentioned that, as is comprehensively recorded, during the colonial era radical and nationalist resistance was at the center of virtually all social movements. Actually, shortly after liberation from the Japanese at the end of World War II, when Korea was in a political vacuum, various sociopolitical organizations seized power in many parts of Korea, and some even demanded the confiscation of property belonging to major landowners who had supported the colonial system. However, the combined effects of the U.S. army occupation and the Korean War (1950-53) took the form of "ideological cleansing," as a result of which capitalist development assumed total dominance as South Korea's development strategy. Socialist and nationalist ideologies were not eradicated completely, however, but remained clearly identifiable in civil movements, such as the April 19th uprising in 1960. One further item that should not be overlooked is that at the root of the political ideology of the developmental dictatorship was an antipathy toward previous regimes. The regime that took power by military coup in 1961 naturally tried to base its legitimacy on the malfeasance of other previous administrations. Under Rhee Sung-man's leadership (1948-60) corrupt cronyism based on personal affiliation had been rampant, "bureaucratic capital" existed as an initial form of collusion between the government and business, and the fiscal deficit had been extremely serious. In contrast, the Park Chung-hee regime would attempt to build new relations with business associations, rather than individual businesses, and avoid fiscal deficits.

Park's developmental dictatorship showed the combined characteristics of political dictatorship and accelerated industrialization. Under his stewardship, of the three elements of modernization — nation-statehood, democracy, and industrialization — the first two were repressed jointly by the Cold War structure (the partition of the Korean peninsula) and by Park himself, whereas only the last element, industrialization, was allowed. Because industrialization was, in effect, accepted as the route by which the Korean people's desire for modernization could be achieved, extraordinarily long working hours and appalling working conditions became the norm, and state support of the *chaebols* met with the general acceptance of the populace. To maintain a minimum level of political support, the regime needed to find some levels of compromise with the wishes of the people or at least appear to be conceding to them. The "Growth first, distribution later" slogan is a prime example of the government dividing political and economic assignments across a time frame. "Distribution later" was a political promise to be realized in the future, and to share those future economic fruits continuous political intervention in the economic sphere would be necessary. Regarding business and capital as the means to achieve modernization also played an important ideological role in justifying the developmental dictatorship system. After the coup, the Park government initially took steps to punish business owners for corruption and antisocial speculation, but the policy was soon abandoned and miscreants were officially pardoned on the pretext of giving them a chance to serve their nation. Political control of the economy and of business and viewing business not as a goal itself, but as a means for social development, were characteristics of the developmental dictatorship; at the same time, they were elements that strengthened and justified the regime itself. This justification evoked less political resistance to the administration's enforcement of long working hours, and provided continuous social support for fostering the *chaebols*.

However, compromise and distortion as in the slogan, "Distribution later, democracy later," pose certain restrictions on a regime's political ideology. At least in the economic sphere, people's social demands tacitly restrained government policymaking and implementation processes and acted as a factor that enabled the government to maintain its political consistency.

Investment in Heavy and Chemical Industries and the Financial System

For the huge investment needed for heavy chemical industrialization the Korean government attracted foreign capital, used policy loans, and, by intervening in the financial market, selectively supported certain industries and businesses. This intervention and selective support initiatives have been evaluated as effectively preventing market failures and narrowing the gap between social and private benefits. If all the fruits of social support had belonged to the private sector, it would have been difficult to continue the huge social investment that used private companies as tools for social development. Therefore, it is rational to think that the government bore the largest part of the high investment risks in heavy chemical industries and, by controlling and managing private companies, returned

138

investment profits in the form of policy loans. By bearing the brunt of the investment risk, the government succeeded in attracting the private sector to become involved in national projects. That is, by lowering the uncertainty of actual investments and sharing investment risks with the private sector, the government increased investment. This meant that the government tacitly provided guarantees that it would save those businesses that cooperated with its economic development plan when they faced low profitability.[1] Although the socialization of investment risk contributed to maximizing the investment needed for heavy chemical industrialization, it also held the danger of returning profits to individuals and losses to society. Therefore, the socialization of investment risks could be justified, as long as there was national sympathy for industrialization and businesses were viewed as a tool to achieve industrialization.

The government itself evaluated company profits. It could intervene in private companies' management and investment activities because it provided payment guarantees and bore investment risks incurred through the activities of those companies. Payment guarantees by the government and banks were an important tool in socializing investment risks. Though foreign capital was essential for heavy chemical industrialization, international financial institutions held negative views on the ability of Korean companies to invest in the industry. Despite their negative inclinations, foreign institutions did lend huge sums of investment capital on the basis of the payment guarantees provided by the South Korean government and banks. In effect, the Korean national economy itself served as collateral for the loans because, in practical terms, the government had no choice

---

[1] In 1975, when the shipbuilding industry was faced with a worldwide recession, the shipbuilding division of the Hyundai *Chaebol* was able to continue only because of government support. The government forced oil refineries to deliver oil only in Korean tankers. In the 1980s, the government allowed 78 companies faced with financial difficulties caused by excessive investment in facilities to extend the terms of redemption, and also provided new loans. As a result, failed bonds increased greatly, and the Central Bank had to provide loans to banks in which the profits had decreased because of low loan rates and nonprofit loans.

other than to guarantee payments when foreign financial institutions were wary of accommodating Korean companies. In 1975, government-owned or controlled domestic banks provided payment guarantees for 88% of the total commercial loans (Table 5.1). In fact, throughout the heavy chemical industrialization period the government guaranteed the great majority of foreign loans. Payment guarantees based on government and bank credit were also needed domestically to help build trust in the financial system itself. To foster investment in the heavy chemical industry, the government encouraged savings and gave depositors assurances that financial institutes would be protected from bankruptcy.

Table 5.1 Commercial Loan Repayment Guarantees (1975)

	Amount ($US million)
Korean Exchange Bank	1,786.070
Commercial banks*	92.491
Local banks	12.093
Korean Industrial Bank	302.550
Total amount of repayment guarantee (A)	2,193.204
Total amount of commercial loan (B)	2,491
A/B	88.0%

Source: Kim Chan-jin (1976).

* Commercial banks are those that operated nationwide. There were two local banks in Korea at the time.

Payment guarantees based on the credit of the government and banks were possible because of cohesion among three parties – the state, the banks, and big businesses. During the heavy chemical investment period, owners of businesses or business groups who received benefits from industrial and financial arrangements had to put up private property as collateral for loans. If the investments had failed, they could have lost everything. However, they had little choice but to participate in the government's developmental projects because had any of them demurred, the government would simply have awarded the projects to competitors, and the reluctant companies or groups would likely have been excluded from future projects.[2] Because the government had to succeed in its program of heavy chemical industrialization for political reasons, it needed those private organizations that could carry out government projects successfully, but they did not necessarily have to be those who provided the largest contributions to political funds. Unlike a Western-type corporate corruption structure in which individual projects are linked to individual political funds, in Korea collusive ties between the government and businesses were formed collectively.[3]

Political Economy of Financial Repression

Throughout the 1960s large companies were established, but few of them could command the huge capital sums required to finance the building of facilities needed for heavy chemical industrialization. To promote the necessary investment, which was beyond the capability of the private sector and which could not be achieved spontaneously through the market, the government used the financial system. This was an institutional structure that Shaw (1973) refers to as a "repressed system," meaning that the government artificially lowered interest rates and managed credit allocation.

---

[2] From the following statement by Park Byeng-yun (1980), we can glimpse the then-competitive situation: 맜ince the heavy chemical industry requires huge facilities and capital, high technology, and sophisticated management skills, only the big *Chaebols* can go into the field. In that sense, the shortcut for expanding a *Chaebol* is to foster the heavy chemical industry. The industry is the best and at the same time the last opportunity for *Chaebol*'s growth.... When the economy passes the stage of heavy chemical development, there will be no chance to build big companies and *Chaebols*.... Heavy and chemical industries guarantee both government support and protection, and the growth of the companies."

[3] Provision of political funds through a company association, such as the Federation of Korean Industries, was a prime example.

During the heavy chemical investment period, the Korean government was deeply involved in the allocation of financial resources to facilitate investment in priority industries. Credit allocation and interest rate ceiling policies were the primary tools used, and the allocation of underpriced credit was one of the most important "micro" tools. Korean corporations were heavily dependent on external capital to the extent that two-thirds of their cash flow came from borrowed capital (Table 5.2). According to Jones and Sakong (1980), "Actual bank interest rates were in negative numbers in many cases, and lower than when capital opportunity costs were most conservatively estimated."

Though various political measures were attempted, financial policies were used as though they were merely a part of industrial policy. Loans and credits provided by government-controlled banks and the bank-based financial system were the most important tools in the package of industrial policy. Banks were operated just like public enterprises. Bank management rights, although legally still remaining with the banks, were, for all practical purposes, assumed by the government. For those banks in which the government was not a major shareholder, a temporary act introduced in 1961 gave it absolute control. The rights of private shareholders were restricted, and after banking legislation amendments were made in 1981, bank equities held by individuals and related shareholders could not exceed 8%. For policy loans and the effective use of foreign capital, the *primary trading bank system* was introduced in 1974. In concert with this system, the policy loan system was completed, and the government was able to accelerate its efforts to foster priority industries. Inflows of foreign capital and outflows of capital also had to be managed and controlled strictly to control domestic and foreign capital.[4]

---

[4] Strict controls on capital outflows were carried out by a concentrated management system for foreign currency. Under this system all foreign currency had to be transferred to the central bank. The Foreign Currency Management Act also strictly controlled the use of foreign currency. This system started to be relaxed in the late 1980s.

Table 5.2 Capital Required by Major Heavy Chemical Companies

Year	1979	1980
Required capital (A)	1,907 (billion KRW)	1,698 (billion KRW)
Self-financing (B)	562	551
Mobilization of foreign capital	554	395
Required domestic capital	791	753
Policy funds	158	200
Other	151	190
Shorts in domestic capital	483	363
B/A	29.5%	32.5%

Source: Park Byeng-yun (1980).

However, financial repression meant repression not only of interest rates through market intervention but also of the interests of the financial rentier class. The financial repression system was underpinned by the philosophy that regarded the financial rentier class not only as a necessary evil but also as a group that hampered corporate development. This conviction is well reflected in the following extracts from the Park Chung-hee government's, *The Summary Report of the 1st Economic Development Plan*; it concerns the circumstances that existed in Korea before the 1961 military coup:

> A few privileged groups that were able to receive loans from banks could enjoy profits.... Instead of putting honest and creative effort into improving production technology and management, a number of businesses accumulated easy wealth through collusive ties with politicians and bureaucrats.... Industries could not help looking for loan-sharking and the usury market was prevalent.... The corrupt banking system not only hampered economic development, but also systematically distorted the national foundation and social justice.

To understand the Korean financial system as it existed before the 1990s, it is useful to keep in mind the very popular sentiments expressed in the above quotation. The financial repression policy had an ideological function that justified government intervention and drew support for the economic development plan, because it appeared as if part of the ruling classes were bearing the costs of industrial development against their own best interests.

The political characteristics of financial repression can be well understood through special measures that alleviated the financial burdens on the manufacturing sector and sacrificed the interests of financial rentiers and the ordinary working people. Postponement of payments on the bond market, the so called August 3rd Order, announced in 1972, was one of these special measures. This instrument was a countermeasure to deal with a financial crisis brought about by the MacKinnon-Shaw-type financial liberalization policies in the mid- and late 1960s, and it had a severe impact on the financial interests of rentiers.

With the financial reform that occurred in 1965, interest rates on domestic capital far exceeded those on foreign capital, a situation that caused many to seek foreign capital for investment purposes. However, with the high interest rates, the current account deficit, and excessive foreign loans that appeared after the 1965 liberalization, the profitability of nonfinancial businesses plummeted, and bad loans in the banking sector increased. A growing number of companies went bankrupt, and a foreign exchange crisis was in evidence until 1972. Because many companies that went bankrupt during this period had external loans, the government implemented special measures. The August 3rd Order salvaged manufacturing companies by postponing the liabilities of all companies for 3 years. It is arguably one of the most extreme cases of financial repression in the history of world capitalism.

Policy loan resources that had been focused intensively on selected industries were mainly obtained from the Central Bank and deposit banks. For example, to deal with reverse margins (when interest rates on deposits exceed those on loans) that resulted from the interest rate ceilings on policy loans, the Central Bank provided automatic discounts and adjusted the rediscount rate according to the cash inflows and outflows of commercial banks. The rediscount rate tune-up of the Central Bank also acted as an important tool in giving loans to strategic industries. Between 1973 and 1991 the proportion of commercial bills rediscounted at the Central Bank was nearly 50%. In policy loans, there was considerable dependence on the reserve base of the Bank of Korea, and direct dependence on fiscal funds was rather low. This is one of the differences from Japan and Taiwan, and it is likely to have arisen out of negative views on fiscal deficits based on historical experience. In any case, it is worth pointing out that the use of the private capital and credit of the Central Bank was justified to support private investment in line with government policy directions. The success of selective financial support is greatly dependent on whether the projects concerned are able to acquire the level of political justification that can be obtained only through public cooperation. Other issues are who should bear the required costs and how they should be allocated. If policies pursue a free market, those who understand the market better can benefit. Costs can be borne either by politics or by the market. One of the fundamental differences between the two options is that the functioning of the latter is accepted by most people as unavoidable "natural law."

III. LIMITS OF MARKET-ORIENTED THEORY: ON THE RELATIONSHIPS OF FINANCIAL INSTITUTIONS TO ECONOMIC GROWTH

Without discriminating between developing and late industrialized countries, much theoretical and political interest has been shown in the correlations between the financial market system and economic growth, which has been, in fact, a main research topic of development economics. In terms of theory, MacKinnon (1973) and Shaw (1973) have been engaged most actively in studies on this subject, and in terms of politics, the international liability crisis in the 1980s, triggered by Mexico's suspension of foreign loan payments in October 1982, was an important motivation that developed political interest in the subject. The fragility of an economy dependent on foreign loans was demonstrated clearly, and the domestic mobilization of financial resources became an important issue. It is widely accepted that if the domestic financial market and system is not well developed, long-term economic growth is negatively affected.

The rapid political and economic changes that took place in Eastern Europe and in the former Soviet Union in the late 1980s and early 1990s reemphasized the importance of the financial market in economic development and drew attention to the ways in which to build and implement a financial market and system. Those countries did not have the financial markets and systems found and expected in capitalist economies. The Asian financial crisis in the late 1990s brought up all the theoretical and political problems raised in the MacKinnon-Shaw approach to understanding financial liberalization and in the establishment of new financial systems and regulations in Eastern Europe. However, unlike South America, Asia has demonstrated excellent economic results in industrialization over the last 20 to 30 years, and unlike Eastern Europe and the former USSR, it has established a capitalist financial market and system. Financial problems in Asian countries were not identical to those experienced in South America and Eastern Europe, and they placed in stark relief many of the theoretical and political limits implicit in Asia.

Financial Liberalization in Developing Countries: Financial Repression versus Financial Restraint

After the work of MacKinnon and Shaw, free market financial systems and depressed financial systems were seen as two mutually exclusive concepts. In the real world, it has often been recognized that the free market financial system appears in financial structures to be based on a capital market, whereas depressed financial systems can be seen in bank-based relationship banking. MacKinnon and Shaw point out that unsophisticated financial intermediaries and systematic structures were found in financial systems in developing countries. Because of this lack of sophistication, savings could not be mobilized easily, and mobilized resources could not be allocated efficiently, a state of affairs that, in turn, leads to the delay of financial deepening. In particular, they argue that fixing interest rates at a low level by administrative order represses financial intermediaries. Because they also argue that governments were mainly involved in the financial sector in an attempt to acquire loan rents, most discussions on the financial development of developing countries taking place after MacKinnon and Shaw have presented competitive financial markets without government intervention as desirable and have focused on the liberalization of interest rates.

However, the liberalization of interest rates turns out to be much more complicated in actuality than had been anticipated theoretically. Post-war Japan and the newly emerging industrial countries in Asia after the 1960s showed high growth rates over a considerable period, yet the working mechanisms of their financial systems and markets were quite different from those of free financial markets. In contrast, in the 1960s South American countries, such as Argentina, Chile, and Uruguay, stopped financial repression and carried out financial liberalization and internalization in attempts to increase savings and investments. However, contrary to their expectations, they witnessed declines in savings, increasing numbers of bankruptcies in the financial sector, and the nationalization of private banks, and all this chaos concluded with government intervention. To those who believed in the laissez-faire approach it was very disappointing that the former Soviet Union and Eastern European countries that adopted capitalism based on the enthusiastic advice and support of market advocates following the collapse of the Soviet Union have not been able to extricate themselves from long-term recession.

These consequences were enough to raise questions concerning the simple viewpoint that regarded depressed financial systems as a cause of economic problems and free market financial systems as a solution. Many studies find that the ostensibly desirable financial market under MacKinnon and Shaw's theory might not be desirable in real situations (Fry 1988). Some researchers, such as Hellman, Murdock, and Stiglitz (1996), encouraged by the instances of East Asian countries achieving rapid industrialization under financial repression, have tried to answer the question of how and in what conditions government intervention in the private financial market could be more efficient than a laissez-faire policy. Arguing that some kind of restrictions on interest rates and on competition in the financial sector could contribute effectively to industrialization, they call this "financial restraint" as compared to MacKinnon and Shaw's "financial repression." Their main argument is that governments created the opportunities for private capital to acquire loan rents, rather than governments themselves acquiring the rents. This argument highlights the differences between forms of government intervention in South America and Asia that had outward similarities, such as restrictions on interest rates and competition. When the financial market (especially the capital market) is underdeveloped and incomplete, interest rates are regulated in an appropriate manner, and opportunities to acquire excess profits are provided through permitted monopoly, private banks can have a stronger motivation to mobilize savings and locate investment opportunities. These are the conditions that explain East Asia's very rapid industrialization. The theoretical position of those who have suggested that financial restraint is not opposed to free market theory might simply be acknowledging the fundamental limits of financial markets. However, this new approach provides important opportunities to take a close look into government intervention and its effects and to put forward compromise suggestions, such as a "market-friendly approach" that allows a certain level of government intervention, rather than a purely market-centered theory (Haggard and Lee 1993; Haggard and Maxfield 1993a, b; World Bank 1993).

Given that it acknowledged government intervention could be more effective than a free financial market, the theory of financial restraint, rather than of financial repression, better corresponds to the realities and experiences of East Asia. However, because financial restraint advocates agree that without an effective market the impact of government intervention in the process of industrialization is only temporary and valid under special conditions, it does not quite correspond to the experiences of Korea. Though there were some variations, in Korea the government directed more than half of bank credit, owned most of the major banks, and controlled interest rates.

In so doing, it went far beyond merely supplementing the defects of the market.

Theory of Financial Liberalization and Financial Systems in the Period of Rapid Industrialization

The major financial systems of the Korean economic structure during the dictator-led development period stemmed from the financial crisis in the late 1960s and early 1970s, the August 3rd Order, and its follow-up measures (Chang and Yoo 1999). The Korean economic development model that existed until the late 1980s had the features of a repressive financial structure. As mentioned earlier, repression meant repression not only of interest rates but also of the interests of the rentier class. This financial repression was reinforced by the conviction that the rentier class was a group that hampered corporate development. In the process of forming financial systems, financial interests were repressed and shareholders' rights were restricted. Restrictions imposed on shareholders' rights were fundamental in shoring up the repressive financial system and were extended over a long period through government credit provisions and the socialization of investment risks. As mentioned previously, repressive financial policies justified government intervention and served an ideological function in motivating people to acquiesce in the economic development plan, because they were viewed as forcing the ruling classes also to bear the costs of industrial development against their own vested interests.

From the neo-classical economic perspective that advocates the principles of laissez-faire, financial repression and government intervention tend to distort effective resource allocation. According to this viewpoint, financial repression and preferential credit (or lending) schemes reduce savings by controlling deposit interest rates and restrict the ability to attract foreign loans. Reduced savings and foreign loans cause difficulties in attracting investment resources, which leads to reduced investment and a slowing down of economic growth. Artificially reduced capital costs send misleading messages regarding the scarcity of resources, and developing countries are likely to adopt capital-intensive technologies that are not in accord with their circumstances. The government that carries out credit allocation is unlikely to select the most effective capital users. Government officials do not have enough of the information needed to allocate credit effectively, nor do they have any motivation to do so. Because financial repression creates economic rents on loans, the government always faces noneconomic problems, including pressure from rent-seeking groups. Financial repression causes companies that have received benefits to be interested in acquiring additional bank credit, rather than making efforts to improve capital productivity. It also has a negative impact on the growth of the financial sector and its competitiveness by repressing the motivation to improve competitiveness and the productivity of financial institutions. Scholars who support the market-centered theory believe that in developing countries or countries in the process of system transformation, financial repression contributes to preserving the fiscal deficit. From that point of view, therefore, financial liberalization is essential for economic development.

However, as many have pointed out, Korea's economic development process was inconsistent with the outcomes suggested in MacKinnon and Shaw's traditional financial repression theory. Though Korea had a repressive financial system and the government was deeply involved in credit allocation, economic results were very positive. They were quite different from the chaos brought about by rapid financial liberalization in Argentina, Chile, and Uruguay (Diaz-Alejandro 1988). In addition government financial repression in countries in the process of system transformation, such as the former Soviet Union and Eastern European nations, was carried out not to preserve the fiscal deficit but to allocate foreign capital to appropriate industries.

Against this backdrop, several studies that supplement traditional financial repression theory are underway. Some emphasize financial infrastructure elements, such as prudential supervision, information systems that minimize uncertainty and financial intermediary costs, and regulations to protect depositors. Based on new institutional economics, others take a close look into the "quasi-internal organization" that exists among the government, financial intermediaries, and businesses that have received selective financing. In particular, advocates of the latter view, based on case studies, acknowledge that the elimination of restrictions on interest rates and on free entry into the financial sector triggers fierce competition and, as a result, can send interest rates soaring to levels beyond control; the financial sector becomes monopolized, and excessive loans are granted to selected industries and businesses (Dalla and Khatkhate 1995; Haggard and Lee 1993; Haggard and Maxfield 1993a, b). They also point out that the systemic environment in which financial liberalization policies take place and the implementation tools used differ depending on the country concerned, and consequently, the results also differ. In addition, they note that initial conditions (the macroeconomic situation, the financial situation, and the debt structure) at the beginning of industrialization and liberalization exert continuous effects on procedures subsequently. They argue that the neoclassic financial liberalization theory has failed to take institutional problems into account.

Their new theoretical approach to institutions better explains the East Asian experience, though it is still not sufficient to explain Korean financial systems during the rapid economic growth period. According to the new institutional economics, the element that eventually breaks the vertical ties among business, politicians, bureaucrats, and financial rentiers does not come from within the nexus. However, in Korea it was the *chaebols* that were the engine of financial liberalization in the late 1980s. In the new institutional economics approach, it is difficult to explain why the *chaebols*, which were the main beneficiaries of the existing repressive financial order, played an active role in breaking the ties. Korea's financial liberalization, unlike those processes in South American countries, was not based on financial crisis, and businesses, the main beneficiaries of the existing selective financing system, actively supported financial liberalization. It should be reemphasized that the government-*chaebols*-banks coalition was based not only on common interest but also on the compromise with social powers. This was the same compromise with social aspirations that existed both tacitly and explicitly in South Korean society after the liberation from colonial rule.

IV. CONCLUSION

Unlike existing studies that have emphasized the individual effects of each institution, this chapter has focused on the complex social and political conditions that determined the outcomes of certain policies. As for the conditions that enabled Korea's industrialization, some studies have concentrated on favorable international market situations (e.g., Cumings 1987), and others have emphasized the strong government role (e.g., Amsden 1989). However, none of these studies can fully explain the Korean industrialization case. After World War II, most developing countries and newly industrialized countries implemented economic development plans and used outwardly similar financial institutions and policies. However, these similar investment plans and financial policies brought different levels of industrialization to each country, and existing studies cannot explain those differences satisfactorily.

To find the answer to this difficult question it is necessary to look more closely into the common will of society, a kind of social agreement or social consensus. This factor tends to be ignored in economic literature. Instead of achieving democracy, a fair distribution of wealth, and the establishment of a unified nation, achievements unlikely to be accomplished under the Cold War structure and dictatorship, Korean society agreed to focus on economic growth. Because of this consensus, the Korean people may not have resisted the government's social control and suppression of workers as strongly as they might otherwise have done, and as a result, resource mobilization was accomplished more easily.

Currently, an increasing number of nations use integration into the world market and a development strategy for the national economy as concepts with the same meaning in their political ideology. They have been forced to believe that markets bring the best results. However, the most fundamental reason why some do not share that idea is the belief that social problems are the products of society and can only be resolved or diminished through the internal movement and will of society.

Chapter 6

Labor Policy and Industrial Relations in the Park Chung-hee Era

Kim Sam-soo

I. INTRODUCTION

The primary objective of this chapter is to define, from an industrial relations perspective, the salient features of the labor system in place during the 18-year incumbency of President Park Chung-hee. As is well known, South Korea experienced unprecedented annual economic growth of between 8 and 9% in the 1960s and 1970s largely as a result of the export-oriented industrial policy implemented during the Park era (1961-79). By adopting industrialization strategies focused on manufacturing, especially in regard to the heavy and chemical industries in the 1970s, and through structural reforms, Korea entered an era of industrialization in earnest. As a mark of the success of this endeavor, the number of employees in the national workforce almost tripled from 2.3 million in 1962 to 6.5 million by 1980.

As has often been the case in the industrial relations of advanced capitalist countries in the world, labor problems related to employment relations occurred in the process of industrialization in Korea, and as a consequence, regulations and systems for dealing with such problems were instituted. According to Kerr et al. (1960), one of the main features of a modern economy is that it is impossible to run an industrial society without proper industrial relations systems built on an ideology that is shared by the concerned parties.

An industrial relations system has various levels, including work-place, company, industry, and national levels, and to understand fully the labor regime in Korea in the 1960s it is necessary to analyze comprehensively all these levels. However, this chapter focuses only on the government's labor policies, especially those related to collective industrial relations. Although this restricts the analysis of the labor regime of the era to the standpoint of the national economy, this approach helps identify the essential historical characteristics of the development of the Korean capitalist economy.

A collective industrial relations policy, namely a *combination policy* that is related to the workers' right to organize, is one that defines whether the bargaining power of workers can be admitted in the labor market by the state (government). The point in question is whether or not trade unions and their functions should be prescribed by law. Legally sanctioning the establishment of unions means granting bargaining power to workers. From this point of view, legalizing the right of workers to collectively withdraw their labor, which is the right to strike, constitutes a logical foundation for the formation of a nation-state in which workers are incorporated as citizens (Bendix 1964; Marshall 1950; Nakanishi 1982; Shibata 1983).

Fundamental to understanding the labor policies enforced by the Park Chung-hee regime is the question of whether those policies were meant to *legally* sanction the independent combination of workers in the form of trade union organization. Although this issue is discussed throughout the chapter, it can be stated here quite un-equivocally that the labor policies of the Yushin regime, instituted from 1972, were never meant to authorize labor unions by law. Many studies on the subject have been published, including Kiyomizu (1987/1988), Choi Jang-jip (1988), Song Ho-geun (1991), and Kim Jun (1993, 1999). Choi Jang-jip, one of the most prominent labor relations researchers in Korea, sees the labor control system under the Park regime as having been one of state-driven authoritarian corporatism. He notes, "The government successfully changed labor unions into company-controlled bodies under the protection of the state to ensure structural safety of the official labor unions" (Choi Jang-jip 1988:34); namely under the regime of the Federation of Korean Trade Unions, which itself was then newly reorganized by the military government power. Song Ho-geun contests Choi's theory, claiming that although corporatism, as first conceived for Latin American countries, is distinctively a state-driven system, it does not fit into the Korean situation because it is a control system designed to obviate direct confrontation between individual workers and the state by utilizing intermediary groups. He offers an alternative approach based on "control (suppression) through market mechanisms." The state controlled individual workers directly while either making labor unions powerless or not authorizing their existence (Song Ho-geun 1991).

The studies referred to above, like other relevant works, all have problems. First, they attempt to understand the labor situation during the Park era as a single entity, rather than differentiating between the 1960s and the 1970s. Although it may appear that the Choi and Song studies, for example, focus on the 1970s at some specific points to establish a distinction between the two decades, this is merely a descriptive effect. The fact is that both authors deliberately avoid classifying the two periods separately.[1] When the 1960s are compared with the 1970s, however, there are certain intrinsic differences in the state's policy regarding the workers' right to organize, as is discussed in more detail below. Second, a more important point is whether their arguments on the labor system were appropriate in Korea under the Yushin regime, from 1972 on. Although the purpose of Choi Jang-jip's argument is to differentiate labor unions from "official" labor unions, he fails to make a clear distinction between them. Moreover, he is in error in deducing that the Park government approved the formation of labor unions, whether company-dominated or not. Song Ho-geun (1991:311-3) is persuasive in his objection to this contention and is surely correct when he argues that labor policy in the Yushin era differed from the "suppression based on corporatism" model in Latin American countries and that the Korean government did not approve the formation of labor. However, Song does not

---

[1] Song Ho-guen (1991:314) categorizes the labor policies in Korea after 1961 collectively as measures to "suppress workers through market mechanisms" like those of Taiwan after 1948.

seem to understand clearly the historical implications, in a comparative perspective, of the state's policy to ban the right to organize
trade unions in the capitalist development process. If he considers
the labor policy at that time as having been a means to suppress
workers through market mechanisms, another form of authoritarianism, that raises the problem of whether the long-established labor
systems without labor unions that commonly existed in developed
countries before they authorized labor unions should be considered
as a form of authoritarianism.

To resolve these problems this chapter analyzes separately the
labor policies enforced in the 1960s and 1970s in Sections II and III,
thereby clarifying the true nature of the combination policy in each
era. Clearly, labor policies implemented under the rule of President
Park, those in force in the 1970s, were meant to replace labor unions
and collective bargaining rights with Joint Industrial Relations Con-
ferences, which were established as part of the New Community
Movement (see below), and organized in a top-down manner. Although labor unions did exist de facto, the government did not legally
sanction them nor their functions. The Korean government at first
authorized the right to organize, though only in the private sector, on
the basis of the Constitution of 1948 and the Labor Relations Acts
of 1953. Despite its limitations, the Labor Relations Acts had significant historical implications because they were enacted as a means of
mediating class conflicts and dealing with labor-related problems
caused by the chaotic political situation after the liberation from Japan, the partition of the peninsula, and the Korean War. The acts
were not visionary, and they have undoubtedly affected the labor
policies of modern South Korea.[2]

After thoroughly analyzing labor policy, this chapter examines
the establishment and functions of the Federation of Korean Trade
Unions (FKTU) and the characteristics of Korean trade unions un-

---

[2] Based on the legislation process of labor policies in 1953, the South Korean capitalist regime after the truce was signed can be categorized as *a
pseudo-nation and authoritarian state*. For the development stage theory of the
capitalist nation-state based on labor policies and the historical restrictions
of labor laws of 1953, see Kim Sam-soo (1993).

der the leadership of the FKTU. Finally, the authoritarian integration mechanism and some economic factors under the Yushin regime are analyzed by examining crucial aspects of the industrial relations of the era. Some of the important features of Korean industrial relations, which have taken shape through the introduction of mass production techniques, enterprise-based labor unionism, and the joint labor-management consultation mechanism, are also addressed.

II. LABOR POLICY IN THE 1960s[3]

Legislative Revision and the Right to Organize

Shortly after seizing power by military coup on May 16, 1961, Park Chung-hee issued an edict that, inter alia, prohibited strikes and dissolved all trade unions in Korea. However, the military government did allow unions to register anew, in accordance with the Revised Act on the Registration of Social Organizations and the Interim Act on Workers' Organized Activities, both of which statutory instruments came into force on August 3, 1961. Although these measures laid the foundation for the establishment of the FKTU regime, workers were deprived of their right to strike until it was restored by the Revised Labor Laws in April 1963.

Subsequently, some provisions concerning the three primary rights of workers — to organize, to bargain collectively, and to withdraw their labor — were amended in a comprehensive revision of the Constitution of South Korea on December 26, 1962. The clause concerning the workers' right to share profits in private companies was abolished in the new Constitution. Prior to the revision public officials had been denied those three basic rights not by express provisions in the Constitution but by related laws. With the revision, however, and except for some officials who were defined to have the rights by subsequent acts, public officials were deprived of all the

---

[3] For a detailed analysis of labor policy in the 1960s see Kim Sam-soo (1999a). The description here is based on that source, unless otherwise noted.

rights according to provisions in the Constitution itself. The revised Constitution meant to suppress open public debate on the teachers' union movement and the public officials' right to organize, a debate that began in the late 1950s and peaked around the time of the uprising on April 19, 1960. Although the right to organize was specified more clearly in the labor relations acts — the Public Officials Law and the Act on Private Schools — the government's guarantees of workers' rights to organize in the 1960s were no different from those in the 1950s. Only the private sector was given such rights. However, even teachers in private schools were denied the right to organize. Public sector workers who were not classified as public officials, in effect, were denied the right to strike by a mandatory arbitration system.

Collective Labor Relations Policy

Although the revisions of labor law in the 1960s were relatively bland, the following elements are noteworthy: (1) the premise or pursuit of a unitary form of nationwide industrial union by enacting related provisions and terms, (2) the virtual impossibility of establishing multiple unions because of provisions for disqualification, (3) the pursuance of a *government concession system* to regulate trade unions by reinforcing a system requiring them to report their establishment, (4) the setting up of Joint Labor-Management Councils (JLMCs), (5) the prohibition of political activities by trade unions, and (6) the reinforcement of restrictions on labor dispute participation by enlarging the extent of public services and introducing an emergency arbitration system.

Compared to the law of 1953 the most important feature of the revised law of 1963 was its inclusion of the concept of an industrial union system, as symbolized by such expressions as "a national scale labor union" and "an umbrella labor organization (branch)" in the text of the statute. However, it must be stated that an industrial union system was not forced by law on the basis of this inclusion. The significance here is that the law was actually constructed on the basis of the revision of the trade union system under the Interim Act on Organized Activities of August 1961. That is, the law was based on the *industrial union system* of the FKTU, an organization imposed on the Korean labor force by military political power. The provisions pertaining to the restriction of the establishment of competitive unions and the reinforcement of the requirement to report the establishment of labor unions played important roles in securing by law the FKTU as a unitary and monopolistic representative institution.

Despite these changes, however, the two laws had a number of features in common, and the essential character of the law of 1953 remained intact. Both laws gave the right to organize only to limited groups, closely regulated activities related to workers' combination, and suppressed industrial action. On the other hand, national safeguards for labor unions, such as the prohibition of the arrest of strikers, except for flagrant offenses, and the restriction on supplementary labor while a strike is in progress, which surpassed by far the boundaries of the civil law, were maintained. However, the more important fact was that, although limited to the private sector (except for public utilities), the policy authorizing the workers' rights to organize and strike was also retained. This suggests that the drafters of the 1963 legislation were unable to escape the historical restraints put in place by the law of the previous decade, insofar as they could not legally deprive workers of their right to organize — in its essence the right to strike. In hindsight, the FKTU regime to which unitary industrial unions were affiliated was chosen and established in an orderly manner by industry as an alternative means of negotiating such restrictions. It must be borne in mind, however, that the union structure headed by the FKTU differed considerably in many respects from the industrial trade union systems prevalent in Western countries, especially Germany, as is explained later.

III. LABOR POLICY IN THE 1970s

Denial of the Right to Organize

Despite the implementation of a revised labor law in April 1963, legislation governing the administration of Korean labor in the 1960s retained the essential characteristics of the 1953 Labor Relations Acts. There was, however, a definitive change at the beginning of the 1970s. One of the most important characteristics of labor policy in that decade was that although extant laws authorized workers' rights, in practice the government denied the rights to organize and to bargain collectively through the enactment and enforcement of special laws. Cases in point are the Temporary Special Act on Labor Unions and Disputes Involving Foreign Invested Firms, dated January 1, 1970, and Article 9 of the Act on Special Measures for National Security issued on December 27, 1971. The effect of these special laws was that the most important policy measures contained in existing labor-related laws lost their functions; in other words, the existing laws were downgraded to supplementary status. The provision in Article 29 of the Yushin Constitution of 1972 guaranteeing the three major rights actually imposed more restrictions on workers' rights to organize and act collectively than the related provision contained in the Constitution of the 1960s. By introducing such special laws prior to the declaration of the Yushin Constitution, the Park Chung-hee government compromised the three major rights of laborers guaranteed by the Constitution.

The Act on Special Measures for National Security of 1971 granted legitimacy to the declaration of a State of National Emergency, which had already been imposed on December 6 in the same year. On the strength of this act the President was afforded unlimited emergency powers to mobilize manpower and equipment and restrict basic civil rights, including economic rights, merely by observing the formality of review by the State Council.[4] This special act, enacted at first for a limited period of time and abolished on December 27, 1981, was pivotal to the continuation of the Yushin regime. From the standpoint of relations between the state and its citizens, the law effectively rendered the Constitution nugatory and brought about an

[4] The following elements were included in the law: freedom to choose and change residence (Article 6); freedom of assembly (Article 7); freedom of speech and publication (Article 8); regulation of collective bargaining rights (Article 9); regulation of prices, wages, and rents; the right to change budget expenditure (penalty: more than 1 year but less than 7 years imprisonment).

era in which, to all intents and purposes, there was no Constitution. On this basis, it can be said that the Yushin Constitution was no longer a Constitution, and the Yushin government ceased to function in a constitutional manner.[5]

Therefore, the 1970s was an era in which the Constitution was replaced with the Act on Special Measures for National Security and labor relations laws were replaced by the two special laws. From a standpoint of modern legislative structure, it can be said that the cart was put before the horse. The pivotal labor legislation of the era was Article 9 of the Act on Special Measures for National Security. The enactment of the Temporary Special Act on Labor Unions and Disputes involving Foreign Invested Firms had important implications as well. The Temporary Special Act was passed with the aim of boosting foreign investment by enhancing cooperation between labor and management. Under its terms foreign investment companies were required to report the establishment of labor unions and labor disputes to the National Labor Administration, and the Central Labor Council was empowered to conduct mandatory arbitration in labor disputes. After the National Security Act was added to the statute book, this arbitration system ceased to function and was replaced by an administrative settlement system, which remained until the National Security Act was finally rescinded in 1981. The aim of the Temporary Special Act was to make the National Labor Administration the competent office dealing with the establishment of labor unions. Under this system, in reality, Korean workers employed by foreign-owned companies or companies in which foreign capital was invested found it difficult even to attempt to establish enterprise trade unions in the 1970s.[6]

---

[5] My views on the Yushin regime are related to the nature of the nation-state from the perspective of state theory, and not to its formation background. For a detailed thesis addressing the background to the declaration of national emergency and the Yushin regime and to contemporary economic development, see Kim Won-jung (1997).

[6] Sumiya (1993:124) notes that no companies in the Masan Free Export Zone had formed a labor union by the middle of the 1970s. Workers were prevented from doing so by the passive attitude of the Labor Administra-

Thus, although labor policy after 1971 might not, on the surface, appear to have prohibited workers in the private sector, workers in public service companies, or blue-collar government public officials from setting up labor unions, in practice such endeavors were effectively precluded by the fact that all workers were deprived of the rights to bargain and act collectively, the essential functions of a labor union. This fact means that the workers' right to organize itself was virtually prohibited.

Article 9 of the Act of Special Measures for National Security

Administrative Settlement

Article 9 of the Security Act is the only provision directly related to labor. Clause 1 states, "Workers must file a settlement with the competent office before exercising their rights to bargain and act collectively and should follow the decision of that office." Clause 2 reads, "The President can take special measures to regulate the right to act collectively of workers employed by national government organizations, local autonomous entities, government enterprises, public service companies, and companies that may exert important influence on the national economy." This second clause in the act was reflected directly in the Yushin Constitution, but of greater significance, at this juncture, is the first clause. Although it did not preclude the rights to bargain and act collectively, it did regulate the procedures for executing those rights by the application of an administrative settlement system; in doing so, it had the potential to deny completely the essential purposes of the right to organize, which include the right to bargain and act collectively. The provision was enforced without a proper enforcement ordinance being put in place, but on the basis of established National Labor Administration regulations. Such an illegitimate procedure illustrates clearly why the law should be regarded as unconstitutional. Indeed, because a political office managed the

---

tion and unfair labor practices of employers. Workers and the general public thought that it was impossible to establish labor unions.

provision arbitrarily and unsystematically, the provision cannot be considered a law at all.

To consider the characteristics of the administrative settlement system of the 1970s, which was managed in accordance with established regulations of the National Labor Administration, it is appropriate to look into the details of two of those regulations, Numbers 103 (February 29, 1973) and 105 (March 25, 1973).

1. The initiation of settlement in collective bargaining: Concerned parties should submit an application form for settlement in collective bargaining to the competent office when exercising their collective bargaining rights. Details required: the parties for settlement, matters for settlement, and the arguments of the concerned parties.

2. Settlement body (competent office): Governors of cities and provinces (companies registered in either a city or a province); President of the National Labor Administration (companies registered in more than two cities or provinces and foreign invested companies).

3. Settlement Decision: After receiving application forms, the settlement body should inform concerned parties of decisions within 30 days. The settlement body should document its decisions and send them to concerned parties. If concerned parties reach agreement on certain points while awaiting a settlement decision, the settlement body shall reflect those agreements in its decision even after receiving the application forms (Regulation 105).

4. Legal effect of a settlement decision: After an settlement decision has been handed down, concerned parties may not apply for a new trial or administrative litigation. The decision is final and legally binding.

5. The right to act collectively: Workers must not exercise the right to act collectively until the settlement body makes its decision.

It can be seen from the above extract that the settlement system was a *compulsory arbitration system* insofar as its initiation was mandatory and the settlement body's decisions had final, legally binding effect. Moreover, it was impossible for workers to stage a strike because they were prevented by law from exercising their rights to act collectively before the administrative settlement body had made its decision. This was a policy structure that in reality denied the right to act collectively, including the right to strike, throughout all industrial sectors. It was far more than a simple procedural regulation, as it imposed serious restrictions on both the public and private sectors. In this respect, it can be said that all the functions of labor relations laws, including the Labor Union Act, were almost entirely suspended by the state. Moreover, the fact that the concerned parties had to request an administrative settlement (arbitration) from the start and accept the decision of the competent office confirms that workers did not have free collective bargaining rights.

Settlement Realities

What then were the realities of the administrative settlement method under the Act of Special Measures for National Security? One means of answering this question is to examine the record of the settlement decisions made by the "competent office." Table 6.1 shows the actual results of settlement, as compiled by the Ministry of Labor and based on reports filed by the arbitration body. The competent office was obliged to submit such reports on a monthly basis either to the President of Labor Administration or the Ministry of Labor.

Three types of settlement decision are shown: a compulsory arbitration, a mediation agreement, and an agreement between labor and management. A compulsory arbitration was one enforced by the competent office; a mediation agreement was one reached after mediation by the competent office when concerned parties failed to agree after requesting settlement, and when they failed to reach a mediation agreement, the case was to be referred to a compulsory arbitration process. An agreement between labor and management was a unique form of settlement. Although such an agreement could not be considered a result of mediation (settlement) by the "competent office," in reality it should be deemed as a form of settlement since sometimes concerned parties reported to the competent office even after reaching an agreement in advance, and still wanted to be treated as if their disputes had been settled by the competent office (Kim Su-gon 1983:41-3).

Table 6.1 Results of Administrative Settlements of Collective Bargaining

	1972	1973	1974	1975	1976	1977	1978	1979	1980	1981	Total (1972-81)	Total (1976-81)
Total number of settlements	452	566	942	1,139	1,448	2,042	2,131	2.149	2.216	2,216	452	452
Agreements between labor & management	401	561	883	1,092	958	1,306	1,488	1,607	1,596	1,838	401	401
Mediation Agreements	-	-	-	-	423	573	544	472	479	356	-	-
Compulsory arbitrations	51	5	59	47	67	163	99	70	141	22	51	51
Percentage of agreements between Labor & Management	88.7	99.1	93.7	95.9	66.2	64.0	69.8	74.8	72.0	82.9	88.7	88.7
Percentage of mediation agreements	-	-	-	-	29.2	28.0	25.6	21.9	21.6	16.1	-	-
Percentage of compulsory arbitrations	11.3	0.9	6.3	4.1	4.6	8.0	4.6	3.3	6.3	10	11.3	11.3

Source: Internal records of the Labor Policy Bureau of the Ministry of Labor.

The average percentage of compulsory arbitrations from 1972 to 1978, during which time the Act of Special Measures for National Security was enforced, was 4.7%. Judging from Table 6.1, there was a high possibility that the cases of mediation agreements were classified as agreements between labor and management. When this possibility is taken into consideration, the percentages of the three categories from 1976 to 1981 are as follow: agreements between labor and management: 72.1%, mediation agreements: 23.3%, and compulsory arbitration: 4.6%. The percentage of settlements by the administrative office, including compulsory arbitrations and mediation agreements, is approximately 28%. This is not a small percentage. Considering the consequences that might ensue from arbitration and the conventional methods used by labor and management to solve labor disputes, the administrative settlement system undoubtedly had a major influence on the relations between labor and management.

One of the most important points to take into account when evaluating the administrative settlement system devised by the Park Chung-hee regime is how to interpret the meanings of agreements between labor and management and mediation agreements as recorded in Table 6.1. As Kim Su-gon points out, it is possible that most cases of agreement between labor and management at that time were not the results of settlement by the administrative office at all. Concerned parties could have reached agreement before they requested formal administrative settlement, but still proceeded with the request because of regulatory implications. As shown previously in the examination of Labor Administration Regulations 103 and 105, although arbitration was mandatory, it might have been the case that the administrative office did not rule out the possibility of agreement to mediation agreement between concerned parties being reached during the settlement procedure, and in reality, some disputes were indeed resolved by the parties themselves while the process was under way. This suggests that a prior arbitration practice was in place at that time. Taking note of the fact that the administrative office authorized agreement between concerned parties during settlement process, Hagiwara (1998) argues that this type of administrative settlement was a *system of obligatory mediation in advance of strike* (prior mediation system) and that the system was not devised to rule out collective bargaining. He also argues that the Park government intervened in labor disputes only at the last stage of collective bargaining and that the purpose of mediation was to promote mutual agreement between labor and management. Even if this argument is accepted, can it be deduced that the prior mediation practice was systematized and that the purpose of administrative settlement during the period in question was to promote collective bargaining?

It is difficult to concur with this view. First, as is shown in the regulations of the Labor Administration, the procedures for prior mediation were not systematized. The competent office handled labor dispute cases at its discretion and had the power to resort to compulsory arbitrations if needed.[7] It introduced the prior mediation system simply because there were too many applications to exercise collective bargaining rights for them all to be dealt with through compulsory arbitration (Park Yeong-gi 1983:144-5).

Second, the more important consideration is that the mutual agreements between labor and management during the period were not the results of exercising collective bargaining rights. Even if concerned parties reached an agreement before requesting arbitration by the competent office, it was only as a result of consultation between labor and management because the workers' right to strike was ruled out from the outset. Needless to say, labor unions would have achieved more if they had been in a position to exercise freely their collective bargaining rights.

Third, Hagiwara's assertion that the compulsory arbitration system was never unfavorable to Korean workers appears to be seriously flawed. It is certainly erroneous to suggest that compulsory arbitration systems always function in a one-sided manner, against the interests of workers. On the contrary, the system in some countries, including Australia, is clearly beneficial to workers. However, this only occurs after labor unions have been recognized in law as legitimate entities in society and when the arbitration bodies and systems are

---

[7] Only in 1980, the year of the Spring of Seoul, did various levels of legal labor committees begin to participate systematically in a deliberate process of settlement decision based on Ministry of Labor Regulation 237, which was enacted on March 7 of the same year. However, the committees were still unable to influence matters related to arbitration agreements, which remained at the discretion of administrative authorities (Federation of Korean Trade Unions 1981:53-4).

genuinely independent. Neither of these circumstances applied at that time in Korea.[8]

As has been explained, the labor policies stipulated in the Act of Special Measures for National Security were essentially based on the compulsory arbitration system, a single trial system, under which the government dealt with labor and management problems arbitrarily after depriving workers in all industries, in both the public and private sectors, of their rights to act collectively and to strike. It is clear that the Act was designed to remove workers' collective bargaining rights by depriving them of the right to strike. In the Park era, therefore, the significance of collective bargaining was reduced to little more than a means of communication between labor and management. Although establishing labor unions was not disapproved by specific provisions, union organizing activities and unions' functions were severely compromised. The regime never allowed workers to form labor unions of their own or to freely exercise their collective bargaining entitlement.[9] Although the actual establishment of a trade union was not illegal, the resultant organizations were merely "representative groups of workers" in joint consultation between employees and management.

Revisions to the Labor-Related Acts

As previously described, under the Act of Special Measures for National Security other labor-related laws were maintained intact, pro-

---

[8] According to Hicks (1963:131-4), in cases of compulsory arbitration, which in reality are government interventions, adjudicators tend to make decisions in favor of labor unions, because they have to make judgments based on *fairness* rather than on conflicts of interest between concerned. When labor unions lost cases in a series of labor disputes in the late 19th century, Australia introduced a compulsory arbitration system to correct such problems (see Macintyre and Mitchell 1989).

[9] The fact that 87.2% of 342 labor dispute cases handled by local labor committees between 1971 and 1974 were related to unfair labor practices by employers shows the seriousness of the government's policy banning the workers' right to organize (Choi Jang-jip 1988:98).

viding they did not conflict with it. However, the aforementioned labor-related acts were revised in 1973 and 1974. Although the revisions covered many issues, such as introducing a broader application of compulsory arbitration to public service companies and strengthening the intervention authority of the administrative office to deal with labor-management relations, the most significant items addressed in the revision process were related to the organizational structure of labor unions and to Joint Labor-Management Consultation Councils (JLMCCs).

First, the expressions used in the text of the article concerning the requirement to report on the establishment of trade unions were changed. The term "a labor union on a national scale" was changed to "an associated union and a trade union which crosses more than two provinces," and the term "an umbrella labor organization affiliated to a national scale labor union" was deleted. One effect of these revisions was that the previous policy to pursue *unitary* organization of nationwide industrial union was abandoned by law. Instead, the organizational structure of the industrial union was perceived as a nationwide association (federation) of independent enterprise-level unions by law. Thus, by the terms of the revision, the Park government gave up the organizational form of *pseudo-industrial unions*, which had been established on the basis of the Revised Labor Act of 1963, and finally accepted the organizational form of enterprise unionism, which already appeared in the mid-1960s in the regulations of the National Labor Administration.[10]

A more noteworthy change, however, was the fact that provisions relating to JLMCCs were reinforced in Article 6:

---

[10] The regulation that required workers to first obtain the permission of a national-level trade union before taking industrial action was abolished. In addition, the regulation that specially allowed "umbrella organizations affiliated to a national-level union" to act as one of the bodies handling collective bargaining rights was also abolished. For a detailed analysis of the various regulations of the Labor Administration in the 1960s, see Kim Sam-soo (1999a:206ff).

1. An employer and a labor union shall establish a Joint Labor-Management Consultation Council in order to promote productivity through mutual cooperation.

2. Members of the Joint Labor-Management Consultation Council shall discuss issues such as production, education, training, work environment, grievances, and the prevention of industrial relations disputes within the scope of collective agreements and regulations on employment.

3. Relevant matters concerning the management of the Joint Labor-Management Consultation Council shall be decided by Presidential decree.

The main participants in JLMCCs were the employer and the relevant trade union, and only companies with labor unions were obliged to set up JLMCCs. The remarkable fact was the deletion of the provision that in the previous law read "'the representative of a JLMCC shall be entrusted with the representation right to make decisions in collective bargaining." Although it may seem that the revised act drew a distinction between collective bargaining and the JLMCC, in fact, the deletion was only a formality. It was inevitable that the scopes of the two organizations coincided with each other, and thus the functions of them were almost the same in the enterprise union system. Considering that the functions of labor unions had all been removed by Clause 9 of the Act of Special Measures for National Security, it can be said that JLMCCs eventually began to replace the role of bona fide trade unions.[11]

---

[11] The JLMCC is essentially identical to Japan's factory council system, which was introduced after World War I. The factory councils were voluntarily established mainly in large companies to replace already existing labor unions (see Hyodo 1971). Trade unions were first legalized in Japan after World War II by the Labor Union Act of December 1945.

IV. FEDERATION OF KOREAN TRADE UNIONS (FKTU)

Organizational Characteristics of the FKTU in the 1960s

The Committee for the Reconstruction of Korean Labor Organizations, set up and directed by the Park Chung-hee military government, led the effort to rebuild all South Korean labor unions after August 3, 1961. One outcome of the rebuilding process was the establishment of the Federation of Korean Trade Unions (FKTU) on August 30, 1961. The FKTU was a federation of unitary national-level unions by industry, consisting of 11 industrial affiliates. The military government was deeply involved in the establishment of the FKTU and the other industrial federations, from the drawing up of organizational plans to the selection of members. By December 12, 1970 the FKTU had increased its number of members to 16.[12]

The structure of the FKTU had very important implications for labor organizing. First, it is important to note that it was impossible for workers to establish labor unions without joining one of the nationwide industrial unions affiliated with the FKTU. In other words, the authorization of an industrial-level union was an essential prerequisite to the formation of an enterprise-level trade union (branch). The industrial-level unions had monopolistic rights because they were established according to a provision prohibiting the establishment of their rival union, and by dint of this monopoly they were able to exert considerable power over their affiliated enterprise-level branches and chapters.

Second, and according to one of the rules of industrial unions under the FKTU, although workers might join the industrial-level union by individuals, in reality, however, the unitary industrial union was just like a federation of enterprise unions. It had branches and chapters mainly at the enterprise level that worked as unit trade unions. In a large enterprise, a branch would be set up, and if the enterprise had multiple business locations they would be accommodated

---

[12] Unless otherwise noted, this description of the formation and characteristics of the FKTU in the 1960s is based on Kim Sam-soo (1999a:210-9).

by separate chapters. In a small company, a chapter would be established under the control of an industrial-level union's branch. It is of fundamental importance to note that the system of so-called unitary industrial unions in Korea, which was a peculiar organizational form in the Park era, was essentially different from the "cross-company" industrial union system prevalent in European countries. In Korea, workers had to be on the payrolls of specific companies in an industry to become members of a trade union, because almost all union branches or chapters were established at the company level. When the worker ceased to be employed by that enterprise, he or she automatically relinquished union membership. Workers paid their union member dues according to the rules of the branch or chapter concerned. The branch or chapter then paid a small part of the accumulated revenue, usually a specific amount per person, to the relevant industrial-level union. The finances of trade union were heavily concentrated in the branches of enterprise-level unions.

Finally, bargaining at the enterprise level was the main form of collective bargaining, regardless of the existence of industrial-level trade unions. Because the labor unions of the government monopolies, such as the railroad network and electricity generation and distribution, were by themselves unitary nationwide organizations, they had to negotiate at the national level. The Textile Industry Union and the Mining Industry Union were actively involved in collective bargaining at the cross-company level. Indeed, the former set an exemplary standard when it started industry-level bargaining with the National Association of Cotton Spinners in 1966 and then concluded an agreement. It also tried to negotiate at the industry level with the National Association of Silk Reelers. However, this type of industry bargaining was exceptional. In private sectors, usually, the branches and chapters of the industrial union negotiated separately with their relevant companies. It was common for the industrial-level unions to hold the right to bargain and the right to conclude agreements according to their internal rules, but they normally entrusted their branches and chapters with those rights.[13]

---

[13] It should be noted that some commentators hold the view that regional branches of industrial unions exercised collective bargaining rights and the

In this respect, although an industrial-level union took the unitary form of organization by industry, in essence, it was no more than a federation of enterprise-level unions that acted almost autonomously. Accordingly, the dominant organizational structures of labor unions in the 1960s were based on the enterprise union system, regardless of the revisions of law and union names. For this reason, it is useful to consider the organizational structures of trade unions under the FKTU as *a pseudo-industrial union and enterprise union system.*

Industrial relations in the 1960s were comparatively stable thanks largely to the above- mentioned labor policies and the leadership of the FKTU. However, by the end of the decade employees at some cotton spinning companies, the Korean Shipbuilding Corporation, and foreign-owned companies, such as Oak Electronics and Signetics Electronics, staged prolonged labor disputes. In the first two cases the disputes developed even into industrial actions including strikes. As worker solidarity was authorized by law regardless of its limitations in the 1960s, the actual occurrence of disputes and strikes became the topic of much public discussion, and in a negative way, the industrial actions paved the way for the changes in labor policy that took effect in the 1970s (Kim Sam-soo 1999a:226-8). The FKTU also took up a more active attitude toward labor movements under the leadership of Chairman Lee Chan-hyok. This did not accord with the intentions of the government, however, and Choi Yong-soo replaced Lee at the helm of the FKTU in October 1970 as the result of intervention by the Korean Central Intelligence Agency (KCIA; Song Ho-geun 2000:217-8).

---

right to conclude collective agreements on behalf of their affiliated chapters (interview with the Planning Manager of the Federation of National Textile Labor Unions, March 9, 2001). However, these were small companies.

FKTU under the Act of Special Measures for National Security in the 1970s

Supporting organization of the Yushin regime

Policies of the FKTU and its affiliated industrial-level unions were changed significantly after the enactment of the Act of Special Measures for National Security. When a State of National Emergency was declared on December 6, 1971, the chairmen of the FKTU and its affiliates signed a statement supporting the declaration. In October 1972, the federations organized national-scale "'Enlightenment Circles" with the dual aim of supporting the policies of the Yushin regime and persuading the public to endorse the ratification of the Yushin Constitution (National Council of Churches in Korea 1984:234). The FKTU and its affiliated industrial federations were the first organizations to officially support the declaration of national emergency (Choi Jang-jip 1988:168). The contents of the policy included the renunciation of unreasonable demands for higher wages, and increasing the source of allocations by improving productivity and cooperation between labor and management. In return for the cooperation of workers in the productivity growth drive, the FKTU devised policies to create or extend social security provisions under the slogan of an "equal allotment of welfare benefits" (National Council of Churches in Korea 1984:239-40).

JLMCCs and the New Community Movement

The FKTU, in its support for the Act of Special Measures for National Security and the Yushin regime, unilaterally abandoned the rights to organize and strike, the ultimate sanctions of labor unions. Considering the imperative for the FKTU to accommodate itself to the political changes taking place under the dictatorship, it was inevitable for its leadership to take this step. However, considering that it afforded virtually no meaningful service of any sort to the Korean trade union movement throughout the 1970s, the FKTU effectively surrendered all the core functions of a labor union.

Yet, the FKTU actively promoted the establishment and management JLMCCs, which were introduced to replace the roles of labor unions, and it participated in the New Community Movement in the factories. The FKTU was also involved in the policymaking process of the government by participating in various government-led deliberative committees.

The number of JLMCCs increased sharply during the 1970s. In 1970, 63.4% of target companies had instituted JLMCCs, and the percentages rose to 96.1% in 1975 and 97.8% in 1978 (Cho Seung-hyok 1984:207; Choi Jang-jip 1988:181). The dramatic increase is explained by the fact that companies with labor unions were obliged by law to set up JLMCCs. The point to be explored is how they functioned. Members of a JLMCC discussed issues prescribed by statute, such as technical education, the working environment, and the handling of grievances. In addition, discussion inevitably took place on other issues related to labor conditions and wage increases. Lacking the rights to bargain collectively and strike, however, JLMCCs acted merely as gatherings of labor and management representatives. The councils were not systematized. If anything, the JLMCCs of the 1970s played only a very minor role in backing up the New Community Movement, which was presented as a Korean-style movement aimed at promoting cooperation between labor and management.

This New Community Movement had its origin in the quality control movement initiated by company management at the beginning of the 1970s. It was a nationwide productivity improvement strategy modeled on the Saemaul (New Village) Movement, which was developed in rural communities after the oil crisis in the latter half of 1973. The Chamber of Commerce and Industry led the initiative under the direction of the Ministry of Commerce and Industry. Small unit circles, each consisting of a leader and between 8 and 15 members, were the main organizational building blocks for the movement. By 1977, 10,000 factories were participating, and the number of small unit circles reached 70,000 by the beginning of 1980. Activities of the circles were focused on matters of production and quality management, such as the improvement of production processes, quality control, the zero-defect movement, cost reductions in energy and materials, and technological innovation; in other words, a Korean-style quality control movement (Choi Jang-jip 1988:187-9). Intent on maintaining the momentum of the movement, the Park Chung-hee government provided group education sessions to promote a diligent work ethic and to instill in all workers the spirit of loyalty and filial duty. Group education was provided mainly to New Community Movement leaders, upper and middle management, and foremen class workers (Kim Ho-gi 1999:187).

What is important in the context of this chapter is that the activities of the New Community Movement in the factories inevitably overlapped with those of the JLMCCs, or labor unions, both in terms of the issues and the people who were in leadership positions. In fact, labor unions teamed up with management representatives to organize and administer steering bodies for the movement.[14] At that time, the FKTU also took an active part in the movement, educating workers on the doctrines of the Yushin regime, the New Community Movement and trade union movement, and Korean-style industrial relations. At the same time, the FKTU attempted to reinforce its power by denouncing such organizations as the Urban Industrial Mission (UIM), the Young Christian Workers (JOC), and opposition parties.

Although further research will be needed to identify and assess the achievements of the New Community Movement, it certainly played a significant role in maintaining and consolidating traditional labor practices, such as early clock-in and late clock-out without pay, unpaid holidays, and the reduction of bonuses (Choi Jang-jip 1988:189-92). Under the circumstances, the JLMCCs played only a supplementary role in helping management promote the New Community Movement as a productivity improvement movement.

Realities of Workers' Participation in Policymaking

Regardless of the fact that the FKTU and its affiliated industrial federations were in no sense well-functioning representatives of worker

---

[14] As was the case at the Korea Electric Power Corporation (Korea Electric Power Corporation 1981).

interests, they gained their status as labor unions by law, and by participating in the Yushin regime and the productivity improvement movement they accrued certain benefits. For example, Choi Yong-soo, then chairman of the FKTU, became a member of the National Assembly by dint of being placed on the proportional representation list of the ruling Democratic Republican Party. However, the political power of the FKTU was weak, and the FKTU members could not participate in the organization of the Political Friends of the Yushin Regime, a floor negotiation group in the National Assembly, which was established as a safety net for the Yushin regime (Kiyomizu 1987/1988:500-1). Furthermore, the FKTU leadership's hope that, in return for its support of the Park regime, the government might expand the social security system for the equal allotment of welfare benefits was not realized.

The only policymaking participation of note in the 1970s was inclusion in the meetings of both the Central Consultative Assembly of Labor and Management and the Deliberation Committee for the Welfare of Workers. The Central Consultative Assembly was established in August 1975 and was an unofficial organization consisting of representatives of labor unions, management, and the government. However, it focused its agenda on relatively insignificant issues related, in the main, to industrial accidents and the New Community Movement. Between 1978 and 1979 the Central Assembly lost its functions entirely (Kiyomizu 1988:504). The government was bent on encouraging the establishment of JLMCCs at the company level and, as a consequence, adopted a negative attitude toward the setting up of JLMCsC at the industry or central level, thus preventing workers from participating further in policymaking.

Meanwhile, under the leadership of the government minister responsible for the administration of the Economic Planning Board, the Deliberation Committee for the Welfare of Workers, which was established in June 1978 and comprising top class officials of labor unions, management, and the government, set up various sectional committees in the Labor Administration and carried out labor-related activities. However, the Committee also focused its agenda on relatively insignificant and limited issues related to production. Its first plenary session was held in January 1979, long after its initial establishment (Kiyomizu 1988:505-6). The Committee achieved only meager results in its field, including the resolution of some issues concerning social insurance.

V. INDUSTRIAL RELATIONS IN THE 1970s

Mechanisms of Integration and Accommodation

FKTU regime as an Institution to Control Labor

Industrial relations were relatively stable throughout the Park era; a condition that became more apparent when the possibility of new leadership for the FKTU trade union movement was ruled out in the late 1960s. In the male-dominated heavy and chemical industries, which were at the center of the economic development plan at that time, there was not one strike of any real significance. Although the industrial action, including a strike at Hyundai Shipbuilding, which occurred in September 1974, sent a shockwave through Korean society, it was staged spontaneously and without the involvement of a labor union. The most significant reasons for stability in the relations between labor and management in the 1970s were the preparedness of the government to intervene, as is evidenced by the forceful suppression of strikes in the late 1960s; the reorganization of the leadership structure of the FKTU in 1970; and the repressive labor policy that, under the umbrella of the Act of Special Measures for National Security, denied workers the right of combination through labor union. As described above, the Park Chung-hee regime obviated worker solidarity to maintain social calm and keep a tight grip on the levers of power so that no obstacles could block the path to economic development.

Scrutiny of the official records of the number of labor union members and the proportion of labor union establishment in the 1970s shows that trade unions not only existed then, but that their numbers actually increased. In addition, a number of labor disputes were staged (Kim Geum-soo 1986:173). However, the point to be noted here is that company-level disputes were the main component, it being difficult to trace industrial action led or directed by the nationwide industry-level unions. Female workers in labor-intensive industries, such as the textile and garment industry, played a leading role in staging strikes of note in the 1970s, such as those at Wonpung Textiles, Dongil Textiles, and YH Trading. The actions were staged by company (enterprise)-level unions without the involvement or support of the industrial unions. What is worse, the industry-level unions actually restricted the endeavors of the "democratic" trade unions at the branch level, as graphically revealed in the case of the strike at Dongil.[15] It is of the greatest importance to note that the actions at Dongil paved the way for the birth of a two-tiered trade union system in Korea in which democratic unions at the enterprise level, which had considerably strong connections with religious organizations, such as the Urban Industrial Mission and the Young Christian Workers, confronted the nationwide official industry-level unions under the FKTU.

Wage Increases

The average annual increase rate in real wages from 1973 to 1979 reached 12.7%, which was 2.4% higher than the increase in GDP

---

[15] On the surface, the disputes at Dongil in 1976 and 1978 were based on attempts of different employee factions to obtain the leadership of the enterprise-level labor union (branch). In reality, they were an outcome of workers' desire to establish a female-led democratic trade union empowered to act in the interests of the workers. The aim of the management of the company was clear: They wanted a union favorable in all respects to the interests of the company. Skilled male workers, the foremen class workers were the main members of the company-led faction in opposition to the then-newly elected female-led democratic leadership. The Ministry of Labor, the KCIA, and the courts consistently supported management's stance. Moreover, the National Textile Workers' Union (NTWU) intervened and exercised its regulations defining the means of dealing with "troublesome branches." In so doing, the NTWU took the lead in the destruction of the Dongil Union (Dongil Corporation Campaign Committee for the Reinstatement of Discharged Workers 1985).

over the same period. The trend of average annual increase in real wages from 1964 to 1970 was roughly similar. The wages of blue-collar workers increased more than those of white-collar workers. Workers at the larger enterprises in capital-intensive industries and male workers gained the most from the wage increases (Amsden 1989:222; Yu Jong-il 1997:92).

The steep increase in wages was due, almost entirely, to particular factors in the labor market. The trade unions could not play their customary role in securing wage increases because of the government's ban on the right of combination through labor union. Some have argued that the Korean economy turned from one in which there was an unlimited supply of labor to one with limited labor resources, based on the "turning point" theory suggested by A. Lewis (Bae Moo-gi 1991; Lewis 1954). However, it is hard to accept that such a change was structural, considering the fact that the country suffered serious but temporary labor shortages from 1976 to 1979 because the government sent a large number of workers to the Middle East to meet the demands of the construction boom in that region.

In addition to energetic labor policies, the increase in wages made a great contribution to stable labor–management relations in Korean industries in the 1970s. Male workers at large companies in the heavy and chemical industries enjoyed especially good relations with management. Some major enterprises, such as the steel conglomerate POSCO, started to pay high wages to workers in recognition of the efficiency and enterprise internalization of the labor market (Amsden 1989:229-30). However, the internal labor market, which began to take shape within the larger enterprises, was still in its infancy. Judging from available statistics on labor conditions, there was not a great deal of difference between the wages of production workers at large enterprises and those of production workers at smaller ones. Moreover, major large companies had not systematized any strategies and procedures to nurture skilled workers at the enterprise level (Yokoda 1998).

Enterprise Unionism and the JLMCC System

Mass Production System and Shop-Floor Reorganization

One of the most important factors in the economic development of South Korea during the period under consideration was the introduction from more developed countries of advanced production equipment and technologies. Until then, large enterprises in the heavy chemical industry had focused, in the main, on processing and assembling (i.e., processes and equipment most suited to mass production; Kim Hyong-gi 1988). This systemic change in technology and production method was accompanied by a commensurate shortage of new skilled workers acquainted with the latest techniques and contributed to render useless the traditional skills.

To deal with this problem, the government first enacted the Vocational Training Act in 1967 and implemented a public vocational training policy. However, it soon introduced a Special Act on Vocational Training in 1974, which obligated companies to carry out in-house vocational training (Lee Ju-ho 1996:229-31).

Following the introduction of new technologies, the shift from traditional skills progressed with little friction, mainly because workers who fell into that category were not numerous and did not have the tradition of having established Western-style craft unions. The top-down system of the JLMCCs and the New Community Movement (quality circles) in the factories were instrumental in enabling workers to cope flexibly with the changed work organizations and work environments caused by the introduction of the new schemes.

The introduction of mass production methods brought about significant changes in industrial relations through shop-floor reorganization because it was accompanied by the importation of scientific management techniques. Traditional field foremen were reduced to the lowest rank in their company's managerial structure, and field supervisors now assumed the role of controlling workplaces, taking orders from staff members (engineers) with university degrees, including engineers in nonmanagerial positions. The fact that in most cases it was field supervisors who became leaders of trade unions

181

(branches or chapters) explains how the adhesive relationship between unions and management was maintained.[16] Although the mainstream organizational structure of Korean trade unions had been at the enterprise level, this structure was reinforced when companies, especially the larger ones, needed workers with firm-specific skills and created internal labor markets. However, the unions played only limited roles as consultative institutions within companies during the period from 1971 to 1987 when the "labor uprising" occurred.

Seniority Wage System

Of necessity, employment and personnel management systems changed their salient characteristics to cope with the introduction of mass production methods. A large number of companies, especially the bigger ones, applied industrial engineering methods to conduct scientific management. Some companies implemented pioneering personnel management systems, such as a pay-for-job system in which the results of job analyses were reflected in the wages and promotions of workers (Kim Hyong-gi 1988; Yang Byong-moo et al. 1992:143-9). However, full implementation of the pay-for-job system failed, as was shown in the pioneering case of the Korea Electric Power Corporation, which introduced the system in 1968, or the system was changed into a Japanese style pay-for-job competency system, which in essence was a wage-attached-to-a-person system (Korea Electric Power Corporation 1981).

The seniority wage system was expanded and also began to be applied to production workers in the 1970s. Not until 1980s, however, was the annual regular wage increase institutionalized to production

---

[16] Before 1987, executive members of the enterprise trade union at KIA Motors had exceptional opportunities for promotion to managerial positions under the strictly educational-based status system (Kim Sam-soo 1999b). Under such circumstances, it is reasonable to assume that the managements of Korean companies at that time might well have established practices, such as recognition of the full-time positions as employees and full remuneration paid by the company, to the executive members of trade unions.

workers. The internal markets of companies were still immature, and the employment retention rate of workers to company was not very high.

VI. CONCLUSION

The social scientific and historical significance of the labor regime in the 1970s, with a focus on labor policies and industrial relations, is considered here.

To sum up from the labor structural viewpoint, Korean workers during the period were deprived essentially of the right of combination through labor unions, and for that reason they were effectively disqualified from full membership in the nation-state. The deprivation of workers' rights was, in essence, related to the true character of the Yushin regime, which, in fact, also disenfranchised the wider population totally or partially through such anti-democratic political institutions as the National Conference for Unification and the Political Friends of the Yushin Regime. The labor policies in the Labor Standards Act and the Livelihood Protection Act were no better than the collective labor relations acts in terms of guaranteeing labor rights. Although the government of Park Chung-hee revised the Labor Standards Act in 1961 and 1973, it failed to raise the minimum labor standards of its 1953 predecessor. It is far from clear whether the functions of labor inspectors, whose role was to ensure and enforce the implementation of statutory labor standards, were actually performed in accordance with the principles of the law. The Livelihood Protection Act of 1963 failed to establish positively the right to relief of the poor, and the institution of the social security system at that time that, in principle, should cover all citizens including poor people, fell far short of the justifiable standards.

From the historical perspective, labor policy in the 1970s regressed to the policies extant prior to the revision of the Labor Relations Acts in 1953. Those policies in force during the State of National Emergency declared by the Yushin regime were even worse than the policy to ban the right of combination through labor union, which was implemented under a State of National Emergency at the very inception of the American Military Government (Kim Sam-soo 1993). This labor policy of prohibiting the right of combination was, in its essence, still maintained until 1987 during the regime of President Chun Doo-hwan, who, as a "legal son" of the Yushin regime, came to power after the assassination of Park Chung-hee in 1979.[17] Undoubtedly, throughout the period under review, the South Korean state achieved high economic growth on the foundation of the state's labor policy.

It has been shown in this chapter that the Yushin regime failed to incorporate the workers into the body of the nation as citizens, although it advocated nationalist ideals while making the people recite the National Charter of Education, learn about the spirit of loyalty and filial piety, and participate in the New Community Movement. Under such a regime, the JLMCC system was fundamentally weak. Companies did not systematically carry out labor management measures fictitiously based on a paternalistic relationship with workers as family members.[18] Workers, especially blue-collar workers, were precluded from full membership in a company community. Workers lodged a significant objection against such a system and made their feelings clear in the extensive labor disputes of 1987 that in turn fueled the process of democratization in Korea.

---

[17] The democratization and social reform processes after 1987 have been geared to promote positive aspects of the concept of a nation state. However, the processes are still continuing, since some negative aspects have also been remained and newly generated. For the characteristics and problems of the current Revised Labor Relations Acts of 1997, see Kim Sam-soo (1999).

[18] There is some dissent on the issue concerning the views of Amsden (1989) and Yu Jong-il (1998), both of whom see industrial relations under the Park regime as having been based on paternalism. For details see Sumiya (1976). However, it is considered inappropriate for Sumiya to regard the labor–management relations in that era as having been based on a master-servant relationship, since he did not take into consideration the historical facts or constraints that Korean workers already had already received, though partially and unsystematically, the baptism of nation state since around the Second World War. For details, see Kim Sam-soo (1993).

Chapter 7

Developmental Dictatorship:
Disparity between
the "Haves" and the "Have-nots"

Lee Joung-woo

I. INTRODUCTION

Year after year, an increasing number of South Koreans hearken with a growing sense of nostalgia to the 18-year period of rule by the autocratic former president, Park Chung-hee (1961-79). In opinion polls, Park has emerged as the most respected leader in the modern history of the nation, even topping Kim Ku, the great freedom fighter,[1] and Ahn Chung-gun, another revered fighter for the cause of Korean independence.[2] The reason for Park Chung-hee's popularity is mainly one of comparison; that is, he is outstanding not so much because of his own achievements but because of the perceived weaknesses of his "competitors." Much of the nostalgia seems to be related to widespread feelings of disillusionment, anger, and antipathy that were generated when former presidents Kim Young-sam and Kim Dae-jung's apparent early successes in the democratization process fizzled out and the later

---

[1] Korea was occupied by Japan when Kim Ku became the head of the Korean Provisional Government, in exile in China, in 1926. In 1945, following the defeat of Japan, Kim returned to Korea, but his Provisional Government was not recognized by the American Military Government.
[2] Ahn Chung-gun assassinated Hirobumi Ito, the first Japanese Governor-general of Korea. He was executed by the Japanese in 1910.

185

parts of their tenures became deeply flawed. This disenchantment was particularly acute when the Korean people saw the sons of the two presidents getting involved in corrupt practices and subsequently being imprisoned for their crimes. Such popular sentiment, however, carries with it the risks of undervaluing the fight for democracy, of becoming skeptical about democracy itself, and of overvaluing economic growth, political nihilism, and "the worship of Mammon."

Rapid economic growth is said to be President Park's signature achievement. This is another reason he is popular. Many believe that most of the credit for South Korea's relative affluence and general well-being, which are outcomes of rapid economic growth, should rightly go to him, despite the enormous harm he did to the Korean people in the process. Park was pro-Japanese. He seized power by military coup d'état, created a dictatorship, and abused human rights. It is simply the fact of the rapid economic growth that he motivated and engineered and the lower-than-expected performances of his successors that together explain his popularity. It is necessary to reflect, however, on three crucial factors: whether Park's developmental dictatorship itself actually brought about the economic development, whether his autocracy was indispensable, and what impact the economic development had on the gap between the "haves" and the "have-nots" in South Korea. Accordingly, this chapter addresses the trinity of economic development, democracy, and distribution.

Complaints regarding income distribution have been voiced increasingly for many years. The economic development that brought growing inequality has concerned many commentators, and there is a widespread consensus among the general public over the deleterious implications of the widening gap between those in society who have and those who do not. The gap between the rich and the poor has always been identified as one of the more serious problems in opinion polls throughout Korea. The question of whether income distribution is, in fact, a serious problem, however, is not easy to answer. What cannot be ignored is that South Korea has been consistently identified by observers as a country that epitomizes rapid growth and relatively fair distribution. Previous assessments of the Korean economy have been largely positive, and many studies conducted both inside the country and abroad have argued that the problem of income inequality has not been as serious as in some other countries nor has it been aggravated during the early growth period. It is, therefore, necessary to reflect on whether this is in fact the case, whether South Korea's developmental dictatorship has not aggravated wealth distribution, and whether the gap between the poor and the rich is not wider than that of foreign countries. As there are substantial differences among the many perspectives on this issue, an objective approach is imperative.

II. DICTATORSHIP, DEVELOPMENT, AND DISTRIBUTION

Brazil in the 1960s well demonstrates the impact of a developmental dictatorship on income distribution. Contrary to the political propaganda on its "economic miracle," Brazil's already wide gap between rich and poor become even wider, and real wages fell. The aggravated and distorted income distribution was explained by two different analyses. The first, based on the Chicago School's human capital theory, saw education as an important variable and analyzed the input and output of education. The other theory focused on the pro-wealthy economic policies of the developmental dictatorship after the Brazilian military coup. Although studies of the relationship between dictatorship and distribution are rare, it can be reasonably assumed that a dictatorship would tend to have a negative impact on income distribution because, for many developmental dictatorships, growth precedes equitable distribution. Here the underlying assumptions are that a bigger pie would facilitate a bigger share for all and that the benefits of economic growth through consumption cuts and rising investment would inevitably trickle down to the lowest rungs of the social ladder.

In reality, those of a conservative persuasion are convinced that savings and investments should take preference over any concepts of fair distribution in order to make the economy grow and that money should be channeled to high-income earners who can afford to increase their savings, rather than to low-income earners.

Meanwhile, advocates of dictatorship claim that it is a form of societal management that actually helps economic growth. An economy begins to grow only when investment reaches a certain level.[3] To increase investment, they say, a dictatorship is needed to force the public to cut spending. Lacking the massive surpluses that industrialized Western countries expropriated from their colonies to enrich their economies in the 19th century, Third World countries have had to create dictatorships to exploit a specific group of people, usually farmers.

The Soviet Union under Joseph Stalin is seen as a case in point. Since the Socialist Revolution in 1917, wage workers in the USSR had been forced to refrain from spending for 20 years, from 1920 to1940, to an unbelievable extent. As a consequence, average spending fell to 30% of the pre-revolution level (Amin 1987, 1994, 1995). Soviet farmers suffered even greater restrictions on spending, which plummeted to between 15- 20% of pre-revolution levels. An enormously high number of people died from starvation and persecution after the 1917 revolution. Bolshevik leftists, including Trotsky, championed Evgenii Preobrazhensky, a representative Revolution theorist who justified the exploitation of farmers. In his theory of socialist primitive accumulation, Preobrazhensky asserted that putting the surplus gained from the temporary exploitation of farmers into factories is a policy strategy indispensable in developing a socialist economy. The argument, however, seems to be a poor excuse for justifying dictatorship. In addition, economic growth in development-oriented poor countries almost always entails a widening gap between the underprivileged and the privileged, without making the slightest improvement in the livelihoods of the have-nots and sometimes making the poor even poorer.

As far as the impact of Soviet developmental dictatorship on income distribution is concerned, more often than not communism is equated with egalitarianism and, therefore, fair distribution. This perception is far from, and even contrary to, reality. Stalin regarded

---

[3] In his "take-off theory" Rostow designates the doubling in investment rate of original 5% to 10% as one of the conditions to make an economy take-off.

egalitarianism as anti-Marxist and advocated performance-based remuneration. As a consequence, income inequality grew during his regime. It was not until Nikita Khrushchev took office and started putting major reforms into place after Stalin's death in 1953 that Soviet elites began cautiously to support egalitarianism, and the income gap, which had fluctuated according to time and conditions in the Soviet Union, began to narrow. The marked differences in income inequality between 1932 and 1979 can be readily observed in Table 7.1.

Table 7.1 Income Inequality in the Soviet Union

	1932	1979
Blue-collar workers	100	100
Gold-collar workers	263	116
White-collar workers	150	79

Source: Rein 1983.

Statistics were suppressed during the period of the Stalin regime (1927-53), and data on income in the USSR were not released until after his death. The ratio of the top 10% to the bottom 10% income bracket fell from a factor of 4.4 in 1956 to 3.4 in 1975. The decrease in the level of inequality is especially noteworthy in the context of this chapter because it was achieved through democratization.

The economic models of Park Chung-hee and Joseph Stalin do exhibit common characteristics, as Paul Krugman (1994), the distinguished American economist, argued a few years ago when noting how East Asian economies resembled that of the Soviet Union. Considering the distance between the ideologies of the two leaders, the similarities are striking. First, both economies were high investment economies. Stalin raised the Soviet investment rate to over 30%, the highest in the world at that time. Such an increase in investment, however, impoverished factory workers and farmers to an unbearable degree. The 30% investment rate was seen again in Japan, Korea, and

Taiwan in the 1960s. Second, both economies advocated policies for strong economic and military muscle. Although some may consider that such policies protected the Soviet Union from invasion by Hitler's Germany, they undoubtedly placed the country under great strain and claimed millions of lives. South Korea also had a powerful and extensive military capability and began to put emphasis on the growth of heavy industry in the 1970s. Military costs absorbed as much as 13% of the national income of the Soviet Union, compared to 6% in Korea, which was still high by international standards. Third, both regimes favored big business, a preference that left small and medium-sized companies relatively underdeveloped. Indeed, Stalin is famous for his order to build a factory so huge that it could be seen even from the moon. The Korean economy was also centered on its unique type of conglomerates, the *chaebols*, which had the advantage of being able to mass produce a small range of items, but which lacked flexibility and could not produce a wider variety of specially designed items in small numbers. Fourth, both economic models spurred growth in quantitative terms, but hampered growth in qualitative terms. Both economies achieved rapid economic growth by putting large numbers of idle workers to work and by facilitating high levels of savings and investment, relatively easy steps in the early stages of development. However, the question that then had to be addressed was how to raise efficiency and productivity after idle resources had been used to the limit. Both modes were undemocratic and rigid in regulation and effectively reached a dead end. Both mobilized resources efficiently, but failed to attract voluntary participation, creativity, and the spirit of cooperation from the general public. Finally, both regimes failed to keep pace with advancing technologies.

An extremely useful lesson can be learned from the decline and eventual collapse of the Soviet Union economy after 1960, despite Khrushchev pounding with his shoe on the podium at the UN annual meeting and blustering that the Soviet Union would bury the United States economically. The Korean economy under Park Chung-hee also arrived at a dead end caused by fundamental flaws inherent in the system. Despite this and its undemocratic and inhumane practices, there remains a body of opinion that still favors the Park

Chung-hee regime without reservation. It is difficult not to conclude that those who hold such predilections are either ignorant of history or profited from patronage under the Park regime or both.

It is the case that the credit for fighting abject poverty must go to Park, who mobilized the entire country to create jobs in a manner reminiscent of the latter part of Japanese colonial rule. Economic growth, however, can be achieved in more humane and democratic ways. The Korean people lost more than they gained. The legacy of the Park Chung-hee era includes the following: hostile industrial relations across the society; an economy dependent on conglomerates; a "cramming" ethos in education that frequently imposed intolerable burdens on teachers and young students; and a society of distrust, social injustice, corruption reflected in self-regarding materialism, and environmental degradation. The damage all this has done to Korean society will take a considerable amount of time to repair.

Dialogues, experiments, and errors — the building blocks of experience — may appear to delay progress, but they are indispensable to the development of democracy, and together constitute a process that will eventually guide society in the right direction. Impatience with the democratic system and the preference for dictatorship are myopic, and sometimes dangerous, conditions. It must be understood that an economy will grow in a coherent and humanitarian way only when democratic administration succeeds in attracting voluntary participation and creativity from the population at large. When that truism is accepted, there remains no other choice but to abandon any vestige of nostalgia for the era of Park Chung-hee.

III. ECONOMIC MODEL OF PARK CHUNG-HEE

In general, the international community seems to hold the view that East Asian countries have achieved rapid economic growth and an equal distribution of income at the same time. The World Bank emphasized this point, releasing a report entitled "East Asian Miracle," in which it concluded that East Asian countries such as South Korea had succeeded in realizing "shared growth." If Korea had, indeed, attained not only rapid economic growth but also fair income distribution at the same time, praise for such a success would have been well deserved. Historical reality presents a very different story, however.

To understand the true characteristics of Park Chung-hee's developmental dictatorship, it is necessary, inter alia, to clarify the definition of economic development. The field of economics has a variety of interpretations of the concepts of growth and development, and some economists do not differentiate between those concepts, using those two terms as though they were synonymous and interchangeable. Economic growth refers only to income growth, and specifically per capita income growth, in order to reflect population growth as a variable. Most champions of neoclassical economics feel at ease using this concept.

However, many economists believe that there has to be a clear distinction between economic growth and economic development. In this context, economic development can be considered as the condition in which economic growth is accompanied by significant changes taking place in concert with per capita income growth. Depending on individual philosophical viewpoints, these changes can have different implications. Attention should be paid to the concept of "development as freedom," which has recently been proposed by the Indian economist and Nobel laureate, Amartya Sen. The International Confederation of Free Trade Unions (ICFTU) and the Food and Agriculture Organization of the United Nations (FAO) together issued an unprecedented communiqué acknowledging and welcoming his winning the Nobel Prize. In one of his studies, Sen introduces his innovative perspective and proposes that the promotion of freedom is itself the main objective of development, as well as being one of the main ways of achieving it. He opposes the notion that particular freedoms, such as political freedom, need to be curtailed en route to the full realization of social and economic development. In Sen's words, "Development calls for the abolition of the major causes of the lack of freedom. In short, development asks for the eradication of poverty, tyranny, restricted economic opportunity, systematic deprivation, the lack of public facilities, and a nation's excessive oppression" (Sen 1999).

In the 1960s, Jagdish Bhagwati, another Indian economist, submitted an opposing thesis on the correlation between democracy and economic development (Bhagwati 1966). He claimed that democracy was detrimental to economic development and regarded the conflictual relationship between them as a cruel dilemma. Admitting his lack of empirical evidence for an overgeneralized theory, however, he later abandoned this position and accepted a potential compatibility between democracy and economic development.

Sen calls the insistence on a conflictual relationship between democracy and development "the Lee thesis," after Lee Kuan-yew, the former premier of Singapore. Lee was a great advocate of "Asian values" and believed that, to some extent and in some circumstances, a deviation from full democracy must be tolerated.[4] In the same context, Lee often expressed his admiration for Park Chung-hee. Sen attempts to prove that there is no correlation between political rights and economic performance by citing the outcomes of current economic and political research, gleaned from many countries, into the potentially negative relationship between democracy and development. Based on this evidence, Sen asserts, "On balance, the hypothesis that there is no relation between them in either direction is hard to reject. Since political liberty and freedom have importance of their own, the case for them remains unaffected" (Sen 1999:150).

If democracy does not stand in the way of economic development, then there is no reason to abandon it. Against the claim that freedom must be sacrificed for development, Sen sees political freedom, freedom from disease, and freedom from ignorance as elements of development. Furthermore, some freedom, and instrumental freedom in particular, will not only allow people to live more liberated lives but will also facilitate development.

Sen divides freedom into five categories. First is political freedom, which empowers people to form a government and retain

---

[4] In 1994 Lee Kuan-yew and Kim Dae-jung, then President of South Korea, joined in open debate. They held opposing views. Lee emphasized "Asian values," while Kim preferred "universal values." It may well be that, in many cases, "Asian values" are merely an excuse for dictatorship, or some other form of authoritarian government.

responsibility for it. Second is economic convenience, whereby individuals are provided with the opportunity to use resources in consumption, production, and exchange. Third are social opportunities, meaning health and education institutions. These represent both intrinsic freedom and instrumental freedom, which serve as a means of delivering political and economic freedom. Fourth is the facility to secure transparency. Openness in public affairs restricts the ease with which corruption can spread and creates a degree of trust in public administration. Fifth is a system of social security, which will constitute a reassuring social safety net for those who genuinely need help.

Sen contends that it is only when the absence or diminution of freedom is addressed and the restoration and maintenance of freedom are guaranteed that people can pursue their individual development, as well as the development of society, through economic and productive activities. In this regard, the nation and society as a whole play a bigger role in enhancing and promoting the capabilities of all citizens.

From this perspective, Sen criticizes slavery in the United States. He counters the claim that under such a system the living standards of the enslaved were higher than those of salaried workers at that time (Fogel and Engenman 1974) by writing:

> Even though African American slaves in the pre-Civil War South may have had pecuniary incomes as large as (or even larger than) those of wage laborers elsewhere and may even have lived longer than the urban workers in the North, there was still a fundamental deprivation in the fact of slavery itself (no matter what incomes or utilities it might or might not have generated). The loss of freedom in the absence of employment choice and in the tyrannical form of work can itself be a major deprivation (Sen 1999:113).

When Sen's freedom perspective is applied to the South Korean economy, it raises the question of how to evaluate the nation's rapid economic growth. Several definitions of development were noted earlier, and it was found that Korea was regarded as an exemplar of successful development. As such, it can be readily appreciated why foreign institutions like the World Bank looked favorably on Korea's economic model. To what extent, then, does the introduction of this new definition, "development as freedom," change the conventional wisdom that places Korea as a resounding success story of development?

Considering the first freedom suggested by Sen, political freedom, it is clear that neither the Park Chung-hee regime nor that of its successor, led by Chun Doo-hwan, can be awarded high scores in political freedom and regard for human rights. During those eras, the freedoms of the press, of assembly, and of association were comprehensively undermined, and innocent people were routinely accused of being political offenders and punished. It is, in fact, no exaggeration to say this was an age of lawlessness (Kim and Park 1985; Lee 1986; Park Se-gil 1989).

From the late 1960s until the last 1980s, not a single month passed peacefully on the campuses of Korea's universities. A large number of students were expelled, imprisoned, and tortured. Workers suffered from low wages and excessively long working hours and in protest against their dire circumstances put their jobs and lives at risk by organizing democratic trade unions. It is well known that during the dictatorship of Park Chung-hee, democratic activists, including students, intellectuals, labor leaders, and politicians from opposition parties, were subjected to all manner of hardship and suffering; arbitrary arrest, torture, imprisonment, and enforced conscription into military service were relatively common impositions. In addition to the treatment meted out to those opposed to his regime, consideration of how Park treated his own loyal subordinates graphically reveals both his true character and the atmosphere he created. It is, indeed, striking to note the low regard in which the dictator held prominent politicians in his own ruling party[5] and the

---

[5] Kim Sung-gon, Gil Jae-ho, Baik Nam-uk and Kim Jin-man, four big players of the ruling party, were behind the disobedience. Once the disobedience took place, intelligence agents stormed the houses of Kim Sung-gon and Gil Jae-ho, beat and dragged them like dogs. Soon they were expelled from the political arena. Even though he was always in good shape

extent to which intelligence agents, on the instructions of the President, tortured and humiliated those who showed the slightest concern about the conduct of government. After the ratification of the Yushin Constitution in November 1972 and the beginning of the Yushin regime, Park's quest for absolute power was complete, and he was then in a position to eradicate the last vestiges of democracy in South Korea.

The extent to which human rights were abused and the people's basic rights were stripped is illustrated by the fact that there was no freedom for the Korean electorate to oppose the provisions placed into law by the 1972 Constitutional revisions. One-third of the members of the National Assembly were appointed by the President, who himself was elected by an electoral college of 2,359 voters with a 99.9% approval rating. When the Yushin Constitution was announced in 1972, even Kim Jae-kyu, who came from the same home town as Park Chung-hee and was his classmate at the Korean Military Academy in the 1940s, threw down the newspaper he had been reading and shouted, "What the hell is the Constitution all about? Park has a dangerous ambition to cling to power for the rest of his life!"[6]

It is fair to say that South Korea under the Yushin regime was an "asylum of horror." The cumulative outcome of the nine Presidential Emergency Decrees issued by Park was to effectively gag the Korean people to such an extent that they could barely breathe. In that era of tyranny, only the President himself was safe from illegal arrest and torture. This is the true picture of the Korean "democracy" created by Park Chung-hee, and it would not be until 1987, 8 years after his death, that genuine democracy would begin to enter the lives of the long-suffering Korean population.

Sen claims that when even the minimum freedom is not permitted, the growth of income alone cannot be considered as real development. In the period under review, no matter how much exports

---

as a judo master, Kim Sung-gon died of the aftermaths of this torture three years later. Kim was a close friend of Park Sang-hee, third eldest brother of Park Chung-hee.

[6] On 26 October 1979, Kim Jae-kyu assassinated Park Chung-hee.

and incomes were increased, the absence of any guarantees of the most fundamental human rights and political freedoms rendered income and economic opportunities meaningless. Though the economy grew rapidly at this time, the growth was accompanied by the widespread side effects of reckless development policies. For example, once the basic humanity of the culture had been eroded, ordinary Koreans began to adopt selfish and self-oriented attitudes, and there was a marked increase in the incidences of frustration and temper loss that took a violent turn. Such phenomena stemmed from the dictatorship itself because it was irrational for the institutions of the state to ask the people to respect morality while the President himself was seen frequently to be in overt contempt of the law.

It is accepted that the Park regime pushed ahead with economic growth in an effort to soothe the public's discontent, and its efforts were highly acclaimed by members of the international community. However, from the point of view of many foreign observers, issues of political freedom and human rights in Korea were not of the utmost importance. Although those self-same observers might well be prepared to risk their lives for their own freedoms and rights, they tended to remain silent on the matter of people in other countries seeking the same privileges. It is simpler, and perhaps more profitable, to talk instead about income and economic indices. It goes without saying that this is a classic case of a double standard, which cannot be tolerated by the Korean public. Those Koreans who have endured decades of dictatorship hold, perhaps understandably, a somewhat different view. It is safe to assume that the differences that are sometimes evident between foreign and indigenous evaluations of the Park Chung-hee regime are largely the result of differing interpretations of development. Thus, it is rational, at least from a South Korean perspective, to define the rapid growth in the period of development-oriented dictatorship from 1961 to 1979 not as economic development but simply as quantitative growth. It is now time to consider the relationship between development-oriented dictatorship and distribution.

IV. DICTATORSHIP AND INCOME DISTRIBUTION

Wage Levels and Differentials

Relevant and reliable information on income distribution is scarce, so it is necessary to consider wage levels and wage differentials based on the limited income distribution data that are available. Data on income have been accumulated over a longer period than that on income distribution, and as a consequence, more statistics have been assembled than for income distribution. Yet, wage levels themselves constitute a major indicator of workers' living standards. What is essential is the comparison between wages and productivity. To put it simply, when real wage increases outpace the increases in real labor productivity, workers' incomes also rise. In all other cases, workers' incomes decline. Table 7.2 shows wages in the nonagricultural sector, consumer prices, and labor productivity indices from 1970 to 1980 when the Yushin reforms were in place and Korea's development-oriented dictatorship was at its height.

Table 7.2 Wages, Inflation, and Labor Productivity

Year	Nominal wage index	Consumer price index	Real wage index	Physical labor productivity index
1970	17831 (100)	(100)	17831 (100)	(100)
1980	176058 (987)	(451)	39063 (219)	(259)
Growth rate (%) 1970-1980	25.7	16.3	8.2	10.0

Source: Bank of Korea, Economic Statistics Database; Ministry of Labor, Labor Statistics Database; Korea Labor Institute, Labor Bulletin Analysis

Note: Labor productivity calculations cover only the manufacturing, mining, and electrical industries.

Over this period, nominal wages increased by a factor of 10, and consumer prices increased by 4.5 times, leading to a 2.2 times increase in real wages. What is most compelling, however, is the comparison between real wage increases and labor productivity. Given that labor productivity increased by 2.6 times, it can be seen that real wage increases failed to keep up with productivity increases and, as a result, the share of labor income decreased. Table 7.2 shows that if we set growth rate as a standard, the average nominal wage annual increase was 25.7%, whereas the real wage annual average increase was 8.2%. In addition, labor productivity's annual average increase was 10%, outstripping the increase in the real wage. Thus, it can be assumed that the controllers of capital received higher rewards and received those rewards faster than did workers in the nonagricultural sectors, driving the share of labor income down. Clearly, this had a negative impact on income distribution.

It is also constructive to compare the remuneration of Korean workers with that of foreign workers. A study on this issue shows that as of 1975, when the Yushin regime peaked, the treatment meted out to Korean workers was much less favorable than that afforded to their counterparts in other countries (Cho U-hyon 1985).

Table 7.3 reflects Cho U-hyon's findings, which incorporate Japanese and International Labor Organization data. This table shows that the productivity achieved by Korean workers was not matched by their remuneration. In short, the income gap between advanced nations and Korea was more than double the magnitude of the labor productivity gap. In a nutshell, Korean workers received barely half of what they deserved.

Table 7.3 Manufacturing Labor Productivity and Income Indices in Selected Countries (1975)

	Korea	Taiwan	Singapore	Japan	United States	Germany
Labor productivity index	100	-	233.2	442.5	614.6	512.4
Wage per hour index	100	133.3	405.6	913.9	1341.7	1026.6
Wage per hour	0.36	1.48	1.46	1.46	4.83	3.70

Source: Cho U-hyon 1985.

The disparity between labor productivity and wages inevitably meant that the income share of Korean workers was relatively smaller. This can be verified by comparing the labor shares of various countries. In 1979, Park Chan-il compared the 1960s and 1970s labor share of Korea's manufacturing industry with those of industrialized nations (Table 7.4).

Table 7.4 Labor Share in the Manufacturing Sector: International Comparison

Countries	1962	1970	1973
Korea	26.1*	25.0	23.0
Japan	37.1	32.0	35.0
West Germany	38.0	40.9	44.1
United States	52.6	47.3	44.1
United Kingdom	53.0**	52.6	49.0
Canada	52.0	53.1	-

Source: Park Chan-il 1979:331.

* 1963 figure provided by the Korea Development Bank
** 1963 figures.

It can be seen that the 1970s labor share for the United States, Canada, and Europe were all in excess of 40%, whereas those for Japan and Korea were 32% and 25%, respectively.[7] Park Chan-il believes that Korea's low rate was due to these factors: labor market supply monopoly, labor oversupply, labor's low mobility, the government's low-priced food staples policy, the ability of the corporate monopoly to translate wage increases into price increases and to hamper real wage increases, and restrictions on labor movement (Park Chan-il 1979:331-2).

On the same subject, there is an interesting study that draws the conclusion that a nation's level of democracy is an important factor in the setting of wage levels (Rodrik 1999). This finding implies that when labor productivity, income level, and other variables associated with wage determination are controlled, the level of democracy is closely related to wage levels in the manufacturing sector. This relationship is easy to locate not only in cross-sectional data but also in time-series data. As an example of time-series data, the experiences of Spain, Greece, South Korea, and Taiwan all confirm that wage increases went hand in hand with the advance of democracy.

Thus Rodrik insists that a nation's democracy advance drives up wage levels. Meanwhile, labor share also is influenced by the level of democratization. Rodrik comments that, although four nations in which democracy has been retrogressive show a marked decrease in labor share, six of the eight nations where the transformation from an authoritarian regime into a democracy has taken place show increases in labor share.

In particular, Rodrik takes South Korea and Taiwan as examples of countries in which democracy has advanced since 1987. About Korea he says, "The case of Korea is especially striking, as this country went from being a relatively low wage country (relative to its per-capita GDP) prior to democracy to one with high wages by the mid-1990s" (Rodrik 1999:725).

---

[7] It has been noted that 1979 Korean employees' incomes were lower than those in Japan in 1952 and in the U.S. in 1929 (Park 1982:134).

In answer to the question of how democracy favors workers, Rodrik arrives at four conclusions. First, a democratic system can more readily accommodate the rule of law, thereby strengthening a labor union's negotiating power. Second, democracy tends to be accompanied by political stability that, in turn, engenders higher wage levels and reservation wages for labor unions. Third, democracy promotes freedom of organizing labor unions and entering into collective agreement, thus further enhancing negotiation power. Fourth, as the median voter model illustrates, increased political participation and competition facilitate the development of institutional systems that serve workers' interests.

When Rodrik's theory is considered in respect to South Korea in the 1960s and 1970s, it can be seen that the low wage and low labor share in that period were closely associated with the hostility of the Park Chung-hee dictatorship to trade unionism and its favorable attitude to business entrepreneurs and the *chaebol* conglomerates. It can, therefore, be deduced that the very fact of the vigorous suppression of democracy by the Park regime was a crucial factor in the structure of working conditions and remuneration.

A closer look at wage gaps, rather than wage levels, among workers reveals a serious income inequality. Taking the wage gaps classified by occupation as an index, Table 7.5 sets the wages of production workers as the benchmark (100) against which other occupations are measured. Such positions as managerial staff, professionals, engineers, and office workers were better rewarded than production workers.

Table 7.5 Wage Rates by Occupation (Nonagricultural Sectors)

	Managerial staff	Professionals	Office workers	Sales personnel	Service workers	Manufacturing
1971	359	250	204	118	90	100
1976	474	292	222	112	103	100
1980	395	246	162	89	100	100

Source: Ministry of Labor.

During this period, manual jobs carried a negative connotation for many young workers, both male and female. One outcome of this discrimination was that production workers tended to be neglected and ignored. What is more, this treatment confirms the view that the developmental dictatorship held production workers in relatively low regard. This inequitable institutional attitude has decreased somewhat in intensity over the intervening years, but remains deeply rooted to this day.

The wage gap between production workers and nonproduction workers under the South Korean dictatorship was markedly greater than that of other nations, reaching its greatest extent in 1976. As of that year, the remuneration of managerial workers was five times, and for office workers double, that of production workers, a gap that was almost twice as big as in other industrialized nations. Fortunately, since 1976 the disparity has steadily declined. When educational background is taken as the classifying variable, the wage gap in Korea is wider than in other advanced nations, but since the peak year of 1976 it also has shown a decreasing trend.

Income Distribution

As has been noted, statistical studies on the subject of income distribution during the period under consideration are rare; however, among the few that have been conducted, the work of Choo Hak-chung, from the Korea Development Institute (KDI) and Surjit Bhalla, of the World Bank, are regarded as two of the most sophisticated. Choo Hak-chung's study is particularly appropriate because it is based on a careful reassessment of the available data, unlike much previous research into Korea's income distribution, which tended to put data problems aside. He carefully reviewed the problems of statistical data and introduced new assumptions. By doing so, he modified a great deal of raw data, from which he then conducted his analysis.

Table 7.6 Income Inequalities in Korea (Gini coefficient)

	Nationwide	Farmers	Non-farmers	Workers' households	Self-employed and business owners
1965	0.344	0.285	0.417	0.399	0.384
1970	0.332	0.295	0.346	0.304	0.353
1976	0.391	0.327	0.412	0.355	0.449
1982	0.357	0.306	0.371	0.309	0.445

Source: Choo 1992; Choo and Yoon 1984.

Choo Hak-chung's analysis shows that income inequality dwindled in the late 1960s, increased in the early 1970s, and decreased again since then (Table 7.6). As has been highlighted, the level of inequality peaked in 1976. When all the households in the nation are divided into three categories — farming households, urban workers, and urban self-employed and managers — income inequality in all income brackets moves in the same direction.

One of the most serious problems encountered when attempting to analyze Korea's income distribution is a lack of reliable data on high-income households. However, rather than make assumptions on patently unreliable statistics, an alternative is to consider critically income distribution on the basis of distributive justice (Lee Chun-gu 1992). When income distribution data are limited or nonexistent, basic philosophical approaches may prove more efficacious.

In the time of rapid growth after the 1960s, the Korean *chaebol* conglomerates, those huge enterprises synonymous with Korea's wealthy class, expanded exponentially. Their explosive growth was grounded on state patronage and favors, collusion with government, and corrupt business practices, facts that were widely known and that generated much social discord. The question whether many of South Korea's wealthiest men can justify their asset accumulation in accordance with any principle of distributive justice is unavoidable.

Furthermore, the *chaebols* are still run by the owner families who started them, thereby maintaining a direct connection between business ownership and the income gap between social classes. In some other industrialized nations there have been owner-run conglomerates in the past, but owner families are now quite rare. As it is unlikely that *chaebol* households would be included in any household income survey, it is reasonable to assume that statistics on income inequality in Korea are underestimated. It is also reasonable to claim that the *chaebols'* monopoly of economic power, their inequitable industrial relations, poor working and living conditions, long working hours, and relatively high rate of industrial accidents all add to the perceived inequality (Cho Sun 1989).

When it comes to dealing with the issue of South Korea's income distribution, it is essential to consider the expansion of unearned income, which is not included in income statistics but which is a major contributor to income inequality. Various categories of unearned income, none of which are recorded in household income surveys, snowballed in the period of developmental dictatorship. Whether considered as a normal income or as a supplement to income, unearned income can exacerbate greatly income inequality, so much so that it should be considered separately.

V. SOARING LAND PRICES AND UNEARNED INCOME

There are three ways through which wealth distribution affects income distribution. First, it is a truism that wealth as such exercises great power and generates economic disparity between the rich and the poor. Second, wealth-induced property income leads to income inequality. Third, when property prices rise, income in the form of capital gains goes to property owners. With this income, owners can acquire additional property, making wealth inequality and income inequality closely related and magnifying economic inequality. When land prices continue to increase, as has been the case in Korea, the price rise itself not only brings about economic power inequality but also greatly exacerbates income inequality.

One of the most serious problems concerning Korea's wealth inequality is the issue of land. Real estate makes up about 60% of inherited property and, therefore, constitutes a significant proportion of household assets. Land statistics are not maintained systematically in South Korea or in many other advanced nations. However, despite the paucity of comparative data, there can be little doubt that land prices in Korea are among the highest in the world. The Korean Ministry of Construction released annual land price trends in 1975, but prior to that there was only very sparse information available. Adjustments to what little data are available are shown in Table 7.7, in which a clear trend toward a huge increase in land price can be detected.

Table 7.7 Land Price Trends

	Nominal interest rate (%)	Rate of increase in land price in major cities (%)	Land price index
1964	15.0	-	100
1965	15.0	50.0	150
1966	30.0	35.3	201
1967	30.0	41.4	329
1968	30.0	43.6	407
1969	25.2	48.5	613
1970	22.8	80.7	1,152
1970	22.8	29.7	1,236
1971	21.3	33.4	1,918
1972	12.6	7.5	2,067
1973	12.6	5.8	2,181
1974	15.0	18.7	2,587
1975	15.0	25.5	3,449
1976	16.2	24.9	4,547
1977	14.4	50.0	5,872
1978	18.6	79.1	10,700
1979	18.6	22.0	18,734

Source: Korea Appraisal Board, *Urban Land Price Index*, 1963-74; Korea Appraisal Board, *Land Market Price Table*, 1975-79.

When the 1963 Korean major cities land price is set as the standard (100), it can be seen that prices have increased exponentially every year. Between 1963 and 1979 there were only 2 years in which single-digit increases were recorded and there were 4 years in which the increase was 50% or higher. Particularly extreme increases were evident in the late 1960s and late 1970s. It took only 17 years for land to increase in price by a factor of 180 or even more; no other commodity returned anything approaching such a performance.

Comparing land prices to bank deposits, which represent the preferred assets for people in the low-income bracket, Table 7.7 illustrates that if 100 *won* had been deposited in a bank in 1963 it would have grown to 1,760 *won* by 1979. In contrast, if a piece of land had been purchased with that 100 *won*, its value would have increased to 18,700 *won*, 10 times higher than the bank deposit. On this basis, it is not difficult to recognize how great have been the gains in land ownership in Korea.

There are two fundamental prerequisites for purchasing land. First, it is necessary either to have sufficient capital or to have access to sufficient capital. Second, sufficient funds are of no use unless they are accompanied by advance information on land availability and its potential. It is, therefore, a simple matter for those in power in a development-oriented dictatorship to take maximum advantage of their position and engage in land speculation. During the period under review, South Korea was embroiled in a frenzy of national development, yet the government failed to ensure that appropriate land policy statutes were put in place to properly manage land usage and control land prices. As a direct result of this failure, huge windfall fortunes were made, with a commensurate increase in asset values and unearned income.

To gain a deeper understanding of the realities of the asset redistribution stimulated by soaring land prices at this time, it is necessary to be aware not only of their actual price levels but also of other details of land ownership. Though there is very little information on these matters, one study affirms that 5% of households with one *pyong*[8] or more land owned 65% of national private land (Research Committee on the Public Concept of Land 1988). This figure merely represents the ratio of actual landowners. Thus, when those without land are taken into consideration, the monopoly of land ownership is far greater. Assuming that the condition of land ownership in the 1960s and 1970s was similar to that of the 1980s, those who benefited most from escalating land prices were confined to the top income bracket.

A brief analysis of the situation in 1988, conducted by the author, found that the capital gains based on land accounted for approximately 20 to 30 trillion *won*, which represented roughly half of the 55 trillion *won* earned by 10 million employed workers annually. Given this finding, it is clear how serious was the problem caused by land-based unearned income (Lee Joung-woo 1991).

Park Chung-hee's presidential style was modeled on that of the Japanese colonial rulers during the Manchu Dynasty. He regulated and intervened in almost every economic activity, with the exception of land, where all he did was to introduce a "green-belt" system. It is not clear what motivation underpinned his land management policy. He may simply have unwittingly ignored the issue or perhaps left it in the hands of his acolytes. In either case, his choice in this area of governance invites criticism. Gains and losses from land price changes are a zero-sum game. While soaring prices remained unchecked, an astronomical amount of wealth was concentrated in the hands of a limited number of individuals; concurrently, similarly extreme effects, although of a markedly different nature, were visited on the poor. No matter how hard they tried to tighten their belts, the vast majority of those who did not own their own houses experienced great difficulty in entering the property market and, as a consequence, faced the growing burden of housing rents. In this regard, the policy adopted by the Park regime must be considered as a failure.

---

[8] The *pyong* is the standard unit of land measurement in Korea (1 *pyong* equals 3.954 square yards).

Although issues of income and wage distribution are of great significance, issues related to real estate dwarf them. The real wealth disparity, which is not represented by the Gini coefficient of income distribution, stems from land-associated issues, and it has been on the rise. Low-income families are not aware that their assets are being redistributed gradually to high-income families and are, therefore, not in a position to stop it. One of the major difficulties is that losses induced by land price changes tend not to be noticed by the untutored eye, and so nothing is done to counter them. Nevertheless, they are the main cause of wealth disparity, paving the way for the rich to get richer and the poor to get poorer. Once the facts are realized, it will be impossible to accept the proclamation of the World Bank that South Korea's income distribution is in sound shape, and the real cause of the nation's wealth disparity will become apparent.

VI. CONCLUSION

This chapter has addressed some of the effects of former President Park Chung-hee's developmental dictatorship. Here was an autocratic leader who revised the Constitution to enable him to remain in power for life. He considered himself to be above the law and, unhindered by the normal institutional checks and balances, followed the dictates of his own highly idiosyncratic notions of justice, conscience, politics, and democracy. There are those within society who admire Park Chung-hee; in part because they think that although he was a dictator, he did achieve rapid economic growth and an ostensibly fair distribution of wealth. The rapid economic growth cannot be denied, but if the question, Was the dictatorship really necessary?, is asked, the answer must be "No." The cost of his economic achievements was far too high and included such deleterious effects as a government-led economy, government-led lending, abuse of power by the *chaebols*, institutionalized corruption, environmental degradation, the collapse of community, mistrust throughout society, dehumanization, and social injustices. Given that these side effects will remain part of the fabric of South Korea for many years to come, it is very much open to question whether the rapid economic growth set in motion by

Park Chung-hee will prove, in the long run, to have really served the nation's best interests. It is submitted that, had the growth followed a relatively slower but more soundly based evolutionary course, South Korea would have been all the better for it.

Distribution-related issues are complex; reliable data are scarce, and that which does exist has important omissions and underestimations. There is, however, clear evidence to show that workers and low-income families were severely penalized under the dictatorship in regard to wage distribution, wage gap, and income distribution. As wage rates were lower than labor productivity, the portion of the collective "pie" that went to labor was smaller, whereas the portion seized by capital was substantially larger. Wage gaps and income inequalities were at their extremes in the late 1970s, when Park's autocratic Yushin (revitalizing) regime was at its peak.

When consideration is turned to the degree of wealth disparity during the era, the issue of investment in such commodities as land and real estate is of greater importance than that of wages and incomes. From 1963 to 1979, Korea's land prices soared by 180 times, but only to the advantage of a small number of those in the high-income bracket. The lives of the majority of Koreans, who were not property owners, were made much harsher. In this regard, Park Chung-hee's regime deserves to be criticized because it failed to tackle escalating land prices and subsequent asset redistribution, which are related issues, and focused instead only on economic growth. The scope of the phenomenon of how land prices enabled the rich to get richer and the poor to get poorer is almost beyond imagination and is really the root cause of South Korea's wealth disparity. Thus, when some in society, using only flow indices of the kind produced by the World Bank as supporting evidence, conclude that distribution in Korea was fair during the Park era, it is because they are blind to the full circumstances.

Park Chung-hee's development-oriented dictatorship did not allow the least amount of freedom for which people yearn. Therefore it was able to realize only quantitative growth, rather than real and comprehensive economic development. In addition, because of the way the regime distributed the fruits of growth, it created severe inequalities. It is imperative for society to learn the priceless lesson that the upholding of human rights and personal dignity is utterly incompatible with a development-oriented dictatorship. It is a matter of profound regret that so many people are still unable to absorb this lesson, even after paying such an exorbitant price. They should keep forever in mind that "Human beings may forget history, but history will always remember human beings."

PART THREE

Political Sociology
of the Developmental
Dictatorship Regime

Chapter 8

The Yushin Regime
and the National Division Structure:

Antagonistic Interdependence
and the Mirror Image Effect

Lee Chong-suk

I. INTRODUCTION

The establishment of the Yushin (revitalizing reform) system made it possible for the Park Chung-hee administration to hold onto political power virtually indefinitely. Although many factors, both at home and abroad, contributed to the formation of the Yushin system, the relationship between South Korea and North Korea undoubtedly played an important part. That this assertion is correct is demonstrated by the fact that the bedrock of the Yushin system — namely, the mobilization and industrialization of South Korean society — was underpinned and justified by constant reference to South-North relations.

In describing that relationship, it is usual to speak of a division structure, with the term "division" having multiple meanings including the physical geographic division between the South and the North, diverse disruptive aspects created by this division, and the complex nature of the overall situation on the Korean peninsula (Lee Chong-suk 1995a:339). In addition, we use the term "division structure" to refer to the political, economic, and social components of the relationship, which are created by the realities of division (Lee Chong-suk 1998).

The division structure of the Cold War era was based on mutual feelings of enmity and distrust toward each other, which were embedded in both societies and supplemented the ideological and military confrontation. What is more, very little has really changed even now, in the post-Cold War period. Accordingly, tensions between South and North under the division structure affected political and social processes within both countries and often played a role in making a particular system more autocratic than it might otherwise have been. This phenomenon could also be found in the counter-measures against international changes that impinged on inter-Korean relations. A typical example is the Park Chung-hee administration. Lacking a sound ideological base or appropriate security capability regarding the external situation, it was expedient for Park to interpret détente between the East and the West as a crisis and to use it to strengthen his autocracy.

The co-relationship between the division and the domestic structures is referred to as *antagonistic interdependent relations*; in other words, the situation in which the South and the North each created tensions or engineered confrontations with their counterpart and then used the resultant situation to strengthen domestic unity and enhance the integration or stabilization of political power (Lee Chong-suk 1998:22). These circumstances suggest a core notion for characterizing inter-Korean relations during the Cold War era and were quite obvious when the legitimacy of political power was weak and the instability of the social system increased. In this situation, each administration thought of division as an important means for maintaining political power while paradoxically, stressing incessantly the importance of unification almost as a matter of course. Naturally, these spurious exhortations eventually become mere empty echoes. The actual partition circumstances became increasingly established and entrenched because of their repeated use in the maintenance of political power. In short, the two regimes used inter-Korean relations as a means to stabilize and consolidate their authority: thus, the co-relationships of the two antagonistic administrations under the division structure were both antagonistic and dependent.

The *mirror image effect*, which can be defined as the antagonistic activities of one party that cause the other party to react, resulting in both parties becoming reactive, can explain the interrelation between division and domestic structures. For example, it explains why military enhancement by one nation can spur a similar policy in another. Such mirror image effects can be found in the inter-Korean arms race and in various political, economic, social, and cultural confrontations between the North and South. It is also a concept that explains relations between the Soviet Union and the United States during the Cold War era (i.e., there is "no difference between the distorted cognition of the other party regarding me, and my distorted cognition regarding the other party"; Bronfenbrenner 1961:46). In other words, "Because the two parties regard each other as foes, the image of the other and the image of oneself are opposite in terms of position, but identical in appearance, just like images reflected in a mirror vis-à-vis actual appearances" (Park Gwang-ju 1990:339).

Such effects clearly show why the inter-Korean systems look so similar, though the images of the relationship during the 1970s were of a distorted shape and, therefore, somewhat different from that described by the original theory. The one-man dictatorship system of North Korea and the Yushin system, established in 1972 in South Korea, bore similarities to each other in the formation process, although the influence of the North on the South was greater than that of the South on the North. Because of the asymmetrical nature of this relationship, the mirror image effect cannot be applied in full to it. In addition, though there were similarities between the two systems, there were also significant differences in terms of their specific characteristics and degrees of despotism. Generally, however, the paradox that the South and the North tended to resemble each other in the diverse processes of inter-Korean confrontations during the Cold War era can be explained through the paradigm of the mirror image.

On the one hand, the Park Chung-hee administration, in devising the Yushin system, cleverly made the most of the effects of the division structure, which, in the 1970s, basically encouraged caution toward the North and granted justification for Park to insist on strengthening national security. The practice of attempting to stabilize political power domestically by using the threat of communism continued up until 1972, and the July 4 South-North Joint Communiqué. The division structure was also used by the Park regime to generate tolerance of the ruler's excessive, unification-oriented speeches that played on the national zeal to overcome division. In the process, less notice was paid by the South Korean population to the establishment of absolute rule by Park. Evidence of these effects can be located in a plethora of discussions about unification and attempts to justify the Yushin system from the time of the issuance of the July 4, 1972 joint communiqué until the establishment of the Yushin system at the end of 1972.

Although within the division structure of the Cold War era, discussions about both anti-communism and reunification appear mutually exclusive, they were, in fact, mutually reinforcing. They are also said to have affected the actual establishment of the Yushin system. The fact that Park Chung-hee could turn away from discussions on unification and address the issue of anti-communism suggests that both topics played contributory roles in justifying his dictatorship. From a theoretical perspective, this chapter examines the effects that the Yushin system had on the division structure.

II. TOWARD INTER-KOREAN TALKS

Opening Dialogues

The first Inter-Korean Red Cross talks, at which delegations from South and North met for the first time since the signing of the armistice at the end of the Korean War in 1953, began at Panmunjom on August 20, 1971. The 56-minute session was spent in little more than exchanging opinions surrounding issues of ceremony, procedure, and location, and the like.[1] However, the meeting was a transitional event, showing that détente between East and West was having a direct impact on the Korean peninsula and suggesting that

---

[1] See *Historical Documents for Inter-Korean Dialogues*, Ministry of National Unification (1987a), Book 2: 178-90.

218

an era of negotiation between South and North was beginning that would supersede a period that, until then, had been dominated by a mass of military issues, conflicts, and tensions.

Interestingly, these talks were not entered into after the way had been paved, and reciprocal sympathy was gained by engaging in a lengthy period of deliberation and secret diplomatic meetings. In fact, neither the South nor the North had any intentions of entering into dialogue, even up until early 1971. In his New Year Message for that year, President Park emphasized that the nation's goal was victory over communism, not unification, saying, "The shortcut to a victory over communism is the construction of our economy."[2] He also insisted that the basis for peaceful reunification would be the nurturance and fostering of national power that would overwhelm the North Korean communist regime from a position of strength in all respects. His administration was dedicated to "unification only after economic development" (Kim Chong-ryom 1997:147). Neither was North Korea interested in inter-Korean dialogue until early 1971.

On April 12, 1971, North Korean Foreign Minister Huh Dam suggested eight clauses for a "Peaceful Unification Plan" (the April 12th proposal), including "the withdrawal of U.S. troops stationed in South Korea, free inter-Korean general elections, and the establishment of a federal system." The proposal did not contain any formal recognition of the South Korean authority nor offer hope for negotiations with the South Korean government.[3]

However, U.S. National Security Advisor Henry Kissinger's visit to China triggered changes in the atmosphere in July 1971, when U.S. President Richard Nixon's plan to visit China was announced. The movement for reconciliation between the United States and China, an axis of the Cold War in East Asia, affected inter-Korean relations virtually overnight. In addition to the suggestions in the April 12th proposal, at a welcoming address for the Cambodian King Shianouk,

---

[2] President Park Chung-hee Digital Library.
[3] At that time, the South Korean Minister of Foreign Affairs, Choi Gyu-ha, responded to the North's suggestion by saying, "It was outrageous and unrealizable insistence" and "It was a new kind of harassing tactic toward the South, targeting the two elections ahead" (*Donga Ilbo*, April 14, 1971).

North Korean leader Kim Il-sung broached the subject of inter-Korean contacts, saying that the North was willing to contact all parties at any time, including Park Chung-hee's Democratic Republican Party, social organizations, and individual persons. During his speech, in which unconditional inter-Korean dialogues were actually suggested, Kim Il-sung insisted that the South accept this "initial contact between the South and the North."

South Korea did not respond in a negative way to the offer of dialogue by the North. On the contrary, the Park administration examined closely the North's intentions in proposing the talks and wanted to take the initiative by suggesting inter-Korean Red Cross talks instead. In this context, the South proposed a campaign for the reuniting of Korean families who had been separated by the North-South border. On August 12, 1971, the President of the South Korean Red Cross, Choi Doo-sun, proposed inter-Korean Red Cross talks in Geneva by October of that year, aimed specifically at discussing the separated families issue. Two days later, North Korea welcomed the proposal and suggested that the talks be held in Panmunjom and that preliminary talks be advanced to September. At this time, the real era of inter-Korean dialogue began.[4]

However, because the authorities in both the South and North were under pressure at that time from their allies amid a global atmosphere of détente, they wanted a higher level of contact and dialogue than was afforded by the Red Cross talks, which only had the limited topic of the divided families on the agenda.

While government staff on each side of the border endeavored to sound out and clarify the other's views, the South offered private contacts at the 9th Inter-Korean Red Cross preliminary talks, held on November 19, 1971. The head of the Korean Central Intelligence Agency (KCIA), Chung Hong-jin, who attended the talks as the administrative chief for the South, offered to engage in private discussions with Kim Duk-hyun, the leader of the Central Committee of the [North] Korean Worker's Party. The North cordially accepted the South's offer. Accordingly, the first contact was made in

---

[4] *Historical Documents for Inter-Korean Dialogues*, Book 2: 41-3

the meeting room of the Neutral Nations Supervisory Commission, at Panmunjom, on November 20, 1971.[5]

At this first meeting both sides confirmed their willingness to engage in further private talks. The North proposed, at the second private contact on December 10, that high-level private contacts should be initiated by leading figures of the Korean Worker's Party and Park Chung-hee's Democratic Republican Party and that these private talks should be held by "trusted men from the highest positions." At the third session of talks, held a week later, two people involved openly revealed their identities to each other.[6]

In this way, messengers from the South and the North increased the number of private contacts and, in the process, agreed that high-level political talks would be held between Lee Hu-rak, the Director of the KCIA, and Kim Young-joo, chief of the guidance division of the Korean Worker's Party.

Background

Observing the process of inter-Korean dialogue starting from the autumn of 1971, two questions spring immediately to mind: Why did the Park government, which had consistently characterized the North Korean government as a puppet regime and had insisted that unification follow development, agree so promptly and unexpectedly to the proposals for inter-Korean dialogue? By the same token, why did the North Korean administration, which did not even formally recognize the Park administration and which had repeatedly engaged in anti-South adventurism, including the infiltration of guerrilla forces into the South, also react so positively? The first answer to these questions can be found in international changes that had occurred since the end of the 1960s.

The global situation began to undergo change with the so-called thawing of relations between East and West beginning in the latter part of the 1960s. The Soviet Union and the United States were

---

[5] Ibid., Book 7 (1987b:25).
[6] Ibid., 26-7.

making progress in the Strategic Arms Limitation Talks (SALT); Germany, a divided country, was seeking peaceful coexistence with the communist bloc, as well as improvement in the inter-German relationship. In July 1969, President Nixon announced the "Guam Doctrine," which asserted that Asian countries should be responsible for their own security in the Asian region. That doctrine triggered rapid changes in the Northeast Asian situation and was expanded to include the rest of the world in February of the following year.

In April 1971, the U.S. table tennis team visited China, heralding the opening of détente between the two countries. Taking advantage of this opportunity, Henry Kissinger traveled secretly to China in July. In October, China was admitted to the United Nations and Taiwan was expelled. In February 1972, President Nixon paid his historic visit to China, in the course of which the two leaders confirmed the "One-China Principle."

At that time, the United States was trying to escape from the quagmire of the Vietnam War. At the same time, China, because ideological and military tensions with the Soviet Union were worsening, needed a device for checking the Soviet Union while trying to recover from the domestic turmoil in the aftermath of the Cultural Revolution. Because the United States and China thus shared common interests, a thaw in their relationship was generated.

Meanwhile, during these shifts in the global situation, U.S. policy toward the Korean peninsula also began to change. The United States announced a plan to reduce the number of troops stationed in South Korea, and in fact, the 7th Division of the U.S. Army left the peninsula in March 1971. In such circumstances, the United States could not avoid being concerned about the possibility of a sudden untoward event endangering the Nixon Doctrine and the thawing process, which was underway in Northeast Asia. Against this backdrop, the United States was thought to have strongly urged the South Korean government to begin dialogue with the North.

In fact, the South, in concert with the United States, was considered to have orchestrated in advance the confidential inter-Korean contacts and Lee Hu-rak's visit to the North. The collection of historical documents concerning the dialogues suggests that Lee Hu-rak met with John Richardson, the head of the Seoul branch of the American CIA, on April 18 and 25, 1972. In a personal conversation, Richardson appraised the inter-Korean dialogues as a positive sign and was said to be encouraged by Lee's visit to the North. Just after the announcement of the South-North joint communiqué, U.S. State Department spokesman Charles Bray issued a statement welcoming the communiqué as "most encouraging news." He added that the United States had played no role in reaching the agreement between South and North and expressed gratitude that the South Korean government had notified the U.S. government of the South-North negotiations (*Chosun Ilbo*, July 5, 1972). This demonstrates the extent of U.S. interest in inter-Korean negotiations.

China, an ally of the North, may have also thought that inter-Korean dialogue would be beneficial to China's interests on the Korean peninsula, the tensest area in Northeast Asia. Such a preference could have been transmitted easily to the North because the North Korea-China relations that had worsened because of the Cultural Revolution were in the process of improving after the end of 1969.

The South was scarcely feeling the necessity for inter-Korean dialogue because it was achieving rapid economic growth under the U.S. security umbrella. However, the North was different. The North was thought to have needed dialogue to "relieve anxiety on the part of the U.S. and the South's leaders, who were worried about the perceived power vacuum that might have been caused by the withdrawal of U.S. troops from the peninsula. At home, the North had achieved relatively poor economic development and suffered from constrained internal resources because of military adventurism that had extended into the late 1960s. Against this backdrop and to overcome these obstacles to economic growth, the North needed an easing of tensions, external aid for economic development, and a transfer of military expenditure into the economic sector. For this, it required inter-Korean dialogue.

As was widely known, North Korea had been engaged in an armaments race in the 1960s. From the early to mid-1960s it strengthened its military power. From the global standpoint, the confrontation over Cuba in 1962 had had an enormous impact on the North, because its circumstances bore close similarities to those of Cuba. The North judged that a comparable situation could occur on the Korean peninsula, noting that the Soviet Union had retreated from placing missiles in Cuba in the face of the hard-line policy of the United States. In other words, it had witnessed the cruel reality that, to avoid global confrontation with the United States, the Soviet Union was prepared to disregard the interests of regional revolutionary forces and adopt a compromise.

Furthermore, the North was feeling increasingly uneasy because of the growing tensions between the Soviet Union and China, with China holding the crucial role of an ally who was supposed to oppose the United States and help the North in an emergency. Amid such a complexity of issues, the military coup in the South, led by Park Chung-hee, took place on May 16, 1961. Subsequently, the normalization of diplomatic relations between South Korea and Japan provided the impetus for establishing political, military, and economic cooperation, thereby linking the United States, Japan, and South Korea. What was worse, the Vietnam War was escalating, and the plan to send South Korean troops there was progressing.

Faced by these external developments, North Korea's leaders initiated a massive armaments build-up. In October 1962, immediately following the Cuban missile crisis, the North Korean government started building up its military power in earnest. Because of a serious confrontation with the Soviet Union, the North was unable to obtain the military or economic assistance that had previously been available, a factor that forced the North to greatly increase its own defense budget, even though Kim Il-sung knew that such large increases in the defense budgets were sure to delay economic development.[7] In the end, the military build-up led to military adventurism, such as the sending of armed guerrillas to the South in 1968, as previously mentioned.

---

[7] Kim Il-sung, *Rodong Shinmun*, October 6, 1966.

The crucial point to note from all these machinations is that after the mid-1960s, the North succeeded in building up its military power but failed to achieve simultaneous economic development, its other goal. It has become clear that the North Korean economy would have disintegrated if the military adventurism had continued. The global situation converted confrontation into negotiation from the late 1960s onward, and a real mood favoring the thawing of relations took hold from the start of the 1970s. Such global changes and internal conditions led the North to modify its existing military orientation and embark on inter-Korean dialogue.

III. CHANGES IN THE GLOBAL SITUATION AND THE RESPONSE OF THE TWO LEADERS

It is of considerable interest to assess how Park Chung-hee and Kim Il-sung each coped with the spirit of détente that was sweeping through Northeast Asia in the early 1970s. The answer to this question may give an important clue to the establishment of the Yushin system, insofar as inter-Korean relations traditionally had an important impact on domestic politics.

The ways in which Park Chung-hee and Kim Il-sung responded to shifts in the global situation in the early 1970s stand out in sharp contrast. Kim Il-sung tackled changes in the world situation proactively and began to manage affairs in close cooperation with China. In particular, because the withdrawal of U.S. troops from the Korean peninsula was something that he had long dreamed of, Kim needed an active peace movement to maintain the mood. Taking a very different stance, Park Chung-hee was passive about coping with international changes and became obsessed by a sense of isolation and crisis caused by a perceived failure to cooperate closely with the United States. This sense of crisis resulted ultimately in the reinforcement of South Korean security measures and national mobilization, which, in turn, led to the consolidation of his dictatorship.

Kim Il-sung's Proactive Efforts

Kim Il-sung's positive response to the easing of international tensions may have been based on a sense of the superiority of the North Korean system over the regime in the South. This comparison would likely have included many factors, but especially those connected with economic and military power. Together with this superior attitude, the self-confidence Kim felt from having total control of the North Korean system may well have played some part in his proactive efforts. In addition, the global thaw and the almost simultaneous normalization of North Korea-China relations, which, up to that point, had been very strained, encouraged him to redouble his efforts.

Kim Il-sung's relations with China had been under serious strain largely because of the issues of assistance in the Vietnam War and the Cultural Revolution in China. In 1965, to cope with the escalating conflict in Vietnam, the Soviet Union proposed that leaders of socialist states, including the Soviet Union, China, and North Vietnam, should work together to achieve a coordinated socialist bloc. Leading Chinese figures refused to accept this offer on the pretext of the "revised attitude" of the Communist Party in the Soviet Union. However, North Korea, as part of a divided nation that was in a situation similar to that of Vietnam, took the standpoint that the world's progressive groups should join hands together to develop collective countermeasures concerning the Vietnam War.

China condemned the North Korean position, claiming it to be "opportunism, middle-of-the-roadism, and eclecticism,"[8] and tried to force North Korea to accept the Chinese position. North Korea refused China's demands, proclaimed its own ideology of "self-reliance," and attacked the dogmatic attitude of the Chinese Communist Party.[9]

These major differences of opinion drove the two countries into a seriously antagonistic relationship. When China accused Kim Il-sung of being a revisionist, the North responded by criticizing China

---

[8] Ibid.
[9] Editorial, *Rodong Shinmun*, August 12, 1966.

as doctrinaire and sectarian. Tension between the two reached its height in 1967-68, but the diplomatic climate began to warm in the autumn of 1969. Kim Il-sung, who had last visited China in November 1964, visited privately each year from 1970 to 1973 and sought a joint strategy with Mao Tse-tung and Chou En-lai amid the rapidly shifting global situation.

For its part, China did not want to continue the bickering with North Korea any longer and so took a positive attitude toward restoring its symbiotic relations. Indeed, China needed joint cooperation with North Korea to set up a new order for Northeast Asia, including the improvement of U.S.-China relations. Furthermore, China was engaged in a troublesome boundary dispute with the Soviet Union in 1969. Accordingly, the Chinese leadership dispatched a delegation, led by Chou En-lai, to Pyongyang in April 1970, aimed at demonstrating that good relations with the North had been restored. Responding to the visit, Kim Il-sung traveled to China privately and met Mao Tse-tung on October 8-10, 1970, his first such visit since 1964. At this meeting, where North Korea and China agreed on a compromise, Mao withdrew his criticisms of Kim Il-sung, made during the Cultural Revolution and criticized himself, saying that during the Cultural Revolution ultra-leftists had made mistakes in their methods.[10]

North Korea and China pulled together during the early stages of improvement in U.S.-China relations and began to link this cooperation with inter-Korean matters. Before the announcement of the July 4 North-South Joint Communiqué in 1971, China sent Chou En-lai to Pyongyang to explain to Kim Il-sung about National Security Advisor Henry Kissinger's private visit to Beijing and the agreement concerning President Nixon's visit to China.[11] Chou emphasized that China had insisted on maintaining its stance, had stuck to its principles, and pinned its hopes on the American people (Wang 1999:40). Kim responded by saying that he supported China,

---

[10] China Central Research Institute for Documents, *Chronological Record of Chou En-lai 1949-1976*, Vol. 2.

[11] Chou En-Lai visited Vietnam, for the same purpose, before visiting North Korea.

but that the Korean Workers' Party would need to educate the North Korean population because Nixon's visit to China posed new problems for his country.

In fact, Nixon's visit to China, as well as Chou and Kissinger's meeting, perplexed the ruling circles in the North, largely because the North Korean people had been taught to regard the United States as a perpetual enemy, and the leadership was now at something of a loss as to how to explain the change. Furthermore, the North was deeply concerned lest China abandon its anti-imperialist stance. A policy decision was made that involved the drawing up of a list of suggestions, which were presented to Chou En-lai by First Deputy Prime Minister Kim Il at a meeting in Beijing on July 30. At this meeting, Kim Il made it clear that the Political Committee of the Korean Workers' Party had discussed Nixon's visit to China very seriously, that all political members fully understood China's invitation to Nixon and the Chou-Kissinger meeting, that these circumstances were favorable for the world revolution, and that there was no change in China's anti-imperialist line or any variance in the North's belief in China's intentions (Wang 1999:40).

At the same time, Kim Il produced a list of the following demands that it wanted China to hand to the United States at their meeting: (1) the complete withdrawal of U.S. troops from South Korea; (2) a complete and immediate withdrawal of the U.S. offer to supply nuclear missiles, nonnuclear missiles, and various other kinds of weaponry to the South; (3) a halt to all encroachment, espionage, and reconnaissance on the part of the United States; (4) a halt to joint military exercises involving South Korea, the United States, and Japan and the disbanding of the U.S.-Korea Allied Force; (5) a guarantee that the United States would not allow the revival of Japanese militarism and would not replace U.S. or foreign troops on the peninsula with Japanese troops; (6) a disbanding of the United Nations Committee for the Unification and Rehabilitation of Korea (UNCURK); (7) a halt to U.S. interference in inter-Korean negotiations; and (8) the U.S. acceptance of the participation of North Korea in all discussions at the UN concerning the two Koreas and the cancellation of any conditions attached to such participation (Wang 1999:40).

Meanwhile, Kim Il-sung stipulated that "Nixon should visit Beijing with a white flag, as if the U.S. aggressors who had failed to win the Korean War had come to Panmunjom with a flag of truce" and that "Nixon's visit to China was the act of a loser, not a winner, and the great victory was that of the Chinese people, as well as the victory of revolutionary people throughout the world."[12] Concerning Nixon's visit to China, though, Kim made it clear that he "was not thinking that he should change foreign policy much," but that "foreign policy could change, according to changes in the global situation."[13] Contrary to its previously held position, North Korea suggested unconditional inter-Korean dialogue.

Henry Kissinger's second visit to Beijing to discuss Nixon's visit to China was held from October 20-26, 1971.[14] At this meeting, both countries exchanged opinions about issues concerning Taiwan and the Korean peninsula, and Chou En-lai delivered North Korea's eight demands to the United States, to which Kissinger made no response (Wang 1999:40).

Kim Il-sung was in a hurry to hear the results of the meeting, and he also wanted to discuss the improvement of foreign relations and the issue of inter-Korean dialogue, because China's admission to the United Nations would soon be accomplished. Accordingly, Kim visited Beijing privately on November 1-3, 1971 and listened while Mao and Chou relayed the substance of the confidential meeting and the U.S. reaction to North Korea's demands.[15]

On January 26, 1972, the Second Deputy Prime Minister of North Korea, Park Sung-chul, visited Beijing and had talks with Chou En-lai and Lee Shen-nan.[16] The particulars deliberated on during

[12] *The Works of Kim Il-sung*, Book 26: 225.
[13] Ibid., Book 26: 306.
[14] *Chronological Record of Chou En-Lai 1949-1976*, Vol. 2, 490-91; *Donga Ilbo*, October 25, 1971.
[15] Ibid., 493.
[16] Ibid., 511.

these talks are not known, but both sides were, after all, supposed to be aligning their positions vis-à-vis the Korean peninsula in advance of Nixon's impending visit to China and the subsequent summit talks. The Chinese position on the issue of the Korean peninsula, announced in a joint communiqué issued after the summit talks, was certainly thought to derive from discussions with the North.

From March 7-9, immediately after the communiqué spelled out the results of Nixon's visit to China, Chou En-lai visited Pyongyang to discuss the summit talks with Kim Il-sung.[17] At the meeting, Chou informed Kim of Nixon's tacit agreement, albeit not reflected in the joint communiqué, that the United States would not tolerate Japan's entry into Taiwan or into South Korea. This affirmation by the American president appeared to provide a full answer to Article 5 of the eight demands that Kim Il had taken to China before the summit. Chou also confirmed that, in regard to the article that specified that no country shall negotiate for a third country, China had explained to the United States that "this article shall apply to the Korean peninsula" and that "China was the friend of North Korea" (Wang 1999: 40).

Kim Il-sung thanked China for its special concern over the issue of the Korean peninsula, and 20 days after the summit talks, inter-Korean private contacts developed further, with the result that Chung Hong-in secretly visited North Korea.

Meanwhile, Kim Il-sung devised both a justification and a theory to rationalize the events that had occurred. First, to justify the dialogues with the Park Chung-hee administration, the North Korean leader addressed the frequency of the usage of the word "independence" in the South. At the first meeting with Chung Hong-in, Kim Duk-hyun asked, "Is there a signboard reading 'Independence' in Namdaemun Market?"[18] During a secret visit to North Korea, and in response to Kim Young-ju, who regarded the Park administration as an "agent" of the United States and Japan, Lee Hu-rak emphasized

---

[17] *Chronological Record of Chou En-lai*, Vol. 2, 515.
[18] *Historical Documents for Inter-Korean Dialogues*, Book 7:26. (Namdaemun Market is a very large commercial market in the center of Seoul.)

that the South was adopting an "independent line." Lee explained, "The basic line of the South Korean government is independence, self-reliance, and self-defense" and that "some day the South will not depend on foreign countries."[19] Kim Il-sung noted, "Recently, administrators in the South have emphasized independent reunification, talking of independence, self-reliance, and self-defense. When these words are interpreted in a good sense, they can be thought to show our common idea of independence, self-reliance, and self-defense, to some degree. If we can find common points and develop them one by one, we can reach an agreement to materialize Korean unity."[20]

At that time, the North did not regard the South as being a fully capitalist society. It thought that in the South there were only a few comprador capitalists, not great monopolized capital. The North was against such comprador capitalists but was not against small and medium-sized capitalists.[21] With these few points, the North found a justification and logic for establishing a united front with the "leading circles" of the South and sought inter-Korean dialogue as part of this endeavor.

The North's intentions were plainly shown in the contents of dialogues between Kim Il-sung and the Chinese leadership, as well as in the records of secret inter-Korean dialogues. Kim Young-ju said to KCIA Director Lee Hu-rak that monopoly capitalists did not exist in the South, that an absolute majority of them were "national" capitalists, and that neither President Park nor Lee Hu-rak himself was a capitalist, so they were not "combat targets."[22] From August 22-25, 1972, immediately after the publication of the July 4 North-South joint communiqué, Kim Il-sung visited China privately and exchanged opinions with Chou En-lai. Chou emphasized the application of the "united front" principle, saying, "When we break up with the propertied classes, we are likely to make the mistake of sticking to a leftist line, so we should fight them, not unite with them." He

[19] Ibid., 90.
[20] *Works of Kim Il-sung*, Book 27: 228.
[21] Ibid.
[22] *Historical Documents for Inter-Korean Dialogues*, Book 7: 96.

added, "When we unite with the propertied classes, we are likely to make the mistake of sticking to a rightist line, so we should unite with them, not fight."[23]

North Korea began reinforcing the international united front, focusing on the UN and the nonaligned organizations, and utilizing fully the reduction in global tension from the early 1970s, as well as pursuing the united front in the inter-Korean relationship. These measures were adopted because the global situation was changing and the scope for competing with the South was widening. As a result, the North made moves to mend the relationship with Yugoslavia, a country that North Korea had previously regarded as "revisionist," and took active steps to improve relations with Western capitalist countries. From April to July 1973, it established diplomatic links with northern European countries, such as Sweden, Finland, Norway, Denmark, and Iceland; with Austria and Switzerland in December 1974; and with Portugal in April 1975 (Park Tae-ho 1985:185). During 1972 and 1973, delegations from the Supreme People's Assembly visited Northern Europe for the first time. In the autumn of 1973, the Mansoodae Arts Company acted as a spearhead in the campaign to improve relations by giving performances in Great Britain, Italy, and other countries. The company's first performance was given in France in February 1972 (Park Tae-ho 1985:184). Throughout this period, the North Korean authorities placed advertisements in leading U.S. newspapers, including the *New York Times* and the *Washington Post*, extolling the virtues of Kim Il-sung. Before this flurry of activity, the only Western countries in which North Korea had trade representatives were France and Finland.[24]

The North paid particular attention to setting up relationships with the nongovernmental sector in the United States. It also wanted government-level dialogues with the United States and divulged this desire to the U.S. government through China. However, in considera-

---

[23] *Chronological Record of Chou En-lai*, Vol. 2, 546.
[24] North Korea concluded a trade agreement with France in April 1967 and established a trade representative in Paris in April 1968. A trade agreement was concluded with Finland in October 1969, and a trade representative was sent to Helsinki in the same month.

tion of the relationship with South Korea, the United States did not respond. The Korean Workers' Party published a joint communiqué, with a delegation of the Japanese Socialist Party that visited the North in August 1970, and Kim Il-sung gave interviews to the leading Japanese press, including the *Asahi Shimbun* (September 25, 1971), the *Kyoto Press* (October 8, 1971), and the *Yomiuri Shimbun* (January 10, 1972). In June 1972, delegations from the Chosun Foreign Cultural Exchange Association and Japan's Clean Govern-ance Party also published a communiqué (*Rodong Shinmun*, June 7, 1972).

On May 26, 1972, in an interview with reporter Barry Solz of the *New York Times*, Kim Il-sung insisted that to improve the North Korea-U.S. relationship, the United States should change its "non-friendly" policy that it had assumed in its dealings with the North thus far, a policy that included unwarranted intervention in North Korea's domestic affairs, U.S. troops stationed in South Korea, and assistance in the revival of Japanese militarism. In addition, Kim emphasized that the United States should keep its promise to support inter-Korean contacts, as had been announced in the U.S.-China joint communiqué (*Rodong Shinmun*, June 2, 1972).

Park Chung-hee's Mounting Anxiety

Unlike Kim Il-sung, Park Chung-hee faced the thawing international mood with mounting feelings of alienation and anxiety. He had to accept a new international environment and reconciliation with the communist bloc under circumstances in which the South was inferior to the North both militarily and economically. He also had to begin negotiations with North Korea from a somewhat inconsistent position insofar as the South regarded anti-communism as the national policy, both domestically and diplomatically. Furthermore, Park's political status was considerably less stable than that of Kim Il-sung.

However, more than anything else, the perceived inhospitable treatment by the United States made the South Korean president uneasy. Although Kim Il-sung occasionally met privately with Chinese leaders and talked over the world situation and inter-Korean relations, Park Chung-hee was viewing an immediate future dominated by the potential withdrawal of U.S. troops from his country. The Park administration was not notified of the secret visit of Henry Kissinger, ahead of Nixon's visit to China, before its public announcement. It was only afterward, in March 1972, that Secretary of State Rogers reported the event to the South Korean Ambassador to the United States (Oberdorfer 1998:29-30). It is not difficult to guess the extent to which Park Chung-hee felt estranged from the United States when he considered that Prime Minister Chou En-Lai visited Pyongyang twice and Kim Il-sung visited Beijing once, as did First Deputy Prime Minister Kim Il and Deputy Prime Minister Park Sung-Chul.

In fact, it is known that Park felt considerable unease because of the improved U.S.-China relationship, and the United States appeared to do little to relieve the discomfort. For example, U.S. Vice President Spiro Agnew promised Park Chung-hee that the United States would not reduce its troop numbers by more than 20,000. However, soon after giving that assurance, Agnew told U.S. reporters on an airplane taking them from Seoul to Taiwan, "Maybe after five years, when full modernization of the South Korean military has been realized, U.S. troops stationed in the South would withdraw entirely" (Kim Chong-ryom 1997:29).

Park was also deeply concerned about the position and role of China. Scrutiny of the content of many of his 1960s speeches makes it clear that he considered both China and North Korea enemies capable of causing similar levels of direct intimidation; he said, for example, "The North might re-attack the South at any time at the instigation of China"[25] and "the North Korean puppet regime and China" stood face to face against the South.[26] The reinforcement of national security and enhanced political power were what Park wanted most to achieve as he faced the changing world situation, and to achieve those ends he used a combination of strategies: first, accelerating the reinforcement of the South Korean military capabil-

[25] Park Chung-hee, 18 December 1965, Electronics Library.
[26] Park Chung-hee, 19 July 1968, Electronics Library.

ity, and second, strengthening the authoritarian nature of his administration on the dual pretext of national defense and reunification.

On the issue of national defense, Park's major concern was the proposed withdrawal of U.S. troops from the peninsula before the South had secured an adequate and appropriate self-defense capability. He met with U.S Vice President Agnew in July 1970 after two divisions of South Korean troops had already been dispatched to Vietnam and won promises concerning the modernization of South Korean military equipment, long-term military assistance, and the U.S. withdrawal of no more than 20,000 troops. Both countries continued military and diplomatic negotiations aimed at realizing these promises until mid-January 1971, and one of the outcomes was the U.S. government's agreement to provide $1.5 billion of assistance for the "five-year-term modernization of South Korean forces."[27] This grant aid was later converted to credit assistance.[28]

One of the major crises of the Park Chung-hee regime stemmed from the secret amendment to the South Korean Constitution enabling the President to remain in office for a third term. In the April 27, 1971 presidential election after the amendment had been enacted, Park defeated the opposition candidate Kim Dae-jung by a relatively narrow margin. His victory was greatly facilitated by the use, or misuse, of state power and by the application of financial influence. In the general election held the following month, Park's Democratic Republican Party won only 113 seats, well below two-thirds of the total, the quorum for a Constitutional amendment. The main opposition New Democratic Party practically swept the board in the major cities of Seoul, Pusan, and Taegu and captured 89 seats.

Directly after the elections, during the second half of 1971, a series of events occurred that jeopardized the Park government. In August of that year, a protest against government policy took place in a massive housing complex in Kwangju city, and a riot by market traders opposed to taxation measures followed shortly afterward. As university campuses began their second semester of the year, the

---

[27] Oh Won-chul, *Shindonga*, June 1995, 482.
[28] Sun Woo-hui, *Monthly Chosun*, March 1993, 176.

voices of students protesting against compulsory military exercises became louder, and the focus of their demonstrations soon widened to include demands for a cessation of state irregularities and corruption. In the meantime, the bill of disposition against the Minister of Home Affairs, Oh Chi-sung, instigated by the opposition New Democratic Party, was passed with the aid of "insubordination votes" cast from within the ruling Democratic Republican Party. To cope with the series of emergencies, Park Chung-hee invoked the Garrison Act around universities in October 1971 and took harsh measures against those in his party whom he deemed guilty of insubordination.

The crises were not easily overcome, however, largely because they were of a structural origin and could only be resolved fully by the realization of democratic and economic justice. Unfortunately, both for himself and for South Korea, Park Chung-hee was not inclined toward either democracy or justice. Instead, he declared a State of National Emergency on December 6, 1971, citing national security issues as the justification for such a drastic step; this was a ruse he would use on numerous occasions. His announcement stipulated that the situation represented "quasi-wartime conditions" and insisted, "I must protect the Republic of Korea." It was a phrase taken directly from the presidential oath of office, as written in the Constitution. "After watching over the trend of North Korea to favor the invasion of South Korea, the government came to conclude that the Republic of Korea was now in an acute phase in terms of national security," wrote Park Hankook Ilbo on December 7, 1971.

In summary, the December declaration of a State of National Emergency and the July South-North joint communiqué had far different characteristics and were, to all intents and purposes, mutually exclusive. Park Chung-hee was getting support from the United States and moving forward with secret inter-Korean negotiations while inflicting terror on the South Korean population in the name of anti-communism. However, this apparent anomaly did not pose a serious problem for Park who, it is suggested, had never conceived of coexistence with the North from the outset.

IV. SOUTH-NORTH JOINT COMMUNIQUÉ AND THE YUSHIN REGIME

The preparation process

At 10 a.m. on July 4, 1972, huge numbers of South Korean people gathered around their radios and televisions as a result of the government's announcement that a broadcast was to be made about a vital matter. Journalists from the *Washington Post* believed firmly that the announcement would be a scoop and kept the front page of the newspaper open. The chief of the Korean Central Intelligence Agency (KCIA) Lee Hu-rak began the announcement by saying, "I have been to Pyongyang." This came as a great shock to most listeners, but the surprise turned to excitement and delight as the broadcast progressed and the South Korean people realized that 27 years of misunderstanding and distrust could be coming to an end and they became aware that there was a distinct possibility of a peaceful reunification with North Korea.

The communiqué, which was agreed to by Lee Hu-rak and Kim Young-ju, Director of the Organizing and Guidance Division of the North Korean Worker's Party, was released simultaneously in Seoul and Pyongyang. It included the proclamation of "unification principles," such as independent and peaceful reunification and racial unity, both of which concept extended beyond the confines of political system and ideology; the end of mutual provocation; the enforcement of inter-Korean exchanges in many fields; and the early implementation of inter-Korean Red Cross talks based on the reuniting of divided families. Lee Hu-rak announced that a South-North Coordinating Committee, co-chaired by himself and Kim Young-ju, would be established and given the task of resolving all the issues connected with reunification and addressing all the diverse problems that had existed for so long between the South and the North (*Joongang Ilbo*, July 5, 1972).

As can be readily appreciated, the implications of the communiqué meant a 180-degree reversal in inter-Korean relationships, which had been so dominated by tension and confrontation. The establishment of the South-North Coordinating Committee was the core of the communiqué, and although some hardliners in the South expressed dissatisfaction, most citizens welcomed the news and felt genuinely hopeful that the day of reunification would arrive in the not-too-distant future.

However, although welcoming the unexpected turn of international events, many among the South Korean population were confused by the apparent contradiction implicit in the Park regime's position. The joint communiqué announcing imminent reconciliation with the North was wonderful news. Yet, barely 6 months previously, in December 1971, Park Chung-hee had ignored the Constitution under the pretext of the necessity to prepare for an invasion from the North, declared a State of National Emergency, and put in place the pernicious National Security Law. In an effort to assuage public uncertainty, Lee Hu-rak invented the following bizarre theory:

> No-one can deny that the North would hold a 60th birthday banquet in Seoul for Kim Il-sung this year, as it has talked about for a long time, had it not been for the declaration of a State of National Emergency at the end of last year. However, six months after the proclamation, we have consolidated national security. Facing each other across the demilitarized zone, the South and the North are trying to enhance their defense power against each other. So tensions are mounting. The government perceives intuitively that inter-Korean relations have been strained to a breaking point (*Joongang Ilbo*, July 5, 1972).

His words can be taken to mean that the Park administration succeeded in preventing the North from attacking the South, thanks to the imposition of the State of National Emergency at the end of 1971. However, more tension mounted between the two countries a few months later, so a strategy of the likes of the joint communiqué was needed to prevent a war. In other words, 6 months earlier Park Chung-hee adopted one strategy in preparation for the North's attack and was now adopting a virtually diametrically opposed policy to achieve the same end.

Meanwhile, the inter-Korean secret dialogues based on the joint communiqué progressed, including reciprocal visits completed by the end of March 1972, immediately after Nixon's visit to China. On March 7, at the fifth secret meeting, Chung Hong-jin suggested that Lee Hu-rak and Kim Young-ju should be jointly responsible for arranging secret contacts between high-ranking officials from each side; the North Korean representative accepted this offer at the next secret meeting, on March 10.[29] Both sides agreed that high-ranking figures, trusted by Lee and Kim, would make reciprocal visits to Pyongyang and Seoul. Accordingly, Chung Hong-jin informed the North at the seventh secret contact that Jang Gi-young would carry the credentials of Lee Hu-rak and visit North Korea.

On May 2, 1972, Lee Hu-rak accompanied Jung Hong-jin and traveled to Pyongyang for a 4-day, 3-night visit. Interestingly, Lee took with him a vial of poison that he intended to administer to himself should any "unexpected event" occur. However, he was received with warmth by the leading figures he encountered. He had two meetings with Kim Il-sung, at which both men confirmed that the South accepted the imperative to "drive out foreign powers" and the North promised to "give up attacking the South."

Second Deputy Prime Minister Park Sung-chul visited Seoul on May 29 in place of Kim Young-ju, who was said to be suffering from "a rare nervous disorder." During his stay he agreed on the details on the formation of the South-North Coordinating Committee and paid a courtesy visit to Park Chung-hee in the Blue House. It was at this stage that both sides finally reached agreement on the preparation of the July 4 Joint Communiqué and the establishment of the Coordinating Committee as an executive institution.

The Birth of "Antagonistic Twins"

Broadcast of the July 4 South-North Joint Communiqué imbued the South Korean populace with a great feeling of anticipation for peace and unification on the Korean peninsula. However, the practical

---

[29] *Historical Documents for Inter-Korean Dialogues*, Book 7: 31-3.

effect of the announcement was less clear because it took place at a time when inter-Korean trust was noticeable by its absence and when domestic conditions in the South remained uncertain. In fact, immediately after the broadcast, contradictory events started to occur across the country. One citizen, excited after listening to the communiqué in the street, was arrested on the charge of saying, "Who will arrest me if I shout 'Long live Kim Il-sung!'?" (*Chosun Ilbo*, July 6, 1972). On July 5, Prime Minister Kim Chong-pil denied the principle of Article 1 in the communiqué by saying, "The July 4 South-North Joint Communiqué does not mean coexistence with North Korea." Kim Gyu-nam, who was involved in a case involving secret agents based in Europe, was executed on July 13, despite widespread expectation that his execution might be postponed because of the communiqué. Park No-su, who had studied at Cambridge University in England, was also executed, on July 28. In addition, it was known that about 30 "political offenders" were executed just before and just after the communiqué was broadcast.

One fact is clear, however. The Park administration had achieved at least one goal by means of the joint communiqué: The political crisis had been circumvented. What was needed then for Park to grasp lifelong political power was to enlarge on the concept of "preparation for the era of unification" and to make it real. With this objective in mind, he devised a political concept new to the Korean peninsula, the Yushin system, by skillfully combining South Korean society's wariness about the North, the spirit of anti-communism that he had been largely responsible for nurturing, and the natural desire of the Korean people for the reestablishment of a once-unified country. He chose as his "D-Day" October 17, 1972. On this date all constitutional functions were terminated and the following special statement was issued:

> Irresponsible political parties have betrayed a national mission, and the parliamentary system has also fallen victim to political tactics. In this situation, who can trust that they will achieve peaceful unification, the dearest wish of Korean people, and will hold inter-Korean dialogues?...Our Constitution, various kinds of laws, and the existing system were made in the Cold War era, un-

der the influence of both East and West. More than ever before, under these changing circumstances we need a revitalizing reform in order to adapt ourselves to these changing circumstances (*Donga Ilbo*, October 18, 1972).

In the formulation of Yushin, Park used the notion of preparation for reunification to an excessive degree. Indeed, he actually used the word "unification" 18 times in his initial statement (*Donga Ilbo*, October 19, 1972). Subsequently, he set up all kinds of unification-related, government-controlled organizations, including the National Congress for Unification and Independence. In addition, Park positioned military personnel within the major institutions of the government, asking them for "wisdom and impregnable solidarity." So Yushin was created, and President Park Chung-hee had grasped lifelong political power.

There have been many debates on the details of the Yushin system's genesis, but all of them emphasize its linkage to the division of the peninsula. People who served close to Park generally recollect the impact of the inter-Korean dialogues, and Kim Chung-ryum, who was then Chief Secretary to the President, identified the process of the Red Cross talks as the deciding factor that persuaded Park of the necessity for Yushin:

> When the North Korean delegation visited Seoul for preliminary talks, the South Korean delegates and other people of the South who were invited to dinner all expressed their feelings frankly but presented different opinions, whereas all the North Korean people spoke with the same voice....hen the North Korean delegation arrived in Seoul, some people welcomed them, some people were uneasy, and some people were very alert. Public sentiment in the South was thrown into confusion. President Park Chung-hee also saw that North Korean Deputy Prime Minister Park Sung-chul spoke from notes written in his pocketbook, and felt how strong the one-man system of rule in the North was (Kim Chong-ryom 1997:166-7).

In these circumstances, "the central government proposed the necessity for a political system to drive inter-Korean dialogues and negotiations to our advantage, we need internal unity, and to strengthen internal unity we must consolidate the political system. Park agreed with Lee Hu-rak on this suggestion" (Kim Chong-ryom 1997:168). Kim Chong-ryom also remembered that Park gave instructions to prepare for the Yushin reforms immediately after either Chung Hong-jin or Lee Hu-rak returned from the North, in April or May of 1972 (Kim Chong-ryom 1997:377). Judging from these factors, it can be concluded that although absolute, lifetime rule had long been a goal for Park Chung-hee, the materialization of the Yushin system, which would facilitate its achievement, was much influenced, if not actually triggered, by the intricacies of the inter-Korean relationship. In his Presidential Message on Armed Forces Day in October 1974, Park noted, "The [Yushin] system was to defend our freedom from communist aggressors," and he insisted further, "For greater freedom, we should sacrifice temporarily a little of our freedom."

Previously, in December 1972, both the South and the North had "modified" their existing Constitutions; with each revised national system effectively guaranteeing one-man, absolute rule. The Yushin system in the South and the one-man dictatorship system in the North were thus created. It is important to recognize, however, that the two systems were based on fundamentally incompatible and antagonistic systems: capitalism and socialism. Accordingly, there are radical differences between the basic tenets of the two systems and between their formation processes: Yushin emerged from a societal atmosphere colored by the sudden application of state oppression, and the North's one-man dictatorship system was formed much earlier, during the socially and culturally distorted period of 1967.[30] In other words, the realization of the Yushin Constitution in the South heralded the birth of the Yushin system, whereas the enactment of a new Constitution in the North meant the completion of the one-man dictatorship system. One characteristic quite clearly shared by the two systems, however, is that they were both unequivocally despotic.

It is a far from inconsequential matter when dictatorships appear, in concert, in neighboring countries under symmetric yet incompati-

---

[30] See Lee Chong-sok (1995b: 296-315).

ble systems. Yet, despite the enormous societal impact of these events, the general public, particularly in South Korea, did not raise their voices in protest at the prospect of the unremitting repression signaled by the Yushin "coup in office."

To examine this lack of protest, it is necessary to return, yet again, to the overarching issue of the physical, geographical division of the Korean peninsula. It can be said that the South made the best of the division from a purely defensive perspective, whereas the North appeared to focus more on an offensive posture. The threat of invasion from the North was certainly used to its fullest by the Park Chung-hee regime to facilitate social mobilization and validate its authority. In particular, such events as the North-led creation of the Unification and Revolution Party in the South and the series of armed guerrilla infiltrations into South Korea in 1968 had a significant impact on South Korean society. State authorities in the South made the most of these occurrences and succeeded in generating a social atmosphere conducive to the acceptance even of violent authority in the face of the perceived threat from the North.

For example, South Korean society entered into a period of mobilization on April 1, 1968 with the formation of local reserve forces, introduced to counter the "provocative military adventurism of the North," as described by the Park authorities. On the basis of the January 21 Red guerrilla Infiltration and the hijacking of the USS Pueblo, the South Korean government sought to establish the need for this civil defense system manned by local reserve personnel. From a political and social standpoint, such measures exceeded mere military or national defense needs and can be regarded instead as important indicators of a social mobilization imperative. In addition to the inception of this local reserve force element, the Park administration introduced compulsory military training for senior high-school and university students in March 1969. Before this, in December 1968, the government had declared the National Charter of Education, a euphemism for the mobilization of public thought.

In the midst of this mass mobilization, Park Chung-hee proclaimed a State of National Emergency as a means of escaping from the December 1971 administration crisis. Unlike in the mid-1960s, however, when the general public had some degree of democratic sensibility and was able to offer some resistance to state injustice, the South Korean people were now in a predominantly passive state and adapted themselves to the new circumstances. There lies a clue to why it was difficult for the great mass of the population in the South to resist the October Yushin.

The unprecedented silence in the North with regard to the political situation in the South can be interpreted as underlining the connection between the position of Kim Il-sung and the inception of the Yushin system. In other words, the Yushin Constitution, in its prescription of the conditions for absolute rule by one man, had clear resonance with the head of state system in the North. In this regard, December 27, 1972 can reasonably be regarded as the "birthday of antagonistic twins": the date of the creation of the Yushin and the one-man dictatorship systems.

V. MIRROR IMAGE EFFECTS: NORTH KOREAN ELEMENTS ABSORBED BY THE YUSHIN SYSTEM

The division structure thus greatly affected the birth of the Yushin System. In the sudden global thawing of the Cold War, Park Chung-hee tried to strengthen his defensive power and mobilize a social system for the survival of the country. Using the circumstances of division, he laid the foundation for the Yushin system, sometimes through the theory of national security reinforcement and sometimes through unification-oriented words. The division structure itself enabled Park to materialize his subjective intention for absolute power. Furthermore, division of the Korean Peninsula had an important impact on the economic structure that the Yushin system pursued; namely, creating the defense industry and the heavy and chemical industries. The Park Administration pushed ahead, enabling the defense industry to attain self-reliance in preparation for the withdrawal of the U.S. Seventh Division stationed in South Korea and for détente. Park thought that the South needed its own power to cope with potential invasion from the North. To realize these policies, he chose to simultaneously cultivate the defense industry and the heavy and chemical industries needed to support the defense industry in the second defense industry meeting held in October 1972. (Kim Chong-ryom 1997:289)

According to Kim Chong-ryom, the cultivation of the heavy and chemical industries was initially not included in a 5-year economic development plan, but amid a fast-changing situation, it was pushed forward as a means to achieve self-defense capabilities and to overwhelm "the industrial power of the North, particularly, the heavy and chemical industries." Because the Park Administration judged that the South lagged behind the North in terms of heavy and chemical industries, it regarded this plan as a way to "secure superiority in all aspects and fundamentally stop the North from provoking a war" (Kim Chong-ryom 1997:289). In addition, this plan had another security justification: "The U.S. will not give up the heavy and chemical country in any case."[31]

Meanwhile, the division structure caused both the South and North to engage in antagonistic competition and to become similar in many respects through the mirror image effect. In the 1970s, both regimes established mobilization systems that were identical to a wartime mobilization system and strongly asserted an independent line against foreign countries. So many slogans they shouted sounded very similar.

In particular, as an illustration of this mirror image effect, the Yushin system that keenly competed with the one-man dictatorship adopted characteristics of the North as its own. From the late 1960s, the Park Administration started frequently using such terms as independence, self-support, self-defense, identity, defense and economic development — words that the North Korean government had enjoyed using in the 1960s. After the formation of the Yushin system, these words were generalized and used even more frequently.

In 1968, the slogan, "While Working, Fight and Work, While Fighting" had been advocated; this led to the governing indicator of the government that meant defense on one side, construction on the

---

[31] "The True History of the Blue House, "Kim Jung-Ryum, *Monthly Chosun*, May 1991, 397

other side: "Defense and economy are different in words but are identical in meaning. If defense goes well, economic development comes out well. If construction goes well, defense power becomes stronger. Now, it's time that we should reinforce wealth and military power" (*Donga Ilbo*, April, 12, 1971). The slogan, "The line of advancing defense and construction together," which the North had coined and advocated from 1962, appeared in the South as well.

In 1969, Park Chung-hee stipulated "defense on one side, construction on the other side and the attainment of self-reliant defense and self-supporting economy as the highest task and goal that we should achieve today." [32] The first and foremost reason why he emphasized a self-supporting economy and self-reliant defense was to reinforce and build up the power of absolute superiority over the North's. [33] Even when entering the 1970s, he continuously focused on "the intention of independence and self-support and endeavors of self-help and self-defense." [34] In particular, he always talked about "self-defense, independence, and self-help," which became the slogan of the Saemaul (New Village) Movement.

The emphasis on independence that Kim Il-Sung had used as an heirloom sword was also used by Park Chung-hee, but only partially. Park was very disappointed because the United States took a negotiation stance with the North against his will concerning the capture of the USS Pueblo. Afterward, he emphasized "the independence of national defense" by saying that "we must not expect that others can defend us for us." [35] He emphasized self-reliant defense, encouraged servicemen to "defend our country by and for ourselves," and advocated "the establishment of independent capabilities and

---

[32] Presidential Message of Park Chung-hee on Armed Forces Day, October 1, 1969, Digital Library, National Defense/Sayings.

[33] Park Chung-hee, Export Promotion Meeting of Diplomatic Offices in Foreign Countries by Region, February 9, 1970, Digital Library, Industry & Economy/Sayings.

[34] Park Chung-hee, Message to Brothers & Sisters Abroad, January 1, 1970, Digital Library, Politics & Diplomacy/Sayings.

[35] Park Chung-hee, Graduation Address in Seoul National University, February 26, 1968, Digital Library, National Defense/Sayings.

independence."[36] As the North emphasized thoughts, he stressed "national mental power" against the North. He also stressed independence and autonomy, by saying that the South would be a castle in the air without the spirit of thorough independence and the spirit of racial independence (*Donga Ilbo*, April 12, 1971).

In this regard, Park established the Yushin system by confronting the North and regarding it as a good target. Consequently, the system did not transcend the character of an antagonistic twin and started looking like the North Korean system. Strategies and measures that the South drove forward and carried out to surpass the North began resembling those of the North in the end. Based on this similarity, this system and the division structure, which can be explained by antagonistic dependent relations and the mirror image effect, had a special causal relationship.

[36] Presidential Message of Park Chung-hee on the Graduation Day of National Defense College in 1970 and the 14th Graduation Day of the Joint Forces Staff College, July 23, 1970, Digital Library, National Defense/Sayings.

Chapter 9

South Korea and the Vietnam War

Han Hong-koo

I. INTRODUCTION

The Korean War (1950-53) is regarded by most Americans as the "forgotten war," whereas for most South Koreans it is the Vietnam War (1964-73) that merits that soubriquet. The Vietnam War was indeed a forgotten war for Korea, at least in part because it took place far from home and because South Vietnam, the side supported by the Army of the Republic of Korea (ROKA), eventually fell. It was also forgotten despite the huge cost it represented to the nation. Park Chung-hee, who was the Korean president throughout the war, deployed a total of 320,000 Korean soldiers, 50,000 of whom were permanently garrisoned in Vietnam: This manpower commitment was second only to that of the United States itself. The involvement, during which ROKA suffered 5,000 dead and 10,000 wounded, would have remained largely forgotten in Korea had it not been for articles published in the autumn of 1999 in the magazine *Hankyoreh21*, reporting details of a massacre of Vietnamese civilians allegedly committed by South Korean soldiers.

The collective amnesia concerning Vietnam may have begun when South Korea first started sending troops there. Neither the fact nor the nature of the deployment was seriously questioned by most Koreans, even as tens of thousands of young men were being shipped to the distant combat area. Instead, the Park Chung-hee propaganda machine succeeded in effectively brainwashing the population into believing that Korea was a peace-loving nation that would never invade another country. The paradox is that, regardless of the collective amnesia, the Vietnam experience has left an indelible mark on South Korea and has had a significant effect on its subsequent history.

During the 9 years of ROKA participation in Vietnam, from September 1964, when Mobile Army Surgical Hospital (MASH) units and a Taekwondo instructor unit were deployed, to March 1973, when the last troops left Vietnam, many important changes took place on the Korean peninsula. Those changes included the strengthened military ties between South Korea and the United States, evidenced by the commitment of Korean forces to Vietnam; anticommunist military activities in South Korea; and President Park's apparent inclination to "militarize" South Korean society, particularly within universities and high schools. Such policy shifts clearly had an impact on North Korea as well and therefore were of great importance. There is, nevertheless, a surprising lack of research on how the Vietnam War influenced the pattern and progress of South Korea's modern history. Although debate in recent times has focused on the broader aspects of Park Chung-hee's 18-year national stewardship, the issue of the extent to which the Vietnam involvement defined Park's regime has not received the attention it deserves.

This chapter reviews, retrospectively, how South Korea was affected by the Vietnam War, and how the Park regime controlled and mobilized the general public during the course of the conflict. It discusses the circumstances in which the Park regime decided on the troop deployment and addresses what effect the deployment had on Korean society, Korea-U.S. relations, and North Korea-South Korea relations. The final section of the chapter deals with the deployment itself and how the inter-Korean tension caused by it shaped South Korean policy.

II. THE PARK CHUNG-HEE GOVERNMENT

Park Chung-hee seized power through a military coup on May 16, 1961, toppling a legitimate, elected democratic government in the process. As with other military regimes around the world that have replaced democratic governments, the lack of legitimacy was the Achilles heel of Park's regime from the outset, and the destruction of democracy was its congenital defect. These were flaws that could be rectified neither by democratic rhetoric nor an orchestrated series of gestures. As a consequence, Park attempted to win public favor by pursuing economic development, instead of struggling with the issue of a legitimacy that he knew could not be attained.

Another fundamental drawback of the regime was the "left-leaning" track records of many of the people who led the coup. Park Chung-hee was himself court-martialed and sentenced to life imprisonment in 1949 for his secret connection with the South Korean Workers Party, a communist underground movement that had infiltrated the military. Partly because of the enthusiasm with which he collaborated with the military authorities investigating his charge, Park was pardoned and reinstated. The fact that the military coup leaders were so fervent anti-communists had much to do with their self-conscious reaction against their past proclivities.

The first priority for the regime after the coup was to gain a seal of approval from the U.S. government. To this end, Park bent over backward to appear worthy of formal recognition by the United States, a difficult task bearing in mind that the United States was understandably deeply suspicious of his past record. After much diplomatic maneuvering, Park finally succeeded in arranging an invitation to a summit meeting with the then-U.S. President, John F. Kennedy. However, in the following month and shortly before the date of the summit meeting, an unexpected incident occurred. North Korea's President, Kim Il-sung, sent Whang Tae-sung, a former North Korean Deputy Trade Minister, to South Korea as an emissary. This overt signal of what might be interpreted as a precursor of a closer relationship with North Korea could not have appeared at a worse time for Park in terms of his efforts to reassure the U.S. administration of his probity. It was with this potential embarrassment in mind that, when the two leaders met during Park's state visit to the United States from November 13-25, 1961, Park Chung-hee offered Kennedy the support of South Korean forces in the Vietnam conflict. As the United States had not, at that stage, decided to commit its own forces on a large scale to Vietnam, it could not have pressured the South Korean regime to send its troops too. Nonetheless, Park volunteered to deploy Korean troops under the pretext of "helping to relieve the U.S. of its burden as a member of the free world," adding, "The U.S. alone has a disproportionate share of the burden." President Kennedy commended Park and said that he was very pleased with the proposal. Thus, Park had every right to believe that he had handled the summit very successfully.

Unlike the first president of South Korea, Rhee Sung-man, and as a further indicator of his desire to please the United States, Park Chung-hee acquiesced to the U.S. demand for the normalization of Korea-Japan relations. It was, however, not only the insistence of the United States that propelled him to pursue this goal, the achievement of which would certainly make a dent in his treasured ideology of a "nationalistic democracy." It was imperative for Park to develop the South Korean economy if he was to stand a chance of gaining any vestige of domestic and international legitimacy, and normalization of relations with Japan was an inevitable step toward resolving his nation's lack of capital and industrial technology.

In the meantime, and somewhat paradoxically, Park also had to deal with pressure from the United States to reduce the size of the South Korean military force that it was supporting financially. This pressure had begun in 1955, when the United States started to look at ways of reducing its deficit and balancing the budget. In the 1960s, however, encouragement to reduce U.S. military spending on South Korea reflected more the Kennedy administration's hopes for the development of the South Korean economy, as it was the view in U.S. government circles that it was impossible to boost the Korean economy while, at the same time, financing the 600,000-strong military forces. In addition, in the early 1960s, when an array of newly independent countries in Asia and Africa emerged, the United States felt compelled to render economic aid to them in an effort to gain advantage in the Cold War balance of power; and the expansion of economic aid presupposed the reduction of military aid. Park, however, could not afford to accept the U.S. demand for a reduction of the ROKA forces. As is apparent from a series of so-called anti-revolution incidents, the Park regime did not have as tight a control of the military as it wanted, and plainly, any reduction under such circumstances would further enhance the complaints emanating from the military, seriously undermining the regime's control over it.

Yet, many still argue that pressure from the United States was behind the South Korea's decision to deploy its troops to Vietnam. They claim that this pressure was irresistible at a time when the South Korea was so dependent on the United States for its survival. However, research based on recently declassified U.S. government documents shows unequivocally that, as stated above, it was not the United States but Park Chung-hee himself who initiated the move.

III. DEPLOYMENT OF THE FORCES AND
MOBILIZATION OF THE PEOPLE

Public Opinion

By the end of 1964, local newspapers in South Korea were carrying reports to the effect that the government was considering an issue of great significance, but details were not made public because of state censorship. On January 8 in the following year, the Park government announced that it had submitted a bill to the National Assembly that would enable the deployment to Vietnam of 2,000 troops in transportation and civil engineering units. This deployment would supplement the medical personnel who were already dispatched to Vietnam. The issue of South Korean troops going to Vietnam, which had been known to the rest of the world via announcements from the U.S. State Department and frequent international media coverage, finally came to the attention of the South Korean general public. By the time the deployment bill was introduced in the National Assembly, 2,000 troops of the Doves Unit were already being trained in Kyungi-do province in preparation for their departure.

What is particularly interesting about the deployment is that, in the beginning, members of Park's Democratic Republican Party expressed the most caution or were positively against the decision, whereas the opposition parties were generally in favor of it, at least in principle. There were two dominant concerns at the time. The first was concern that the deployment of the Doves Unit would soon be followed by the deployment of combat forces, given the nature of the guerrilla warfare in Vietnam in which it was difficult, if not impossible, to demarcate front and rear combat areas. The other concern, of which the opposition in particular made an issue, was whether the troop deployment was a fully independent decision of the South Korean government or whether it was as a result of a "sincere request" from the U.S. government. Chung Sung-tae, then floor leader of the Democratic Justice Party in the National Assembly, said, "We will object to the deployment if is pursued by the South Korean government on its own. If it is pursued because of a U.S. request, we may consider the matter favorably, taking into account the relations between the U.S. and South Korea."

The bill for the second deployment passed the National Assembly on January 26, 1965, with 106 votes for, 11 against, and 8 abstaining. The *Chosun Daily*, a leading newspaper in South Korea at the time, commented in its editorial on the bill being passed with an absolute majority, "The result strikes us as a kind of surprise in view of the 'turmoil surrounding the matter' and 'the public doubt as to the wisdom of the deployment,'" citing remarks made by a Republican assemblyman who was supposed to speak in favor of the deployment at the hearing: "The deployment does not do us any good diplomatically, militarily, or economically." The unexpected result of the vote was credited to the U.S. ambassador to South Korea, Winthrop G. Brown, who had made concerted efforts to persuade the opposition members of the merits of the proposal.

As soon as the bill was passed, Park Chung-hee issued a statement on the deployment in which he argued, "If a free Vietnam falls into the hands of communists, the anti-communism front of the free world will suffer a setback" and "If Vietnam collapses, communism will launch open and rapid provocations against the free nations in the Pacific area, including South Korea." He went on to say, "We have to determine whether we will wait and see, or whether we take preventive measures." He cited three reasons for the deployment. First, it was a partial fulfillment of South Korea's moral duty to safeguard the collective security guarantee of peace and freedom in all of Asia. Second, the communist invasion of free Vietnam posed a serious threat to South Korea's security and, therefore, its support of Vietnam was an indirect act of national defense. Third, as a nation that had been able to defeat communist forces itself, with the help of 16 allies, we could not turn a blind eye to one of our friends, who was falling victim to a communist invasion.

The deployment of the Doves Unit, which was already under way, proceeded in a speedy fashion. At 2 PM on February 9, 1965, a ceremony, with a crowd of 30,000 well-wishers in attendance, was held with much fanfare at Seoul stadium to wish the departing troops good luck. Park Chung-hee commended them as "crusaders for freedom, who are about to start a historic mission for the first time in our nation's history," adding, "Even though our nation has been invaded many times by surrounding powers during its 5,000-year history, our country has never invaded another country." After a farewell song sung by high-school girls, and the shouting of three hurrahs, the troops began their march through the streets.

Disputes surrounding the sending of combat troops to Vietnam arose immediately after the Doves Unit had departed. Within the restrictions of state censorship, the general opinion expressed in the media was that South Korea had already done its part by sending noncombat forces to Vietnam. However, the Park regime, which had used the deployment as a powerful card in negotiations to win support from the United States immediately after the coup, could not now withdraw it. In May 1965, Park returned from a U.S. red-carpet reception, and on July 2, he chaired a cabinet meeting at which it was resolved to deploy one division and the necessary support units. On July 12, he had the bill for approval of the deployment submitted to the National Assembly.

Given the security situation in which South Korea was confronting North Korea along the Demilitarized Zone (DMZ), deployment of combat forces drew more criticism than was leveled at the departure of the Doves Unit. Son Won-il, a former defense minister in the Rhee Sung-man government, objected to the sending of combat forces, although he accepted the deployment of the noncombatant units. There were voices among the media and from within the National Assembly urging that reservists be dispatched instead of combat troops. This suggestion did not gain widespread approval, however, partly because South Korea might then be criticized for sending mercenaries and partly because the United States would have to pay them compensation commensurate with that for civilians attached to the military.

Cha Ji-chol, a Republican assemblyman who would later become Park Chung-hee's chief bodyguard and be assassinated with him in 1979, was opposed to the dispatch of combat forces; in contrast, assemblymen of the opposition Democratic Peoples Party, Cho Yun-hyung and Kim Chun-hyun, actively supported the initiative. Cho Yun-hyung stated, "Aware that the U.S. is intervening in Vietnam at the risk of having the People's Republic of China or the Soviet Union participate in the Vietnam conflict, touching off a third world war, we should back the U.S. on the premise that we may have a chance to realize the national goal of reunification." With respect to compensation for the deployed forces, the subject of heated debate, he said that he was concerned that "too much interest in economic gain may eclipse the noble cause and the crux of the matter." Cho criticized some ruling party members who demanded increased compensation for the deployed troops and a clear guarantee of South Korean security, saying, "Near-sighted behavior of some ruling party members is likely to stoke anti-Americanism among the public, whose sense of anti-communism may suffer in the future." He went so far as to say, "We should take advantage of this opportunity to enhance South Korea's international standing and to reunify the nation by defeating the communist North."

When the bill for a third round of troop deployment was submitted to the National Assembly, the ruling camp and the opposition were locking horns over the issue of approval of the normalization treaty between Japan and Korea. When these two extremely sensitive pieces of legislation were placed before the National Assembly on the evening of July 14, 1965, pandemonium ensued, including fistfights between members, which continued for some 10 minutes. The reason for the more vociferous objections to the bill enabling a third deployment was a report from overseas to the effect that South Korea stood to gain little economic benefit from such a commitment. Even though the government expressed the hope that South Korea would be able to export military supplies via a tripartite trade agreement with the United States and Vietnam itself, the report that the United States had placed a military order in Japan tended to cast doubt on that hope. There ensued loud objections to the deployment on the grounds that "South Korea sowed the seed, and Japan reaped the harvest." U.S. Ambassador Brown again contacted opposition members behind the scenes, and the bill passed the National Assembly on August 13, with 101 votes for, 1 against, and 2 abstentions. The opposition members were absent.

Having got the bill successfully onto the statute book, albeit unilaterally, the Park regime established the Blue Dragon Unit based at the Second Marine Brigade and created the Tiger Unit within the Capital Division of the Army. The deployment meant that a total of 20,000 combat troops would follow the initial deployment of the 2,000-strong Doves Unit. This number was huge, considering South Korea's level of economic and military power at that time. On October 12, a farewell ceremony for the departing Tiger Unit was held in Yoido, Seoul, and attended by some 300,000 spectators, more than 10 times the size of the crowd that had gathered to bid farewell to the Doves Unit. Park Chung-hee praised the departing soldiers as "the descendants of Hwarang, the elite young men of the Shilla Dynasty" and urged them to "show your mettle to the world as the proud youths of a great country." Three hundred doves were released, famous actresses such as Choi Eun-hee presented bouquets of flowers, and more than 30,000 balloons filled the sky. For 12 kilometers the streets leading to the ceremonial site were decorated with colorful placards and giant balloons. The columns of Tiger Unit troops marching along the streets stretched 1 kilometer in length, and from television sets that had just come into household use in South Korea people could hear the Tiger Unit song, which goes, "Let's defend our fatherland to build a reunified free country. You have been called in the name of the fatherland. Your name is Tiger Unit. Hurrah for the Tiger Unit." Also blaring out from televisions and radios was the Blue Dragon song, which praised the Marines "in dappled military fatigues catching ghosts in the jungle."

The deployment of military personnel did not stop at the 20,000 figure that was reached in October 1965, just as many people had feared that it would not, and the issue of an enhanced commitment of South Korean forces emerged as early as the end of November. U.S. Vice-President Hubert Humphrey visited Seoul on January 1, 1966 and again the following month. Five days after his second visit the Park cabinet decided on the fourth round of deployment, and on March 20, the National Assembly passed the bill approving that decision. The *Chosun Daily* arranged for literary figures like Lee Ho-chul, Shin Dong-moon, and Park Kyung-lee to sit in on the process of the bill's passage, and it carried their observations. Lee Ho-chul said in his piece that the National Assembly had turned into a rubber stamp and that the Korean public was showing "a great display of indifference." He deplored this indifference, saying, "Isn't this too much, considering the grave nature of the issue?" Park Kyung-lee agreed that those who were opposed to the deployment "looked as though they were resigned" to not blocking the passage of the bill because it was a fait accompli. She went on to report that there had been many vacant seats in the National Assembly, and even those members who were present were mostly dozing. She concluded by noting, "The assemblymen seemed more indifferent than the general public were, and merely waited for the gavel to fall."

Confronted with the fourth round of deployment the South Korean people did, indeed, display a surprising lack of concern. The collective attitude of resignation seemed to signal that, now the decision had been made, the general public assumed that there was no choice other than to accept the inevitable. This mass acceptance proved to be a great obstacle to forming any kind of coherent opposition to the deployment. Park Kyung-lee wrote, "The blood of our youths is more pathetic than holy" when drawing attention to the fact that a small, divided country, relying on the United States for its defense, had to deploy 20,000 troops in addition to the already deployed 22,000.

The opposition that was evoked by the fourth deployment came from women, which was unexpected, and part of that opposition was based on the issue of equitable remuneration. Park Chung-hee had not demanded fair compensation for South Korean troops during the deployment period, although Lee Dong-won, then Minister of Foreign Affairs, did suggest that South Korea seek economic gain from the situation: "Vietnam is not only a battleground, but also a market." Park's response to that comment was this: "If we try to take advantage of the U.S. quandary, it would be unbecoming of an ally." The result was that Korean troops received a salary that was one-sixth of that paid to U.S. troops of comparable rank and one-fourth of that received by soldiers from the Philippines and Thailand; it was lower even than the remuneration of personnel in the South Vietnamese army. The Association of Korean Wives went public on February 22, 1966, with this statement in the names of 15 million Korean women: "Unless appropriate compensation for Korean soldiers is fully guaranteed, the Association of Korean Wives is opposed to any further deployment of Korean troops." Writer Kang Shin-jae contributed an article to the women's section of a national newspaper in which she asserted that it was totally unreasonable for an army of one country to employ an army of another country without compensation. She said that there could be no rational reason for this inequality.

Grounds for Deployment

Park Chung-hee's reasons for agreeing to the commitment of so many Korean troops, his "anti-communist crusaders," to Vietnam were to express gratitude to the United States for its support and recognition, to defend the second front line against the perceived threat of communism, and to enhance South Korea's standing in the international community. Both the ruling Democratic Republican Party and the opposition parties were well aware that the deployment lacked substantial grounds, and elements of the national media had argued from the beginning that it was unjust. Commentators claimed that the sending of combat troops had not received the endorsement of an international body such as the United Nations and was not in accordance with any mutual defense agreement or formal military alliance between South Korea and South Vietnam.

In response, Park argued that the country should help South Vietnam as a way to repay the debt owed to the "16 free allies" who had come to the aid of South Korea a decade earlier, during the Korean War. His argument was countered by the claim that, in view of its relative size and strength, and its own serious security concerns, South Korea had already done its share by sending the 2,000 Doves troops.

One of the most prevalent components of Cold War ideology was the *domino theory*, which held that if South Vietnam succumbed to the communist advance, neighboring countries would fall in turn and suffer the same "communized" fate. The theory of the *second front line*, as championed by the Park regime, could be regarded as a Korean version of the domino theory. In a farewell speech delivered on the occasion of the deployment of the Tiger Unit to Vietnam on October 12, 1965, Park said, "Unless we deter the communist aggression in free South Vietnam, the whole of South East Asia will be lost in the near future, and the security of the Republic of Korea could not be assured." On February 9, 1965, in another speech marking the deployment of more troops, he asked rhetorically, "If we sit idly by when our neighbor's house is broken into, isn't our own house going to be broken into next?" On September 20, 1965, at the inaugural ceremony for the Blue Dragon Unit, he claimed, "Just as we would give a helping hand when our neighbor's house is on fire, so should we help South Vietnam win in this war." These extracts are examples of how Park Chung-hee conveyed the concept of the domino theory to the general public. Later, and using the same basis for his argument, he claimed, "There is a direct link between the anti-communist front line of free South Vietnam and our own Demilitarized Zone." He went so far as to insist that Vietnam was, in fact, the "second front line" of the Korean War.

One intriguing factor about the so-called second front line is that Park criticized communist China and used it in justifying the deployment. Park defined the Vietnam War as "being waged through the despicable attack by North Vietnam supported by the People's Republic of China." He argued, "China is behind North Vietnam, as it was behind North Korea during the Korean War....Therefore, Koreans were fighting the Chinese again in Vietnam." He was trying to establish a link between the Korean War and the Vietnam War, but his argument that the South Vietnamese People's Liberation Front and North Vietnamese regime were underpinned by China was simply untrue. It was a theory frequently used by the Park regime in 1965, but one that was effectively repudiated by Park himself in August 1966, at the time of the fourth round of troop deployment, when he said, "The culprits who control and support the Vietcong and the North Vietnamese army and destroy peace are the international communists who instigated the North Korean invasion of the South."

The argument that "the deployment enhances the nation's international standing" was one of Park's favorite ploys. On January 26, 1965, he bellowed,: "Now is the time for South Korea to wean itself from a passive position of receiving help or suffering intervention, and to assume a proactive role of taking responsibility on major international issues." The statement was followed on Christmas Day 1965 by a message delivered to the Korean troops serving in Vietnam, in which Park said, "By deploying our troops, we have become a benefactor for the free world, including Vietnam. We are emerging from the past history of relying on outside help to stand at the crossroads of opening a glorious new chapter in the nation's history." He praised the departing soldiers as "the vanguard, who are extricating the nation from the tradition of stagnation and retrogression to blaze a trail of prosperity and glory." In October 1966, after returning from a visit to South Vietnam, Park was delighted to say, "We have become an international leader in the new age, a truly sovereign country that has left behind its history of submission and disgrace." That set the tone for the Charter for People's Education, drawn up in December 1968.

However, it was not long before the rationales for the commitment of combat troops began to fall on deaf ears as it became increasingly clear that the deployment was actually beyond South

Korea's capability, constituted a threat to domestic security, and was being roundly criticized by the rest of the world for its lack of legitimate justification. In the run-up to the presidential election in 1967, Yun Bo-sun, an opposition candidate, denounced the Park regime for "waging a proxy war." In response to that accusation, Park Chung-hee raised the issue of the withdrawal of U.S. troops from the Korean peninsula, thereby weakening somewhat the rationales he had employed until then.

On April 17, 1967, while campaigning in Daejeon, he stated, "I will give you a more frank reason for the troop deployment instead of saying, as I have been, that we have to repay our debt or that communization of South East Asia will affect us adversely." He went on, "We could have chosen not to deploy our troops when asked. Then the two U.S. divisions deployed in South Korea would have been transferred to Vietnam. How could we have been able to stop them while not sending our own forces? We could not have." Thus, he asked, "Could we not help but deploy for the sake of our own security?" He said that if the U.S. troops were pulled out of South Korea, it would give "the communist North another chance to invade the South, causing political and psychological unrest, a reduction in foreign investment, and make it difficult for us to obtain foreign loans." That was why the deployment was inevitable, and the opposition was "causing the government a lot of trouble by trying to find fault, and saying that it was waging a proxy war or sacrificing the blood of our youth."

Actually, not all those in the opposition were against the government's Vietnam policy. Park Soon-chon, chairman of the Democratic People's Party, the main opposition party, said during her inspection tour of Vietnam in September 1966, "I withdraw my objection to the deployment" and added that she was now personally in favor of the deployment, although her party adopted an opposing position. She said, "Now that the country has deployed the troops, shouldn't we support them as subjects of the country. If I were in military fatigues, I would stay here."

As can be deduced from the statements of Cho Yun-hyung, Park Soon-chon, and Kim Jun-yon, the opposition at that time was, in a sense, more conservative, more anti-communist, and more pro-American than the ruling party. With regard to the deployment, it did not question the nature of the Vietnam War, nor did it ask whether the South Vietnamese government was legitimately supported by the general public. Park's regime drummed up support for deployment under the slogan, "Let's build the nation while fighting." Vietnam, though in southern Asia and far away from home, was a theater of war from which South Korean people could still feel the heat of battle. Koreans were not as enthusiastic about the war in Vietnam as the Japanese had been about the China-Japan War and the Russia-Japan War, but neither were they against it in a unified and clearly defined manner. The war allowance for the South Korean troops was certainly an issue at home, but the amount of US$50 received by each South Korean soldier was not paltry, in light of South Korea's relatively poor economy. The TV sets, radios, cameras, and tape recorders that South Korean soldiers brought home after their periods of service made Vietnam seem like a land of opportunity. Reports that the express highway between Seoul and Pusan was built with hard currency remitted by the deployed soldiers and the foreign loans granted in exchange for the deployment deprived many South Koreans of an opportunity to question the nature of the war.

The absence of concerted opposition to the Vietnam War by the majority of the South Korean populace was also caused by the general misconception of the toll it took on Korean youth. A popular song, "Sun-tanned Master Sergeant Kim from Vietnam," sung by Kim Choo-ja, gave the impression that everyone returned from Vietnam safe and sound, with nobody seeming to notice the many "Kims" who did not return at all. The human cost of the war was the main concern of the Park government and could have sparked serious anti-war popular sentiment in the most direct way. As late as 1965 the number of South Korean troops killed in action was reported regularly by the newspapers. As the total passed 300, however, the statistics were no longer printed. In their place details of victories achieved by South Korean forces made the headlines.

IV. IMPACT OF THE DEPLOYMENT

South Korean Society

The most talked-about by-product of the military deployment was the so-called Vietnam War bonanza, through which South Korea was able to earn about one billion U.S. dollars and secure additional benefits from the United States, including loans and special trade privileges. The one billion dollars provided a major boost to the South Korean economy, and it is safe to say that the sum laid the foundation for rapid economic development. Vietnam certainly made an important contribution to the fledgling export industry of the nation, but even so, its importance should not be overemphasized. There were many other factors in addition to the Vietnam War bonanza that made South Korea's subsequent dynamic growth possible.

In addition to the question of whether it is morally acceptable to take economic advantage of the unfortunate situation of another country involved in a war, the *opportunity cost* should also be taken into account when assessing the economic gain from the deployment; that is, an economic gain that would have arisen even in the absence of a large-scale deployment. Had South Korea not deployed its troops, would it have been excluded completely from the economic advantage gained from the Vietnam War bonanza? Would the United States have opened its market to South Korea without the deployment? The greatest beneficiary of the war bonanza was Japan, whose armed forces did not shed a single drop of blood in Vietnam. Japan earned more each year than South Korea managed to gross during the entire time it was involved in Vietnam. Taiwan, which deployed only 20 soldiers at the request of the United States, who wanted to see more national flags flying in Vietnam, enjoyed the benefits of the war bonanza. Neither was it excluded from the list of subsequent beneficiaries of the United States, who selectively opened its markets on the basis of the political and economic calculations dictated by the Cold War ideology. That "favored nation" list also included Singapore and Hong Kong, neither of which committed troops. The economic gain accrued by South Korea, which suffered a major loss of human life beyond monetary calculation, which acquired a bad reputation for having committed a civilian massacre, and which was the object of much criticism to the effect that its troops were "the mercenaries of the United States" was only slightly more than that accrued by Taiwan, which sent the nominal quota of 20 troops.

It was on the army of South Korea that the Vietnam deployment had the most direct impact. First, it helped the army neutralize the perpetual pressure to reduce its size. However, there were other considerations as well. In the days immediately following the 1961 military coup, Park Chung-hee could not help but focus attention on the eradication of corruption within the military; not least to alter the South Korean public's generally negative perception of its armed forces. Many high-ranking officers and noncommissioned officers who had served in Vietnam had made fortunes by engaging in the black market in U.S. supplies. In a number of instances corrupt military personnel bribed their way to promotions and other benefits when they returned to South Korea, using the money they had accrued while serving abroad. The incidences of widespread corruption and malfeasance in the forces, which had begun to taper off in the early part of the 1960s, started to become more prevalent, largely on the basis of illicitly acquired money. At that time, senior commanding officers had the power to appoint staff officers and commanding officers of units under their command; this practice led to the formation of cliques and exclusive groups within the overall military structure. After the withdrawal of Korean troops from Vietnam in 1973, and as a sort of reward for the army, Park Chung-hee established 20 additional divisions to create more positions for officers of the rank of general. After his assassination in 1979, the greatly enhanced officer corps elite that he had created quickly grasped political power by means of two military coups.

The involvement in Vietnam marked a turning point in relations between South Korea and the United States. The administration of President Lyndon Johnson withdrew its reservations concerning the legitimacy of Park Chung-hee and began to praise his ruling capability. The U.S. government also stopped intervening in South Korean domestic affairs, a practice in which it had engaged since 1948. Park was greatly encouraged by both the overt support of the United States and the extent to which South Korea's economic development was invigorated by benefits accrued from the Vietnam deployment. Buoyed by this increased confidence, he sought to revise the Constitution to enable him to run for a third term in office; a move that would pave the way for him to rule for even longer.

From that time onward, the United States did not constitute any form of deterrent to Park as he maneuvered himself inexorably into a position of enormous autocratic power, nor did the United States appear to make any effort to restrain the activities of the KCIA. William Porter, a former U.S. ambassador to the Republic of Korea, testified that U.S. inaction in South Korea was due to the consideration afforded to Park Chung-hee in return for South Korea's contribution in the Vietnam War. This endorses the view that in agreeing to send Korean combat troops to Vietnam, Park was able to consolidate his grip on power.

South Korean-U.S. Relations

When the United States began its involvement in the Vietnam War in earnest, it adopted a policy of "more flags." Realizing that it was impossible to mobilize international support through the United Nations, as had been the case in the Korean War, the United States attempted to get as many of its allies as possible involved in the conflict to make the venture appear justified and endorsed by the international community. To the dismay of the United States, however, it was only South Korea and Taiwan, 2 of 25 possible allies, that offered active support. These contributions were not entirely palatable to the United States because both countries were divided and, as a consequence, were considered to have defense problems of their own. Furthermore, support from Taiwan was likely to provoke the People's Republic of China and add fuel to the traditional anti-Chinese sentiment among the Vietnamese. As has been noted above, Taiwan actually sent only a nominal number of troops but, despite U.S. reservations, did help it realize the "more flags" objective.

Because international support for the Vietnam War was lacking, the role of South Korea in Vietnam was destined to grow. To the United States, eager to counter the criticism that the war was a racial invasion of "the white on the yellow" and to project instead the illusion that it was waging an ideological war to contain communist expansionism, the involvement of South Korean combat troops, men who belonged to the same race as the Vietnamese, was a matter of major import. When Park Chung-hee first offered the idea of South Korean participation, it was intended as a token favor. Yet, its total of 50,000 troops was three times the combined contributions of Australia, New Zealand, Thailand, the Philippines, Taiwan, and Spain. This helped catapult South Korea into being, in effect, a partner of the United States, at least as far as the war in Vietnam was concerned, even though, in many Third World countries through which strong waves of nationalism were sweeping, South Korea was regarded as something of a "cat's paw."

Initially, Park Chung-hee did not ask for much in return for the relatively huge troop commitment. As he remarked, "We must not become too selfish." The quid pro quo from the United States included sentiments expressed by Vice-President Hubert Humphrey in February 1966 at the end of a visit to South Korea: "We are friends and allies. South Korea is as strong as the combination of the U.S. and South Korea, and the U.S. is as strong as the combination of South Korea and the U.S. If North Korea attacks the South, we will consider it an aggression on the U.S. mainland, and retaliate at once." However, this somewhat fulsome rhetoric was considered by Senator J. William Fulbright, chairman of the Senate Foreign Relations Committee, to be "full of flowery words never heard of in the history of the U.S."

One noteworthy gain that South Korea did secure from the United States in 1967 was the Status of Forces Agreement (SOFA). Before this agreement was reached, uniformed U.S. personnel stationed on the Korean peninsula could not be charged with criminal offenses in a South Korean court. However, Park Chung-hee failed to secure a firm commitment from the United States to continue to deploy its forces on the peninsula indefinitely, and to intervene automatically in the event of an aggressive act by North Korea.

Inter-Korean Relations

North Korea reacted strongly to the Vietnam deployment, regarding the normalization of relations between South Korea and Japan as consolidation of a tripartite military alliance among the United States, Japan, and South Korea and as the signal for a resurrection of Japanese militarism. Kim Il-sung stressed, "The Vietnam War is a touchstone that distinguishes between a revolutionary position and opportunism, between proletarian internationalism and national selfishness." He went on to say that the Korean Workers' Party "considers the struggle of South Vietnamese people as its own" and "is willing to fight along with them by deploying its forces when the South Vietnamese government requests it." Kim Il-sung's intimation that he was ready to help the Vietnamese gave rise to heightened tension along the demarcation line between North and South. The number of skirmishes in the region soared from 88 in 1965 and 80 in 1966 to 784 in 1967 and 985 in 1968. January 1968 saw two grave incidents occur in succession: a failed attack on the Blue House, the South Korean president's official residence in Seoul, and the capture of the USS Pueblo, a U.S. naval vessel.[1] Neither Washington nor Seoul failed to recognize the "message" from Pyongyang, which was clearly intended to apply pressure on South Korea. In any event, a proposal to actually increase the size of the South Korean deployment did not come to fruition precisely because of the heightened tension on the peninsula. Thus, it can be deduced that the deployment to Vietnam helped reinforce and underpin authoritarian rule in both Koreas.

---

[1] The USS Pueblo was a U.S. Navy intelligence-gathering vessel on a mission off the coast of North Korea. On January 23, 1968 it was attacked by North Korean ships and aircraft. The 82 survivors were captured and imprisoned for 11 months.

V. CONCLUSION

In the year 1968 the anti-war movement and general social revolution were sweeping through countries across the world. In contrast, in South Korea it was a year of the militarization of the society, especially on university campuses, and in North Korea it saw the burgeoning of the Kim Il-sung personality cult. The global anti-war movement was not in evidence on the Korean peninsula, where even the poet Kim Soo-young could not exercise "a right to object to the deployment," but could simply exclaim, "Wind, Dust, Grass!!! How small I am!!!"

Thirty years after the Vietnam War, Korea is confronting the wounds resulting from its intervention in the war. This is not just because tens of Vietnamese equivalents of "Nogunri," the massacre of South Koreans by U.S. forces during the Korean War, are coming to light. Park Chung-hee boasted of his troops because of their abundant experience in the counterinsurgent warfare of the Korean War. Unfortunately, however, these experiences were accompanied by atrocities and civilian massacres. The same commanders, after their mission in Vietnam, returned home and repeated their ritual in the Kwangju Uprising. Side effects from exposure to defoliants, in the form of frequent sickness, blotches on the skin, and birth defects in their offspring, are not the only scars of service in Vietnam. The impact of South Korean involvement is much more profound and far reaching. The war and the deployment of South Korean troops destroyed democracy in South Korea, intensified South Korea's dependence on the United States, and turned the country into a garrison state.

The past decade of democratization in South Korea is merely the restoration of procedural democracy. Despite the absence of a military dictatorship, militarism, which demands absolute obedience to a higher authority, remains the order of the day, and sovereignty is still far from being restored fully. No coherent attempts have been made to heal the wounds of the Vietnam War; it has simply been "celebrated." In the mid-1960s, South Korea set foot in the wrong place, not as an ally of Vietnam but as an ally of the United States,

268

and it did so without arousing the slightest vestige of anti-war activism. The brouhaha surrounding the deployment of South Korean forces to Iraq in 2003 proves that the government has learned nothing from the Vietnam experience. Since Vietnam, South Korea has sent troops to the Gulf area during the Gulf War, to Angola during its civil war, to Afghanistan, and recently to Iraq. No other country among the U.S. allies has participated in all the wars that the United States has waged. It is true that the argument that the deployment to Vietnam was a repayment of a debt is not entirely groundless. What is deeply regrettable, however, is the fact that, despite the loss of 5,000 young South Korean men in a war waged by the United States, similar arguments, expressed in slogans like "Korea-U.S. Blood Allies," remain popular currency.

Despite South Korea's support for the United States in Vietnam, the United States withdrew its own troops from the Korean peninsula during the Vietnam War. They went home to America. Had they been redeployed to Vietnam instead, such a transfer would have been understandable in view of the difficult circumstances in Vietnam at that time. The revision of the South Korea-U.S. Mutual Defense Treaty, aimed at ensuring an automatic commitment of U.S. forces to the Korean peninsula in the event of a crisis, did not materialize, even though it was the most pressing concern of Park Chung-hee and even after the deployment of so many Korean troops. Under the circumstances, it is unreasonable to expect that South Korea's deployment of troops to Iraq will help create a situation helpful for solving the North Korean nuclear issue. Nonetheless, yet again South Korea is trying to exchange the lives of its young generation for uncertain economic benefits in the name of the national interest.

South Korea sent its troops to Vietnam on a large scale, and to other places, at the demand of the United States, because it had more troops than were strictly necessary. Still a highly militarized country, even after a significant level of democratization has been reached, South Korea maintains a large military force, an inappropriate policy in the age of modern warfare. This is why there is a continual demand from the United States for further deployments. In its failure to learn any lessons from the Vietnam experience, South Korea will certainly find itself, at some stage in the future, the first to be asked to comply with a U.S. demand for military commitment if and when it wages war against another country.

Chapter 10

Oppressive Modernization and the Risk Society

Hong Seong-tae

I. INTRODUCTION

Industrial power is a key component of modernization. Modernization is a very complex societal change, so it has a component of historical transformation. However, history is changed not only by advancements in human reason but also by material changes. In this regard, the fundamental factor that differentiates modern times from earlier eras is the presence of new productive power, which is referred to as industrial power. Productive power is at the center of modernization.

The new society that emerges as a result of modernization is generally referred to as an industrial society.[1] Sometimes the terms "modern society" and "industrial society" are used interchangeably. Industrial power is regarded as the main characteristic of modern society because it is the productive power to effectively change the world. By having access to and controlling such power, human beings can be the ruler of the world.

Yet, industrial power can be destructive as well (Kim Jin-gyun and Hong Song tae 1996). Two world wars and the recent global eco-crisis clearly support that fact.[2] In particular, the eco-crisis, which

---

[1] The term "industrial society" emphasizes the changes brought about by industrial power.

[2] The World War II gave birth to Horkheimer and Adorno's *Dialectic of*

seriously worsened in the 1980s, gave rise to the concept of *risikoge-sellschaft* (risk society), as formulated by German sociologist Ulrich Beck (1992), as a means of focusing attention on the fundamental problems embedded in modern society. He argues that industrial society would be transformed into a risk society as "a result of the success of modernization, and not from a crisis of it" (Beck 1992:45).[3]

Beck's proposition can be summarized as follows: pre-modernization → classical modernization → one modern society (classical industrial society → new industrial society = risk society) → reflexive modernization → another modern society. Beck does not identify industrial society with modern society. According to his argument, as a result of the success of classical modernization, the classical industrial society that puts economic equality at its center turns into a risk society with social safety at its center. To respond effectively to these changes, classical modernization itself should be the subject of modernization. This is reflexive modernization, and it leads to another new modern society.

The theory of the risk society was structured in Germany, an advanced industrial state. There are, therefore, some difficulties in adapting this theory to either developing or underdeveloped countries. However, insofar as the theory highlights the inherent problems within classical modernization, it does offer some explanatory power to all societies that have recently entered on the path of modernization. Contemporary Korean society can be assessed using this theory, as can its predecessor, the society shaped by the developmental dictatorship exercised by Park Chung-hee between 1961 and 1979.

Ulrich Beck created the theory while focusing on the faith in science and the development of individualism. The same framework

---

Enlightenment (1947), whereas the recent ecocrisis motivated Beck's *Risk Society* (1986). Both works deal with the dark side of modern times, and both were written by Germans.

[3] Beck's *Risikogesellschaft* was translated to English in 1992. I translated the English version into Korean in 1997. I refer to the English version in this chapter.

can be applied to current Korean society and to that under Park, but there are many differences. For example, the change in gender relationships, the weakness of family relationships and the prevalence of job insecurity — intrinsic to Beck's study of individualism — are closely related to the rise of neo-liberalism and are clearly found in Korean society after the mid-1990s. In this regard, it can be said that although West Germany became a risk society during the early 1970s (Beck 1992:54), Korea reached that stage in the mid-1990s.

However, because this comparison only emphasizes the external similarities in the process of moving toward a risk society, it does not fully reflect the contextual differences that could occur in the concrete process of modernization. It is, therefore, essential to consider those differences.

II. THE PARK CHUNG-HEE ERA AND OPPRESSIVE MODERNIZATION

Beck's risk society study examines Western "advanced societies" in which concerns about poverty have decreased and have begun to be replaced by concerns about newly emerging risk factors. Beck views the rise of the risk society not as an abnormality, but as a normal consequence of classical modernization. In other words, the risk society is not the offspring of corruption and irrationality, but a normal outcome. From this position, it can be assumed that the risk society refers to the so-called advanced society. Beck argues that advanced society is governed by a blind faith in science per se, that its regulating system constituted by family and occupation has collapsed, and that its members confront the enormous dangers incurred as a result of classical modernization.

It would be both a theoretical and a political mistake to adopt the theory of risk society in the Korean case without any adjustment whatsoever; partly because, as is plain from Beck's explanation, the risk society does indeed refer to an advanced society. Neither during the Park Chung-hee era[4] nor at the current time can the Korean

---

[4] This refers to the era of 1961-1979 during which Park ruled Korea as

society be regarded as advanced. Thus, attention is drawn to structural differentiation between an advanced society and Korean society.

There are two main structural differences between the two types of societies. One is status in the world system. Compared with an advanced society, Korea still has a nearly dependent status (dependency). So Korea is vulnerable to external changes effected by advanced societies; in fact, this weakness itself poses a very important risk to Korea. The other difference is the relative degree of political democratization, the core of classical modernization. Unlike an advanced society, Korea began and strongly drove the process of classical modernization under the repressive circumstances of dictatorship (oppressiveness). Thus, Korea is immature in adjusting to a plurality of opinions and caring for its minorities. This immaturity itself is another important risk to Korea. We cannot apply the risk society theory to Korea without paying attention to these differences.

From the viewpoint of risk theory, blind faith in science is more evident in Korea than in advanced societies, and the regulating system of industrial society is less developed in Korea. Therefore, Korea does not have the social mechanisms needed to control the risks triggered by science nor the social safety network to support the regulating system of industrial society, as do advanced societies. These features stem from the structural differences (dependency and oppressiveness) between advanced society and Korean society, which were generated in the process of classical modernization carried out under Japan imperialism's colonization and the Park Chung-hee regime's oppression. During those periods, dependency and oppressiveness were strengthened: As classical modernization proceeded, more and larger risk elements were rapidly generated than in an advanced society.

In Korea, classical modernization was aggressively pursued by Park Chung-hee under the slogan, "National Modernization." [5]

president with very oppressive state apparatus in one hand, and with a very developmental state apparatus in the other.

[5] In a press conference held on January 9, 1970, Park Chung-hee said, "The 1970s will be the time to achieve national modernization" (*Cheongsa*

According to Beck's theory, it was an endeavor on the state level to realize classical modernization by mimicking Western societies, and the objective was to catch up to them. Because this modernization was carried out very rapidly, it is called *compressed modernization*. It could be achieved in such a short time mainly because Park Chung-hee pushed the Korean people so remorselessly. In this regard, it is more appropriate to refer to the process not as compressed modernization, but as *oppressive modernization* (Hong Yun-gi 2000:55-6). However, national modernization under Park Chung-hee produced many problems, not only because of the speed with which it was carried out but also because of the manner.

The term "oppressive modernization" emphasizes the salient characteristics of governmental power that directed the process.[6] It was not the process that differed from classical modernization, but the fact that it was realized rapidly in a violent manner. In Western societies, classical modernization took place in concert with civil revolution, whereas in Korea it was carried out in an oppressive manner. The most important fact regarding oppressive modernization is that political democratization, a primary tenet of modernization, is circumscribed by violence. From the viewpoint of the ideal type of modernization, political modernization is the core element. Therefore, oppressive modernization is modernization that distorts the core element of modernization. Of course, not one single country has fully realized the ideal type of modernization. Regardless of the degree of development, all states remain at some distance from the ideal, and, thus, all modern societies are distorted to an extent. However, although Western societies that have achieved political democratization through mutual consent have moved closer to the ideal, Korean society has failed to cover the same ground. In evaluating both the Park Chung-hee era and current circumstances in Korea, this difference is far from insignificant.

Publication 1984: 9).

[6] Actually, all states are violent. Violent power is a physical basis of political power. At this point, all states should be a legitimate holder of violent power. State power that is unjust is far more dangerous than other types of violent organization.

No matter how comprehensively it is realized, classical modernization has limits, and the risk society theory emphasizes this point. Oppressive modernization realizes classical modernization by using violence as a main means. In this way, the various limits of classical modernization are often ignored; thus, oppressive modernization more obviously illustrates the limits of classical modernization.[7] In this context, the developmental dictatorship in pursuit of oppressive modernization becomes a dictatorship of *destructive development*, meaning that many aspects of society are destroyed in the name of development. All the damage manifested by Park Chung-hee has led to massive social and ecological degradation, and Korean society has become markedly more of a risk society than Western societies.

This destructive development of oppressive modernization was facilitated by the overt use of state violence. Those citizens who did not follow the Park Chung-hee line were regarded as anti-regime, which went beyond being anti-government, and many were forced to sacrifice their lives or to endure torture, prison, and other hardships. Of course, any social change cannot be sustained only by violence. Two predominant arguments were used to justify this process of destructive modernization. One was the imperative to mobilize scientific logic; that is, the diverse components of destructive development were promoted as scientific necessities on the path to becoming an advanced society. Nuclear power generation is a prime example of this argument. The other justification was grounded on post-colonialism and posited that Korea had been colonized because its society had a collectively outdated way of thinking and it could only attain advanced society status through national modernization. The notion of *Yeopjeonism* is a representative example of "colonial discourse" that can be understood in this context.[8]

---

[7] The reason why many call Korea a "construction republic" or an "accident republic" can be explained in this context. Because modernization was carried out in such a short time, and in an oppressive manner, there were several accidents in which a bridge and many buildings that looked superficially satisfactory suddenly collapsed.

[8] A *yeopjeon* is a Korean brass coin of little value, and *Yeopjeonism* bears the

Undeniably, Park Chung-hee's developmental dictatorship brought economic growth. Those who value this achievement highly underscore Park's achievement by labeling the 1950s as the "the era of ruin" and the 1970s as "the era of development."

> Imagine we are walking through the streets of Seoul in 1953, and again in 1970. We could easily find extreme differences between the two situations.... In 20 years, depression and hopelessness had turned into vitality and growth.... The 1970s was obviously the time that brought big historical change to Korean society, and it was a time of excitement. Just like in "The Thousand and One Nights," many changes took place, bringing much excitement to Korean people (Shinhan Research Center 1991:25-6).

It can indeed be said that the 1970s was a decade of excitement. However, it was also a decade of terror, which was generated by the violence of the Park Chung-hee government and the extraordinary expansion of classical modernization.

Park's oppressive modernization was aimed at building a classical industrial society in a way that would achieve classical modernization. From the viewpoint of risk society theory, Park's excessive focus on external factors precluded the achievement of classical modernization. As a result, the limits of classical modernization were highlighted more clearly in Korean society. Developmental dictatorship did not transform Korean society into the risk society as presented in Beck's theory, but it did make it more risky than Western risk societies. At this juncture let us consider the various risks associated with oppressive modernization. They are addressed from two perspectives: environmental destruction and social destruction.

---

connotation that nothing of substance can be derived from Korean history and tradition. Shin Chung-hyon, Korea's leading rock musician, named his group "The Yeopjeons" in a critical reference to this notion. He ceased to imitate American rock music and tried instead to express Korean sentiments in his compositions.

III. ENVIRONMENTAL DESTRUCTION

Environmental destruction is the modern risk that is most commonly generated in the process of modernization in both developed and underdeveloped states. Environmental destruction has been evident from ancient times, but has changed markedly in impact and scope in modern times. Park Chung-hee's oppressive modernization achieved substantial and explosive economic growth, but a huge price: The sacrifice of the natural environment paid for the achievement. This ecological sacrifice is considered in terms of industrialization and the perspective of nature.

Industrialization

There is no difference between consensus modernization and oppressive modernization, insofar as industrial power is the core of both processes. Industrial power is also at the center of reflexive modernization, such as classical modernization. However, because this same industrial power is at the physical core of risk society, the main goal of reflexive modernization in escaping from being a risk society is securing a new control mechanism to regulate industrial power.

Park Chung-hee's developmental dictatorship pursued rapid industrialization as the single most important vehicle to achieve modernization. Power plants and industrial complexes sprang up across the state with extraordinary speed, and many new highways were carved out of the landscape: "Every day, exciting news was delivered. Whenever monumental achievements, such as the completion of the Gyongbu highway or the Pohang steelworks, were broadcast, people got excited and brimmed with confidence. Traffic networks, enormous dams, power plants, and industrial complexes were built one after another" (Shinhan Research Centre 1991:27).

However, these outstanding achievements also brought huge environmental degradation, and one of the most crucial changes at this time that can be related to the theory of the risk society was the establishment of nuclear power plants. Nuclear power generation

278

began to be universally adopted after U.S. President Eisenhower delivered a speech on its peaceful use at the United Nation's annual meeting on December 8, 1953. The International Atomic Energy Agency (IAEA) was established after this speech, in 1954, and the United States revised its Atomic Power Generation Act to enable nuclear power agreements with other nations. On the basis of the revised act, the United States proposed a nuclear power agreement between itself and Korea for "nonmilitary purposes." Korea accepted this proposal in February 1956 and joined the IAEA in August 1957. In August 1958, Korean delegations visited the United States in a bid to purchase an atomic reactor for research purposes, and the first installation went into operation in March 1962. The Atomic Power Generation Committee was established in November of the same year. The Atomic Power Society was founded in March 1969, and the Korean Atomic Industry Council was created in December 1970. Meanwhile, the Atomic Power Generation Committee selected Gori, in Gyongnam province, as the site for the first full-scale nuclear power plant and began purchasing land in October 1969. A 120,000-pyong site (approximately 480,000 square yards) was secured after forcibly evacuating 162 households. Construction began in March 1971 and was completed in July 1978, making Korea the world's 22nd nuclear power nation.

Ulrich Beck's risk society theory was written against the background of the catastrophic accident at Chernobyl in Ukraine on April 26, 1986.[9] Before Chernobyl, the capacity to generate nuclear power was seen as a symbol of an advanced society. In particular, developing nations, such as Korea, which were handicapped by inadequate energy resources, viewed the acquisition of nuclear power generation

---

[9] Many safety procedures were disregarded during the testing of one of the four reactors at the Chernobyl nuclear power plant, 80 miles north of Kiev, on April 25-26, 1986. As a consequence, the nuclear chain reaction process went out of control, and there were massive explosions. Thirty people were killed immediately, and as a result of high radiation in the surrounding area, 135,000 people had to be evacuated. Since this accident, societies that develop "alternative" energy sources are now considered to be the advanced societies.

capacity as a means of becoming one of those advanced societies. However, the disaster at Chernobyl changed attitudes not only in the West but also in Korea. In fact, the potential dangers of nuclear power generation had been known for a long time. For example, radioactive contamination occurred over a 200-square mile area after a leakage of radioactive iodine at the Windscale atomic plant in the United Kingdom in 1957, and radioactive fallout had became a political issue in the United States as early as 1956. Despite the well-known dangers, nuclear power generation proceeded and finally led to the Chernobyl disaster.

In Korea, spurred on by Park Chung-hee's strong desire to possess nuclear weapons,[10] a nuclear power policy was pursued with such vigor that it would have been extremely difficult to oppose or divert. After nuclear power plants had been constructed and began operation, some unprecedented occurrences began to be recorded. Deformed fish, calves and, finally, even babies, were born at locations adjacent to power plant sites. Among the most publicized were the cases of babies born either with no brain or with an excessively large brain. These deformed babies were borne by women who worked near the Yeonggwang nuclear power plant in Chunnam province. Experts who conducted studies on these incidents said that they had nothing to do with the nuclear power plants. However, American biologist and environmental activist Barry Commoner (1971) had stated long before that there was not a single radiation exposure that was not harmful. Which of these positions is correct? What does it mean that all the abnormal incidents happened after the construction of nuclear power plants and that the victims were the most vulnerable in Korean society?

The Park Chung-hee government was a false institution without political legitimacy. On the one hand, it oppressed the great mass of the Korean people with indiscriminate and arbitrary violence, and on

[10] At the time when Park Chung-hee's dictatorship was developing, U.S. nuclear weapons were already deployed in South Korea. On March 10, 1970, it was reported that the United States had five such weapons in Korea (*Cheongsa Publication* 1984: 13).

the other hand, it tried to seduce the Korean people by promising splendid changes. In the 1970s the nation was still extremely poor, and Park was not slow to exploit this condition.[11] He succeeded in implanting into people's minds the firm belief that they could also be well-off; in the process, however, he sacrificed democracy and created systems of new modern risks. Through the Park Chung-hee model of oppressive modernization, the equation "modernization = economic development = industrialization" became firmly established as the governing idea throughout Korean society (Shinhan Research Centre 1991:28). Embedded risks in classical modernization were ignored, and any active protest on the part of the general public was brutally suppressed. As industrialization proceeded, a once beautiful nation was turned into a contaminated nation, and its people were confronted with even greater risks.

Views on Nature

What was destroyed through industrialization was not only the natural environment but also the traditional Korean way of looking at nature. Though not a large country, Korea has a variety of ecosystems in its many mountains and rivers, and the traditional attitude to nature has been shaped by people living in and adjacent to those systems (Bak 1999; Joh 1993). The overriding cultural imperative was to consider the natural world as something that should be protected and lived with in harmony. This attitude constituted a significant part of Korean social wisdom; it was a folk knowledge that should have been treasured and preserved.

Sadly, Park Chung-hee's modernization model destroyed all of this. The Saemaul New Village Movement, a program to build new villages that was instituted by the Park government, is a good example. Straw-thatched houses were demolished, and roads were widened

---

[11] This was the so-called barley hump period, from May to June annually, when many households suffered extreme shortages of food. According to a research in 1969 by the Health and Social Department, the calorific intake per person in 1969 was 2105 calories, which is 300 calories less than the recommended intake (*Cheongsa Publication* 1984: 9).

as part of the program, and these projects disrupted the natural cycle and created new modern risks. What were the consequences of this widening of roads and replacement of traditional houses? Agricultural communities across the nation collapsed less than a generation after the Saemaul movement began as farmers left the land and farming villages were destroyed. More fundamentally, the natural characteristics of agriculture were greatly contaminated.

Traditionally, agriculture was regarded as a way for people to work in harmony with nature, but with the proliferation of chemical farming that was encouraged by the Park regime, agriculture was degraded into just another form of industry. Chemical fertilizers, chemical insecticides, and vinyl plastic came to be a necessary part of agriculture under the Park Chung-hee developmental dictatorship. The government paid little attention to the consequences of their increasing use. The slogan, "nature protects man, man protects nature," coined toward the end of Park's reign, carried with it a suggestion of the realization that environmental degradation had reached a serious level, but the government had little intention of putting this message into practice. Although systematic research conducted in the early 1970s highlighted the problems (Yu In-ho 1973), the government continued with its obsession for development and regarded the researchers as nothing more than troublemakers.

In many advanced societies, environmental protection movements aimed at correcting the destructive influences of industrialization were already under way by the 1970s,[12] but Park Chung-hee's philosophy of industrialization did not embrace such entities. From the world history point of view, his approach was thoroughly outmoded. Although it is true that developing nations tend to pursue rapid economic growth at the expense of nature, Park's policies

---

[12] *Silent Spring* by Rachel Carson drew attention to environmental issues, and environmental movements began to proliferate in Western societies. U.S. President Richard Nixon said in 1970 that the society that poured millions of dollars into developing weapons was taking the wrong path and environmental degradation should become America's top concern (Gim 1991: 341).

generated a plethora of social and natural problems. Nevertheless, eager to show off his achievements through spectacular outcomes, Park paid little attention to what he perceived to be such trivial consequences.

Ulsan, situated in the far southeast of the Korean peninsula, was a small fishing village until the mid-1960s when it was transformed into a primary industrial city as part of Park's industrialization blueprint. A monument erected in the new city bears the following passage written by Park Chung-hee (Hong 2004): "As long as black smoke from industrial factories can be seen in the air, we will also see hope for the development of our nation."

Indeed, Park saw hope for the development of the nation in the black smoke from industrial factories, which was already regarded as dangerous and outmoded in advanced societies. Park was obsessed with development. The filing of the first lawsuit on the grounds of environmental pollution, on February 22, 1973, did not shake his resolve or give cause for reflection. While engaged on a tour of inspection of the Sangyong Cement Company on March 2, 1973, Park commented that it would be better not to pay too much attention to pollution problems for industrial development (*Cheongsa Publication* 1984: 141-2).

Park's industrialization policy destroyed Koreans' perspective on nature, as well as nature itself. This destruction was characterized by a combination of violence and science. Park's oppressive modernization spread the worship of power. The source of power was military power and industrial power. Military power produces a very blunt sort of violence, but industrial power is far more subtle. Park Chung-hee cunningly used violence and science at the same time, and the chimera of violence and science wedded to his oppressive modernization sought to instill in the Korean people the belief that their traditional views on nature were scientifically wrong.[13]

---

[13] Park's dichotomy was that Traditional = Korea and Modern = Western. Democracy is at the political core of the Modern=Western equation. Though he pursued the Modern=Western equation, he refused to contem-

However, the science put forward by Park's government to justify violence was itself another form of violence. As the risk society theory explains so well, science is used to rationalize and justify risks through knowledge monopolization of professional systems. The modern science as a form of monopolized knowledge was an *uncivilized science* that regarded ecological thinking as superstition and environmental destruction as a privilege of a great civilization. Park Chung-hee exercised his influence on professional systems, and uncivilized science had a powerful impact. In the same way that Japan used the pseudo-science of eugenics to justify its colonization, Park Chung-hee used uncivilized science to justify his violence and destruction. In taking this course, Korean traditional wisdom was polluted and destroyed, and oppressive modernization created yet more risks.

IV. SOCIAL DESTRUCTION

From the viewpoint of world history, classical modernization was an unavoidable trend. Oppressive modernization was a process of brutal transformation using classical modernization to realize Park Chung-hee's political ambition and his supporters' interests, as well as economic growth. Social destruction was the gravest outcome of the process. Risk society theory explains that new social risks emerge as a result of successfully completing classical modernization. The goal of oppressive modernization was to build a classical industrial society, but, with the social destruction incurred during the process, the Korean society became more of a risk society than Western risk society.

Inter-Regional Antagonism

Inter-regional antagonism is one of the major problems that oppressive modernization exacerbated in Korean society. If regional division is a characteristic of pre-modern society, regional unification is a

plate Democracy. The political basic contradiction of his regime lies here.

core element of modern society. Modern society can be a political product of unified regions. Regionalism prevents both regional unification and the full formation of a modern society and tends to prevent citizens from keeping a watchful eye out for the state. In a society in which regionalism is a significant component, the people cannot be sovereign, and the state power has become degraded to regional power.

There is no society that does not have regional differences. The cultural and ecological uniqueness of each region is very important because it helps make the broader society more diverse and vibrant. However, regionalism is a cancer of modern society that distorts further social development. The Park Chung-hee government tried to establish its power using regionalism because it lacked legitimacy. The material basis of the regionalism was the unequal regional development. However, this inequality is in the nature of capitalism. To some extent, intensive investment in the Youngnam region of Korea, Park's birthplace, was an inevitable decision in view of the overall economic plan to connect with Japan. However, the policy to exclude everyone else from virtually all key posts in the military, government, and associated public spheres reflected the political limits of the Park's government. In terms of this political and economic discrimination, the Park Chung-hee government was unequivocally a "Youngnam government," and the unequal regional development was quite intentional.

The fact that ruinous regionalism is a very serious political obstacle to contemporary Korean society is a clear demonstration of the success of Park's oppressive modernization. The Honam region came to the forefront of challengers to Youngnam's supremacy after the presidential election in 1971, in which the Shinmin party candidate, Kim Dae-jung, actually defeated Park Chung-hee in the Honam constituency. It sent a clear signal to Park that Honam was a region that needed special attention, and an illusory confrontation between Youngnam and Honam emerged from this defeat. Park's political ambition was to keep his unjust power using Youngnam and discriminating against Honam.

Though Park Chung-hee was killed by a member of his senior staff on October 26, 1979, the regionalism he generated still lingers in Korean society. Even those who openly deplore the regionalism seem unable to escape from it. The regionalism is a spell that Park cast on Korean society to keep his power and to hamper development of this society. Driving away this ghost is key for further development of Korea.

Refugee Society

The Park government single-mindedly pursued economic growth as though its achievement could justify all wrongdoings. In the course of this pursuit, environmental degradation escalated, workers were treated as slaves, and the exercise of arbitrary state violence was commonplace. Meanwhile, the mantras, "Ten billion dollars exports and one thousand dollars national income by 1980," were intoned endlessly. As a result of the state's obsession with economic performance, the goals were achieved ahead of schedule." Aided by this passion for economic growth, Korea witnessed GNP growth from $8.1 billion in 1970 to $51.3 billion in 1978. GNP per capita exceeded $1000 in 1977, from $252 in 1970. With exports increased from $1.6 billion in 1972 to $10 billion in 1977, national targets were finally achieved (Shinhan Research Center 1991:27).

But what did this achievement mean to the people of Korea? Those who aligned themselves with the regime could gain great advantage, but those who could not or would not had to struggle to adapt to the new social condition.

Being a professional soldier, Park Chung-hee treated his declared economic goals in precisely the same way that he treated any military target: The task was identified and clear, and everyone involved had to be coerced to participate in its successful execution. The term "industrial fighter" reflects accurately the mood of the time, a social atmosphere in which citizens had to work as though they were on the battlefield and in which those who could not adapt were branded as social failures. People were forced into circumstances characterized

286

by the fiercest competition of capitalism. They were farmers from time immemorial who had regulated their working hours to harmonize with the rhythms of the land and the seasons, but now they were required to adjust their body cycles more in accordance with the movement of a machine as a profit slave of capital.

As a direct result of industrialization, very many people were forced to abandon their farms and move to the cities. The population of Seoul was 2.4 million in 1960; it increased to six million in 1972 and to eight million in the late 1970s (Shinhan Research Center 1991:40). The population and resources gravitated to the capital city, which soon assumed the role of refuge for the tens of thousands of Koreans who had lost their livelihoods in the countryside. Refugees are those who have lost all possessions and for whom distrust becomes a natural instinct. They have to struggle to survive. If the 1950s was the period of the war refugee, the 1970s was the period of the industrial refugee.

Regionalism is closely connected with the notion of the refugee society. Those who suddenly became refugees were placed in a position where they had to use all the connections they had to survive, and the first thing most of them could think of was their home town. The nostalgic impact and magnetic potency of the concept of the home town or home region can exert great psychological influence on a society; an influence that is not always for the good.

Distrust Society

In a distrust society, people distrust not only each other but also all the institutional structures around which their society has evolved. If a refugee society is the offspring of excessive dependency on the economy, a distrust society is the offspring of excessive dependency on power. Park Chung-hee's oppressive modernization pushed people into fierce competition through the demands of its economic policy and forced them to succumb to excessive power through its authoritarian nature. Park's image was almost god-like, and his subordinates lined up around him to put into effect his "divine" will. For lesser beings to achieve success, it was essential for them to make the appropriate connections with those acolytes. The official system was distorted and distrusted; but power, or even the shadow of it, can become an object of trust. Despite it being a distrust society, there had to be something in which people could place a modicum of belief. This is a defining characteristic of the distrust society.

The bitter assertion, "Everyone is a thief," entered into common parlance during the Rhee Sung-man period (1948-60), so it is self-evident that a society marked by collective distrust was not created by Park Chung-hee. In terms of arbitrary changes to the Constitution, electoral corruption, and the illegal use of state power to extend the presidential term of office, Rhee Sung-man can be regarded as Park Chung-hee's teacher. In all too many respects, however, it is clear that Park was a pupil who excelled his master.[14]

First, he had a Japanese name, Dakaki Masao, and unlike Rhee Sung-man who joined an independence movement, Park faithfully served Japanese imperialism. He graduated from Japanese military schools with good marks and spearheaded the liquidation of those who worked for Korean independence. Despite his subsequent insistence on extreme anti-communist policies, he himself had a communist background. Regardless of his pledge not to stand for any further terms as president, he did precisely that, mobilizing money and using violence in the process. Park's word could not be believed, but the mere threat of his power was enough to quiet most doubts. Money and violence were the bases of his oppressive modernization.

Second, it is said that both Rhee Sung-man and Park Chung-hee were men of integrity, and the blame for any wrongdoing during their incumbencies should rightly be placed at the doors of their subordinates. However, this question must be asked: If they were truly men with clean hands, from where did all the money they needed to

---

14 Those who choose to make a hero of Park Chung-hee tend also to regard Rhee Sung-man as a great Korean modernizer. It is difficult to find the logic in their contention.

maintain their organizations and win elections come? They were chiefs of power and chiefs of corruption. The following statement is the epitome of clarity: "In the Park Chung-hee regime, the state set the scope of corruption, and corruption worked as a dynamic factor for development (Jung 2000:45). The only real differences between the two autocrats were their scope and method.

The Park Chung-hee era was a time when the iron fist was the only reliable factor. Park believed in the law of the jungle and thought that history was written by and for the winner. Modern laws and systems were constructed and put in place, but they simply camouflaged the corruption, inconsistencies, and irrationalities of his stewardship. The distrust society in Park's Korea was one devoid of a rational framework.

Military Society

To draw attention from the problems of his oppressive modernization, Park Chung-hee exploited to its fullest extent the partition of the Korean peninsula. By manipulation of the National Security Law, he devised "anti-communist" legislation under which all who opposed the policies and methods of his government were branded as communist. Park claimed that communist spies constituted a major and constant threat to Korea and had carried out numerous seditious acts throughout the country. His well-orchestrated scare tactics succeeded in instilling fear into the minds of many, and he used this ploy to its utmost as a means of consolidating his grip on state power. The words "spy" and "communism" became synonymous with "enemy," and the enemy was not a human being, but simply an entity that must be destroyed. The crux of the matter, however, was that the right to stipulate precisely who was the enemy was afforded exclusively to Park Chung-hee.

National division and anti-communism provided the fundamental justification both for oppressive modernization and Park Chung-hee's permanent hold on power. He wished to transform the nation into a military nation and to make each of its citizens a staunch and dedicated fighter against communism. Children and adults were domesticated either through education or by violence. Park wanted to inculcate the population with the belief that it was their duty to embrace with enthusiasm whatever he did, because they could be assured that every decision he made was for the good of the nation. He achieved an extraordinary degree of success in this endeavor, so much so that, even today, there are many Koreans who remain enchanted with the spell Park Chung-hee cast.

Violent Society

The astonishing magnitude of the so-called miracle of the Han River was only made possible by the systematic and routine use of violence. Park Chung-hee was a master of violence. He was very good at using it and very good at ensuring that it would facilitate his retention of power. All of this state-orchestrated violence was directed at his own people.

For example, the opposition leader Kim Dae-jung was abducted by agents of the KCIA in Japan and very narrowly escaped death. Chang Chun-ha, a distinguished political figure, was found dead in mysterious circumstances on a mountain path. Even Professor Choi Jong-gil of Seoul National University was cruelly murdered after being tortured in the KCIA building. Kim Hyong-wook, a close presidential aide, disappeared in Paris after showing disloyalty to the President; his whereabouts are still unknown. It was claimed that Kim was abducted, killed, and his body destroyed with acid. Whether the claim is true is not the issue here; what is important is the fact that the event occurred at a time when such rumors could be spread and gain widespread credence. Even if untrue, it remains an exemplar of how oppressive the Park government was, an image that many Korean people still hold in their minds. The entire ethos of the Park Chung-hee era was dominated by violence.

When Park Chung-hee could not be regarded as a beloved king like Rhee Sung-man, he tried to make himself appear as the Messiah. In his efforts to justify a constitutional amendment aimed at securing his third term in office, he mobilized shaman fortune-tellers and "physiognomists." Those who were connected with the Park Chung-hee government started to claim that Park Chung-hee was indeed the Messiah, and the wise retainer of Buddha. Yun Chi-young, the leader of the Republican Party, was sent to Kwangju and instructed to announce that our great leader Park Chung-hee was the only person who could deal with current hardships. Mass mobilization and fabrication were possible due to the connections Park had with criminal gangs.... When a government does not have legitimacy, it is inevitable that it will be the same as the Mafia.... We have seen this too much from the "military Mafia," which seized the power through coup d'état (Han Sang-bom 2002).

Against such a violent and threatening background, it might be regarded as appropriate that ultimately Park Chung-hee himself suffered a Mafia-like death. Unfortunately, however, Park's termination only gave birth to yet another military Mafia. Therefore, it can be said that Park's death was not just. He should have lived to face the Korean people and answer for his crimes in a legitimate and fully democratic, court of justice.

When people live so long under violence, they become accustomed to it and come to accept it; a culture of violence becomes well established. Those who learn from experience that violence is a foundation of power regard it as a key factor for success. Park Chung-hee created a culture in which violence was respected rather that disdained, and he was the originator of what could be called the *gang syndrome*.

V. CONCLUSION

Ulrich Beck argues that a risk society emerges when the problem of poverty is solved and concerns about risks start to grow. In other words, risks itself already exist in a society long before people notice them. Discussion of the so-called new poverty, such as environmental degradation and traffic pollution, is one way to deal with risks normally produced in a social system. Though Korean society already harbored all the risks while progressing through the 1990s, it can be said that the country did not then enter the risk society, as neither the government nor civic society attended to those risks and the level of democracy remained low.

According to Beck, as classical modernization matures, a classical industrial society turns into a new industrial society, which equals the risk society. Park Chung-hee's oppressive modernization was markedly inferior to the modernization based on mutual agreement. From outside, oppressive modernization seems to achieve more than that based on mutual agreement, but it instead brings natural and social destruction and strengthens the risks embedded in classical modernization. Collapsed bridges and buildings were among the inevitable manifestations of oppressive modernization. Oppressive modernization created many abnormal consequences in its wake and forced people to accept this abnormality as normal. These erroneous assumptions should be addressed with urgency; otherwise, the Korean society of the future will stand in far greater risks.

To address these consequences, the reform of politics is the most urgent task. Power through injustice gives rise to the most pernicious and insidious violence. Park Chung-hee proved this proposition over a period of almost two decades. Conversely, an open and honest political culture produces an open and honest nation; but such a transformation is not easy to accomplish. Korea has to struggle with the many negative legacies from the process of oppressive modernization.

Sadly, the reality of the current situation in Korea is epitomized by the fact that the government is not supporting a campaign with the admirable and essential purpose of bringing to justice those who served Japanese colonialism.[15] If past misdemeanors are allowed to

---

[15] Park Chung-hee is a symbol of this problem. It is considered irrational and retrogressive to commemorate an individual who graduated from the Japanese military schools and crushed the Korean independence movements. He is a dark stain on Korean history, and an open, honest political culture will not be fully achievable while he continues to be held in reverence.

go unacknowledged, history will repeat itself, and state malfeasance will, once again, be regarded as legitimate conduct.

When citizen politics are activated, reflexive modernization can proceed, and a new form of modern society can emerge to overcome the problems of the risk society. Circumstances in Korea may differ from those in advanced societies, but those differences could constitute the reason why the imperative for citizen politics is even more pressing here than anywhere else. At this point, Korean citizen politics, which has been very active from the mid-1990s, is deepening democracy and paving the way to move beyond the risk society.

Chapter 11

The Dead Dictator's Society:
An Analysis of
the "Park Chung-hee Syndrome"

Chin Jung-kwon

I. INTRODUCTION

Park Chung-hee belongs to the past. The recent, intense controversy surrounding the establishment of a Park Chung-hee Memorial Hall is nothing more than a trivial and tiresome squabble over the shadow of his memory. The levels of political, economic, and cultural development that are enjoyed in Korea today greatly exceed those of the Park Chung-hee era, and every rational citizen is well aware that the "Korean-type democracy" and developmental dictatorship that characterized the Park Chung-hee ideology can never return. Even those who continue to revere Park accept this as a truism. Although there may be some temporary setbacks, the historical development of South Korea is irreversible. Karl Marx's aphorism suggesting that history repeats itself twice — once as a tragedy and the second time as a comedy — begs the question why history should repeat itself in comedic form. One response might be that it does so to facilitate a joyful farewell to the past.

All the diverse happenings of the Park Chung-hee era that have been featured in the media seem to have been assessed as a comedy or perhaps more accurately as a comedy of errors. They constitute a dramatic production promoted by the media, supported by *soi-disant* intellectuals, and used by opportunist politicians. However, now the show is over, and to refer again to Marx, a happy goodbye seems to have been bidden to the past.

Circumstances are not quite as simple as that, however, because the show was not merely the outpourings of a few political tacticians or quasi-intellectuals. The reality is that people throughout South Korean society supported the military dictator. Many even praised him and wish to mark that regard by the construction of a permanent and substantial memorial.

Discourse, Public Opinion, and Habitus

The so-called Park Chung-hee syndrome is neither a transient phenomenon nor a figment of the imaginations of a few politicians. Rather, it is a clinical condition, a disease even, that exists in South Korean society and that reappears under certain, specific circumstances. In precisely the same way that a doctor will diagnose an illness by observing its symptoms, what ails Korean society in this context may be ascertained by close examination of the symptom or symptoms of Park Chung-hee syndrome. A quality that renders dictatorship especially problematic is that it is harmful not only when it is exercised but also when it collapses. In the case of Park Chung-hee syndrome, there appears a powerful and inveterate tendency toward a sequel.

Although much political analysis has been focused on the subject of Park Chung-hee's military dictatorship, there has been no published research on how the trajectory of the dictatorship distorted individual human character and obfuscated social interaction. This shortcoming is important because the ways in which a military regime affects society are of far greater, long-term significance than whether the regime was fascist or not. Park Chung-hee and his philosophy may have receded into the past, but in terms of social and psychological perspectives he still casts a shadow.

To address this perceived lacuna, the following questions require answering: What was the ideological basis of Park Chung-hee's policy strategy? How was that policy strategy modified or distorted by the U.S. occupation? How was the strategy fulfilled after the imposition of the Yushin (revitalizing) reforms? The most important question in the context of this chapter is: What effects did Park Chung-hee's ideology have on the minds of the South Korean people during the 1960s and 1970s, and how do those influences reveal themselves today? To answer these and other questions, it is necessary to consider the mental characteristics of the hypothetical *Homo Koreanicus*, a monster of Park Chung-hee's own creation.

As has been pointed out above, the Park Chung-hee syndrome is not an ephemeral phenomenon, but is grounded on a consistent, tripartite ideology. The first stage is discourse, in which discussion is rationally conducted and, as a consequence, relatively few people express their unequivocal support for the dictator. The second level is public opinion (Gerede), mediated through the electronic media or other avenues of public discourse. True ideology, of a caliber capable of motivating and energizing a society, resides in public opinion, and Park Chung-hee's ideology also existed there. The final level is habitus. Park Chung-hee's ideology exists not only in the forms of the written and spoken word but it is also encoded within the collective psyche. Unfortunately, this set of encoded notions causes communication problems in many parts of contemporary South Korean society.

The Park era was the period during which salient characteristics of Korean society were formed, both in the positive and in the negative. Thus, because the Park Chung-hee regime had the power to change people's mental structures, it is essential to examine more closely the nature of the biological code embedded by him, if an attempt is to be made to try to change it.

II. SOCIAL PSYCHOLOGY OF THE SYNDROME

Cause

The Korean economic boom in the 1990s revived the memory of Park Chung-hee. Korean companies advanced aggressively into the world, especially Eastern Europe, establishing automobile plants and the like and achieving substantial external growth by acquiring major foreign companies. As the wave of globalization swept ahead during the presidency of Kim Young-sam (1993-98), South Koreans became greatly excited and began to believe that they could lead the world. The optimism about Korea's economic growth potential was further strengthened by the collapse of socialism and by the ever more impoverished economy of North Korea. When regarding the areas of the world that they hoped to conquer, Koreans remembered one of Park Chung-hee's favorite mottos, "We can do it, if we do it." In recalling him, they began to see Park Chung-hee not as an assassinated dictator, but as a man of great prescience.

The chaotic economic situation just prior to the Asian financial crisis in 1997 also brought Park to the minds of many Koreans. As it became increasingly clear that political incumbents were incapable of resolving the mounting problems, the general public began to yearn for strong and charismatic leadership. The failure of the so-called people's government to cope effectively with the disaster led to widespread distrust of the power that drove the democratic movement, and Park Chung-hee's "Messianic" image became further enhanced.

Politicians were not slow to exploit this mood for their own interests. One presidential candidate announced proudly that he had been central to the Yushin reforms, and another stressed that he was actually a relative of President Park. One hopeful claimed to belong to the party that drove national modernization, and someone else went so far as to pledge to build a Park Chung-hee Memorial Hall. Clearly, these political opportunists recognized the mood of a growing number of voters and the increased popular nostalgia for the dead dictator and believed that there was mileage to be gained from jumping on the bandwagon. Furthermore, by lending it additional publicity with their declarations of affinity for Park, they reinforced the Park Chung-hee syndrome itself.

Idolization

Although the concept of a Park syndrome did not carry much weight in Korean academic circles, attempts were made by a few intellectuals to spread and strengthen the notion. Novelist Lee In-hwa presented the image of Park Chung-hee through the character of a reformist emperor in his novel, *Eternal Empire*, and openly praised and flattered him in another book, *The Path Taken by Man* (1997a). The *Chosun Daily* newspaper serialized Park's biography, written by right-wing journalist Cho Gab-je (1998), and devoted many more column inches to Park's "imperial" credentials in the magazine, *Monthly Chosun*. It is of interest to note this use of popular literature to generate the idolization of a national personality. The directness and immediacy of the impact on a broad swathe of the general public and the overt appeal to instinct and emotion were quite commonplace strategies in fascist regimes.

Park Chung-hee can, with some justification, be considered to be the "father" of South Korean rightists. Although Rhee Sung-man was himself a dictator, he nevertheless claimed American liberalism as the basis of his political belief. In that regard he was clearly at a distance from those who served the interests of Japanese colonialism. In contrast, Park Chung-hee absorbed the Japanese spirit while undergoing training in a Japanese military school. Subsequently, he gravitated to the core of the Korean right-wing group, and the entire pattern of his opportunistic behavior reflected the history of that grouping. As a consequence of this overt ideological alignment, those in the right wing in South Korea set out to revive the messianic aspect of the Park Chung-hee collective memory and to bathe themselves in its reflected glory. As far as they were concerned, the reawakening in the public arena of the Park mythology meant that the rightists in Korean political society no longer felt it necessary to apologize for their past wrongdoings. On the contrary, they now give the impression that they actually merit public appreciation for their efforts on the nation's behalf.

By presenting Park Chung-hee as a mythological, omnipotent being who achieved unprecedented economic development and by dismissing his less savory conduct as simply the inevitable consequence of the "trial-and-error" governmental mindset so essential to successful development, those of the Korean right hope to acquire historical legitimacy. By cleverly extending their logic and weaving it into the fabric of a blueprint for a powerful nation, they effectively paralyzed much of the South Korean people's political consciousness and systematically embedded the Park Chung-hee syndrome into the collective psyche. Having for so long been portrayed as having only a negative ideology of anti-communism, the right needed a more positive identity. Furthermore, the collapse of socialism signaled a marked diminution in the impact of anti-communist rhetoric; thus, the Park Chung-hee syndrome provided an opportune and expedient route to an ideological reincarnation.

Emergence of Fascist Ideology

The ideology propounded by Korean rightists consisted of little more than a concoction of worldly wisdom and rabid anti-communism, and the Park Chung-hee syndrome was utilized to help create their view of the world. The writers already referred to, Lee In-hwa and Cho Gab-je, helped build that crucial bridge between discussion and public opinion through the medium of their work. They gathered stories and topics circulating among the general public and developed them into a form of discussion while, at the same time actually molding public opinion by means of their popular writings. Because their work touched the public consciousness at so many points and at so many levels, it was possible both to detect the ebb and flow of ideological thinking within the wider society; because the writings were also vehicles for the dissemination of right-wing political aims, it was also possible to identify the direction in which the right wished to lead the public.

The work of these two individuals clearly functioned in a complementary relationship, and, when viewed together, presented a coherent view of the world. Interestingly, it is a view quite similar to fascist philosophy, insofar as it includes leader worship, public stoicism, military ethos, intuitionism, racism, political theology, paterfamilias, fanatical anti-communism, and nationalism.

299

World history suggests that the reason why these and other similar elements appear repeatedly across time and space is that the fascist mentality is a phenomenon intrinsic to every society. Those with conservative inclinations may well possess some of these characteristics, and it is not entirely unreasonable to presuppose that possession of all of the traits listed constitutes the definition of fascist. In normal times, these personal predilections are scattered like pieces of a puzzle. A fascist movement can be said to be in evidence when those puzzle pieces are systematically organized and purposefully promoted among the public. In that sense, the texts emanating from Lee In-hwa and Cho Gab-je provide South Korea's first examples of the theoretical expression both of fascist ideology in South Korea and of fascist sedition.

This fascist sedition ended as a somewhat minor drama because the charismatic personality who should have been the object of leader worship was one who no longer existed. To seduce the majority of people into following the fascist cause, it is crucial to present the leader in person. A few politicians did attempt to fill the role by imitating Park Chung-hee, but when the economic crisis swept across Asia and the consequential disintegration of the image of invincible Korean economic development took place, the myth of Park Chung-hee also collapsed. The fascist movement could not take off in South Korea, partly because South Koreans already had a strong antipathy toward the extreme right wing, but mainly because the severity of the economic crisis actually being endured presented a "reality" of Park Chung-hee that no propaganda could dispel.

What is really important to bear in mind, however, is that these considerations are not about historical events, but reflect the reality of current obstacles that continue to preclude sound political dialogue in Korean society. Park Chung-hee departed this mortal coil a quarter of a century ago, but his memory lingers on and the mindset he tried so hard to make an integral part of national character still has resonance. That is why he continues to be the subject of so much debate.

III. JAPANESE RIGHTISTS

Extension of Fascism

During the period of military dictatorship, Korean student protestors frequently chanted "Down with fascio," and "fascio" was not an academic term, but a pejorative directed at the dictator. This raises the question of whether fascism itself has ever really existed in Korea. This is not a simple question because, as is so often the case in social affairs, the answer depends on the definition of terms. In its narrowest sense, fascism refers only to the movement that Benito Mussolini led to power in Italy in 1922. By the same token, the Hitler regime and the Japanese regime are differentiated as Nazism and militarism, respectively. However, the term has a wider connotation, within which all three national phenomena can be embraced by the title of fascism. In some Third World countries, the label of fascism is also used to refer to a military dictatorship.

Fascist-like elements came to Korea from Japan, as is only to be expected given that Korea's modernization took place under Japanese colonialism. However, it is important to recognize that Japanese fascism differs from the brand that appeared in Europe. Although fascism in Europe was characterized by the active participation of the populace, Japanese society was deeply rooted in feudalism and the general population was still relatively passive as far as political movements were concerned. In other words, Western fascism can be described as the result of a transformation from political masochism to sadism, whereas Japanese militarism remained at the stage of political masochism. As a result, Japanese militarists barely managed to mobilize the public by utilizing the "emperor ideology." However, the emperor, who was the very epitome of charisma, did not have any actual power, and even when the military faction seized power, the cabinet only existed for the sake of formality. Despite repeated coups, Japanese fascists failed to seize power and served only to help the military grasp it. Therefore, Japanese militarism can reasonably be regarded as fascism according to the broader interpretation of the concept.

If fascism has indeed ever existed in any real form in Korea, it can only have begun under the Park Chung-hee regime, but it would certainly be irrational to attempt to characterize the entire period from May 1961 to October 1979 as fascist. Although the nation was militarized and showed distinct fascist traits after the imposition of the Yushin reforms in 1972, Park Chung-hee did not deny liberal democracy itself, the media retained at least some of its voice, and powerful political opponents continued to exist in the National Assembly. In that sense, the Park Chung-hee regime and the Park Chung-hee ideology should be differentiated. Given his educational background and mindset, it is evident that he was a fascist, whereas the actual conduct of his regime was clearly influenced by American liberal democratic principles, in conjunction with Japanese-style fascism. The Yushin system came to an end subsequent to Park's removal from the National Assembly of the leader of the main opposition, Kim Young-sam, and the denial of proper parliamentary government.

Kita Ikki

With regard to the actual source of Park Chung-hee's fascist political ideology, the only text that provides meaningful clues is that found in *Spit on My Grave*, written by the aforementioned Park Chung-hee specialist, Cho Gab-je (1998). The book contains many biographical details about Park that had not previously been revealed and therefore provides material invaluable to the study of the man. However, the text should be treated with a degree of caution, because the abundant "facts" it presents are subjectively interpreted by the author who, it must be said, has an extremely reverential regard for the late President. Just as in the works of Cho Gab-je, one of the salient characteristics of Japanese rightist literature is the tendency to disguise subjective opinion by presenting it with objective facts. The concept of using popular writings to propagate specific ideas to the public, a strategy that has been referred to before, also came from Japan.

To return to the origin of Park Chung-hee's ideology, Cho Gab-je notes the following in *Spit on My Grave*: "On February 26,[1] young officers launched a coup only to be suppressed after a short time. Park Chung-hee refers to this incident in launching his 16 May 1961 military coup in South Korea." At the time, in 1936, Japan was in chaos caused by a series of coups and widespread violence similar in nature to the activities of the "brown shirts" in Germany and the "black shirts" in Italy during the 1920s and 1930s. Adolf Hitler himself once participated in a fascist coup, and although he was subsequently imprisoned when the attempt failed, he later seized power by way of a legal and democratic process. In Japan also, a coup attempt by fascists failed, but unlike the German case, the Japanese fascists did eventually gain power.

Kita Ikki (1884-1937), the Japanese author of *The Plan for the Reorganization of Japan*, was the source of inspiration for the young fascist officers in the Japanese military. If Park Chung-hee was influenced by the actions of those young officers, it follows that the writing of Kita Ikki must also have had an impact on him. A study of the Kita Ikki text provides a clear indication of the steps that Japanese fascists planned to take to rebuild the country after their seizure of power: First, proclaim martial law, dismantle Parliament, and return power to the emperor; second, limit the assets of any single family to 1 million yen and those of any single company to 10 million yen; and third, declare a preparedness to go to war in the defense of any nation being oppressed.

The first step indicates the imperative to revert to an emperor-centered political structure, the second implies the implementation of petit bourgeois-centered economic policies, and the third hints at an intention to wage war in Asia. Even today, Japan's right wing still insists that the Pacific War in the 1940s was fought to free Asians from Western imperialism. Kita Ikki's text expresses antipathy toward corrupt politicians and incompetent parliamentary politics, a hatred of *chaebol*-centered economics, and dissatisfaction with American and

---

[1] This refers to the *niniroku* or incident of February 26, 1936 when a Japanese army uprising occurred in Tokyo.

303

British foreign policy that precluded Japan from advancing into Asia. A particularly interesting inclusion in the text is the article limiting private economic activity; in which can be detected socialist characteristics. This pseudo-socialism is one of the essential features of fascism; indeed, Hitler called his Nazi ideology "National Socialism," whereas Kita Ikki claimed himself to be a "pure socialist."

It is, perhaps, this pure socialism that had a significant influence on the evolution of Park Chung-hee's sociopolitical mentality. Both Park and Kita Ikki shared a personal history of vacillating between left and right, and it is indeed the case that fascist ideology itself is "conservative revolutionary theory" that embraces both leftist and rightist ideas. In one of Park Chung-hee's speeches he said, "Have you ever seen the hands of the 1% of privileged people in or society? Delicate hands are our enemy. Those hands damage our minds." This has the ring of traditional leftist rhetoric, but actually reflects Kita Ikki's pure socialism.

There are other indications that the roots of Park Chung-hee's ideology lie in the realm of the Japanese rightists. For example, Park's Saemaul (or New Village) Movement was a copy of Japanese Governor-General Ugaki's Farming Village Promotion Movement. Park's Revitalizing Reform (the Yushin system) in 1972 was derived from the Meiji Reforms. The National Charter of Education, drafted by philosopher Park Chong-hong at Park's behest, is an imitation of the Japanese Imperial Message on Education. The introduction of military training classes in schools was inspired by the Japanese military education that Park received. In Park's highly critical evaluation on the Chosun dynasty in Korea, the Japanese colonial view of Korean history can be clearly detected. Park composed a few anthems, all of them based on the Japanese musical scale. Finally, Park's adoption of a Japanese name underlines the extent of the Japanese influence on his personal development.

Observing the role played by the Japanese army in the unfolding of Japanese modern history and in setting up the puppet government with the last emperor, Pui, persuaded Park Chung-hee of the importance of the military as a means of national reform. Up until the time of the downfall of Rhee Sung-man in April 1960, the Korean army had been politically neutral, which means, in effect, that it functioned in accordance with American ideology. After the Park Chung-hee coup in May 1961, however, the South Korean sociopolitical agenda would be dominated by the military and would remain so for more than a quarter-century. In contrast, after its defeat in the Second World War, Japan was occupied, demilitarized, and transformed into a liberal nation. That is one reason why South Korea is more militaristic in outlook and character than is Japan.

IV. LINEAGE OF THE RIGHT

After World War II the United States occupied Japan and undertook extensive reforms to liberalize the erstwhile fascist nation. They downgraded the status of the emperor, disarmed the country and drafted a Peace Constitution, dismantled the massive industrial conglomerates that had supported the war, punished war criminals, and broke up the rightist groups that had formed under the militarist regime. In the early stages of the occupation the U.S. military administration systematically oppressed the rightist elements to rid the post-war scene of fascism and militarism and reinstated leftist groups to achieve a modicum of balance. However, this was all taking place at the time when the United States and the former Soviet Union were confronting each other and when communism, rather than fascism, was emerging as the major threat. It was in this time of global uncertainty and instability that the Korean War broke out in 1950. It was also at this time that the U.S. occupation forces in Japan stopped hounding the Japanese right and began instead to focus on the left.

Members of right-wing groups, who had until then been considered by the American authorities as war criminals or fascists, now assumed the role of anti-communism fighters. A similar transformation took place in U.S.-occupied South Korea. Korean rightists were metamorphosed from shameful "Japanophiles" to valued anti-communists, deserving of the protection and patronage of both the United States and the Rhee Sung-man government, which was eager to impede the spread of the political left. To both Japanese and

Korean rightists, anti-communism was a concept and a commitment that could ensure survival. Old Japanese rightists who had instigated the Pacific War were transmogrified into staunch protectors of liberal democracy; all in the cause of anti-communism.

Rightists who were revived after the U.S. occupation are generally referred to as "post-war rightists," and part of the price of their revival was the acceptance of both the superiority of liberal democracy and U.S. hegemony. Their previously held fascist predilections did not survive, and they were defined, from then on, by the extreme nature of their anti-communism. Old rightists boycotted Western liberal democracy as a foreign culture and argued that it should be replaced by an oriental ideology or emperor-centered system to protect the Japanese spirit. They also claimed that Japan had the responsibility to liberate Asian countries from Western colonialism. However, the reality of the situation was that, after the defeat in 1945, the only way for Japanese rightists to survive was to accept American hegemony and values. It was a clear case of a Hobson's choice.

Although the post-war rightists were effectively "tamed" by the acceptance of American liberal democracy, the new rightists, who emerged after the self-disembowelment of novelist and playwright Yukio Mishima[2] exhibited very different characteristics. In the 1970s, Japan had already reached the level of industrial development of Western societies. As the country achieved even greater economic success, internal dissatisfaction with its diplomatic and political status increased, and voices calling for the withdrawal of U.S. forces and for rearmament grew louder. It must also be recognized that for Japan, liberal democracy was a foreign political concept imposed by an external agency, and to some Japanese it served as a constant reminder of the humiliation that had been heaped on the nation after its defeat in World War II. Those Japanese who saw themselves as represented by Yukio Mishima insisted on a return to an emperor-

---

[2] Yukio Mishima was the pseudonym of Kimitake Hiraoka, whose central literary theme was the dichotomy between traditional and contemporary Japanese life. He committed suicide on November 25, 1970 after calling on the Japanese military to rise up in defense of traditional Japanese culture.

centered system, and many of the younger generation, raised in a consumer-oriented society, acquired a romantic yearning for the old rightist ideology.

Given their thoughts and predispositions, the new rightists were undeniably fascist and, indeed, differed very little from those in the past who had dreamed of advancing further into Asia. Theoretical distortions, which are emerging as social issues between South Korea and Japan, have occurred not because of the re-emergence of the extreme old rightists, but because the new rightist tendency embedded in Japanese society is slowly and inexorably making its presence felt.

Park Chung-hee and His Successors

If the assertions of Cho Gab-je are correct, Park Chung-hee was very confident in his fascist views. However, with U.S. sensitivities in mind, he could not display his political ambitions in the same overt manner adopted by the Japanese rightists. After the 1961 military coup, he behaved as a hard-core anti-communist and ardent admirer of the United States in order to alleviate any doubts that it might have concerning his left-wing background. Even so, Park quite soon began to deny the core principles of liberal democracy, a shift in attitude that manifested itself in his formulation of the Yushin Constitution and associated system. Such was the extent of the conflict generated with the United States that President Jimmy Carter even suggested the possibility of the withdrawal of U.S. troops from the Korean peninsula. From that point on, Park Chung-hee started to display overtly his anti-American characteristics.

According to Cho Gab-je, Park openly defined Western liberal democracy as corrupt and declared his intention to achieve absolute self-reliance in national defense. If a conservative rightist suddenly expresses anti-American sentiments and decries liberal democracy, it is a sign of fascism in Asia. When dictatorship is promoted as "the establishment of a self-reliance system" and anti-Americanism is interpreted as "protection of national independence," the rightist is not merely a violator of the principles of liberal democracy but a fascist attempting to present a positive conception of dictatorship. As Cho Gab-je points out, if there had been no U.S. control or partition of the Korean peninsula, Park Chung-hee could have extended his ambition as a fascist. In fact, he worked very hard to construct a fascist system that he called "Korean Democracy" and utilized it to maneuver himself into a position where he could seize lifelong power.

However, Park could not make up his mind which path to take: the one followed by the post-war rightists or that followed by the new rightists. That is why it is difficult to define precisely the Park regime era as fascist. Park had the mentality of the old right, yet took the path of the post-war right to hide his true colors. In the process of strengthening his dictatorship he did display his true face, however, and this is a significant difference between him and his immediate successor as President, Chun Doo-hwan, who implemented a liberal economic system along the lines of the post-war right.

In one sense, it could be said that Park Chung-hee's actual successor was not Chun Doo-hwan, but was instead the faction that created nostalgia for Park himself among the South Korean public. For example, Park's biographer, Cho Gab-je, describes Western liberal democracy as "foreign ideology" and argues that the United States was an obstacle preventing South Korea from launching pre-emptive attacks on North Korea. It was the rightists, not the leftists, who suddenly generated anti-Americanism and called for national self-reliance when they wanted independent rights; what they meant by independent rights was the right to declare war without U.S. interference. Cho's *Spit on My Grave* and Lee In-hwa's *The Path Taken by Man* are the first published works by members of the South Korean "new right" who did not experience Japanese colonialism. In that sense, the two can be viewed as Park Chung-hee's ideological successors.

In Japan, the right and the left can join in amicable debate on the issue of the withdrawal of U.S. troops. In Korea, however, right and left show hostility toward each other, and because each faction tends to keep the other in check, the new rightist element is not yet of real significance. There is, however, the potential for it to grow. An example is the success of the novel *Mugunghwa*[3] *is Blooming,* in which Park Chung-hee's nuclear development program is praised as "self-reliance." This is rightist literature based not on political ambition but on pure passion. If this passion should coalesce on a large scale with the nationalism of Cho Gab-je and Lee In-hwa, South Korea will witness the emergence of a new right comparable to that in Japan, which is reason enough to regard the Park Chung-hee syndrome as potentially dangerous.

New Rightists

Unlike Japan, South Korea does not yet have organized fascist groups, although through the Park Chung-hee syndrome and the influence of Japanese rightist literature, fascist ideology has had a chance to be expressed. The reason that Korea's post-war rightists cannot develop into new rightists is the geographical division of the Korean peninsula. Because of the existence of North Korea, with its immense and ominous military power, the South had little choice but to take a pro-American, anti-communist position. For the emergence of organized and coherent new right groups with fascist characteristics, it is necessary for the right wing, consisting of the likes of Cho Gab-je, Lee In-hwa, and those who call for a nuclear program in Korea, to join together with left-wing nationalists. Given the current situation in South Korea, however, such an eventuality is hardly realistic.

In Japan, the number of new right "Uyoku" amounts to some 200,000, many of whom have a connection with the Japanese criminal underworld, the "Yakuza." Though they broadcast their policies through loudspeakers in the streets, their status in Japanese politics is still not very strong. Japanese mainstream conservatives still hold the position of post-war rightists representing anti-communism and pro-Americanism. The problem is that there is a certain connection between the two groups. In reality, conservative politicians are trying to separate themselves from the out-of-power new right, but at

---

[3] Mugunghwa is the national flower of South Korea, the Rose of Sharon.

the same time, they secretly use them to make Japan a more conservative society.

Ishihara Shintaro, elected governor of Tokyo in 1999, is a new rightist who had been in the political wilderness. His election was a somewhat gloomy indicator of Japanese society's drift to the right. However, the group that actually poses the greater danger is not that of the new right on the streets, but that of the post-war rightists in parliament. If post-war rightists who accept parliamentary democracy are the *Datemae* (the outward appearance), the new rightists, out of parliament, are the *Hone* (the inner thought). Thus, rather than the new rightist group itself being dangerous, they are viewed as a threat only because they can be exploited by existing political elements to make Japanese society more conservative.

As a direct consequence of the division of the peninsula, the South Korean right continues to espouse anti-communist and pro-American preferences. As a direct consequence of democracy and liberalization, however, their influence on the government and National Assembly is slowly diminishing, and their only remaining purpose seems to be to fight a rear-guard action in an attempt to protect the National Security Law, an invidious piece of legislation whose time is past. With the collapse of socialism and the decline of North Korea, anti-communism and pro-Americanism are losing the power they once enjoyed, and the ideology that emerged to fill the vacuum was the Park Chung-hee syndrome, with public nostalgia playing a part similar to that played by the new right in Japan.

The syndrome was subject to Japanese influence, at least in the form of its literary expression. For example, Cho Gab-je has argued the superiority of the thoughts of the Chinese philosopher Wang Yangming (1472-1529), which were followed so closely by Japanese warriors and which are fiercely critical of the concepts of human nature and natural law that constituted the main pillars of knowledge in the Chosun dynasty in Korea. This is yet another indication that Cho Gab-je's praise for Park Chung-hee has been influenced by Japanese rightist ideology. According to Cho, it was Park Chung-hee who saved South Korea by introducing the philosophy of Wang

Yangming to a nation that had been gravely damaged by erroneous interpretations of human nature and natural law. It is Cho's contention that "the philosophy of Wang Yangming that valued practical benefits rather than moral obligation" meant military government, whereas the philosophy adopted in the Chosun dynasty, and that was responsible for its ultimate defeat, meant "people's government." In this way, the Park Chung-hee syndrome was used to justify the past military government and its supporters and to lend credence to the proposition that those who delivered democracy were incompetent hypocrites whose only values were based on moral obligation.

V. CONCLUSION

In South Korean politics, the Park Chung-hee syndrome is used for two purposes, and they are both negative. One is to secure ongoing support from Youngnam region conservatives by fostering inter-regional antagonism, and the other is to replace the ideology of anti-communism. The former is utilized tactically to help one political party seize power, whereas the latter is applied to the goal of keeping South Korean society conservative in attitude and aspiration.

The real concern about the phenomenon, however, is its residue in the minds and bodies of the South Korean population. Through his "humane reconstruction" projects, Park Chung-hee constructed an image of the nation he wanted. With his fascist ideology and politics he distorted the collective character of those South Koreans who lived and were educated in his era. Sadly, it is not possible to fully comprehend the magnitude of those character changes. Though Park Chung-hee has been dead for a quarter-century, Korean society is still populated by many who remain fascinated and captivated by both the man and his ideology. The Park Chung-hee syndrome maintains a trace of the dead dictator in the psyche of every South Korean and fosters an inclination toward fascist behavior. This distortion of human character is the most severe damage that Park Chung-hee was ever responsible for because, unlike the political damage he caused, the latent and irrevocable distortion of human mentality is virtually undetectable.

Chapter 12

Park Chung-hee
in the Age of Democratization:

A Critical Analysis of
Deification Discourse on Park Chung-hee

Hong Yun-gi

I. A "NEW" OLD ALTERNATIVE FOR THE FRAGILE DEMOCRACY OF KOREA

No Korean doubts that South Korea has been transformed drastically from an agrarian society to an industrial one during the 18-year period from May 16, 1961 to October 26, 1979, when General Park Chung-hee ruled the nation, first as chairman of the Supreme Council for National Reconstruction and later as dictatorial president. Such change has been driven intentionally through a series of state undertakings called "modernization of the fatherland" aiming at national restoration.

From the contemporary point of view, it appears strange that, throughout the period of his rule, the pejorative term "fascism" was never voiced in critiques of the state apparatus and the modes of domination of Park's type. Instead, such terms as "military dictatorship" and "authoritarianism" were used frequently to describe his political behavior, and "comprador" and "foreign dependency" were terms commonly employed to characterize his economic policies. In no case did public discourses of that time critique Park's regime as "fascist" with its social-scientific implication and practical sincerity.[1] However, in the spring of 1997, when the Park Chung-hee syndrome emerged to expose the insolvency and fragility of the "civilian government" of President Kim Young-sam in almost all its spheres — politics, economy, and society — an anti-fascism discourse concerned with Park Chung-hee became suddenly prevalent. This occurred almost as long after he died as President Park had ruled this country.

The Park Chung-hee syndrome was perceived first as a mass phenomenon. Its genesis was somewhat mischievous. In March 1997, the Korea University newspaper conducted a survey that asked 180 students whom they would most like to clone. The renowned Korean nationalist and independence fighter in the early years of the 20th century, Kim Ku, emerged at the top with 113 votes, followed by Mother Teresa with 7, and Park Chung-hee with 6. At the same time, then-President Kim Young-sam received the most votes of 39 in response to the question, Who is the person you would least like to clone? It was significant that although confidence in the president declined sharply Park, who had been the object of extreme disapproval among university students, received support from them. In a poll conducted by the *Donga Daily* newspaper for its 70th anniversary in the next month, Park Chung-hee was chosen as "the most success-

---

[1] In a statement "Popular, national, democratic Declaration" issued by the National Student Democratic Association which motivated the promulgation of "Emergency Act No. 4" (April 3, 1974), the so-called Park Regime in the age of Yushin was described not as "fascist" but as a "corruptive privileged system" which was condemned by the military prosecutor to repeat the camouflage propaganda of north-Korean puppet regime and to prove itself to be pro-communist propensity. (National Council of Churches in Korea, Human Rights Commission 1987, p. 355) The polemical front in the dimension of national politics and critical discourses on Park's regime was built around the thematically binominal confrontation of "liberal democracy vs. dictatorship" or "self-sustained economy vs. comprador economy," but witnessed no place in which Park Regime was characterized as fascist. Although there were popular records of his oppressive characteristics being compared with those of Hitler and Stalin, there was no record of the regime being described as "fascist."

ful president in his official functions" (75.9%); in another survey, by the Bureau of Public Opinion, he was selected as the most respected political figure, past or present (23.4%). As a result of such burgeoning popularity "each kind of event concerned with President Park which was undertaken covertly in the past is now driven openly and magnificently." In such a mood the Association of Admirers of Park Chung-hee and Yuk Young-su (the former First Lady)[2] was formed, and a Park Chung-hee Web site was launched on the Internet (Jong Hae-gu 1998:52-4).

Rather than evolving by dint of any intrinsic virtue, the Park Chung-hee syndrome was, to a very large extent, a phenomenon artificially manufactured by the South Korean media,[3] which had espoused outspoken antipathy to reform politics as the Korean political arena entered the phase of democratization. Against the background of disillusionment with the slowness of the reform process being undertaken by the so-called civilian government of

---

[2] Park Chung-hee's wife, Yuk Young-su, was assassinated on 15 August 1974.

[3] The method of opinion poll has proved to have such aspect as encouraging the followers of Park Chung-hee even before the Park Chung-hee syndrome. In an opinion poll which was conducted nationally by Media Research on 25 June 1994 and excluded President Kim Young-sam, Park (75.3%) was chosen as the most successful president with his official functions to such a degree that exceeded far the previous Korean presidents, namely, Rhee Sung-man (4.7%), Chun Doo-hwan (3.8%), Roh Tae-woo (1.9%). In the opinion poll conducted by the same opinion research organ two years ago, too, the rank was marked in the order of Park Chung-hee (88.3%), Chun Doo-hwan (3.0%), Rhee Sung-man (2.8%), and Roh Tae-woo (2.2%). Such results of opinion research encouraged the followers of Park in self-consoling way, although the future presidents in the phase of democratization did not yet appear as the compared persons and the popularity of serving president Kim Young-sam driving forth reform politics surpassed marathoner Hwang Young-cho, the Olympic gold medalist. Such results were quoted proudly in the preface of a book titled as "The age of Park Chung-hee: What was it for us?" edited by Kim Seong-jin, the ex-minister for culture and public information and the governmental speaker of Park's rule.

President Kim Young-sam, the media opened cultural discourses on Park Chung-hee.

Lee In-hwa's saga (1997a) and Cho Gab-je's biography of Park Chung-hee[4] (1998) developed a new dimension of deification discourse on Park Chung-hee. This new discourse went far beyond the justification discourse on Park Chung-hee, which used to concentrate on giving proof of his accomplishments and making propaganda based on the governmental record. In contrast, the deification discourse on Park Chung-hee tried to make an idol of him as a material figure who could survive even a society experiencing drastic democratization in direct confrontation with the mass of Korean civil society.

Those who criticized Park regarded the evolution of the syndrome to the level of public discourse as a restorative attempt to resurrect the Park Chung-hee regime, and they tried to counter it by emphasizing the negative aspects of Park's national stewardship. They developed a kind of "cure discourse" that tried to substitute the unhistorical oblivion of the masses with the reactivation of historical memory by presenting Park Chung-hee as a dictator reborn without historical assessment.[5] They failed in this endeavor; not least because the syndrome affected a very broad swathe of the population, including politicians and even his erstwhile political enemies, many of whom had, paradoxically, suffered greatly at his hands. As a measure of the "revival" of Park Chung-hee, at least in the eyes of some politicians, in a campaign speech presidential candidate Kim Dae-jung pledged to build a Park Chung-hee Memorial Hall if he was elected. After the election, and true to his word, Kim provided state-owned land next to the Sangam World Cup Stadium in Seoul as a site

---

[4] See chapter 11.
[5] The Council of the Korean Political Society (1998) presented the "pros and cons" of Park Chung-hee in a series of publications including *The Park Chung-hee Myth*, *The Collapse of Democracy and the Anti-government Movement*, *The Miracle on the Han River* and *Foreign Relations and Dependency*. The purpose of the series was to address what was perceived as a "lapse of memory" on the part of the South Korean general public.

for the memorial hall and allowed funds to be raised privately for its construction. Many in Korean society began to regard the late dictator not merely as a figure from the past, but as a force that could reverse the present wave of actual democracy, in which ex-president Park was perceived as a "new" old alternative of competitive competence against agonizing democracy.

II. TRIPLE IMMORALITIES IN THE FASCISTIZATION OF PARK CHUNG-HEE

In the spring of 1997, when the Park Chung-hee syndrome first emerged, there was a certain degree of instability within Korean society, particularly in the labor movement. The civilian government of Kim Young-sam had introduced revisions to labor laws in an underhanded way through the National Assembly in December 1996, and workers were waging widespread industrial actions in protest. The civilian government had more than a year left in office, and yet its governing potential had reached its nadir. The emergence of the Park syndrome clearly demonstrated the unnecessarily wide spectrum of political and social opinions with respect to the future of the state and nation of Korea, which was on the verge of freeing itself from the Park Chung-hee regime and its legacy.

That is to say, there is no likelihood of Korean society returning to any previous feudal form of monarchy. However, it was evident both during and after the Asian financial crisis of 1997/1998 that the possibility could not be totally excluded for the nation to decline into a "semi-colonized" status reminiscent of the time of Japanese imperialism in the early 20th century. There is no doubt that, at the time of the crisis, many were of the opinion that the Park Chung-hee regime remained an optimal alternative for the insufficient present democracy. The prevalence of such undercurrents, made it apparent that the full realization of true democracy in South Korean society remained at some distance. The fact that the Park syndrome emerged in such a democratized and pluralistic context forced Korean society to confront an almost completely novel image of Park Chung-hee; Park Chung-hee was not simply reborn in the same figure as he had been, but reincarnated as an almost god-like persona. The two Parks were totally different from each other — the mythical Park Chung-hee was not the historical Park Chung-hee who had held Korean society in an iron grip for almost two decades.

Attempts to transmute Park into a national hero have been made almost continuously not only in his lifetime but also since his death. Yet, before the Park Chung-hee syndrome emerged, these attempts expounded rationally on the practical achievements of the Park regime and emphasized the importance of his leadership in the historical context of modern Korea.[6] Much rehabilitation work was undertaken in a quasi-positivist way by the so-called regally subordinate scholars from the humanities and social science areas, whose main point was to defend Park Chung-hee from all adverse criticism. In such justification discourse, Park was portrayed as a leading guide of a developing country who achieved unprecedented national development though industrialization and modernization.[7] In this context Park was brought forth as a man of the people who tried to be friendly to the common people.[8] Viewed through the medium of these collective works, Park Chung-hee became a personality essential to the attainment of the Korean people's political aspirations: He was both a nationalist whose central goal was to liberate the South Korean nation from economic poverty and a democrat bent on freeing his people from the shackles of Western political influence (Chung Jae-kyong 1991).

This endeavor to explain and justify Park Chung-hee had been conducted by elite groups who shared his interests and who, understandably enough, concentrated their efforts on emphasizing Park's

---

[6] The most extensive work on Park Chung-hee's achievements was done by Chung Jae-gyong, who arranged collected materials by date. He wrote two books, one in 1991 and another in 1994, both of which he regarded as supplementary to his previous book *Thought for the Restoration of Korean nation* (1979).

[7] Gu Byom-mo (1978) is representative of the genre.

[8] See Park Won-tak, *Ignition of History: Park Chung-hee's Politics and Philosophy*, (1978), Taeyang Publication, pp. 584-671.

positive achievements, factors long forgotten by the great majority of the public. Because there were so many publications reminding readers of Park's overwhelmingly negative record, such a project for the rational justification of Park's achievement did not gain wide acceptance.[9]

In contrast to the sponsors of these relatively long-running efforts, it was largely the Korean cultural circle of old-liners, and the media in general, that were the instigators of the Park Chung-hee syndrome in 1997. For example, in his novel, *The Path of a Man*, Professor Lee In-hwa (1997a) of Ewha Woman's University presented Park Chung-hee quite unequivocally as a hero, a strategy that immediately caught the attention of the Korean press.[10] Lee, who belongs to the so-called 3-8-6 generation, that age group at the forefront of the anti-dictatorship and pro-democracy movement,[11] presented an image of Park Chung-hee that could not be shared by the overwhelming majority of his generation. Cho Gab-je (1998) gave a kind of heroic aura to the figure of historical Park in his novel, *Spit on My Grave*, which was serialized in the *Chosun Daily* newspaper. Kim Chong-ryom (1977), who had been a close aide of Park's, published stories aimed at arousing sympathy for his deceased employer in his book, *Ah! Park Chung-hee*. These works, and others in a similar vein, set out to manufacture a public perception of Park Chung-hee as not only a leader who had achieved great things for the nation but also as a revolutionary who personified the sorrow of his people in one heroic spirit. His death was also romanticized into a kind of martyrdom. All in all, the picture of Park Chung-hee that was presented at the end of the 1990s differed radically from the reality of the tyrant who was assassinated at the end of the 1970s.

---

[9] Kim Hyong-uk, who spearheaded the Constitutional amendment for Park Chung-hee's third term, wrote a document exposing Park Chung-hee's corruption, which was released after Park's assassination.

[10] Most newspapers reported details of this book, including: *Jungang Daily*, 3 April 1997; *Hankuk Daily*; *Chosun Daily*, 6 April 1997; *Donga Daily*, 8 April 1997; *Munhwa Daily*, 10 April 1997, and *Hangyerai*, 13 May 1997.

[11] This soubriquet refers to South Koreans aged in their 30s, who went to university in the 1980s, and who were born in the 1960s.

The justification of Park Chung-hee and his deification are clearly distinguishable concepts. Those who attempted deification focused on superhuman aspects of Park, rather than on his concrete achievements as a leader. They had a much loftier ambition than those who concentrated on justification because their efforts were aimed at actually revising Korean modern history itself with regard to Park's private life. In their writings, Park appeared to acquire the degree of popular adoration for which he longed, but could not gain during his lifetime. Those whose mission was deification focused on the imperative to fully integrate Park Chung-hee with the Korean people themselves. Reason seemed to be abandoned by those purporting to deify Park Chung-hee's life. This fascist discourse on Park functioned in the imaginary framework of the indivisible oneness of the leader and the masses, seducing the masses immersed in their shabby lives within civil society to transcend their misery at one blow through a moral-free rape done by a superhuman in the network of triple wrongdoings, as described below

1. In the deification process, Park's words and conducts constitute "ideological messages" imbued with the power of incantation, and his heroic life is presented as an object of idolatry for passionate worship by the masses. During his lifetime, Park constantly made clumsy excuses in a perpetual, and largely futile, attempt to rationalize his behavior; after his death, however, he was idealized through this process of deification. Park had idealized Admiral Lee Soon-shin and Great King Sejong into sacred heroes of Korean national history through many cultural projects, but was now made into a heroic figure of the same degree. Characteristically, such deification discourse rejects fully any kind of rational justification. By some alchemy Park was transmogrified into a religious figure, a truly holy being worthy of worship, whose alleged weaknesses and wrongdoings were dismissed as purely anecdotal. Furthermore, the extent to which his virtues were overstated was matched, and even exceeded, by the degree to which the Korean democracy movement, which Park confronted throughout his time in office, was understated. The origins of deification lie in the disillusionment with contemporary South Korean political life, in which corrupted party politics with

"surprise show and force drive" are frequently presented as constituting the democratic process. To some extent, there is an element of truth here, but one of the many problems with deification is that it consistently sneers at the nation's fragile democracy and, in so doing, denies South Korea's identity as a democratic republic and lends justification to political immorality.

Therefore, *the first immorality of deification discourse on Park* has a political flavor as it mocks consistently the fragile democratic modernity of Korean society. The political immorality here is the denial of the identity of South Korea as a democratic republic and the portrayal of the trans-democratic political behaviors of a violent and anti-moral kind in Park's era as an unavoidable necessity. Such a one-sided vision turns from the shabby democracy to the heroic person of Park Chung-hee. Park is brought forth as "a type for a human fate transcending good and evil before which people behold him as a truly great leader of our nation with respecting look." His bending and crooked course of life, "full of unforgivable sins and morally indelible stains" results in "a will to pietism for our state and a lofty will to self-sacrifice" and "sublimes to a force of death spreading to his whole soul like the cells of cancer." This is the man who was a first lieutenant of the Manchurian monarchy who had graduated from a Japanese military academy at age 28, a secret member of the military faction in the South Korean Labor Party who was sentenced to death as a candidate of a red purge from the South Korean militia at age 35, and a prime mover of a military coup d'état who trampled on the constitutional order of liberal democracy.

> This force of death whipped him to run a narrow and sheer path to the national interest without looking around the before and the behind. Only the urgent task of his time leading his nation to flourishing was the sole way of his self-salvation. The highest imperative to achieve an economic development and to keep simultaneously North Korea from provoking war distressed him to break down until he became old and drained (Lee In-hwa 1997a).

The reasonable interest in the legitimacy of his ruling is practically an object of cynicism in the context of his superhuman transcendence in the background of such *metaphysics of death* (Hong Yun-Gi 1997: 150-70.)

2. Many of those who are old enough to have had actual experience of the Park Chung-hee era are, understandably, unfamiliar with the newly created image of Park, a phenomenon that can only be comprehended in the context of pseudo-religious transcendentalism. Statements regarding the dictator's superhuman ability that do not conform with historical truth can only be explained as resulting from the inappropriate use of *aesthetic autonomy* afforded to modern artists; poetic license, in other words. However, the abuse of autonomy added immorality and irrationality to the catalogue of political wrongdoings of which Park Chung-hee was indubitably guilty.

3. The most important factor here is *the inhumane contempt shown to the Korean civil society* on the verge of maturing into a fully coherent, autonomous body in the modern sense, as the fascist discourse on Park was connected to the spontaneous subordination and mobilization of the masses. Those responsible for the deification of Park created an imaginary figure that by definition existed beyond the experience of the Korean people. At the same time, they fabricated the fictitious masses whom we cannot confirm in our historical memory and document. The Park Chung-hee who is remembered painfully by so many Koreans was a leader beset with political crisis after political crisis and who lived in almost constant fear of popular reaction. In contrast, the deified Park Chung-hee was invested with superhuman powers and basked in the love of his people. In the same fashion as Cho Gab-je, Lee In-hwa portrayed Park as a natural rebel with a lifelong burning passion to rebel: "The rebel here is distinguished from a normal resistance. The rebel presupposes solidarity of men from the outset and is eager to win without sacrificing them." "Although a rebel cannot be forgiven, even if the benefits of a rebellion are ascribed to all members of the society," the author "found in Park a power and a courage, which seem not to be able to be found in the human existence, through the Machiavellism of solitude and melancholy being immersed in sins, treacheries, injustices, and falls and pushing on toward his ideal resolutely" (Lee In-hwa 1997a:7). This statement which seems to advise people to value the

sort of "adventurous heroism" that commits crimes rather than the moral courage that fights against them is not his intimate monologue, but is witnessed by the people of Korea. Lee In-hwa agitates the people "to stand up over their own fate not toward a reality, but toward a certain possibility. If we try, we can achieve anything. It was possible before. This time things will be much easier" (p. 8). With messages redolent with moral contradiction and political danger, Lee In-hwa and the others set out to deny the actual experiences of their readers and redraw social attitudes.

The question that demands to be answered, of course, is whether Park Chung-hee's fascist brand of modernization could have had the facility and flexibility to rescue the nation from the verge of collapse and guarantee the ongoing positive development of South Korean society. However, Lee In-hwa does not recognize the need to address such a question. In his effective "canonization" of Park, Lee underlines his emotional antipathy toward the democratic reforms carried out by the civilian government, rather than offering a rational critique of them. This emotion-driven polemic succeeded in arousing the sympathy of others who were, for one reason or another, dissatisfied with the government of the day. In this manner, Lee achieved his primary objective of planting the seed of anti-democratic ideology. For when it comes to the question of ideology, it is frequently the case that it is actually preferable for the iconic figurehead to be dead because it is easier to romanticize about a deceased personality than to deal with the sometimes inconvenient realities of his or her life. If Park Chung-hee had never existed, it is not beyond the realms of possibility that Lee In-hwa and others of his ilk would have had to create someone rather like him.

The political and economic atmosphere conductive to the idealization of Park Chung-hee continued not only in the civilian government of Kim Young-sam but also in the people's government of his successor, Kim Dae-jung. First, there were people who were frustrated by what they perceived to be the excessive tardiness of the democratization process; second, there were writers willing and able to incite and broaden popular discontent; and third, there was a strong ideological social apparatus, the panoply of the media, so adept at spreading selective ideas through all strata of society. In concert with these elements, there were powerful strands within Korean society intent on protecting their particular interests by obfuscating the democratic movement, an endeavor well served by judicious use of the newly created image of Park Chung-hee.

Furthermore, the "imaginary figure" of Park Chung-hee (Ryu Sang-young 1998:18) thus used, the Park Chung-hee in the age of democratization assumes greater significance as the focus of unimaginable force for the drawing together of social groups, and the "ghost" begins to gain in both substance and credence. In a liberal democratic society that allows freedom of expression and artistic creation, it is both impossible and undesirable to censor literature, even if it contradicts historical fact. The possibly deleterious effects of this restriction are exacerbated in proportion to the magnitude of the influence over contemporary society exerted by a newly created image, and the manufactured image of Park Chung-hee not only revises his past but also mocks civic society for its slow progress. Thus, what matters for the fascist discourse on Park is not only the imaginary figure expressed in the style of a historical novel but also the "imaginary masses" that the fascist discourse takes as its target. Fascist arguments from the Park Chung-hee corner are tailored to convince Korean society of its lowly status and to urge its citizens to follow a reliable hero, rather than clinging to the uncertain path on which they currently find themselves: "We humans thrive by following more practical and immediate guidance. We should learn from a great person and imitate his behaviour. This may be the only way people can advance. When a genius shows the path to take, the only thing for others to do is to follow him" (Lee In-hwa 1997a: 6)

Those who undertook the deification of the dictator might well have thought deeply about the thousands of mourners who lined up at temples, churches, old Confucian local schools, and administrative agencies after Park's death in October 1979 or of the two million people who crowded the streets leading to the National Cemetery to witness his funeral cortège in the following month (Chung Jae-kyong 1991:639). They may have attached significance to the fact that the number of people who visited Park's birthplace increased from

29,400 in 1995 to 42,000 in 1996 and to an average of 300 per day in 1997 (Chung Hae-goo 1998:54). Mourners are mistaken hastily for worshipers by those trying to make an idol of Park. They read a religious longing of the weak for the power, or rather an existential beautification of the will of the powerless to the powerful from the life and personality of Park Chung-hee himself, and transfer this will to the powerful to the presumed worshipers: "Tender feelings of love and lingering attachments are things the weak need in order to continue in their miserable lives. The true human beings are all dead. I want to rid this land of superficial ideas, and want to meet a strong god; a god with a tough and simple spirit and vast energy with which he will confront the world." This god is expressed as an "unmerciful god of the wilds where the power, the final providence of the fate, dominates all things brutally.... The god has attributes of tenacious wild vitality and will, transcending all human sensitivity directly against and over the world" (Lee In-hwa 1997a:308-9).

Whatever the author's intention, the wildness is undeceptively closer to barbarism than it is to culture or civilization. In the above quotations, Lee expresses contempt for the weak and a longing for a god driven by the pursuit of power. Under this god it is impossible for the disadvantaged to lead a full life even if they become free from oppression. The only choice the weak have is to seize power and rule even more forcefully. However, in the situation where one cannot avoid defeat, the only recourse is to turn away from losers and attach oneself to winners. At the moment when the winners are exhausted and a small crack in their armor becomes visible, one should take their swords and conquer both winners and losers before they realize what is happening. That is power opportunism, and it is the brand of opportunism that those who developed fascist arguments around Park Chung-hee encourage South Korean society to participate in. They try to reinvigorate the collective mindset about power politics and economic development that once made South Koreans into "power and growth addicts." Such a strategy of escape from the weakness is nothing other than the tactic to join the plunderers of the weaker.

It is truly ironic that the historical Park Chung-hee was gloriously reborn as a fascist and became the object of deification at a time when the democratization process that he had opposed for the greater part of his tenure had reached such an advanced stage; even more ironic is the way in which the anti-Park parody rearranges the fragmented statements of Park that are emphasized selectively in the deification discourses. Jin Chung-gwon's (1998) *The Park Chung-hee Philosophy*, which re-edits the works of Lee In-hwa and Cho Gab-je that make ideology from the materials of Park's life, is itself the epitome of fascism; what it highlights is the added irony that it has taken 20 years from his death for the truth to emerge: Park Chung-hee was indeed a fascist. What is perhaps genuinely surprising, however, is to discover that fascists can become organized and build a power base in South Korea. After all the country's tragic history, a history so recent that it burns within living memory, there emerges a significant number of South Koreans who seem not only to have forgotten but who appear positively eager to dedicate themselves both to a "new" Park Chung-hee and to fascism. However, the most surprising fact is that some Korean intellectuals claim that a strong-rooted force of the masses that have internalized and supported fascism fervently has been already formed in the Korean society since the era of Park's regime.

III. THE ARGUMENTATION DISTORTION OF THE DISCOURSE OF "FASCISM WITHIN OURSELVES"

Virtually every facet of Park Chung-hee, from his political strategies, thought processes, and private life, has been described as fascist, and the Park Chung-hee syndrome is a phenomenon not confined to simply restorative nostalgia, but linked inextricably with his being idealized in the public sphere. The Park Chung-hee in the age of democratization is not a concept created surreptitiously, but a public project in which thousands of citizens overtly participated. The newly created image of Park Chung-hee differs in almost every sense from the historical reality and has gained credence, in large part at least, because of public dissatisfaction with contemporary sociopolitical circumstances. Given this, there is clearly an element of risk in attempting to enlighten those who have been seduced to a pro-Park disposition by reminding them of the real Park Chung-hee. For despite the enormous evidence that proves that the present image of Park Chung-hee is not the Park experienced in the past, there still remains the popular dissatisfaction with the present social process in which ongoing democratization is still immature.

It is also clear that, for Park Chung-hee to be a "perfect" fascist, if that is not a contradiction in terms, and for his political system to be "true" fascism, it would be necessary for there to be *the passionate masses* who identify themselves with Park Chung-hee and hate the naïve and mean democracy. Those masses mentioned before were simply a kind of fictitious masses that were presumed to be or invented artificially. However, the problem of absent masses is solved in an unexpected way.

After the deification discourse on Park Chung-hee swept over the cultural front, a certain speculative question was posed to critical readers in the progressive social movement: Did the masses of a fascist character supporting Park's fascism already exist in Park's era, and even more did almost the entire South Korean population belong to such pro-fascist hard-liners? Such an unexpected discourse on the fascist masses, which ran parallel to the deification discourse on the fascist Park Chung-hee, was proposed by a group who wanted to ascertain fascism within themselves or the presence of fascism in an ordinary life.[12]

---

[12] From the second half of the year 1999 on, the magazine *Dangdaebipyong* (*Criticism of the contemporary age*) in which I also participated as founding member and editor started to talk about "fascism within ourselves" as a reference concept in order to confront directly with the problem of practical regression saturated in the progressive circles. The practical depression of the progressive at that time could not be owed simply to the strong pressure or the reaction from the old-liners. The reflection was spreading widely that it could be explained only by the inner negative factors inside the progressives.

From the late 1990s, as the "progressives" in South Korean society connected daily life with political concepts, the ordinary life in which people actually lived and earned their livelihoods began to be regarded as the proper location for the initiation of social reform and progressive politics. The progressive circles in social and political movement drove the politicalization of ordinary life, going one step further from the class front based on mass organization. Then the diverse fields of civic life that had not been regarded as the places of struggle began to flow into the field of political praxis. Outdated attitudes, immaturity, and irrational behavior, which previously had not attracted overmuch political attention and been accepted in progressive circles, became the targets for changing thinking and for self-reform. To consolidate the achievements of the long struggle for democracy the consciousness had to be clearly brought forth that such undesirable regressive factors operated continuously and could not be overcome because of the long duration of dictatorship. The mechanism of the self-reproduction of these attitudes, even within the progressives, had to be highlighted. Thus, more important, they suggested that the "enemy" was not the old-liners, but something inside themselves that could deflect them from their purpose and make them even fall down decisively.[13]

The concerns raised in the magazine, *Dangdaebipyong* under the title, *Fascism within Ourselves*, did not differ significantly from the sociocritical works of Gang Chun-man (2000), which have been undertaken under the motto, "to challenge the sanctuaries and the taboos of Korean society." However, although Gang maintained a journalistic sensitivity in his approach to specific problems and exposed the fundamental falsehoods and inconsistency of fascism discourse by means of an analysis of comprehensive data, *Dangdae-*

---

[13] *Dangdaebipyong* identified three categories of regression not only in the progressives, but, more correctly, in the whole Korean society: 1) "collective consciousness of anticommunist disciplinary society" inherent especially in the anticommunism, militarism and resident registration; 2) "logic of exclusion based on patriarchal blood lineage" expressed sharply in the discrimination of gender guest workers; and 3) "ordinary culture of fascism" saturated in everyday language, religion, and architecture.

bipyong drew on the critical works of Gang Chun-man and the mass response aroused by the Park Chung-hee parodies of Jin Chung-gwon[14] and categorized certain negative taboos that existed in Korean society as "fascism within ourselves." The magazine's criticism of fascism was the climax of a criticism of power and summarized the self-reflective characteristic of the progressives. Regrettably, in *Chosen Ilbo*, "which was recognized as truly pro-fascist newspaper, the views of the two editors of *Dangdaebipyong*, Im Ji-hyon and Mun Bu-sik (2002), were of questionable validity; because of this , their discussion on the subject of fascism within ourselves, a debate that could have made a meaningful contribution to the overall fascism critique, was oddly presented.

In the editors' distorted view, the criticism of fascism was not directed at fascism itself, but at those who criticized it. The idiosyncratic perspective reached its height when Im Ji-hyon (2000b) described the progressives as those who were infected with fascism and the masses as the proactive bodies of Korean fascism. Im Ji-hyon's "Position of Fascism and Consensus Dictatorship" was regarded as an introduction to "The Masses, Are They Victims or Accomplices?" which was featured in the magazine in 2000; it targeted an issue that could have had important implications for understanding Korean society and revolutionary movements. It discussed the characteristics and functions of fascism as unique political and social phenomenon of a modern society and how fascism appeared in South Korea society. Im wrote about fascism as follows:

> The distinctive difference between "dictatorship" and "despotism" is modernity. Various factors, ranging from a well-established administrative organization and control and mobilization mechanisms, to a mass party to promulgate ideology that controls peoples' everyday thoughts and conduct, clearly demonstrate modernity of dictatorship. The dignity of King Louis XIV,

---

[14] See my analysis of Jin Joong-gwon's Park Chung-hee parodies in my contribution "Uncompleted Fascism and Immature Civil Society in the Context of Multipolar Modernity" to *Society and Philosophy* (2001) Vol. 2, pp. 57-103.

the brutal reigns of the Russian Czars, and the absolute power of the Chinese emperors cannot be compared with Nazism or Stalin's dictatorship that were characterized by modernity.... The modernity of a fascist dictatorship is first witnessed in its sophisticated governing techniques; its modernity is even assessed at the point that it pursues the system of "government by the people....Wilhelm Reich distinguished fascism from other counter-revolutions on the grounds that it is supported and advocated by the people. The George Mosse argument that fascism was the climax of "new politics" based on the popular sovereignty theory in the 18th century can be understood in the same context. Fascism was a popular movement and people's democracy originated from discontent with the representative system and bourgeois parliamentary politics. Renzo de Felice, an Italian researcher on fascism, went so far as to say, in his book *Consensus Time, 1929-1936*, that support for fascism reached the level of national consensus (Im Ji-hyon 2000b:24-5).

Emphasizing "modernity, the popularity of fascism, and national consensus,"[15] Im Ji-hyon argues that the masses should be understood not as resisters or fighters but as those who lend support to the governing hegemony. Im regards the masses in this way because in fascism there is something that cannot be explained by the dichotomy of institutional authoritarianism and sacrifice by the masses. However, it is inaccurate to deduce that Im Ji-hyon viewed the masses simply as accomplices in the fascist project because he also claims that "the masses under fascism are not a passive object that is mobilized by governing fascists, but are those who give passionate support to fascism and who find great hope in the system." It is, however, subject to question whether the support shown by the populace under fascism reflected accurately their preferences or was a direct outcome of the "persuasive" qualities of the governing fascists. In most cases, Im asserts, the masses were a body actively participating in fascism; however, he suggests elsewhere that popular support was

---

[15] Im Ji-hyon refers to the following: W. Reich, *Psychology of Fascism* (1987, 18); G.I. Mosse, *The Nationalization of the Masses* (1977, 1-4); R.D. Felice, *Interpretation of Fascism* (1977).

a direct result of the totalitarian state's ability to unify and mobilize (Im Ji-hyon 2000b:31).

Despite this ambiguity, a "coercion-free" system for mass mobilization is regarded as an "agreed dictatorship" based on consensus and acceptance (Im Ji-hyon 2000b:36). "Voluntary coordination from the bottom" was the basis of fascist dictatorship, and even after fascism lost its power politically it continued to infiltrate deeply into the collective consciousness and affect the daily lives of the people.

The view of fascism as a coercion-free popular revolution was applied to the analysis of the Park Chung-hee regime. In accordance with this view, the Park government-led Saemaul Movement (see Chapter 11) was a "passive revolution" carried out by the masses. As proof of the voluntary nature of popular participation, Hwang Byong-ju argues that the Park Chung-hee regime was fascist or at least "quasi-fascist" (Hwang Byong-ju 2000: 46-68). His reference to the Saemaul Movement as a kind of social revolution is exceptional. He claims that in the process of implementing Saemaul, Korean farmers cooperated with the government that provided developmental resources and, by means of these relations, began to recognize the government as a provider, rather than as an object of direct resistance: "Farmers had a desire to be respected as meaningful social beings, and from their experience with the government they felt they were treated as important beings" (Hwang Byong-ju 2000:58-9).

Though Hwang and Im Ji-hyon share many ideas, they differ in some aspects. As has been shown, Hwang argues that farmers worked willingly with the government to maximize their interests, and although he analyzed the Park regime from a fascism viewpoint, he did not substantiate the assertion that there was a specific agreement between the governing power and the people. The text that supported Im Ji-hyon's Korean fascism was an essay written by Mun Bu-sik (see above in *Dangdaebipyong* magazine):

> Soldiers appeared in front of Kwangju citizens who called for democracy and the lifting of martial law. Chun Doo-hwan ordered them to fire at the citizens. Soldiers who believed the crowd

consisted of rioters wielded bayonets and fired without any hesi-
tation. Terrified Kwangju citizens seized guns. They felt they must
offer resistance, and also believed that if they held out a bit
longer help would come. But no-one came to help. On May 27,
when riot police killed protestors in the crowd without mercy,
Kwangju people could not even help each other.... No-one went
to Kwangju to help them in response to their pleas.... Now people
want to treat the past only as history, they do not want to remember (Mun Bu-sik 2002: 23-4).[16]

It was by means of extreme circumstances like this, and countless
others, that fascism was said by Im and Mun to become deeply
internalized in South Korean society.[17] However, they did not supply
their readers fairly and honestly with statistical results of the last
general election of December 12, 1978 in Park's era under the Yushin
Constitution, in which the governmental party, the Democratic
Republic Party, got 31.6% (4,695,995) of the total votes (14,812,443);
the opposition party, the New Democratic Party, won 32.7%
(4,861,204); and the independent candidates received 20.8%
(4,160,870). However this result could not influence the power
relations in the Parliament, because the Yushin Constitution prescribed the one-third presidential quota under the pseudo-party
Yushin Political Comrades Association (*Yushin Jeong-woo-hoe*) in the
distribution of Parliamentary seats. Yet, the election statistics showed
clearly that the majority of the population in the final stage of Park's
regime began to reject Park's military dictatorship. Even the rural
regions and his home provinces, which had been the traditional
sources of his political support, showed a repugnance toward Park, as
the overwhelming majority from the Youngnam region (Kyoung-
sangnamdo, Kyoungsangbookdo, Busan, and Daegoo) voted for the
independent candidates. Therefore, so-called pro-fascist disposition
had never been internalized so deeply in the masses of Korean

---

[16] This refers to the mass uprising by the citizens of the city of Kwangju in
May 1980, during which great brutality and massacre was used against
civilians by Special Forces troops on the orders of Chun Doo-hwan.
[17] For a critical review of Mun Bu-sik's book see my book review in *Monthly
Characters and Thoughts*, October 2002.

society, as the proponents of the "fascism within ourselves" views wanted people to believe. Rather, the Korean people are politically opportunists, an acquired wisdom from the long tragic experiences of Korean modern history in which their country has been overridden by strong forces from outside and even from inside who were themselves power opportunists.

IV. WAS THE PARK CHUNG-HEE REGIME FASCIST? PARK AS MYTH AND PARK AS HISTORY

Incomplete fascism

The Park Chung-hee whom South Korean society actually experienced was not a fascist, and the governmental and social system that evolved under his stewardship cannot be regarded as fascist either. That said, it is indisputable that Park was a personality very difficult to define. In his own words he was a nationalist, yet by his conduct he appeared to be a self-seeker who worked for foreign capital. Although he "talked the talk" of democracy, his rule was unequivocally anti-democratic. Though national wealth was accumulated and the national income was increased during his reign, the life of the ordinary South Korean citizen was constantly under the threat of state terror.

Park failed in his efforts to build a coherent governing group capable of implementing fascism. He remained in a precarious position from which he could be removed at a time of political crisis. Unlike the North Korean leader Kim Il-sung, Park did not have close comrades who would share his fate. His followers were people who might have shared the same regional background or whom he knew from the army, but there were no close ties, only superficial loyalties (Yang Song-chol 1987:326). Thus, Park Chung-hee's eventual demise was quite different from the heroic deaths that tended to be the lot of other prominent fascists. His assassination on October 26, 1979 [18] was caused by Park Chung-hee's indecisiveness and his aides' disillusionment. It is difficult to accept that the head of the Korean Central

---

[18] The date on which Park was assassinated in 1979.

Intelligence Agency assassinated him just because he was critical of the Yushin reforms (Kim Jae-hong 1998:20) Park Chung-hee failed to secure the full support of powerful collectives who could have protected him.

Because the term "fascism" has such a variety of connotations, it is difficult to define it with any degree of precision. Friche writes, "There was almost no ideology that was not criticized as having fascist-like features. Almost all ideologies, ranging from protectionism to liberalism, social democracy, socialism, and communism, have been accused of fascism" (Friche 1984:226-27). To consider a political phenomenon as fascist there should be, first and foremost, an extensive popular movement and political agreement.[19] Because Park Chung-hee lacked the spontaneous support of the South Korean people, he could not implement fascism, although his leadership had overt fascist characteristics. Despite the fact that he did not attempt to hide his cynicism about democracy, neither did he deny its justness. He could not, therefore, present "democracy in crisis" as a tool to legitimize his dictatorship. Although democracy in South Korea was incomplete and fragile after the civil and student revolt of April 19, 1961 against Rhee Sung-man, the cause of its collapse was not popular rejection and distrust, but a direct result of Park Chung-hee's military coup of May 16.

In the situation in which democracy has not developed so fully as to be able to characterize it as being in crisis, Park Chung-hee felt himself always threatened that he consistently used violence to obstruct his opponents. He responded to resistance not with political negotiation and concession but with military force. During his rule, martial law was proclaimed three times, lasting for 31 months in all. The Garrison Act was implemented three times, for a total period of

---

[19] According to Friche (296), the fascist movement originated in popular resistance against monopolistic capitalism. The movement uses public frustration and aggressiveness to destroy outdated order and set up a new order. This process of building a new order is grounded on subjective ideology. Therefore, it is problematic to claim that the fascist movement has elements that can replace existing political and economic structures.

5 months and an Emergency Act was implemented nine times for 69 months. Altogether, Korean society was under some kind of abnormal governance for 105 months, a period that accounts for half of Park Chung-hee's time in office. Park Chung-hee's reign began with a coup and ended with the Garrison Act. His regime was one of perpetual violence" (Chung Hae-gu 1998:90)

Having said all that, it must be emphasized that in any discussion of the nature of Park Chung-hee's fascism it is essential to recognize the implications that it has for the nation today, rather than focusing simply on making comparisons between the new image of Park and the real man.

The Problem of Taking a Position in the Critique of Fascism

The main reason that Im Ji-hyong's critical logic regarding fascism did not gain wide acclaim is because he adopted an erroneous position. His critique began from the point when he witnessed a mix of "ideological advancement and conservatism" in progressive students. Because "authoritarianism, idol warship, paterfamilias, and closed democracy" were not qualities found only in South Korea's progressive students, his criticism also targeted Marxism and Leninism in Eastern Europe. However, it failed to keep a sense of balance. Having started from a point of self-reflection to find "fascism within ourselves," the narrative changed course abruptly after receiving strong criticism from readers of his writing in the *Chosun Daily* newspaper, and he began to accuse all and sundry of being fascists. Although he was very careful to avoid criticizing the *Chosun Daily* itself for its fascist-like characteristics, he condemned those who criticized the newspaper. However, the damage he did to the popular understanding of the concept can be said to be relatively slight.

Fascism as the "Pathological Irrationality of the Diseased Mass"

Im Ji-hyon clearly defined the boundary of fascism when he identified it as a modern phenomenon in which power originated from

334

popular movements and in which its structure was supported by the agreement of the people. It is widely understood in Italy and Germany, where fascism originated, that it is not a historic phenomenon created by a dictator's charisma and it cannot be explained as oppression by a governing power. However, for historian Im Ji-hyon, it was necessary to study more closely the modernity and popularity aspects of fascism.

When examining how fascism actually gained power in Germany, Italy, and Japan between the World War I and II, it can be seen precisely why it cannot be viewed simply as the product of modernity, popularity, and consensus. Many capitalist countries faced structural crises at the time and were searching for solutions to their societal and economic problems. For Germany, Italy, and Japan, fascism appeared to offer salvation, and according to classical Marxism, dictatorships were formed because monopolistic capital handed over monopolistic power to fascists out of spite. However, this contention does not explain why other advanced nations that had even stronger monopolistic capital did not also adopt fascism as a solution to their own structural crises (Peukert 2003:33-4).

The countries that did adopt fascism are thought to have done so for two main reasons. First, confronted by financial crisis, existing political institutions, such as political parties and interest groups, did not have social and cultural foundations that were sufficiently robust to cope with the coming problems (Peukert 2003:36) Second, the middle classes, including office workers, public servants, business owners, and farmers, seceded from bourgeois parties and joined various fascist movements in large numbers (Peukert 2003:33-4). Clearly, characteristics shared by those who abandoned the more traditional sociopolitical groups should be a matter for the closest scrutiny. Ranging from the mass psychology of W. Reich to Erich Fromm's social psychology, and to the structural approach of the Frankfurt school, many commentators summarize the mental status of the relevant populations as "pathological irrationality."[20] Most of

---

[20] In *Die Massenpsychologie des Faschimus* (1993, 31) W. Reich wrote that while economic foundations were moving toward the left, ideology was moving

those who joined the fascist movement were in unstable social conditions. Many of them had been unable to regain any form of social life after World War I and either changed jobs continuously or remained unemployed as a result of long-term economic recession. Those who had not yet experienced social instability believed that the same problems could soon befall them. Though it is likely that most of them were well aware that simply by joining a fascist movement they could not immediately overcome the crisis and regain some meaning to their lives, the collective and active participation itself made living a bit more bearable. Physical and verbal conflict must have helped fill the social and cultural void and made the participants feel that they were contributing to a great victory for the fascist movement by sacrificing themselves. They also thought that on the day of victory their contributions would be assessed and rewarded (Reich 1993:44-5). Regardless of the fact that the populace was mobilized by consent, the mindset that governed their behavior cannot be considered as being entirely rational.

Yet, pathological irrationality does not render the governing structure and ideology of fascism irrational. To some extent, a mentality dominated by a "voluntary subordination" may be capable of maximizing the effectiveness needed to achieve a particular goal. Though fascist ideology had a pre-modern and irrational goal, the fascist way of political governance was itself a modern and rational entity. In other words, fascism's irrational goals were pursued by the use of highly sophisticated and rational means of modern mechanism. It is, therefore, incomplete to define the characteristics of fascism as "modernity, popularity, and popular agreement." Fascism was the "pathology of modernity" carried out by the masses with a "pathological irrationality" (Reich 1993:11).

---

toward the right. This phenomenon was also found in Russia, when Russian soldiers, who could have seized power themselves, dispersed voluntarily after executing only those for whom they believed they had reason to feel resentment.

V. WAS A SOUTH KOREAN VERSION OF FASCISM POSSIBLE?

In his analysis Jin Chung-gwon (1998) perceived Park Chung-hee as a fascist, yet the Park Chung-hee who appeared in that analysis was not the Park Chung-hee of South Korean history, but a newly created image of Western origin. Im Ji-hyon assessed the entire Park Chung-hee regime as fascist and those who lived in the Park era as having completely internalized fascism. However, did the Park Chung-hee's regime have the necessary modernity and popularity that are prerequisites for a fascist institutional structure? Although he argued that fascism is indeed a modern phenomenon, the fact is that Korean society at the time under consideration patently lacked modernity. On the subject of "fascism within ourselves" he identified a number of structural problems that South Korean society was experiencing at the time, but many were problems that cannot exist in a modern society.

Above all, the Park regime most certainly did not enjoy widespread popularity, and Park could never have achieved his goal of dictatorship on the basis of popular acclaim; it could only be reached by dint of the great fear of communism felt by all those South Koreans who had experienced the Korean War. What did occur, however, was that the seed of social pluralism sprouted rapidly and grew exceptionally well in the economic sector. So Park Chung-hee should be given credit only in terms of the economic modernity he achieved. His dictatorship was not a brand of fascism forged in a semi-developed democratic state and underpinned by mass support. It was more akin to an absolutist state in transition from the monarchy state of a feudal type to the modern nation-state.

At the time of his imposition of the Yushin Constitution in 1972, it is clear that President Park Chung-hee sought to mobilize the people of South Korea and build a state grounded on quasi-fascist ideology, with which he had been acquainted in his youth in the Japanese Military Academy. His National Charter of Education is a prime example of fascist proclivities. Park wanted to create a nation of citizens who would voluntarily respond to a call for national mobilization at any time and voiced on any pretext. However, modernization took hold in South Korea only in the economic sector, and even more in the state-led and *chaebol*-centered way, not in the realm of politics and ordinary economic life. Therefore, any fascist ambitions Park Chung-hee may have embraced were bound to fail. Crucially, however, it is at the present time, when social differentiation is rapidly taking place and when crises are appearing in every sector, that the emergence and blossoming of fascism are most likely to occur.

About the Contributors

Kim Sam-soo
Born in 1955. Ph.D. in Economics at Toyko University, Japan. Professor at Seoul National University of Technology. Researcher at Korea Development Institute and Korea Institute for Industrial Economics and Trade. Major works: *The Realization Process of the Capitalistic State of Korea, 1945-1953* (Tokyo University); *Phenomenon and Possibility of Economic Cooperation in East Asia* (collaboration); *Labour Economy of Korea* (collaboration).

Seo Ick-jin
Born in 1956. Ph.D. in Economics at Universite Pierre Mendes France, Grenoble. Assistant Professor in Department of Economics at Kyungnam University. Major works: *La Corée du Sud: Une Analyse Historique du Processus de Développment* (*South Korea: A Historical Analysis of the Development Process*; Paris, L'Harmattan, 2000). Translated works: *Globalisation of Capital*; *Globalisation of Finance*.

Yoo Chul-gyue
Born in 1961. Ph.D. in Economics at Seoul National University. Professor in Department of Social Sciences, Sungkonghoe University. Editor of *Korean Economic Association*. Worked as guest researcher at Oxford University and London University, England. Major works: *The Formation and Dismantling of the Development Model of Korean Capitalism* (collaboration); *Korean Economy, Is there a Way to Revive?* (collaboration).

Lee Byeong-cheon
Born in 1952. Ph.D. in Economics at Seoul National University. Professor in Department of Economics and International Trade at Kangwon National University. Director of the Institute for Participatory Society. Co-editor of *Citizens and World*. Worked as visiting professor at University of California at Berkeley. Major works: *Crisis and Great Transformation* (collaboration); *J. Stiglitz's Principles of Econom-*

ics (translation). Major theses: *The Regime of Developmental State and Developmental Dilemma; The Trap of Polarization and Broken Promises of Democratization in South Korea.*

Lee Sang-cheol
Born in 1964. Ph.D. in Economics at Seoul National University. Professor in Department of Social Sciences at Sungkonghoe University. Worked as advisor to the Presidential Committee on Northeast Asian Cooperation Initiative and Research Fellow at Inchon Development Institute. Major theses: *Late Industrialization and Industrial Policy of Korea; Development of Industrialization Policy for Import Substitution.*

Lee Joung-woo
Born in 1950. Ph.D in Economics at Harvard University. Professor in the Department of Economics & Commerce, Kyungpook National University. Chairman of the Presidential Commission on Policy Planning. Major works: *Social Problems of Korea; Theory of Income Distribution.* Major thesis: *Land Problem of Korea: Diagnosis and Prescription.*

Lee Chong-suk
Born in 1958. Ph.D. in Politics and Diplomacy at Sungkyunkwan University. Vice secretary-general of National Security Council. Worked as a senior researcher at the Sejong Institute and Leader of North Korea Research Centre. Major works: *Understanding Modern North Korea; Unification in a Divided Era; Relationship between North Korea and China, 1945-2000.*

Cho Young-chol
Born in 1960. Ph.D. in Economics at Korea University. Budget Analyst at the Bureau of National Assembly. Major works: *American-Style Capitalism and Alternative Plans for Social Democracy* (collaboration); *Anatomy of European Capitalism* (collaboration). Major thesis: *The Reason America and Germany Became Different: Focus on the Difference between Possession and Ruling Structure.*

Chin Jung-kwon

Born in 1963. Theorist of Aesthetics. Culture Critic. Editor of *Outsider*. Graduated from the Department of Aesthetics and Graduate School at Seoul National University. Majored in Aesthetics, Analysis, and Language Philosophy at the Department of Philosophy at Freedom University, Berlin, Germany. Major works: *Aesthetics Odyssey*; "'I'll Spit on Your Grave'": Chin Chung-gwon Lecture on Modern Aesthetics.

Han Hong-koo

Born in 1959. Ph.D. in History Department at University of Washington at Seattle. Professor at the Department of Korean History, Sungkonghoe University. Co-Deputy Secretary-General of Promotion Committee of Peace Museum. Co-Chairman of Execution Committee to Improve Alternative Army Service System (and for the recognition of the right to refuse army service). Major works: *History of Korea; A Starfish* (collaboration). Major thesis: *Scarred Nationalism*.

Hong Seong-tae

Born in 1965. Ph.D. in Sociology at Seoul National University. Professor at the Department of Liberal Arts and Science, Sangji University. Chairman of Policy Committee at People's Solidarity for Participatory Society. Representative of Information-Share and Solidarity. Major works: *Anti-America Textbook for Thinking Koreans; Understanding the Real Information Society; Beyond the Risk Society; Culture and Politics of the Cyber World; For the Ecological Society*. Translated work: *Dangerous Society* (Ulrich Beck).

Hong Yun-gi

Born in 1957. Professor in the Department of Philosophy, Dongguk University. Graduated from the Department of Philosophy and Graduate School at Seoul National University. Ph.D. from Free University Berlin, Germany. Major works: *Dialektik-Kritik und Dialektik-Entwurf* (1995); *Habermas's Thought* (collaboration). Translated works: *Hinduismus und Buddhismus* (Max Weber), *The Beautiful New World of Works* (Urlich Beck), *Theorie und Praxis* (J. Habermas), *Vom sinnlichen Eindruck zum symbolischen Ausdruck* (J. Habermas et al.).

Bibliography

A. Korean and Asian-Language Publications

Akira, Suehiro, ed. 1998. *Developmentalism*. Tokyo University Press.
_____. 2000. *The Theory of Catch-up Industrialization: The Path and Prospects of Asian Economy*. Nagoya University Press.
Association for Korean Industrial and Social Studies. 1994. *Studies on Industrial Trade Union*. Mirae Press.
Association for Korea Politics Study. 1998. *Beyond Park Chung-hee*. Green Forest Press.
Bae Jin-han. 1992. Changes in the distribution of Korean labor income. *The Korean Economic Association Economics Study* 40: December.
Bae Moo-gi. 1991. The turning point of the Korean economy. In *Korean Labor Relations and Employment*. Kyongmun Press.
Baek Yong-so. 1993. East Asian civilization in the 20th century and a nation-state. *Changbi Press*, Winter.
Bank of Korea. Economic statistics yearbook. *Analysis of Industrial Relations*.
Beck, Ulrich. 1992. *Dangerous Society: Towards a New Modernity*. (Trans. by Hong Song-tae). New Wave Press.
Byun Hyung-Yoon. 1996. *Korean Economic Theory*. Yupung Press.
Centre for Land Unification. 1987a. *Historical Records of Inter-Korean Meeting*, vol. 2.
_____. 1987b. *Historical Records of Inter-Korean Meeting*, vol. 7.
_____. 1988. *Documents of North Korean Supreme Committee*, vol. 3.
Centre for National Study. 1995. *Review on Korea-Japanese Agreement*. Asea Press.
Chang Ha-won. 1999. Korea's developmental strategy in the 1960s and industrial policy. In *Korean Industrialization and Economic Structure in the 1960s*. Baeksan Press.
Cho Chun-hyon. 2000. *Developmental Model of East Asia and the State*. Shinji Press.

Cho Dong-song. 1990. Studies on Korean *chaebols*. *Maeil Financial Daily*.

Cho Gab-je. 1998. Spit on my grave. *Chosun Daily*.

Cho Hui-yon. 1998. *Korea's Democracy and Social Movement*. Dangdae Press.

_____. 1999. Korean economic growth and political changes. In *Collected Papers of Sungkonghoe University* 13:7-78.

_____. 2001. *Korean Democracy and Social Movement*. Nanum Press.

_____. Political and social changes and democracy. In *Political and Social Discussion in Korea and Democracy*. Hamgge Press.

Cho Seung-hyok. 1984. *Korean Industrialization and the Labor Movement*. Pulbit Press.

Cho Sun. 1989. Equality problems in Korea. *Korean Economic Association Studies on Economics*.

Cho U-hyon. 1985. Wages, labor, productivity, prices, and workers' life. In *Korean Capitalism and Labor Issues*. Dolbeggae Press.

Cho Yong-bom. 1973. *Economic Theory of Underdeveloped Nations*. Parkyeongsa.

Cho Young-chol. 1998. Retreat and changes of Korean economic developmental plan. In *Crisis and a Great Change*, ed. Lee Byeong-chun and Kim Gyun, 137-73. Dangdae Press.

_____. 1999. Loan-dependent economy and *chaebol* reform. *Review on Social Economy* 12:219-50.

_____. 2001. Corporate finance in Germany and outlook on the Rhein model. *Review on Social Economy* 16:57-91.

Choi Jang-jip. 1988. *Korean Labor Movement and the State*. Yeoleum Press.

_____. 1996. *Korean Democracy and Outlook*. Nanam Press.

_____. 2002. *Democracy after Democratization*. Humanitas Press.

Choi Sang-o and Chon Byong-gyu. 1999. Economic stability and the Korean-US argument on exchange rates. *Review of Economic History* 26.

Chong Byong-hyu and Yang Young-sik. 1992. *Economic Analysis of Korean Chaebol*. Korea Development Institute.

Chong Dong-woo and Byeon Young-uk, eds. 1980-1983. *Complete Collection of Labor Law Regulations*. Hongmun Press.

Chong I-hwan. 1987. *The Way Workers Adapt Themselves to Low Wage Structure: Male Production Workers.* Master's Thesis, Sociology Department of Seoul National University.

Chong Jin-ki. 1977. President Park Chung-hee's ideology and philosophy. *Maeil Financial Daily.*

Chong Jong-gil. 1994. Economic leadership of Korean presidents: Economic policies of Park Chung-hee, Chun Doo-hwan, and Roh Tae-woo administrations. *Korean Economic Daily.*

Chong Jong-rak. 1989. *Public Offering and Industrial Democracy.* Centre of Korea Chamber of Commerce and Industry.

Chong Song-jin. 1990. *Marxian Analysis of Korean Economy.* PhD Thesis, Economics Department of Seoul National University.

_____. 2000. The Korean War and the arms race. In *Korean War and Korean Capitalism.* Hanwool Press.

Chong Yun-jae. 2001. Prime Minister Chang Myon's political leadership and the collapse of the Second Republic. In *Chang Myon, Yun Bo-son, and Park Chung-hee.* Baeksan Press.

Chu Hak-chung. 1979, 1982. *Wealth Distribution.* Korean Development Institute.

Chu Hak-chung and Yun Chu-hyon. 1984. Changes in income distribution in 1982 and the cause, *Korea Development Institute,* March.

Chun Byeong-gyu. 1988. *On the Cheonma Meadow.* DongBaeck-Chun Byeong-gyu Publishing Committee.

Chung Hae-gu. 1998. Aspect and characteristics of Park Chung-hee syndrome. In *Beyond Park Chung-hee.* Green Forest Press.

Chun Jae-ho. 1998. *Nationalism of Park Chung-hee Regime.* PhD Thesis, Seogang University.

Chung Jae-kyong. 1991. *Introduction to Park Chung-hee's Ideology.* Jibmun Press.

_____. 1994. *True Records and Documents of Park Chung-hee.* Jibmun Press.

Chung Un-chan. 1997. *Korean Economy.* Baeksan Press.

Chungsa Editorial Department. 1984. *Korea in the 1970s.* Chongsa Press.

Commoner, Barry. 1971. *Nature, Human Nature, and Technology.* (Trans. by Song Sang-yong). Chunpa Science Press.

344

Economic Planning Board. 1968. *Minutes of the Foreign Capital Induce-
ment Committee*. National Archives & Records Service of the
Ministry of Government Administration and Home Affairs.
_____. 1981. *Economic White Paper*.
_____. 1982. *Economic Policies: 20-Year History of Economic Planning
Body*.
Federation of Korean Industries. 1978. *Private Economic White Paper*.
_____. 1983. *20-Year History of the KFI*.
Federation of Korean Trade Unions. 1979. *History of the Korean Labor
Movement*.
_____. 1981. *Annual Report in 1980*.
Friche, Claus. 1984. Fascism: Criticism and outlook. In *Political Theory
and Ideology II*, ed. F. Neumann. (Trans. by Hong Yun-gi and
Kim Mi-hyong). Dolbeggae.
Gang Chun-man. 2000. Im Ji-hyon, your idea reflected in *Chosun
Daily* is "fascism." *Monthly Characters and Thoughts* Feb:19-35.
Gang Gwang-ha. 2000. *Five Year Economic Development Plan: Evaluation
on the Goal and Execution*. Seoul National University Press.
Gu Bom-mo. 1978. *Leader and National Development: President Park
Chung-hee's Leadership*. Presented at the Third Seminar of Mod-
ern Politics Study Centre.
Hagiwara, Susumu. 1998. Historical development of industrial
relations in Korea and the basic problems of the current state.
In *Industrial Relations in Modern Korea*. Ochyanomizu Press. (in
Japanese).
Han Bae-ho. 1993. *Korean Politics and Changes*. Beobmun Press.
Han Hon-gu. 2003. Korean history. *Hangyerai Daily*.
Han Sang-bum. 2002. Korean politics and the Mafia. *Hangyerai Daily*,
January 26.
Hong Jang-pyo. 2001. Developmental nation and the *chaebol*. *Review on
Social Economy* 16.
Hong Seong-tae. 2000a. *Beyond the Dangerous Society*. Saegil Press.
_____. 2000b. Social result of the 50-year war: Normalization of
abnormality. *Culture and Science*, Winter.
_____. 2001. Military growth and collapse of the Songsu Bridge.
In *Barbarity in 20th Century Korea*, ed. Lee Byeong-chun and Lee
Gwang-il. Ilbit Press.

Hong Sok-ryul. 1999. Intellectual trends in the 1960s: Industrialization. In *Modernization and the Intellectual, Studies on Social Changes in the 1960s: 1963-1970*. Baeksan Press.

Hong Yun-gi. 1997. Insolvent power and the waste structure of power. *Dangdaebipyoung*, Fall.

_____. 2000. Position of anti-position. A memorial paper for the Foundation of *Dangdaebipyoung* that could not published in *Dangdaebipyoung*. *Monthly Characters and Thoughts* October:80-9.

_____. 2001. Uncompleted fascism and immature civil society in the context of multi-polar modernity. *Society and Philosophy* 2:57-103.

_____. 2002. Half-broken memory, the way to respect durvivors. *Monthly Characters and Thoughts*, October.

Horkheimer, Max, and Theodor Adorno. 1947. *Enlightenment and Dialectics*. (Trans. by Kim Yu-dong, Chu Gyong-sik, and Lee Sang-hun). Munye Press.

Hukagawa, Yukiko. 1998. *Korean Economy at a Turning Point: Blueprint to Overcome the Crisis*. (Trans. by Park Chan-yok). Nanam Press.

Human Rights Commission of the National Council of Churches in Korea. 1987. *Democracy Movement in the 1970s*.

Hwang Byong-dok. 1990. Current situation of Korean capitalism. *Historic Criticism Press*, Fall.

Hwang Byong-ju. 2000. People and nation in the Park Chung-hee era. *Dangdaebipyoung*, Fall.

Hyodo, Tsutomu. 1971. *Historical Development of Industrial Relations in Japan*. University of Tokyo Press. (in Japanese)

Im Hyon-jin and Song Ho-gun. 1994. Governing ideology of the Park Chung-hee regime. In *Governing Ideology of Korean Politics and Opposition Ideology*. History Criticism Press.

Im Ji-hyom. 1998. Progressive ideology and conservative life. In *1998 Report on the Intellectual: Voice of Korean Leftist*. Mineumsa.

Im Ji-hyon. 2000a. Sad portrait of a mole. *Monthly Characters and Thoughts*, March.

_____. 2000b. Position of fascism and "consensus dictatorship." *Dangdaebipyoung*, Fall.

Ingwageonil. 1989. *Report on Air Pollution: Nuclear Power and Industrial Accidents*. (Trans. by Yuk Hae-young). Gaemagowon Press.

Ishizaki, Nao. 1996. Heavy and chemical industrialization policy in Korea. In *Development Mechanism in Korea and Taiwan*, ed. Hattory Tamio and Sato Yukihito. Institute of Developing Economies.

Jessop, B. 2003. Developmental state and the knowledge-based economy. In *Changes of East Asian Economy and the Role of the State*, ed. Kim Dae-hwan et al. Hanwool Press.

Jin Chung-gwon. 1998. *I Shall Spit on Your Grave*. Gaemagowon.

Kim Byong-tae et al. 1981. *Development of the Korean Economy*. Four Season Press.

Kim Chan-jin. 1976. *Introduction of Foreign Capital*. Iljogak Press.

Kim Chong-chol. 1986. Dependency, dictatorship, and resistance: Politics from 1965 to 1972. In *New Understanding of Liberation*. Dolbegae Press.

Kim Chong-ryom. 1977. *Ah! Park Chung-hee*. Chungang M&B Press.

_____. 1990. 30-year history of Korean economic policy. *Chungang Daily*.

_____. 1994. Was Park's developmental policy a failure? *Chosun Daily*.

_____. 1995. 30-year history of Korean economic policy: Kim Chong-ryom memoirs. *Joongang Daily*.

Kim Dae-hwan. 1987. Changes of international management environment and heavy industry. In *Korean Economics*. Gachi Press.

Kim Dal-hyon. 1962. *Review on the Five Year Economic Development Plan*. Jinmyong Press.

Kim Dong-chun. 1999. People in 20th century Korea. *Changbi Press*, Winter.

Kim Geum-soo. 1986. *Labour Problems in Korea*. Publit Press.

Kim Gi-won. 2002. *Is it the End of the Chaebol Reform?* Hanwool. Press.

Kim Gwang-sok, and Cha Dong-se. 1995. *Historic Evaluation on the Half-Century Korean Economy and its Vision for the 21 Century*. Korea Development Institute.

Kim Gyun, and Lee Byeong-chun. 1998. *Crisis and a Great Change*. Dangdae Press.

Kim Ho-gi. 1985. Economic development and the role of the state: The 1960s and 1970s. In *Korean Capitalism and State*, ed. Choi Jang-jip. Hanwool Press.

_____. 1999a. Changes in social structures and policies in the late 1970s. In *Political and Social Changes in the Late 1970s*. Baeksan Press.

_____. 1999b. Park Chung-hee era and contemporary history. In *Korea's Social Changes*. Nanam Press

_____. 1988. *Monopoly Capital and Wage Labour*. Gachi Press.

_____. 1990. *Monopolistic Capital and Work for Wages in Korea: Analysis of Work for Wages under Monopolistic Capitalism*, 3rd ed. Gachi Press.

Kim Hyong-uk, and Park Sa-wol. 1985. *Kim Hyong-uk's Memoirs*, vol. 3. Achim Press.

Kim Il-gon. 1986. *Theory of Korean Economic Development*. Trade and Management Press.

Kim Il-sung. 1966. Current situation and duty of the party. *Nodong Daily*, October 6.

_____. 1971a. Joint struggle against the US will certainly succeed. In *Kim Il-sung's Work 26*. Pyongyang: Chosun Nodong Press.

_____. 1971b. Problems of Chosun Nodong Party and the government's domestic and foreign policy. In *Kim Il-sung's Work 26*. Pyongyang: Chosun Nodong Press.

_____. 1972. Decision made at the Fifth Meeting of the Central Committee of Chosun Nodong Party. In *Kim Il-sung's Work 27*. Pyongyang: Chosun Nodong Press.

_____. 1984. Conversation with journalists of the *New York Times*. In *Kim Il-sung's Work 27*. Pyongyang: Chosun Nodong Press.

Kim Jae-hong. 1998. *Inheritance of Park Chung-hee*. Green Forest Press.

Kim Ji-ha. 1984. Satire or suicide? In *Song for the Nation and People*. Dongwang Press.

Kim Jin-gyun, and Hong Song-tae. 1996. *The Ruler and the Ruled and Modern Society: Studies on Modern Militarization and the Defense Industry*. Culture and Science Press.

Kim Jin-myong. 1993. *Mugunghwa Is Blooming*. Haenaem Press.

Kim Jin-yob. Formation and breakdown of developmental model of Korean capitalism. *Centre for Social and Culture Studies at Sungkonghoe University, Research Paper 2*. Nanum Press.

Kim Jun. 1993. *Labor Policies and Movement in Asian Authoritarian Nations: Comparison between Korea and Taiwan*. PhD Thesis, Sociology Department of Seoul National University.

_____. 1999. Reorganization of labor unions after 5/16 and formation of the Federation of Korean Trade Unions. *Society and History* 55.

Kim Kwang-Suk. 1984. *The Pattern of Korean Industrialization and the Cause*. Korea Development Institute.

Kim Myong-ja. 1991. *Science in the Western and Eastern Worlds, and the Environmental Movement*. Donga Press.

Kim Nak-nyeon. 1999a. Korea's economic development in the 1960s and the role of the government. *Review of Economic History* 27.

_____. 1999b. Korean industrialization in the 1960s and its characteristics. In *Korean Industrialization in the 1960s and Economic Structure*. Baeksan Press.

Kim Sam-soo. 1993. *The Formation of a Capitalist State in Korea, 1945-53: Political System, Workers' Movement, and Labour Policy*. University of Tokyo Press. (in Japanese)

_____. 1998. The 1997 revision of Korean labour law: Problems and policy alternatives. *Korean Journal of Labour Economics* 21(2).

_____. 1999a. Korea's labor policies in the 1960s and industrial relations. In *The Industrialization and Economic Structure of Korea in the 1960s*. Baeksan Press.

_____. 1999b. Industrial relations in the Korean automobile industry. *Journal of Industrial Relations Review* 9.

Kim Song-jin. 1994. Park Chung-hee era, What does it mean to us? *Chosun Daily*.

Kim Su-gon. 1983a. *Policy Alternatives and the Direction of Industrial Relations*. Korea Development Institute.

Kim Su-gon. 1983b. *Labor Relations and Institutional Improvement Measures*.

Kim Sung-sok. 1996. National capital and the *chaebol*. *Social Science Thesis* 6(2):27-54.

Kim Tae-il. 1985. Studies on the emergence of authoritarianism. In *Korean Capitalism and State*, ed. Choi Jang-jip. Hanwool Press.

Kim Yong-ho. 1999. Korean political movements in the late 1970s. *New Understanding of Korean Modern History 13*. Baeksan Press.

Kim Young-sun. 1988. *Studies on the Revitalizing Reform: Today's Korean Capitalism and State*. Hangil Press.

Kim Yun-tae. 2000. *Chaebol and Power: Looking for a New Economic Model*. New People Press.

Kimiya, Tadashi. 1991. *The Failure of the Inward-Looking Deepening Strategy in South Korea*. PhD Thesis, Korea University.

Kiyomizu (1987/1988). Yushin regime of Park Chung-hee and the development of labour control. *Hokkudai Legal Studies*, 36/37. (in Japanese)

Ko Chong-il. 1989. *Structural Analysis of Korean Economy*. (Trans. by Ko Chong-il). Solbap Press.

Ko Chun-sok. 1989. *Korean Economic History: 1876-1979*. (Trans. by Park Gi-chol). Dongnyok Press.

Ko Song-guk. 2000. Ideal and limit of the Progressive Party. In *Theory of Korean Modern Politics*, ed. Han Bae-ho. Orm Press.

Kong Byong-ho. 1993. *Ups and Downs of Korean Enterprises*. Myongjin Press.

Korea Chemical Fibres Association. 1972. *Minutes of Board Meeting*.

Korea Development Bank. 1984. *30-Year History of the Korean Development Bank*.

Korea Development Institute. 1982. *Industrial Policy and Supporting Measures*. Research Paper 82-09.

Korea Electric Power Corporation. 1981. *20-Year History of KEPCO*.

Korea Institute for Industrial, Economic and Trade. 1997. *Korean Industry: History of Development and Future Vision*.

Lee Byeong-cheon. 1996. Cold War structure and authoritarian capitalism: Korea. *Review on Social Economy* 9.

_____. 1997. Korea's economic development and developmental theory. *Industry and Economy* 7(2).

_____. 1999a. Park Chung-hee regime and the developmental state. *Centre for Economic Development Study* 5(2).

_____. 1999b. Park Chung-hee regime and the formation of a national developmental model. *Research on Economics Development* 5(2).

_____. 2000a. Buma resistance, American hegemony, and democracy. In *Review and Outlook of Korean Democracy*. Hangaram Press.

_____. 2000b. Developmental nation and dilemma. *Economic History* 28.

_____. 2000c. History and outlook of Korean development model: Conservative modernization model dependent on American hegemony. In *Korean Society at a Turning Point*. Semyong Press.

_____. 2000d. Looking back on the national economy 1. *Collected Papers of Centre of Korean Social Science*.

_____. 2003a. Developmental competition and the global standard. Presented at the 10th Mediterranean Scientific Gathering.

_____. 2003b. Overcoming the developmental nation theory. *Economy and Society* 57, Spring.

_____. 1998. Capitalism of developmental nations and its dilemma. In *Crisis and a Great Change*. Dangdae Press.

_____. 1999, Park Chung-hee regime and formation of a developmental state model. *Economic Developmental Study* 5(2):141-87.

Lee Chong-o. 1988. Anti-Japan, nationalism and the 6/3 movement. *History Criticism Press*, Summer.

Lee Chong-sok. 1995a. *Understanding Current North Korea: Ideas, System, and Leadership*. History Criticism Press.

_____. 1995b. *Studies on Chosun Nodong Party: Focused on Changing Ideas and System*. History Criticism Press.

_____. 1998. *Unification Study on the Divided Peninsula*. Hanwool Press.

_____. 2003. Revitalizing reform and the divided country. In *Developmental Dictatorship and the Park Chung-hee Regime*. Changbi Press.

Lee Chong-won. 1995. International politics and the Korean-Japanese meeting. In *Looking Back on the Korean-Japanese Agreement*. Asea Press.

Lee Chun-gu. 1992. *Theory and Current Situation of Income Distribution*. Dasan Press.

Lee Chun-sik. 2002. Formation of governing ideology of the Park Chung-hee regime. In *Studies on the Park Chung-hee Era*. Baeksan Press.

Lee Gwang-il. 1995. Movement against the Korean-Japanese agreement. In *Looking Back on the Korean-Japanese Agreement.* Asea Press.

_____. 2001a. National characteristics and changes under developmental dictatorship. *Economy and Society*, Spring.

_____. 2001b. National and structural characteristics under developmental dictatorship. In *Korean Democracy and Social Movement*, ed. Cho Hae-yon. Nanum Press.

Lee Han-doo. 1986. *Park Chung-hee, Kim Young-sam, and Kim Dae-jung.* Beomjo Press.

Lee Han-gu. 1999. *History of Korean Chaebol.* Bibong Press.

Lee Hang-gyu. 1993. Nuclear energy policy. *Environmental Movement*, September.

Lee In-hwa. 1997a. *The Path of Man.* Sallim.

_____. 1997b. True leader who rises above virtue and vice. *Hangyerai*, May 13, p. 11.

Lee Jae-hui. 1984. Capital accumulation and the role of the state. In *Korean Capitalism*, ed. Lee Dae-gun and Chong Un-young. Gachi Press.

_____. 1999. *Chaebol* and the national economy. In *Korean Chaebol Reform*, ed. Kim Dae-hwan and Kim Gyun. Naman Press.

Lee Jay-min. 1996. Historic type of late industrialization and understanding of Korean industrialization. In *Major Nations' Experience on Economic Development: Assessment and Comparison of Development Model.* Korea Development Economics Association.

_____. 1995. Post-war world structure and Korea's export-oriented industrialization. In *Korean Economy: Issues and Outlook.* Knowledge Industry Press.

Lee Jin-sun. 1993. *Korean Land Problem*, unpublished paper.

Lee Joung-woo. 1991. Wealth in Korea, capital returns and income inequality. In *Collected Papers on Economics*, Economy Research Centre of Seoul National University, September.

_____. 2003. Korea's 50-year economic development. *Studies on Economics*, February.

Lee Joung-woo, and Hwang Song-hyon. 1998. Wealth distribution: Current situation, problems and future policies. *KDI Policy Studies* 22(1&2).

Lee Ju-ho. 1996. *Employment Policy and Human Resource Development: Institutional Approach*. Korea Development Institute.

Lee Sang-cheol. 1998a. Korea's chemical fibre industry and the role of the government (1965-1972). *Economic History* 25, December.

_____. 1998b. Korea's late industrialization and industrial policy: Focused on chemical fibre. *Journal of Korean Economic Development* 4(1).

Lee Sang-woo. 1984. *Inside Story of Park Chung-hee Era*. Chungwon Press.

_____. 1986. 18 years under Park Chung-hee regime. *Donga Daily*.

_____. 1987. *America or American Product*. Jungwon Press.

_____. 1993. *The Third Republic 1*. Jungwon Press.

Lee Song-hyong. 1985. Nation, class, and capital accumulation: Focus on 8/3. In *Korean Capitalism and State*, ed. Choi Jang-jip. Hanwoo Press.

Lee Sung-Hun. 1989. *Korea's Industrial Policy*. Korea Institute for Industrial Economics & Trade.

Lee Won-dok. 1996a. Problems and revision of the Korean-Japanese agreement. In *Looking Back on the Fundamental of Japan*. Hangil Press.

_____. 1996b. The history of the past Korean-Japanese relations. In *Japanese Diplomacy and Korea-Japanese Meeting*. Seoul National University.

Liu Sang-young. 1998. To overcome Park Chung-hee and his era. In *Beyond Park Chung-hee*. Green Forest Press.

Ministry of Finance. 1982. *White Paper on Financial Investment and Loans*.

Mokgungjeongsa. 1991. *Collapse of Korea's Intensive Industrialization*. PhD Thesis, Politics Department of Korea University.

Mun Bu-sik. 2002. *Looking for Lost Memory: Looking Back on the Time of Madness*. Samin.

Mun Myong-ja. 1999. *Park Chung-hee and Kim Dae-jung from My Perspective*. Monthly Mal Press.

Murakami, Yasusuke. 1996. *An Anticlassical Political Economy – A Vision for the Next Century*. (Trans. by Kozo Yamamura). Stanford University Press.

Nakanishi, Yoh. 1982. *Studies of 'Social Policy' and 'Labour Problems' in Japan*. University of Tokyo Press. (in Japanese)

National Council of Churches in Korea. 1984. *Labor and Testimonies in the 1970s*. Pulbit Press.
National Statistics Office. 1991. *Major Economic Statistics*.
O Won-chol. 1994. Inside Story of the defense industry. *Monthly Chosun*, September.
_____. 1995a. *Korean Economic Development: Engineering*. Kia Economic Study Centre.
_____. 1995b. The start of the Yulgok Project: Dispute between Park Chung-hee and Kim Il-sung. *Shindong*, June.
_____. 1996. *Economic Development in Korea*, vols 1-5. Kia Economics Centre.
_____. 1999. *I Am Not Arguing for War!: Korean Type Economic Development*. Centre for Korean Economic Policy.
Oberdorfer, Don. 1998. The two Koreas. *Chungang Daily*.
Office of the Prime Minister. 1967. *Assessment Report on the First Five Year Economic Development Plan*.
Park Byeng-yun. 1980. Heavy chemical industrialization. *Shindonga*. 189.
Park Chan-il. 1979. Income distribution: Federation of Korean Trade Unions. In *Economic Development and Income Distribution*. Literature and Intelligence Press.
Park Chung-hee. 1963. *Nation, Revolution and I*. Jiguchon Press.
_____. 1997. *Nation, Revolution, and I*, 2nd ed. Jiguchon Press.
Park Dong-chol. 1999. Formation and structure of enterprise groups in the 1960s. In *Korea's Industrialization in the 1960s and Economic Structure*. Baeksan Press.
Park Eun-hong. 1999. Review on development theory. *Collection of Treatises of International Politics* 39(3).
Park Gwang-ju. 1990. Searching for Inter-Korean Dialogue. In *Unification Problems at a Turning Point*, ed. Min Byong-chun. Daewang Press.
Park Hui-bom. 1968. *Theory of Korean Economic Development*. Korea University Centre for Asian Studies.
Park Hyon-chae. 1982. Changes in the Korean economy and people's life. In *People and Economy*. Minjung Press.
_____. 1987. Economic and national analysis of 4/19 and 5/16. In *Korean Economics*. Gachi Press.

Park Sang-hwan. 2000. *The Korean War and Philosophy: Anti-Communism Ideology and Inspection.* Culture and Science Press.

Park Se-gil. 1989. *Rewritten Korean Modern History.* Dolbeggae Press.

Park Tae-gyun. 2000a. Amendment of 1961-1964 Economic Development Plan. *Society and History* 57.

_____. 2000b. *Formation of Korean Economic Development Plan 1956-1964: Economic Development Theory and US Policy towards Korea.* Thesis, History Department of Seoul National University.

Park Tae-ho. 1985. *Foreign Relations of the Democratic People's Republic of Korea.* Pyongyang: Social Science Press.

Park Won-tak. 1978. *History, Politics, and Philosophy of President Park Chung-hee.* Taeyang Press.

Park Young-gi. 1983. *Current State of Korean Labour Movement and Improvement Measures.* Kim Su-gon ed.

Peukert, Detlef. 1982. *Ordinary Life under Nazism: Adaptation, Resistance, and Racism.*(Trans. by Kim Hak-ee). Gaemagowon.

Planning Body to Restore National Economy. 1961. *Comprehensive Plan to Restore Economy.*

Presidential Secretary's Office. 1972. *Report on Commerce and Industry.* Document Keeping Centre of the Ministry of Government Administration and Home Affairs.

Reich, Wilhelm. 1933. D*ie Massenpsychologie des Faschismus.* Verlag Kiepenheuer.

Research Committee on Land Possession. 1989. *Research Paper on Land Possession.*

Samir, Amin. 1985. *Future of Motaktong.* (Trans. by Hanulrim Editorial Department). Hanwoollim Press.

Seo Ick-Jin. 1999. Korean crisis and the crisis of the developmental model. *Gyeongsang* 27(1).

_____. 2002. Korea's developmental model, political economics to overcome crisis (1). Presented at Korea's Economic Development: Introspection of Political Economics, Spring Seminar of Social and Economics Association.

Shibata, Michio. 1983. *Modern World and Peoples' Movements.* Iwanami Press. (in Japanese)

Shin Gwang-young. 1999. *Industrialization and Democratization in East Asia.* Literature and Intelligence Press.

Shin Il-ryong. 1985. *Studies on Basic Rights to Labor.* Mirae Press.

Shinhan Research Centre. 1991. *7089: From 1970 to 1989.* Koryowon Press.

Sin Yu-gun. 1992. *Management in Korea: The Phenomenon and Outlook.* Parkyongsa Press.

So Chung-sok. 1994. Political ideology of the democratic government. In *Korean Politics Governing Ideology and a Counter Ideology.* Institute for Korean Historical Studies.

_____. 1999. *Cho Bong-am and the 1950s: The First and Second Volumes.* History Criticism Press.

Son Woo-wi. Park Chung-hee's testimony, vol.1. *Monthly Chosun.*

Song Ho-geun. 1991. *Labour Politics and Market in Korea.* Nanam Press.

_____. 2000. Park Chung-hee regime and labor. *Society and History* 58.

Struggle Committee for the Reinstatement of Discharged Workers at Dongil Corporation. 1985. *History of Labour Union Movement at Dongil Corporation.* Dolbeggae Press.

Sumiya, Mikio. 1976. *Korean Economy.* Iwanami Press. (in Japanese)

Weber, Max. 1975. *Collected Papers of Social Science.* (Trans. by Yang Hoe-soo). Eulyu Press.

Yang Byong-moo et al. 1992. *Wage Management of Korean Enterprises.* Korea Employers Association.

Yang Song-chol. 1987. *Divided Politics, Comparison between Park Chung-hee and Kim Il-sung.* Hanwool.

Yokoda, Nobuko. 1998. Lower class in cities and the labour market in Korea. In *Industrial Relations in Modern Korea.* Ochyanomizu Press. (in Japanese)

Yu Chul-gyue. 1992. Increase of domestic demand in the late 1980s. *Korea Social Research Centre Trend and Outlook*, Winter.

Yu In-ho. 1973. Economic growth and environmental degradation: Rapid growth. *Changbi*, Fall.

Yu Jong-il. 1997. Appraisal of labour policy in the era of Park Chung-hee and direction of labour relations improvement. *Journal of Korean Economic Development* 3.

_____. 1998. Changes in labor relations and political economics. In *Crisis and a Great Change*, ed. Lee Byeng-chun and Kim Gyun. Dangdae Press.

Yu Song-chun. 1997. Possibility and limit of Confucian capitalism. *Tradition and Modern*, Summer.

Yu Sung-min. 1998. Efficiency, democracy, equality, and *chaebol* reform. *Sasang*, Summer.

Yu Won-sik. 1987. *Inside Story of 5/16: Where is the Revolution?* Inmu Press.

Yun Gi-chung. 1997. *Analysis of Inequality of Korean Economy.* Parkyongsa Press.

B. English and Western-Language Publications

Amsden, A.H. 1981. An international comparison of the rate of surplus value in the manufacturing industry. *Cambridge Journal of Economics*, September.

_____. 1989 *Asia's Next Giant: South Korea and Late Industrialization.* Oxford University Press.

_____. 1991. Big business and urban congestion in Taiwan: The origins of small enterprise and regionally decentralized industry. *World Development* 19(9).

Amsden, A. H., and A. Singh,1994. Growth in developing countries: Lessons from East Asian countries. *European Economic Review* 38(3/4):941-51.

Aoki, M., Hyung-ki Kim, and M. Okuno-Hujiwara, eds. 1999. *The Role of Government in East Asian Economic Development: Comparative Institutional Analysis.* Clarendon Press.

Bendix R. 1964. *Nation-Building and Citizenship.* University of California Press.

Bhagwati, Jagdish. 1966. *The Economics of Underdeveloped Countries.* Weidenfeld and Nicolson.

Bhagwati, Jagdish. 1997. Democracy and development: New thoughts on an old question. In *Writings on International Economics*, ed. V. N. Balasubramanyam. Oxford University Press.

Bhalla, Surjit. 1979. The distribution of income in Korea: A critique and a reassessment. Mimeo. World Bank.

Boureile, P. 1994. *Relations entre importations et le dèvelopement: le cas de l'inde*, Ph.D. thesis, Universitè des Sciences Sociales-Grenoble II.

Bronfenbrenner, Urie. 1961. The mirror image in Soviet-American relations: A social psychologist's report. *Journal of Social Issues* 17(3).

Castells, M. 1998. *The Information Age*, vol. 3: *End of Millennium*. Blackwell.

Chandler, Jr., A. D. 1990. *Scale and Scope--The Dynamics of Industrial Capitalism*. Harvard University Press.

Chang, H. J., and C. G. Yoo. 1999. The triumph of the rentiers?: The 1997 Korean crisis in a historical perspective. Presented at the Workshops on the World Financial Authority organized by the Center for Economic Policy Analysis, New School University.

Chang, Ha-Joon, and R. Rowthorn, eds. 1995. *The Role of the State in Economic Change*. Clarendon Press.

Cho, Yoon Je, and Thomas Hellmann. 1994. The government's role in Japanese and Korean credit markets: A new institutional economic perspective. *Seoul Journal of Economics*. 7(4).

Choo, Hanchung. 1992. Income distribution and social equity in Korea. Presented at the KDI/CIER Joint Seminar, April.

Cumings, B. 1984a. The origins and development of the Northeast Asian political economy: Industrial sectors, product cycle, and political consequences. *International Organization* 38(7).

Cumings, B. 1984b. The legacy of Japanese colonialism in Korea. In *Japanese Colonial Empire, 1895~1945*, ed. R.H. Myers and M.R Peattie. Princeton University Press.

Cordova, D. 1994. *Succes et echec de l'industrialisation: Coree du Sud et Peru*. Ph.D. thesis, Universite des Sciences Sociales-Grenoble II.

Cox, R 1987. *Production, Power, and World Order*. Columbia University Press.

Dalla, I., and D. Khatkhate. 1995. Regulated deregulation of the financial system in Korea. *World Bank Discussion Papers* 292.

Davis, E. P. 1992. *Debt, Financial Fragility, and Systemic Risk*. Clarendon Press.

Diamond, L., J.J Linz, and S. M. Lipset. 1989. *Democracy in Developing Countries: Asia*, vol, 3. Lynne Rienner Publishers.

Diaz-Alejandro, Carlos F. 1988. Good-bye repression, hello financial crash. In *Trade, Development and the World Economy*, ed. Andres-Velasco. Basil Backwell.

Eckert, C.J. 1991. *Offspring of Empire*. University of Washington Press.

Eckert, C.J. et al. 1990. *Korea Old and New: A History*. Ilchokak Publishers.

Fishlow, Albert. 1972. Brazilian size distribution of income. *American Economic Review*, May.

_____. 1975. Income distribution and human capital: Some further results for Brazil. In *Contemporary Issues in Economics*, ed. Michael Parkin and A. R. Nobay. Manchester University Press.

Forgel, Robert W., and Stanley L. Engerman. 1974. *Time on the Cross*. Little Brown.

Fukuyama, F. 1995. *Trust: The Social Virtues and the Creation of Prosperity*. The Free Press.

Gelb, A., and P. Honohan. 1989. Financial sector reforms in adjustment programs. *World Bank Policy, Planning, and Research Working Paper* 169.

Gerschenkron, Alexander. 1962. *Economic Backwardness in historical Perspective: A Book of Essays*. Harvard University Press.

Hagen Koo, ed. 1993. *State and Society in Contemporary Korea*. Cornell University Press.

Hagen Koo. 2001. *Korean Workers: The Culture and Politics of Class Formation*. Cornell University Press.

Haggard S., and Chung H. Lee. 1993. The political dimension of finance in economic development. In *The Politics of Finance in Developing Countries*, ed. S. Haggard, C. H. Lee, and S. Maxfield. Cornell University Press.

_____. 1995. *Financial Systems and Economic Policy*. Cornell University Press.

Haggard S., and S. Maxfield. 1993a. Political explanation of financial policy in developing countries. In *The Politics of Finance in Developing Countries*, ed. S. Haggard, C. H. Lee, and S. Maxfield. Cornell University Press.

_____. 1993b. The political economy of capital account liberalization. *Financial Opening*, OECD.

Harley, C. Knick. 1991. Substitution for prerequisites: Endogenous institutions and comparative economic history. In *Patterns of European Industrialization: The Nineteenth Century*, ed. Richard Sylla and Gianni Toniolo. Routledge.

Hart-Landsberg M. 1993. *The Rush to Development: Economic Change and Political Struggle in South Korea*. Monthly Review Press.

Hellman, T., K. Murdock, and J. Stiglitz. 1996. Financial restraints: Toward a new paradigm. In *The Role of Government in East Asian Economic Development*, ed. Masahiko Aoki, Hyung-Ki Kim, and Masahiro Okuno-Fujiwra. Clarendon Press.

Hewlett, Sylvia Ann. 1980. *The Cruel Dilemmas of Development: Twentieth-Century Brazil*. Basic Books.

Hicks J.R. 1963. *The Theory of Wages*. MacMillan.

Hirschman, A.O. 1968. The political economy of import-substituting industrialization in Latin America. *Quarterly Journal of Economics.* 82(1).

Huntington, S. 1968. *Political Order and Changing Societies*. Yale University Press.

Jessop, B. 1990. *State Theory: Putting the Capitalist State in its Place*. Polity Press.

John, Lie. 1998. *Han Unbound: The Political Economy of South Korea*. Stanford University Press.

Johnson, C. 1982. *MITI and the Japanese Miracle*. Stanford University Press.

_____. 1995. *Japan: Who Governs?* W. W. Norton & Company.

Jones, L., and Sakong, I. 1980. *Government, Business and Entrepreneurship in Economic Development: The Korean Case*. Harvard University Press.

Kerr C., J. Dunlop, F. Harbison, and C. Myers. 1960. *Industrialism and Industrial Man*. Harvard University Press.

Kim Jong-gi. 1994. Urban poverty in the Republic of Korea: Critical Issues and political measures. *Asian Development Review* 12(1).

Kim K. S., and Westphal L. E. 1976. *Exchange and trade policies in Korea*. KDI.

Kim Linsu. 1997. *Imitation to Innovation*. Harvard Business Press

_____. 2000. The dynamics of technological learning in industrialization. Discussion paper series 2007. United Nations University, Institute for New Techology.

Kohli, A. 1999. Where do high-growth political economies come from? In *Developmental State*, ed. Woo-Cumings.

Koo, Hagen, ed. 1993. *State and Society in Contemporary Korea*. Cornell University Press.

Kozul-Wright, R., and P. Rayment. 1997. The institutional hiatus in economies in transition and its policy consequences. *Cambridge Journal of Economics* 21.

Krueger, Anne O. 1978. *The Developmental Role of Foreign Sector and Aid*. Harvard Council on East Asian Studies.

Krugman, P. 1994. The myth of Asia's miracle. *Foreign Affairs*, Nov/Dec.

Kuznets, P.W. 1977. *Economic Growth and Structure in the Republic of Korea*. Yale University Press.

Kuznets, Simon. 1955. Economic growth and income inequality. *American Economic Review*.

Kuhnl, Reinhard. 1983. *Der Faschismus*. Heilbronn.

Langoni, Carlos. 1977. Income distribution and economic development: The Brazilian case. In *Frontiers of Quantitative Economics*, vol. 3-B, ed. M. D. Intriligator. North-Holland Publishing.

Lanzarotti, M. 1992a. *La Corée du Sud: Une sortie du sous-développment*. PUF

_____. 1992b. Taux de change et subventions dans la politique de promotion des exportations: le cas de la Corée du Sud. In *Réforme du commerce exterieur et politique de dévelopment*, ed. J.-M. Fontaine. PUF.

Lee C. H., and S. Haggard. 1995. Issues and findings. In *Financial Systems and Economic Policy*, ed. S. Haggard and Chung H. Leeds. Cornell University Press.

Lee Hyo-Yung. 1985. *Processus d'industrialisation et secteur des biens d'équipement en Corée: Une analysis du mode d'industrialisation*. Ph.D. thesis, Université des Sociales Grenoble II,IPER.

Leftwich, Adrian. 1995. Bringing politics back in: Towards a model of the developmental state. *Journal of Developmental Studies* 31(3).

_____. 2000. State of development: On the primacy of politics in development. In *The Distribution of Income and Wealth in Korea*, ed. Danny M, Leipziger, David Dollar, Anthony F. Shorrocks, and Su-Yong Song. World Bank.

Leske, Monica. 1 990. *Philosophen im Dritten Reich*. Leipniz.

Lewis A. 1954. Economic development with unlimited supplies of labour. *Manchester School Economics and Social Studies*, May.

Linz, J. J. 1970. An authoritarian regime: Spain. In *Mass Politics: Studies in Political Sociology*, ed. Erik Allard and Stein Rokkan. Free Press.

Luedde-Neurath, R. 1986. *Imports Controls and Export-Oriented Development: A Reassessment of the South Korean Case*. Westview Press.

Macintyre S., and Mitchell R. 1989. *Foundations of Arbitration*. Oxford University Press.

MacKinnon, Ronald I. 1973. *Money and Capital in Economic Development*. The Brookings Institute.

_____. 1980. Financial policies. In *Policies for Industrial Progress in Developing Countries*, ed. John Cody et al. Oxford University Press.

Marshall, T. H. 1950. *Citizenship, Social Class and Other Essays*. Cambridge University Press.

Migdal, J. S. 1994. *State Power and Social Forces*. Cambridge University Press.

Moran, J. 1999. Patterns of corruption and development in East Asia. *Third World Quarterly* 20(3).

Obstfeld, M. 1995. International capital mobility in the 1990s. In *Understanding Interdependence: The Macroeconomics of the Open Economy*, ed. Peter B. Kenen. Princeton University Press.

Ogel, George E. 1990. *South Korea: Dissent within the Economic Miracle*. Zed Books.

Ominami, C. 1986. *Le Tiers monde dans la crise: Essai sur les transformation récentes des rapports Nord-Sud*. La Découverte.

Rein, David. 1983. *Unequal Structure of Russian Society*. Educational Science Press.

Rodrik, D. 1995a. Trade and industrial policy reform. In *Handbook of Development Economics*, ed. J. Behrman. and T. N. Srinivasan.

_____. 1995b. Taking trade policy seriously: Export subsidization as a case in policy effectiveness. In *New Directions in Trade Policy*, ed. Jim Levinsolm, Alan V. Deardorff, and Robert M. Stern. Michigan University Press.

_____. 1995c. Trade strategy, investment and exports: Another look at East Asia. *NBER Working Paper* 5339.

Rodric, D. 1999. Democracies pay higher wages. *Quarterly Journal of Economics* 114(3). Rueschemeyer, D. et al. 1992. *Capitalist Development and Democracy.* Polity Press.

Sagong, I. 1993. *Korea in the World Economy.* Institute for International Economics.

Salama, P. 1980. Recherche d'une gestion libre de la force de travail et divisions internals du travail. *Critiques de l'Economie Politique.* 13.

Salama, P., and P. Tissier. 1982. *L'industrialisation dans le sous-developpement.* Maspéro.

Schmitt C. 1994. *Die Diktatur.* Duncker & Humblot.

Sen, Amartya K. 1981. Public action and the quality of life in developing countries. *Oxford Bulletin of Economics and Statistics*, November.

_____. 1983. Development: Which way now? *Economic Journal* 93.

_____. 1999. *Development as Freedom.* Knopf.

_____. 2000. *Development as Freedom.* Random House.

Seo Ick-Jin. 2000. *La Corée du Sud: Une analyse historique du processus de développment* L'Harmattan.

_____. 2002. L'expérience coréene dans le domaine du dévelopment-le modele et son application. In *Quel Developpement pour Algérie.* Forum des Chefs d'Entreprises.

Shaw, Edward S. 1973. *Financial Deepening in Economic Development.* Oxford University Press.

ShimYoung-Seop. 1992. *Les capitaux étrangers dans le processus d'industrialisation en Corée du Sud : Une intérpretaon á partir d'une logiaue endogéne.* Ph.D. thesis, Universite des Sciences Sociales Grenoble II,IREP.

Skocpol, T. 1985. *Bringing in the State Back In.* Cambridge University Press.

Stern, Joseph J, et al. 1995. *Industrialization and the State: The Korean Heavy and Chemical Industry Drive.* Harvard Institute for International Development.

Stiglitz, J. E. 1993. Some lessons from the Asian miracle. Mimeo. Stanford University.

_____. 1995. Reform of capital markets. In *Whither Socialism?* MIT Press.

Stiglitz, J. E., and A. Weiss. 1981. Credit rationing in markets with imperfect information. *American Economic Review.*

Suzumura, K. 1997. Industrial policy in developing market economies. In *Development Strategy and Management of Market Economy*, vol. 1, ed. E. Malinvaud, J. E. Stiglitz, and A. Sen. Clarendon Press.

Thala, L. 2002. Théorie de la régulation et développment. In *Théorie de la régulation : l' Etat des savoirs*, ed. R. Boyer et Y. Saillard. La Découverte.

UNDP. 1998. *Human Development Report.* Oxford University Press.

Vittas, Dimitri, and Yoon Je Cho. 1995. Credit policies: Lessons from East Asia. Working Paper 95-04. World Bank.

Wade, R. 1990. *Governing the Market: Economic Theory and the Role of Government in East Asian Industrialization.* Princeton University Press.

Wade, R., and F. Veneroso. 1998. The Asian crisis: The high debt model versus the Wall Street-Treasury-IMF complex. *New Left Review* March/April: 3-23

Weiss, I., and J. M. Hobson. 1995. *State and Economic Development.* Polity Press.

Westphal, Larry. 1978. The Republic of Korea's experience with export led development. *World Development* 6.

Willamson, O. E. 1975. *Markets and Hierarchies: Analysis and Antitrust Implications.* Free Press.

_____. 1985. *The Economic Institutions of Capitalism.* Free Press.

Woo-Cumings, M. 1991. *Race to the Swift: State and Finance in Korean Industrialization.* Columbia University Press.

Woo-Cummings, M. ed. *The Developmental State.* Cornell University Press.

World Bank. 1989. *World Development Report 1989.*

_____. 1990. *Financial Systems and Development.*

_____. 1993. *The East Asian Miracle: Economic Growth and Public Policy.* Oxford University Press.

Yanowitch, Murray. 1997. *Social and Economic Inequality in the Soviet Union: Six Studies.* Sharpe.

Yoo Hak-Sang. 1985. *Le rôle de l'Etat dans le processus d'industrialisation: le cas de l'économie coréenne.* Ph.D. thesis, Université des Sciences Sociales-Grenoble II.

Glossary

Act on illicit asset disposition 부정축재처리법 (不正蓄財處理法)
Act on payment guarantee of foreign borrowing
　　借款支給保證 에 관한 法律
Chaebol (Korean conglomerates) 재벌 (財閥)
Chaebol republic 재벌공화국 (財閥共和國)
Chang Myon 장면 (張勉)
Cheong-Wa-Dae 청와대 (靑瓦臺)
Chil-Sa Nam-Buk Kongdong Sungmyoung (Joint Communique of
　　July 4, 1972) 7.4 남북 공동 성명 (七四南北共同聲明)
Cho Bong Am 조봉암 (曺奉岩)
Chongryeok anbo ("All-Out National Security")
　　총력안보 (總力安保)
Chun Doo-hwan 전두환 (全斗換)
Chun Tae-il 전태일 (全泰壹)
Chung Ju-yung 정주영 (鄭周永)
Chunggye nojo 청계 노조 (淸溪勞組)
Daejung Kyeongje (Mass economy) 대중경제 (大衆經濟)
Daewoo 대우 (大宇)
Developmental dictatorship 개발 독재 (開發 獨裁)
Developmental state 개발 국가 (開發國家)
Developmentalism 개발주의 (開發主義)
Economic Planning Board (EPB) 경제기획원 (經濟企劃院)
Emergency Decree No. 9 긴급 조치 9 호 (緊急措置 9 號)
Emergency decrees 긴급조치 (緊急措置)
Export is to build national power 수출은 국력 (輸出은國力)
Export Promotion Meetings 수출진흥회의 (輸出振興會議)
Fiscal stabilization plan 재정 안정 계획 (財政安定計劃)
General trading company 종합 무역상사 (綜合貿易商社)
Guro-dong export industry complex 구로 공단 (九老工團)

Financial repression 금융 억압 (金融抑壓)
HCI (heavy chemical industrialization)
    중화학 공업화 (重化學工業化)
Hyundai 현대 (現代)
Industrial militant 산업 전사 (産業戰士)
Insolvent companies 부실 기업 (不實企業)
Jal sara bose (Let's live a rich life) 잘 살아 보세
Joguk geundaehwa (Modernizing the Fatherland)
    조국 근대화 (祖國近代化)
Kim Dae-jung 김대중 (金大中)
Kim Il Sung 김일성 (金日成)
Kongdoli (factory boy) 공돌이
Kongsuni (factory girl) 공순이
Korea-Japan normalization treaty 한일 협정 (韓日協定)
Korea-U.S. Economic Cooperation Committee
    한미합동경제위원회 (韓美合同經濟委員會)
Korean Central Intelligence Agency (KCIA)
    한국 중앙정보부 (韓國中央情報部)
Kukga anbo (National Security) 국가 안보 (國家安保)
Kwangju Uprising 광주 항쟁 (光州抗爭)
Kyoung-Bu Highway (from Seoul to Busan Highway)
    경부 고속도로 (京釜高速道路)
Masan Free Export Zone
    마산 수출 자유지역 (馬山自由輸出地域)
Minjok Kyeongjae 민족경제 (民族經濟)
Minju nojo 민주 노조 (民主勞組)
Minjung 민중 (民衆)
Miracle on the Han River 한강의 기적 (漢江의 奇蹟)
National Emergency Situation 국가 비상사태 (國家非常事態)
Observe the Labor Standard Law
    근로기준법(勤勞基準法)을 준수(遵守)하라
O-il-yuk coup d'état (May 16, 1961 military coup d'état) 5.16 쿠데타

Pal-sam Decree (President's Emergency Decree on Economic
  Stability and Growth, August 3rd Order in 1972)
  8.3 조치 (措置)
Park Chung-hee 박정희 (朴正熙)
Park Chung-hee syndrome 박정희 신드롬
Peace market 평화시장 (平和市場)
POSCO (Pohang steel and Iron company)
  포항 종합제철 공장(浦項 綜合製鐵工場)
Rhee Sung-man 이승만 (李承晩)
Risk society 위험 사회 (危險社會)
Saemaul undong (New Community Movement) 새마을運動
Sa-il-gu hyeokmyeong (April 1960 student revolution) 4月革命
Samsung 삼성 (三星)
Seoul Republic 서울 공화국 (서울共和國)
Ulsan Industrial Complex 울산 공업 지구 (蔚山工業地區)
Y.H. incident Y.H. 事件
Yushin regime 유신 체제 (維新體制)

Chronology

Political-economy in the Park Chung-hee Era

Year	Politics and Society	Economy
1961	-May 16. Commencement of military coup -Jun. 10. Proclamation of laws concerning the Supreme Council for National Reconstruction and the Korean Central Intelligence Agency -Jul. 27. Official statement in support of the South Korean military government by U.S. Secretary of State Dean Rusk -Aug. 28. Military court sentenced to death those involved in "nation's daily case" -Nov. 14. Summit talks between Park Chung-hee and U.S. President John F. Kennedy	-Jun. 10. Proclamation of the act on high interest debt liquidation for agricultural and fishing villages -Jun. 14. Promulgation of the act on illicit asset disposition -Jun. 20. Enactment of temporary measure law for financial institutions -Jul. 22. Announcement of 5-year comprehensive economic reconstruction plan and establishment of Economic Planning Board -Aug. 7. Revision of foreign capital inducement promotion act -Aug. 8. Restoration of Korea-U.S. Economic Cooperation Committee -Aug. 14. Enactment of temporary measures concerning workers' collective activities -Oct. 14. Redemption of five commercial banks' shares -Dec. 27. Enactment of the Korea Reconstruction Bank Act

		-Dec. 30. Illicit Asset Disposition Committee's final notification of the amount of illicit accumulation (30 people: 4,228,000,000 won)
1962	-Nov. 12. Kim Jong-pil-Ohira memo agreement on South Korea-Japan normalization talks -Dec. 26. Proclamation of new Constitution (direct presidential elections)	-Jan. 15. Announcement of the first 5-year Economic Development Plan -Feb. 3. Establishment of Ulsan Industrial Complex and ground-breaking ceremony -May. 24. Amendments of the Bank of Korea Act and the Banking Act -Jun. 10. Implementation of the second currency reform -Jul. 31. Enactment of the act on payment guarantee of foreign borrowing -Sep. 28. Outset of development of a economic plan supplementary to the first plan
1963	-Feb.27. President Park's declaration of non-attendance at civil administration -Mar. 6. Announcement of investigation details into the stock-market, Saenara Motors, Walkerhill Hotel, and slot machine cases by the Korean Central Intelligence Agency (KCIA) -Oct. 15. Fifth presidential election	-Jan. 29. Establishment of fiscal stabilization plan -Apr. 17. Amendments to Labor Union Law

	-Nov. 26. Sixth general election (69.8 % participation: Republican Party 110, Democratic Justice Party 41, Democratic Party 13, United Liberty-Democracy Party 9, Nation's Party 2 seats) -Dec. 17. Park Chung-hee's inauguration as fifth President of South Korea (beginning of the 3rd Republic)	
1964	-Mar. 9. Formation of pan-national struggle committee by 200 members of opposition parties and representatives of various circles, in reaction to humiliating diplomatic relations with Japan -Jun. 3. College students demonstrate against Korea-Japan talks (June 3 incident) -Aug. 14. Announcement of results of investigation into People's Revolutionary Party case by KCIA	-Adoption of unitary floating exchange rate system (Official rate: from 130 won/US dollar to 255 won/US dollar) -May. 7. Completion of Ulsan oil refineries -Jun. 24. Announcement of Comprehensive Export Promotion Measures ct. 31. Korea-Vietnam Agreement on dispatch of Korean forces -Dec. 18. Exchange of Korea-Japan Agreement ratification
1965	-Jan. 26. National Assembly passes troop deployment to Vietnam legislation -Apr. 13. Over 4,000 college students demonstrate in Seoul against "humiliating" diplomacy -Jun. 22. Signing of Korea-Japan Normalization Treaty	-Jan. 5. Formulation of the second 5-year Economic Development Plan -Mar. 22. Enforcement of unitary floating exchange rate system -Aug. 14. National Assembly's ratification of Korea-Japan Normalization Treaty

	-Aug. 13. National Assembly passes Korea-Japan treaty ratification and dispatch of Korean combat divisions to Vietnam, in the absence of opposition party members	
1966	-Mar. 7. Korea-US "'Brown Memorandum" consent -Jul. 9. Signing of Status of Forces Agreement (SOFA): effective February 9, 1967, relinquished jurisdiction over U.S. personnel)	-Aug. 3. Enactment of Foreign Capital Inducement Act -Sep. 15. Samsung "Korea Fertilizer" smuggling of saccharine material -Dec. 12. First General Assembly of IECOK in Paris
1967	May. 3. Sixth presidential election -Jun. 8. Seventh general election (70% participation, Republican Party 130, New Democratic Party 44, Ordinary People's Party 1 seats) -Jul. 8. Announcement of investigation into East Berlin-based North Korean "red movement agent group" (Dongbaengnim case)	-Mar. 3. Temporary measure act on textile industry facilities -Mar. 30. Enactment of machinery industry promotion and shipbuilding industry promotion law -Apr. 1. Completion of export industry complex at Guro-dong, Seoul -Apr. 15. South Korea included in GATT -Jul. 25. Introduction of Negative List Import system
1968	-Jan. 21. Armed guerrillas invaded Seoul targeting Cheong-Wa-Dae (the Blue House) (January 21 incident) -Aug. 24. Announcement of investigation into United Revolutionary Party case -Oct. 10. Introduction of	-Feb. 1. Commencement of Kyeongbu Highway construction -Nov. 22. Enactment of the laws on capital market promotion

	certificate of residence system	
1969	-May. 5. New Democratic Party organized pan-national committee against Constitutional amendment for a third term presidency, at YMCA auditorium -Jun. 19. Student demonstration against Constitutional amendment (continued until December) -Oct. 17. National referendum approved Constitutional amendment (77.1% participation, 7,550,655 for, 3,636,369 against)	-Jan. 28. Enactment of Electronic Industry Promotion Act -May. 22. Commercial and Industrial Ministry announced PVC industry-fostering measures -May 25. Announcement of consolidation measures for insolvent enterprises and companies with overdue bank loans -Jun. 3. Completion of Honam refinery -Jun. 4. Consolidation of insolvent companies -Sep. 16. Setting up of Masan Free Export Zone
1970	-Apr. 8. Collapse of Seoul Wau apartment block -Jul. 6. U.S. President Richard Nixon's administration announced withdrawal of one division of U.S. troops from South Korea -Aug. 15. Declaration concerning South-North Reunification (acknowledgement of North Korea's existence and proposal of "benevolent competition") -Nov. 13. Seoul 'Peace Market' worker, Jeon Tae-Il, committed self-immolation	-Jan. 1. Promulgation of temporary special case laws regarding foreign direct investment companies' labor unions and labor disputes. Enactment of free export zone establishment laws, petrochemical-industry-fostering laws and steel-industry-fostering laws -May. 26. Agreement on the final U.S. aid to Korea signed -Jul. 7. Opening of the Kyeongbu Highway -Mid July. Establishment of construction plans for four core plants for heavy and

by fire in protest against inhumane working conditions in the garment industry

chemical industrialization
-Nov. 4. Confirmation of heavy industry construction plans
-Nov. 24. Announcement of electronic-industry-fostering schemes

---

1971

-Mar. 27. Withdrawal from Korea of the 7th U.S. Division
-Apr. 27. Seventh presidential election. Park, Chung-hee won for third-consecutive time, beating Kim Dae-jung by 950,000 votes (79.9% participation)
-May 25. Eighth general election (Republican Party 113 seats, New Democratic Party 89 seats, remaining parties 2 seats)
-Jul. 16. Richard Nixon announced his visit to China
-Aug. 10. Gyeonggido Gwangju large-scale settlement town incident
-Aug. 20. South-North Red Cross talks at Panmunjom
-Dec. 6. Declaration of State of National Emergency
-Dec. 27. Enactment of special measures for national security

-Feb. 9. Announcement of the third 5-year economic development plan
-Mar. 11. Establishment of the Korea Development Institute (KDI)
-Aug. 15. Richard Nixon's suspension of dollar convertibility in gold.
-Oct. 16. Conclusion of Korea-U.S. textile export self - imposed regulation convention
-Oct. 18. Commercial and Industrial Ministry increased export securities reserve ratio
-Oct. 27. Establishment of the first Comprehensive National Physical Development Plan
-Nov. 10. Determination of defense industry promotion strategies (Cheong-Wa-Dae tripartite meeting)
-Nov. 20. Economic Planning Board announced 26 distressed foreign loan companies

---

1972

-Jul. 4. Announcement of July 4th North-South Joint Communiqué

-Jan. 4. Korea-U.S. textile agreement signed
-Aug. 3. Invocation of the

	-Oct. 17. Declaration of martial law nationwide (October Yushin reforms) -Oct. 18. Chosun Ilbo newspaper supports Yushin regime -Nov.21. National referendum on Yushin Constitution (91.9% participation, 91.5% in favor) -Dec. 23. Park, Chung-hee re-elected as the president by National Congress for Reunification (91.99% support)	President's emergency decree on economic stability and growth (August 3rd Order) -Oct. 21. Industry Rationalization Council appointed 15 industry categories, including steel and textiles -Oct. 25. Full implementation of New Community Movement -Dec. 30. Enactment of public offering of Corporation Stocks Inducement Act and amendments to Capital Market Promotion Act
1973	-Feb. 27. Ninth general election (Republican Party 73 seats, New Democratic Party 52 seats, Democratic Reunification Party 2 seats, Independent: 19 seats) -Jun. 23. Park Chung-hee announced special declaration on "Peaceful Reunification Diplomatic Policy" -Aug. 8. KCIA kidnapped Kim Dae-jung, former presidential candidate of the New Democratic Party -Dec. 24. Constitutional Amendment Petition Movement begins campaign for 1 million signatures	- Jan. 6. Announcement of Long-term Development Plan (1973-1981) - Jan. 12. Park Chung-hee proclaimed the age of the heavy and chemical industrialization at a press conference -Mar. 13. Amendments of three labor laws, including restricting the right to strike -Jun. 29. Establishment of plans to foster the heavy and chemical industry -Jul. 3. Completion of Pohang Iron and Steel Company -October. First oil shock -Dec. 14. Enactment of National Investment Fund Act -Dec. 24. Enactment of Industrial Base Development Promotion Act

| 1974 | -Jan. 8. Declaration of Presidential Emergency Decrees, Nos. 1 and 2.
 -Apr. 3. Declaration of Emergency Measure, No. 4.
 -Apr. 25. KCIA announced results of investigation into Democracy Youth and Student League Case
 -May 27. Announcement of investigation into the 2nd People's Revolutionary Party Case
 -Oct. 24. Dong-a Ilbo journalists declared "Press Freedom Practice"
 -Nov. 27. National Council for Democratization declaration convention | -Jan. 14. Presidential Emergency Decree for "stabilization of national life" (Emergency Decree, No. 3)
 - May 29. Implementation of measures to reform the financial structures of the enterprises and to mobilize domestic capitals (May 29th measures)
 -May 30. Countermeasures for loan advance and concentration of enterprise ownership
 -May 31. Korean banking syndicate conclusion of credit management agreement on *chaebols*
 -Jun. 26. Announcement of Korea-U.S. nuclear energy agreement
 -Jul. 13. Ministry of Finance introduction of Employee Stock Ownership Plan
 -December. Foreign exchange concentration system
 -Dec. 7. Government raise exchange rate (398 won/US dollar to 484 won/US dollar)
 -Dec. 14. Enactment of National Investment Fund Act |
| 1975 | -Feb. 12. National referendum on Yushin Constitution enforcement (79% participation, 73% in favor)
 -March. Chosun Ilbo and Dong-a Ilbo journalists struggle for press freedom | -Apr. 29. Introduction of a general trading company system
 -Jul. 16. Defense tax law
 -Aug. 8. Announcement of government complementary measures for Public Offering |

	and their dismissal -Apr. 9. Death penalty for eight people connected with the 2nd People's Revolutionary Party Case -South Vietnam collapsed -May 13. Promulgation of Emergency Decree, No. 9 (ban on all opposition to Yushin Constitution)	of Corporation Stocks Inducement -Oct. 24. Announcement of comprehensive measures for localization of mechanical products -Dec. 5. Announcement of promotion measures for entry into Middle East countries
1976	-Mar. 1. Declaration for Democracy and Nation by Yun Bo-seon, Kim Dae-jung, Ham Seok-heon, and Ham Se-ung (March 1st Declaration for Democracy and Nation) -Aug. 18. Panmunjeom Axe Murder incident	-Mar. 31. Enactment of act on savings increase and support for workers' wealth creation -Jun. 18. Announcement of the fourth 5-year Economic Development Plan (1976-81)
1977	-Mar. 9. U.S. President Jimmy Carter announced prospective withdrawal of U.S. ground forces from Korea "within 4-5 years"	Jul. 1. Implementation of value-added tax and occupational medical insurance systems -Jul. 23. Enactment of special measure laws for construction of a temporary administrative capital
1978	-Feb. 21. Sewage smeared over female workers at Dong-il textile corporation -Dec. 12. Tenth general election (New Democratic Party defeated the Republican Party by 1.1%)	-May, 26. Completion of Yeochon petrochemical complex -July. Second oil shock -Jul. 20. Completion of the Gori nuclear power generator -Aug. 8. Announcement of

	-Dec. 27. Park Chung-hee's inauguration as ninth President of South Korea	comprehensive measures for anti-speculation real estate policy and stabilization of land prices
1979	-Apr. 16. KCIA announced Christian Academy case -Aug. 11. Police forcibly terminated protest demonstration by female workers at YH Trading Company -Oct. 4. Dismissal of Kim Young-sam, opposition party leader, from the National Assembly -Oct. 9. Interior Ministry announced South Korea Nationalist Front case -Oct. 16. Busan citizen's demonstration; start of Busan-Masan Protest Movement -Oct. 18. Proclamation of Martial Law in Busan area -Oct. 20. Garrison decree in Masan and Changwon -Oct. 26. Assassination of President Park Chung-hee by KCIA Director, Kim Jae-gyu -Dec. 12. Commander Chun Doo-hwan arrested former Army Chief of Staff, Jeong Seung-hwa (December 12th Incident)	-Feb. 14. Repeal of the legal minimum wage system -Apr. 17. Announcement of comprehensive measures for economic stabilization -May 25. Finalization of temporary adjustment of heavy chemistry investment plan

Index

5-year Economic Development
  Plan
    first, 81-82, 84-86, 94, 106,
      113, 131
    second, 104, 113
    third, 99, 101
Absolutism, 17-18
Abuse of power, 209
Accumulation regime, xii, 31, 33,
  52-53, 61, 63, 65-67, 78
Administrative settlement, 161-
  67
Advanced society, 273-74, 276,
  279
Aesthetic autonomy, 321
Ah! Park Chung-hee, 318
All-out national security, 24, 27,
  29
America. *See* U.S.
American liberalism, 298
Antagonistic twins, 239, 244
Anti-communism, 4, 22, 24, 26,
  29, 43, 218, 233, 236, 240, 253,
  255, 289, 299-300, 305-6, 309-
  310
Anti-dictatorship, 318
Article 9 of the Security Act, 162
Asia's Next Giant: South Korea
  and Late Industrialization, 59
Authoritarianism, 8-9, 15, 35, 156,
  312, 329, 334
Beck, Ulrich, xvi, 48, 272, 279,
  291
Bhagwati, Jagdish, 193
Blue Dragon Unit, 256, 259

Borrowing economy, 54-55, 57-
  58, 67, 70
Caesarism, 9
Capitalism, 4, 7, 10, 12, 15, 17-19,
  25-26, 33, 38, 42, 83, 91, 106,
  108, 117, 132, 134, 144, 147,
  242, 285, 287, 333
Carter, Jimmy, 307
Cha Ji-chol, 255
Chaebols, xiii, 4, 21-22, 26-28, 31,
  33-35, 37, 40-42, 47, 71, 74-75,
  108-111, 113-26, 128-33, 135-
  38, 141, 151, 190, 205, 209
  banks owned by, 111
  ranking of, 120
  reform of, 108, 132
Chang Ha-won, 113
Chang Myon, 22-23, 30, 110, 114,
  131
Cheap labor force, 61
Chemical fiber manufacturing, 92,
  94, 96
Chiang Kai-shek, 44
China, 15, 29, 32, 40, 185, 219,
  222-34, 239, 255, 259-60, 262,
  265
Cho Gab-je, 298-300, 302, 307-
  310, 315, 318, 321, 325
Cho Yun-hyung, 261
Choi Doo-sun, 220
Choi Jang-jip, 22, 28, 30, 35, 154,
  168, 174-76
Choi Yong-soo, 173
Chong Song-jin, 56
Chosun Daily, 253, 257, 298, 318,
  334

Chou En-lai, 227-32, 234
Chun Byeong-gyu, 83
Chun Doo-hwan, xiv, 39, 47, 184, 195, 308, 314, 330-31
Chun Tae-il, 28, 35
Civilian government, 313-14, 316, 322
Civilian massacre, 264, 268
Cold War, xi-xii, 7-8, 17, 21-22, 24-26, 29-30, 36-38, 40, 45, 48, 137, 152, 216-19, 240, 244, 251, 259
Collapse of socialism, 297, 299, 310
Collective amnesia, 248-49
Collective bargaining, 156, 160, 163-64, 166-70, 172
Collective psyche, xvi, 296, 299
Comedy of errors, 294
Commercial loan, 92, 94-96, 106, 117-18, 140
Compulsory arbitration to public service companies, 169
Compulsory arbitration system, 164, 167-68
Compulsory savings, 74-75
Consensus modernization, 278
Constitutional Amendment, 27, 235, 290
Corrupt politicians, 303
"Cramming-style" education, 65-66, 191
Credit, 22, 39, 89, 91-92, 119-120, 122-23, 140-42, 145, 148-50, 186, 191, 235, 337
Daewoo, 120
Dangdaebipyong, 326-28, 330
Deification discourse, 312, 315, 319-20, 325-26

Deliberation Committee for the Welfare of Workers, 177
Democratization, vi, ix, x, 3, 6, 13, 17-18, 45, 47, 77, 79, 129, 131, 136, 184-85, 189, 201, 268-69, 274, 312, 314-15, 322-23, 325-26
Deprivation of workers' rights, 183
Destructive development, xvi, 276
"Development as freedom," 192, 195
Developmental dictatorship, i, iii, v-viii, x-xiii, 3, 5-9, 11-17, 20-31, 41-48, 51-52, 55, 66, 71-72, 77-79, 108, 125, 130, 133-38, 185, 187-88, 203, 205, 209, 276-78, 282
Developmental state, 11-16, 18-20, 52, 78, 110, 125-26, 274
Developmentalism, 7-8, 15, 17-19, 26, 41
Diplomatic maneuvering, 250
Discourse, xvi-xvii, 18, 28, 276, 295-96, 313, 315, 317, 326-27
Distrust society, 287-89
Division structure, vi, 215-18, 244-45, 247
Donga Daily, 313, 318
Doves Unit, 252-54, 256
Dual double- track theory, A, 62
Economic convenience, 194
Economic development, v, xi, 6-7, 12, 17, 22-23, 30, 49, 51, 71, 83-85, 89, 91-92, 94, 99-100, 104, 110, 112-14, 117, 125-26, 130, 143-44, 146, 149-50, 152, 178, 181, 186, 192-93, 210,

219, 223-25, 245-46, 250, 263, 265, 281, 298, 300, 320, 324

Economic growth, viii, xii, 4-5, 10-12, 19, 24, 26, 29, 43, 56, 58, 60, 67, 74, 82, 86, 100, 109, 113, 132, 146, 151-53, 184, 186-88, 190-92, 194, 209, 223, 277-78, 282, 284, 286, 297

Economic Planning Board, 56, 69, 71, 78, 84, 93, 95, 102, 118, 177

Electronics Industry Promotion Act, 116

Enterprise-level unions, 169, 172-73

Environmental destruction, 277-78, 284

Exchange rate reform, 89

Export-oriented economy, 53-56, 58-60, 63, 65-67, 70-71, 74-75

Facility to secure transparency, 194

Fair distribution, 152, 186-88, 209

"Fascism within ourselves," 325-28, 331, 334, 337

Fascist characteristics, 309, 333

Fascist discourse, 319, 321, 323

Fascist ideology, 299-300, 304, 309, 311, 336

Fascist masses, 326

Federation of Korean Trade Unions, 76, 156, 171

Feudal social structure, 136

Financial liberalization, 73, 108, 144, 146-47, 149-51

Financial reform, 144

Financial repression, v, xiii, 34, 42, 135, 141, 143-44, 147-50

Financial Restraint, 14, 146, 148

Financial systems, 146-47, 149, 151

Fiscal deficits, 137, 145

Foreign capital regulation, 89

Free market, 9, 47, 83, 110, 114-15, 129, 145-48

Gerschenkron, 18, 82

Global depression, 38

Government concession system, 158

Government economic intervention, 135

Government-directed capitalism, 91

"Growth first, distribution later," 35, 47, 109, 125-26, 132, 135, 137-38

Guam doctrine, 28

Hagiwara, 166

Heavy chemical industrialization, xiii, 41, 99, 102-3, 107, 116, 132, 136, 138-41

Hegemony, 10

Human rights, 313

Humphrey, Hubert, 257, 266

Hyundai, 120-21, 139, 178

Idolization, xvi-xvii, 298

Im Ji-hyon, 328-30, 334-35, 337

Imaginary figure, 321, 323

Import substitution industries, 87, 91, 94, 96

Income distribution, xiv, 186-87, 198-99, 203-5, 209-210

Income inequality, 187, 189, 202, 204-5

Incomplete fascism, 332

Industrial Complex, 72, 278

Industrial policy, v, xii, 27, 31-34, 41-42, 80, 131, 142

Industrial power, 245, 271, 278, 283

Industrial relations, v, 153-54, 156-57, 170, 176, 181, 183-84, 205

Industrial society, 18, 153, 271-72, 274, 277, 284, 292

Industrialization, v, ix, xii-xiii, 3-7, 13-14, 17-20, 30-35, 38-39, 41-42, 45-48, 51, 54-57, 59-67, 72-73, 77, 80-82, 91, 99-100, 102-3, 105-7, 109-116, 130-32, 134-41, 146-49, 151-53, 215, 278, 281-83, 287, 317

Industrial-level unions, 171-72, 174

Industry-level bargaining, 172

Initial Public Offering, 118, 126

Interest rates, 41, 73, 89, 106, 122, 135, 141-42, 144, 147-49, 151

Inter-Korean dialogue, 218-21, 223, 225, 229-31, 239-41

Inter-Korean Red Cross talks, 218, 220, 237

Inter-Korean Relations, 29, 216, 219, 225, 232, 237-38, 267

International liability crisis, 145

Inter-regional antagonism, 284

Japan, xvii, 4, 13, 19-20, 22-23, 25-26, 31-32, 36-37, 39, 42-46, 123, 145, 147, 156, 170, 185, 189, 200-201, 224, 228, 230, 251, 255-56, 262-63, 267, 274, 284-85, 290, 301-310, 335

Japanese imperialism, 288

Japanese militarism, 228, 233, 267, 301

Japanese military school, 292, 298

Japanese rightists, 304, 306-7

Jessop, 10, 16

Kennedy, John E., 250-51

Kim Chong-ryom, 219, 241-42, 245

Kim Chun-hyun, 255

Kim Dae-jung, 28, 40-41, 185, 193, 235, 285, 290, 322

Kim Duk-hyun, 220

Kim Il-sung, xv, 32, 40, 220, 224-27, 229-34, 238-40, 244, 246, 250, 267-68, 332

Kim Su-gon, 165-66

Kim, Young-sam, 185, 297, 302, 313-16, 322

Kissinger, Henry, 219, 222, 227, 229

Kita Ikki, 302-4

Korea-Japan Normalization Treaty, 44, 255

Korean model, xii, 47, 79

Korean peninsula, xii, xv-xvi, 4, 21, 40, 46, 48, 137, 215, 219, 222-24, 229-30, 239, 243-44, 249, 261, 266, 268-69, 283, 289, 307-9

Korean War, 21-22, 137, 156, 218, 229, 248, 259-260, 265, 268, 305, 337

Korea-Japan relations, 251

Korea-U.S. relationship, 233

Korea-U.S.-Japan triangle, 36

Korea-U.S. Joint Economic Cooperation Committee, 86

Krugman, Paul, 66, 189

Kwangju Uprising, 268

Labor policy, v, 27, 153, 155-57, 160, 162, 165, 173, 178, 183-84

Labor unions, xiv, 77, 126, 154-56, 159-62, 167-77, 183, 202

Labor-intensive industries, 179

Land price, 205-210

Late industrialization theory, 82

Lee Chan-hyok, 173

Lee Dong-won, 258

Lee Hu-rak, 221-22, 230-31, 237-39, 242

Lee In-hwa, 298, 300, 308-9, 315, 318, 320-25

Lee Kuan-yew, 193

Lee Shen-nan, 229

Linz, Juan, 8

Manchurian state, 20

Mao Tse-tung, 227

Market-oriented theory, 145

Martial law, 27, 29, 35, 39-41, 43, 303, 330, 333

Marx, Karl, 19, 294

Mass mobilization, 243, 330

Mass production system, 181

Mass psychology, 335

Master of violence, 290

Mechanisms of integration and Accommodation, 178

Military dictatorship, 47, 268, 295, 301, 312, 331

Military government, 90, 112-15, 125, 131-32, 155, 157, 171, 184-85, 311

Military power, 224-26, 246, 256, 283, 309

Military society, 289

Miracle on the Han River, xiii, 45, 51

Mirror image effect, 215

Modernization, vii-ix, xii, xvi, 5-7, 9-11, 13-15, 17, 22, 31, 35, 38, 45-48, 80, 114, 137-38, 234-35, 271-78, 281, 284, 292-93, 297, 301, 312, 317, 322, 337

Modernizing the fatherland, 24, 28, 30

Monolithic totalitarianism, 8

Mun Bu-sik, 328, 331

Murakami, 17-18

National Assembly, 92, 177, 196, 252-57, 302, 310, 316

National defense, 100, 235, 243, 246-47, 254, 307

National security, 27, 30, 100, 161, 174, 218-19, 234, 236, 238, 244, 289, 310

Nationalism, xii, 6-7, 18, 21, 24-25, 28-30, 46, 266, 300, 309

Nature, 281

New Community Movement, 174-76, 181, 184

Nixon, Richard, 28, 100, 219, 282

Nuclear power plants, 278, 280

Opportunity cost, 142, 263

Oppressive modernization, vi, xvi, 271, 275-78, 281, 283-85, 287-89, 292

Park Chung-hee
administration of, 215-17, 230
assassination of, 39, 184
era of, iv, ix, xi, xv, 21, 109, 191, 273, 275, 289, 294, 321
ideology, 294
military government, 171
regime, vii, 5, 44, 84, 107, 109, 137, 154, 178, 195, 197, 235, 289, 296, 302, 315-16, 330
syndrome, xvi, 294-97, 299, 309, 316-17, 313-14, 316-18, 325

Park Chung-hee Philosophy, The, 325

Park Hee-bom, 114

Park Soon-chon, 261

Park Sung-chul, 229, 239, 241

Passive revolution, xii, 5, 11, 30-31, 45, 330

Paternalistic relationship, 184
Path Taken by Man, The, 298, 308
Pay-for-job system, 182
Payment guarantees, 89-93, 117-18, 124, 132, 139-40
Peace market, 35
Plan for the Reorganization of Japan, The, 303
Policy loan system, 142
Political democratization, 7, 131, 274-75
Political economy, v, 3, 5-6, 17, 79, 141
Political freedom, 11, 29, 192-93, 195, 197
Political Fund Act, 117
Political pluralism, 8, 15
Political sociology, vi, 14, 213
Popularity of fascism, 329
Post-war rightists, 306, 308-310
"Power and growth addicts," 324
Presidential election, 26, 28, 40, 235, 261, 285
Presidential Emergency Decrees, 196
Primary trading bank system, 123
Private companies, 72, 84, 91-92, 105, 115-16, 118, 138-39, 157
Private ownership, 16, 18
Pseudo-industrial unions, 169
Public discourse, 296, 312, 315
Public officials' right to organize, 158
Public opinion, xvi, 252, 295-96, 299, 314
Pure socialism, 304
Quasi-intellectuals, 295
Raw materials, 54, 64, 70, 72, 87-88, 97-98, 103-7
Refugee society, 286-87

Regionalism, 285-87
Regulation, xii, 16, 41, 51-52, 66-67, 71-72, 75, 77-78, 97-98, 104, 106, 160, 163-64, 167, 169, 190
Rentier class, xiii, 143, 149
"Repressed system," 141
Rhee Sung-man, 110, 114, 137, 251, 254, 288, 290, 298, 305, 314, 333
Richardson, John, 223
Risk Society, vi, xvi, 271-74, 276-79, 284, 291-93
ROKA, 22, 248-49, 251
Saemaul (New Village) Movement, 175, 246
Samsung, 104, 120
Semi-developed democratic state, 337
Sen, Amartya, 192
Shianouk, 220
Shop-floor reorganization, 181
Social destruction, 277, 284, 292
Social opportunities, 194
Social psychology, 335
Son Won-il, 254
Song Ho-geun, 154-55
South Vietnam, 248, 258-60, 262, 267
South-North Coordinating Committee, 238-39
Special Measures for National Security, 160-62, 164, 168, 174
Spit on My Grave, 302-3, 308
Stalin, Joseph, 188-89
State of National Emergency, 160, 174, 183, 236, 238, 243
State-directed banking, 116
State-led regulation, xii, 66-67, 71

Statist-nationalism, 7, 25, 27, 29, 44-45
Student uprising, 22, 25
Summary Report of the 1st Economic Development Plan, The, 143
System of social security, 194
Taiwan, 8, 12, 16, 19, 21, 31, 41-42, 44, 75, 116, 132, 145, 155, 190, 200-222, 229-230, 234, 263-66
Tiger Unit, 256, 259
Troop deployment, 249, 253, 255, 260-61
"Turning point" theory, 180
Uncivilized science, 284
United States of America. *See* U.S.
U.S., iv, xv, 22, 26, 28-29, 37, 40, 44-45, 57, 86, 89, 100, 109, 115, 134, 137, 219, 222-23, 225, 227-29, 232-35, 244-45, 249-58, 261, 263-70, 279-80, 282, 296, 305-8
Vietnam deployment, 264-65, 267

Vietnam War, vi, 23, 25-26, 37, 43-44, 47, 57, 222, 224, 226, 248-49, 259-60, 262-63, 265-69
Vietnam War bonanza, 263
Violent society, 290
Wage gap, 202-3, 210
Wage increases, 65-66, 75, 77, 125, 175, 179-80, 198-99, 201
Wage levels, 75, 198, 201-2
Western colonialism, 306
Whang Tae-sung, 250
World War II, xii, 19, 136, 152, 170, 271, 305-6
Yu Won-sik, 83, 114
Yukio Mishima, 306
Yushin Constitution, 27, 160-62, 174, 196, 242, 244, 307, 331, 337
Yushin regime, vi, xv-xvi, 27, 31, 154-55, 157, 160-61, 174, 176-77, 183-84, 196, 199, 215, 237

Homa & Sekey Books Titles on Korea (1)

East and West: Fusion of Horizons
By Kwang-Sae Lee, Kent State University
ISBN 1931907269, Order No 1030, 6 x 9, Hardcover, $59.95, £35.00
ISBN 1931907331, Order No 1041, 6 x 9, Paperback, $34.95, £22.00
Philosophy/Culture/Comparative Studies, 2006, xii, 522pp

**A Topography of Confucian Discourse: Politico-philosophical
Reflections on Confucian Discourse since Modernity**
By Lee Seung-hwan, Korea University
ISBN 1931907277, Order No 1031, 6 x 9, Hardcover, $49.95, £30.00
ISBN 193190734X, Order No 1042, 6 x 9, Paperback, $29.95, £19.00
History/Culture/Philosophy, 2006, xii, 260pp

**Developmental Dictatorship and the Park Chung-hee Era:
The Shaping of Modernity in the Republic of Korea**
Edited by Lee Byeong-Cheon, Kangwon National University
ISBN 1931907285, Order No 1032, 6 x 9, Hardcover, $54.95, £32.00
ISBN 1931907358, Order No 1043, 6 x 9, Paperback, $32.95, £20.00
History/Politics, 2006, xviii, 384pp

**The Gwangju Uprising: The Pivotal Democratic Movement
That Changed the History of Modern Korea**
By Choi Jung-woon, Seoul National University
ISBN 1931907293, Order No 1033, 6 x 9, Hardcover, $49.95, £31.00
ISBN 1931907366, Order No 1044, 6 x 9, Paperback, $29.95, £19.00
History/Politics, 2006, xx, 326pp

**The Land of Scholars:
Two Thousand Years of Korean Confucianism**
By Kang Jae-Un
ISBN 1931907307, Order No 1034, 6 x 9, Hardcover, $59.95, £35.00
ISBN 1931907374, Order No 1045, 6 x 9, Paperback, $34.95, £22.00
History/Culture/Philosophy, 2006, xxx, 516pp

Korea's Pastimes and Customs: A Social History
By Lee E-Wha. 16 pages of color photos. B&W illustrations throughout.
ISBN 1931907382, Order No 1035, 6 x 9, Paperback, $29.95, £21.00
History/Culture, 2006, x, 264pp

Homa & Sekey Books Titles on Korea (2)

A Love Song for the Earnest: Selected Poems of Shin Kyungrim
ISBN: 1931907390, Order No 1037, 5 ½ x 8 ½, Paperback
Poetry, $11.95, 2006

Cracking the Shell: Three Korean Ecopoets
By Seungho Choi, Chiha Kim, and Hyonjong Chong
ISBN: 1931907404, Order No 1038, 5 ½ x 8 ½, Paperback
Poetry, $12.95, 2006

Sunrise over the East Sea: Selected Poems of Park Hi-jin
ISBN: 1931907412, Order No 1039, 5 ½ x 8 ½, Paperback
Poetry, $10.95, 2006

Fragrance of Poetry: Korean-American Literature.
Ed. by Yearn Hong Choi, Ph.D., 5 ½ x 8 ½, Paperback, 108pp
ISBN: 1931907226, Order No. 1027, **Poetry**, $13.95, 2005

A Floating City on the Water: A Novel by Jang-Soon Sohn
ISBN: 1931907188, Order No: 1025, 5½ x 8½, Paperback, 178pp
Fiction, $14.95, 2005

Korean Drama Under Japanese Occupation:
Plays by Ch'i-jin Yu & Man-sik Ch'ae, 5½ x 8½, Paperback, 178pp
ISBN: 193190717X, Order No: 1026, **Drama**, $16.95, 2004

The Curse of Kim's Daughters: A Novel By Park Kyong-ni
ISBN: 1931907102, Order No: 1018, 5½ x 8½, Paperback, 299pp
Fiction, $18.95, 2004

I Want to Hijack an Airplane: Selected Poems of Kim Seung-Hee
ISBN: 1931907137, Order No: 1021, 5½ x 8½, Paperback, 208pp
Poetry, $15.95, 2004

Flowers in the Toilet Bowl: Selected Poems of Choi Seungho
ISBN: 1931907110, Order No: 1022, 5½ x 8½, Paperback, 112pp
Poetry, $12.95, 2004

Drawing Lines: Selected Poems of Moon Dok-su
ISBN: 1931907129, Order No: 1023, 5½ x 8½, Paperback, 112pp
Poetry, $11.95, 2004

Homa & Sekey Books Titles on Korea (3)

What the Spider Said: Poems of Chang Soo Ko
ISBN: 1931907145, Order No: 1024, 5½ x 8½, Paperback, 96pp
Poetry, $10.95, 2004

Surfacing Sadness:
A Centennial of Korean-American Literature 1903-2003
Ed. by Yearn Hong Choi, Ph.D & Haeng Ja Kim
ISBN: 1931907099, Order No: 1017, 6 x 9, Hardcover, 224pp
Asian-American Studies/Literature, $25.00, 2003

Father and Son: A Novel by Han Sung-won,
ISBN: 1931907048, Order No: 1010, 5½ x 8½, Paperback, 285pp, 2002,
Fiction, $17.95

Reflections on a Mask: Two Novellas by Ch'oe In-hun.
ISBN: 1931907056, Order No: 1011, 5½ x 8½, Paperback, 258pp, 2002,
Fiction, $16.95

Unspoken Voices: Selected Short Stories by Korean Women Writers
By Park Kyong-ni, et al.
ISBN: 1931907064, Order No: 1012, 5½ x 8½, Paperback, 266pp, 2002,
Fiction, $16.95

The General's Beard: Two Novellas by Lee Oyoung,
ISBN: 1931907072, Order No: 1013, 5½ x 8½, Paperback, 182pp, 2002,
Fiction, $14.95

Farmers: A Novel by Lee Mu-young,
ISBN: 1931907080, Order No: 1014, 5½ x 8½, Paperback, 216pp, 2002,
Fiction, $15.95

www.homabooks.com

Ordering Information: Within U.S.: $5.00 for the first item, $1.50 for each additional item. **Outside U.S.:** $10.00 for the first item, $5.00 for each additional item. All major credit cards accepted. You may also send a check or money order in U.S. fund (payable to Homa & Sekey Books) to: Orders Department, Homa & Sekey Books, 138 Veterans Plaza, P. O. Box 103, Dumont, NJ 07628 U.S.A. Tel: 800-870-HOMA, 201-261-8810; Fax: 201-261-8890, 201-384-6055; Email: info@homabooks.com

www.ingramcontent.com/pod-product-compliance
Lightning Source LLC
Chambersburg PA
CBHW021807270326
41932CB00007B/84